www.wadsworth.com

wadsworth.com is the World Wide Web site for Wadsworth Publishing Company and is your direct source to dozens of online resources.

At *wadsworth.com* you can find out about supplements, demonstration software, and student resources. You can also send e-mail to many of our authors and preview new publications and exciting new technologies.

wadsworth.com
Changing the way the world learns®

ESSENTIALS *of* CULTURAL ANTHROPOLOGY

ESSENTIALS *of* CULTURAL ANTHROPOLOGY

Garrick Bailey
University of Tulsa

James Peoples
Ohio Wesleyan University

WADSWORTH

™

THOMSON LEARNING

Australia • Canada • Mexico • Singapore • Spain
United Kingdom • United States

WADSWORTH

THOMSON LEARNING ™

Anthropology Editor: *Lin Marshall*
Development Editor: *Robert Jucha*
Assistant Editor: *Analie Barnett*
Editorial Assistant: *Reilly O'Neal*
Marketing Manager: *Matthew Wright*
**Project Manager, Editorial
  Production:** *Jerilyn Emori*
Print/Media Buyer: *Robert King*
Permissions Editor: *Joohee Lee*
Production Service: *Hockett Editorial Service*

Text Designer: *Ellen Pettengell*
Photo Researcher: *Linda Sykes*
Copy Editor: *Sheryl Rose*
Illustrator: *Lotus Art*
Cover Designer: *Stephen Rapley*
Cover Image: *Jonathan S. Fisher*
Compositor: *Thompson Type*
Text and Cover Printer: *Von Hoffmann Press, Inc./
  Custom Printing*

Wadsworth/Thomson Learning
10 Davis Drive
Belmont, CA 94002-3098
USA

For more information about our products, contact us:
Thomson Learning Academic Resource Center
1-800-423-0563
http://www.wadsworth.com

International Headquarters
Thomson Learning
International Division
290 Harbor Drive, 2nd Floor
Stamford, CT 06902-7477
USA

UK/Europe/Middle East/South Africa
Thomson Learning
Berkshire House
168-173 High Holborn
London WC1V 7AA
United Kingdom

Asia
Thomson Learning
60 Albert Street, #15-01
Albert Complex
Singapore 189969

Canada
Nelson Thomson Learning
1120 Birchmount Road
Toronto, Ontario M1K 5G4
Canada

Library of Congress Cataloging-in-Publication Data
Bailey, Garrick Alan.
  Essentials of Cultural Anthropology/Garrick Bailey,
  James Peoples
    p. cm.
  Rev. ed. of: Introduction to cultural anthropology. 1999.
  Includes bibliographical references and index.
  ISBN 0-534-58626-0 (alk. paper)
    1. Ethnology. I. Peoples, James. II. Bailey, Garrick
    Alan. Introduction to cultural anthropology. III. Title.

GN316.B36 2001
306—dc21   2001022037

CONTENTS

chapter 4

Studying Culture: Approaches and Methods 48

chapter 5

Adaptation: Environment and Cultures 71

chapter 6

Exchange and Economic Systems 96

chapter 7

Domestic Life 110

chapter 8

Kinship   127

chapter 9

Gender   147

chapter 10

Politics and Social Inequality   173

PREFACE

Cultural anthropology is the academic field that focuses on the cultural diversity of the world's peoples. As authors of a comprehensive text, *Humanity: An Introduction to Cultural Anthropology*, now in its fifth edition, we are gratified that so many instructors have adopted this mainstream text for their introductory cultural anthropology course. However, many instructors have told us over the years that the comprehensive textbook does not suit their manner of teaching the beginning cultural anthropology course. For these instructors and their students we have written *Essentials of Cultural Anthropology* as a shorter and less expensive textbook for beginning students. We cover the "essentials": basic concepts, terms, approaches, methods, and facts about cultural variability. Photos are minimal, but the book contains many maps and graphical features. For instructors, we hope the brevity and low cost of this book facilitates the assignment of multiple additional ethnographies, edited volumes, field-work projects, Internet searches, or other kinds of assignments.

At times, condensing everything that should be included in a modern-day first course in cultural anthropology has been difficult. The task is even more problematic given that anthropologists themselves do not always agree on some of the "essentials" of the field. (Probably, professors will find one or more of their own "essentials" absent!)

We have tried to balance the diverse interests and approaches of the many ways of doing anthropology today.

AN OVERVIEW OF CONTENTS

Students and teachers often find a chapter by chapter preview helpful. Chapter 1 ("The Study of Humanity") provides an overview of anthropology as a whole, concentrating on the very broad scope of the discipline and briefly describing the five subfields. It discusses cultural anthropology, focusing on general perspectives of the study of cultures, and on the contributions anthropologists have made to the understanding of humanity.

Chapter 2 ("Culture") introduces the key concepts of the field. We emphasize the distinction between cultural knowledge and behavioral patterns, then provide a definition that is both simple and useful for understanding cultural diversity. The chapter describes some of the underappreciated components of cultural knowledge and their importance in shaping the behavior of individuals and groups. We close by describing the role of culture in adapting to nature, living in groups, and interpreting the world.

Chapter 3 ("Culture and Language") first introduces the power of language and then provides brief technical coverage of descriptive linguistics, focusing on phonology (sounds) and morphology (words and meanings). Anthropologists are interested mainly in the relationship between the culture of a people and the language they speak. Here we cover the relationship between language and three specific aspects of culture: cognitive classifications, world views, and how language use and speaking style reflect and shape social relationships.

Chapter 4 ("Studying Culture: Approaches and Methods") deals with topics that some call "theories and methods." The chapter describes the history of anthropological thought, including orientations such as evolutionism, historicism, and functionalism. The goal is to show how modern anthropological approaches and methods have changed since the nineteenth century. A discussion of the contemporary theoretical division between materialist and idealist approaches will aid student appreciation of the great diversity of modern thought. Ethnographic fieldwork methods, problems, and ethical issues conclude the chapter.

Chapter 5 ("Adaptation: Environment and Cultures") begins coverage of the various ways cultures differ. Hunting/gathering, horticulture, intensive agriculture, and pastoralism are described, using many examples to illustrate general points. For each adaptation, we interweave coverage of the adaptation itself with the broad impacts it has on the cultural systems of peoples who live by it. By the end of the chapter, we hope students will have a broad understanding that adaptation is an important force in shaping (though not "determining") cultures.

Chapter 6 ("Exchange and Economic Systems") covers the exchange forms called reciprocity, redistribution, and market. We emphasize the kinds of societies in which each exchange mode is dominant, reinforcing the knowledge that impersonal buying and selling of products is not characteristic of all economies.

In Chapter 7 ("Domestic Life"), we discuss various forms of marriage, residence, and family organization. Throughout this chapter (and in others as well), we emphasize that beliefs and practices that many students brought up in the Western cultural tradition find strange or even abhorrent do in fact make sense, once students understand the life conditions (context) that give rise to them.

Chapter 8 ("Kinship") begins by discussing the nature and importance of kinship, especially in the social organization of preindustrial peoples. We then note the various ways in which cultures trace descent, and how descent is used to establish differing types of social groups with important functions. Finally, we discuss the five main types of kinship terminologies and the social significance of kinship terms.

Chapter 9 ("Gender") focuses on four themes. First, we discuss the difference between sex (biologically determined) and gender (a cultural construct). Second, we describe gender crossing and alternative gender identities, using some Native American peoples as cases. Third, we address the sexual division of labor, noting cross-cultural differences and similarities, as well as explanations for why such differences exist. Finally, we discuss gender stratification and some factors that influence it.

In Chapter 10 ("Politics and Social Inequality") we cover three interrelated topics. The varying types of social inequalities and stratification found in societies are described. This is followed by a discussion of the diverse forms of political organizations among the world's peoples. Finally, we examine the nature of social control, with an emphasis on the law and legal systems.

Chapter 11 ("Religion and World View") first discusses religion from a cross-cultural perspective and presents major explanations as to why religion is found among all peoples. This is followed by a discussion of the different types of religions found in the preindustrial world. We end with a discussion of sorcery and witchcraft and why such beliefs are so widespread.

In Chapter 12 ("Art and the Aesthetic") we cover artistic expression from an anthropological perspective, especially body arts, visual arts, and performance arts. Integrating many examples throughout, we conclude by discussing relationships between the arts and culture.

Chapter 13 ("Globalization and Ethnicity") addresses the emergence and manifestations of globalization of economies and cultural features. It also provides anthropological insights on ethnic groups and nationalities and on resolving ethnic-based conflicts.

In Chapter 14 ("The Future of Indigenous Peoples") we discuss indigenous peoples and how global forces threaten their physical and cultural survival. We argue that the rights of indigenous peoples should be protected, not just for moral reasons, but for the cultural knowledge transmitted through their traditions that is of value to all peoples of the world.

Instructors may find it useful to have the main subjects of each chapter summarized in as few words as possible. The following list can be useful the first day of class, or in preparing a course syllabus. Briefly, each chapter covers:

Chapter 1 Anthropology as a field of study; approaches and contributions
Chapter 2 The nature of culture; its importance to understanding humankind
Chapter 3 Understanding language; how it relates to culture
Chapter 4 The development of anthropological thought and fieldwork methods
Chapter 5 Types of adaptation; their main impacts on cultures
Chapter 6 Exchanges of products and their social correlates
Chapter 7 Making sense of variations in marriage, residence, and family structure
Chapter 8 Kinship forms and terminologies; how to understand their diversity
Chapter 9 Understanding diversity in gender constructions and practices
Chapter 10 Wealth distribution; the organization of power and social control
Chapter 11 Variability in religions and world views; how anthropologists interpret them
Chapter 12 Forms of artistic expression; their roles and functions in culture
Chapter 13 Emergence and significance of globalization; ethnic groups and conflicts

Chapter 14 Forces threatening indigenous cultures; arguments for their survival

PEDAGOGICAL FEATURES

As befitting a brief introduction, we have kept the text's pedagogical features to a minimum. Each chapter has the following features:

- A topical outline and brief narrative preview of contents
- Key terms, which are boldfaced at their first definition and listed in order of mention at the end of each chapter
- Point by point summaries for each chapter
- Suggested readings at the end of the chapter
- A glossary that defines each of the key terms in alphabetical order

We have tried to minimize the use of anthropological jargon, while providing students with the definitions of key terms that most instructors of the course are likely to use themselves.

In addition to the above, most chapters contain one or more concept reviews, which focus readers' attention on particular issues or key concepts presented. As in the larger text, *Humanity,* we chose to improve the readability and flow of the text by collecting and briefly annotating references at the end of the book, organized by chapter. Finally, we have provided an Internet appendix that links to Wadsworth's home page.

Supplements for Instructors

Instructor's Manual with Test Bank. Written by Bruce P. Wheatley of the University of Alabama at Birmingham, this supplement offers the instructor chapter outlines, lecture suggestions to facilitate in-class discussion, suggested student activities, film/video resources, and Internet and InfoTrac® College Edition exercises for each chapter. The test items consist of 20–25 multiple-choice and 15–20 true/false questions with rejoinders and page references, as well as essay questions for each chapter. In addition, a list of suggested ethnographic studies to accompany the text is included, as is a cumulative video/film resources section with ordering information. A concise user guide for InfoTrac College Edition is provided as an appendix.

A Guide to Visual Anthropology. Prepared by Jayasinhji Jhala of Temple University, this guide provides a compendium of fifty of the most outstanding classic and contemporary anthropological films. The guide describes the films and why they are important, along with suggestions for their use in the classroom.

Wadsworth's Cultural Anthropology Transparency Acetates. A set of four-color acetates is available to help prepare lecture presentations.

AnthroLink 2002: A Microsoft PowerPoint Presentation Tool. AnthroLink 2002 is an easy-to-use CD-ROM with which instructors can create customized lecture PowerPoint presentations for class. AnthroLink 2002 includes nearly 500 pieces of graphic art from all Wadsworth cultural, physical, and archaeological titles. In addition, the user may choose from 400 photographs grouped by standard chapter categories. A unique feature of AnthroLink 2002 is the ability to choose and integrate video segments into lectures. AnthroLink 2002 gives instructors the ability to utilize images from the text to create their own lecture presentations or to use and manipulate the premade lecture presentation already on the CD-ROM.

Classroom Videos

Wadsworth Anthropology Video Library. Qualified adopters may select full-length videos from an extensive library of offerings, drawn from such excellent educational video sources such as NOVA, BBC, Films for the Humanities and Sciences, and The Disappearing World Video Series.

CNN Today Cultural Anthropology Video Series, Volumes I, II, and III. CNN Today Cultural Anthropology Videos is an exclusive series jointly created by Wadsworth and CNN for the cultural anthropology course. Each video in the series consists of approximately 45 minutes of footage originally broadcast on CNN within the last several years. The videos are broken into short two- to seven-minute segments, which are perfect for classroom use as lecture launchers or to illustrate key anthropological concepts. An annotated table of contents accompanies each video with descriptions of the segments and suggestions for their possible use in the course.

Visual Anthropology Video. This video consists of sixteen clips, each three to four minutes in length, from some of the best-known ethnographic films. The shortness of the clips makes for maximum flexibility. Documentary Educational Resources produced the video exclusively for Wadsworth Publishing.

Supplements for Students

Applying Cultural Anthropology: Readings. This reader prepared by Gary Ferraro contains 35 readings in applied anthropology. The readings focus on areas in which anthropology has been used, such as applied business, medicine, education, government and law, criminal justice, and housing.

Researching Anthropology on the Internet. Prepared by David L. Carlson of Texas A&M University, this useful guide is designed to assist anthropology students when doing research on the Internet. Part One contains general information necessary to get started and answers questions about security, the type of material available on the Internet, the information that is reliable and the sites that are not, the best ways to find research, and the best links to take students where they want to go. Part Two looks at each main discipline in the area of anthropology and refers students to sites where the most enlightening research can be obtained. Specific drawbacks and issues to watch out for in each of the different areas are noted, as well as specific resources and subjects that are well represented in the online world.

Internet Resources

Anthropology Online: Wadsworth's Anthropology Resource Center, http://anthropology. wadsworth.com. The Wadsworth Anthropology Resource Center contains a wealth of information and useful tools for both instructors and students. After logging on, click on the Bailey and Peoples *Essentials of Cultural Anthropology* book page and proceed to the Student Resources section. There you will find study aids such as flashcards and online practice quizzes for each chapter. The Anthropology Resource Center contains two special features:

- *A Virtual Tour of Applying Anthropology.* This special section of the Web site serves as an online resource center for the anthropology student. There is an essay, illustrated with video clips, on careers in anthropology written by Wadsworth author Gary Ferraro. The site includes information on careers in anthropology outside the academic setting, including advice on organizations that provide student internships and hot links to graduate programs in applied anthropology.
- *Student Guide to InfoTrac College Edition.* Prepared by Kathryn Coe of the University of Missouri, Columbia, this guide consists of exercises based on 16 core subjects vital to the study of anthropology. These exercises utilize InfoTrac College Edition's huge database of articles. The exercises help students to narrow down the search of articles related to each subject and ask questions that enable them to see the ideas more clearly and pique their interest.

InfoTrac College Edition. Ignite discussions or augment your lectures with the latest developments in anthropology and cultural change. InfoTrac College Edition (available as a free option with newly purchased texts) gives you and your students four months' free access to an easy-to-use online database of reliable, full-length articles (not abstracts) from hundreds of top academic journals and popular sources. Among the journals available 24 hours a day, seven days a week, are *American Anthropologist, Current Anthropology,* and *Canadian Review of Sociology and Anthropology.* Contact your Wadsworth/Thomson learning representative for more information.

ACKNOWLEDGMENTS

We are grateful to those anthropologists who in preparation for this book reviewed the previous version of this text, *Introduction to Cultural Anthropology:*

Cheryl Ajirotutu, University of Wisconsin at Milwaukee
Traci Arden, Florida State University
Howard Campbell, University of Texas at El Paso
Barbara Cook, California Polytechnical State University at San Luis Obispo
Brian M. Donohue-Lynch, Quinebaug Valley Community Technical College
B. James McElroy, Puget Sound Christian College
Mary Jo Schneider, University of Arkansas

In addition we thank Nicholas Freiden (Marshall University), William M. Leons (University of Toledo), Karl F. Rambo (University of Oklahoma), and Mark S. Warner (Miami University) for their criticisms and suggestions for the earlier version.

Members of our departments lent support and, sometimes, comments: Ted Cohen, John Durst, Mary Howard, Akbar Mahdi, and Jan Smith at Ohio Wesleyan; and Monty Lindstrom and Peter Stromberg at the University of Tulsa. Jim also thanks Janice Schroeder and Pam Laucher for their helpful attitude and assistance.

Our editors at Wadsworth, Lin Marshall and Bob Jucha, were extremely helpful in the development of the book. Jerilyn Emori, our project editor; Matthew Wright, the anthropology marketing manager; and Analie Barnett, the assistant editor, all deserve our gratitude for their assistance. Finally, Jim thanks his wife, Deborah, and son, Matthew, for their tolerance, while Garrick thanks his wife, Roberta, for her help and encouragement.

ESSENTIALS *of* CULTURAL ANTHROPOLOGY

chapter 1

THE STUDY *of* HUMANITY

Contents

A couple of million years ago, on the plains of southern Africa, an animal lived that was a lot like us. Its brain was only about half as large, but it walked on two legs, ate both animals and plants, lived in social groups, made crude tools out of stone, and probably fought over mates and resources.

Twenty thousand years ago, on the continent we today call Europe, lived a people virtually indistinguishable from twenty-first century people biologically. They got most of their food from hunting large mammals, were highly skilled at making knives and spearpoints out of stone, kept themselves warm with animal skins and fire, painted images of animals on the walls of caves, and occasionally fought among themselves.

Five thousand years ago, in the place that would later become part of the nation of Iraq, there existed a civilization. Its people got almost all of their food from growing and processing grains and eating the products of livestock, lived in walled cities of several thousands, smelted metals, manufactured pottery, kept records by making marks on tablets of wet clay, and fought among themselves and with other people quite a lot.

Right now, in the city of Los Angeles, people of many different nationalities live. Few of them know how to hunt or grow their own food, make tools or pottery or their own writing utensils, or build houses. Instead of doing these things for themselves, many of them get up at five so they can make it to work by eight, earn $50,000 per year so they can afford their $1,500 monthly mortgage payments, run themselves ragged getting their kids to soccer games, and wonder whether Social Security will be there for them. Few of them actually fight, but they do worry a lot about getting ripped off.

Anthropology is the field that studies all these people. Anthropologists are interested in almost everything about humans: our genetic makeup, our biological evolution, our languages, our emotions, our technologies, our art styles, our families, and our behavior. Within colleges and universities, anthropology is usually classified as a social science, along with disciplines such as

psychology, sociology, economics, geography, and political science. But as we shall see, anthropology has much in common with the natural sciences (such as biology and geology) and the humanities (such as religion and art), as well.

Anthropology, then, is a diverse field. In fact, perhaps the main way anthropology differs from other social sciences is in its broad scope. Anthropology's subject matter is broad in two senses. First, anthropologists are interested in *all human beings:* We study people wherever they are found today and whenever they lived in the past. Second, anthropologists are interested in *many different aspects of humans:* We investigate topics as diverse as skin colors, kinship systems, religions, technologies, cuisines, and practically every other dimension of human life.

SUBFIELDS of ANTHROPOLOGY

Clearly, no individual can become familiar with the enormous range of subjects studied by the whole discipline of anthropology. As a practical matter, almost all modern anthropologists specialize in one of five main subfields: physical anthropology, archaeology, cultural anthropology, anthropological linguistics, and applied anthropology. (The Concept Review summarizes the primary interests of each.) Although cultural anthropology is the main subject of this book, a brief discussion of the other four subfields will help you to understand the whole discipline.

Physical Anthropology

Physical anthropology (also called **biological anthropology**) investigates the evolution of the human species, the behavior and anatomy of monkeys and apes, and the physical variations among and between human groups. Physical anthropology is closely related to the natural sciences in both its goals and its methods.

One goal of physical anthropology is to understand how and why humans evolved from prehuman, apelike ancestors. The investigation of human biological evolution is known as **paleoan-thropology**. Through many decades of searching for and analyzing fossil remains, paleoanthropologists are learning how humans evolved biologically. There remains much disagreement over details, but the outlines of human evolution are becoming clear. Most specialists now agree that the evolutionary line leading to modern humans split from the line leading to modern African apes (chimpanzees and gorillas) at least five million years ago. Biological anthropologists generally agree that the characteristic that first separated the human line from the ape line was *bipedalism* (walking on two legs), rather than an increase in the size of the brain, which is what most people think of as most important. It also appears that fully modern human beings, *Homo sapiens*, came into existence surprisingly recently, probably less than 150,000 years ago.

Another specialization within physical anthropology is **primatology**. Primatologists specialize in the evolution, anatomy, adaptation, and social behavior of primates, the taxonomic order to which humans belong. By conducting field studies of how living primates forage, mate, range over their environment, and interact socially, primatologists hope to shed light on the forces that affected early human populations. Primatological research on the behavior of group-living monkeys and apes has added significantly to the scientific understanding of many aspects of human behavior, including sexuality, parenting, cooperation, tool use, and intergroup conflict and aggression.

Yet another type of biological anthropologist is interested in how and why human populations vary physically. All humans are members of a single species, and one of the basic tenets of anthropology is that the physical similarities among the world's peoples far outweigh the differences. Nonetheless, peoples who trace their ancestry back to Africa, Asia, Europe, the Americas, Australia, and the Pacific islands were once more isolated from one another than they are today. During this separation they evolved differences in overall bodily and facial form, height, skin color, blood chemistry, and other genetically determined features. Anthropologists who study **human variation** seek to measure and explain the differences and similarities among the world's peoples in these and other physical characteristics.

Most physical anthropologists work in universities or museums, as teachers, researchers, writers, and curators. But many also work in "practical" jobs, applying their knowledge of human anatomy to find answers to problems. For instance, **forensic anthropologists** work for or consult with

CONCEPT REVIEW Primary Interests of the Five Subfields of Anthropology

ANTHROPOLOGY				
PHYSICAL/ BIOLOGICAL	**ARCHAEOLOGY**	**CULTURAL**	**ANTHROPOLOGICAL LINGUISTICS**	**APPLIED**
Biological evolution of **Homo sapiens;** physical variation among human populations; comparisons of human anatomy and behavior with other primate species	Changes in human cultures over very long time spans by excavating sites, to reconstruct human prehistory and supplement written historial documents	Differences and similarities in contemporary and historically recent cultures, investigated through intensive fieldwork and careful comparisons	General relation between language and culture; role of language and speaking in cultural and social life of specific peoples; how language shapes cognition and thought	Applications of anthropological skills, knowledge, concepts, and methods to the solution of real-world problems

law enforcement agencies, where they analyze and help identify human skeletal remains. Among their contributions are determining the age, sex, height, and other physical characteristics of crime or accident victims. Forensic anthropologists know how to gather evidence from bones about old injuries or diseases, which are compared with medical histories to identify victims. For example, forensic anthropologist Clyde Snow has worked with governments and human rights investigators to identify victims of atrocities in the Middle East and Eastern Europe. In the 1990s, teams of forensic anthropologists exhumed remains from graves in Bolivia, Guatemala, El Salvador, and Haiti to identify victims of political assassinations and determine the exact causes of their deaths.

Archaeology

Archaeology is the study of the human past by excavating and analyzing material remains. Because it studies the ways in which human life has changed over the centuries, archaeology has much in common with history. It differs, however, in its methods and, to some extent, its goals. Modern archaeology usually is divided into two major kinds of studies: prehistoric and historic.

Prehistoric archaeology investigates cultures that never kept written records of their activities, customs, and beliefs. (The word *prehistory* means literally "before history," or before the development of writing.) Evidence of the ways of life of prehistoric peoples exists in the tools, pottery, ornaments, bones, plant pollen, charcoal, and other materials they left behind in or on the ground. Through tedious excavation and laboratory analysis of these material remains, prehistoric archaeologists reconstruct the way people lived in ancient times and trace how human cultures have changed over the centuries. In fact, research conducted by prehistoric archaeologists provides our main source of information about how people lived before the development of writing.

To learn about the more recent past, historians use written materials such as diaries, letters, newspapers, and tax collection documents. Written records provide useful data, but they typically are fragmentary and provide information only on specific subjects and subgroups within a society. The growing field of **historic archaeology** supplements written materials by excavations of houses, stores, plantations, factories, and other historic structures. Historic archaeologists often uncover hard data on living conditions and other topics lacking in written accounts.

Many modern archaeologists are employed not in universities, but in museums, public agencies, and for-profit corporations. Museums offer jobs as curators of artifacts and as researchers. State highway departments employ archaeologists to conduct surveys of proposed new routes in order to locate and excavate archaeological sites that will be destroyed. The U.S. Forest Service and National Park Service hire archaeologists to find sites on public lands so that decisions about the preservation of cultural materials can be made. Those who work in the growing field of cultural resource management locate sites of prehistoric and historic significance, evaluate their importance, and make recommendations about total or partial preservation. Since the passage of the National Historic Preservation Act in 1966, private corporations and government bodies that wish to construct factories, parking lots, shopping malls, and other structures must file a report on how the construction will affect historical remains and on the steps taken to preserve them. Because of this law, the business of contract archaeology has boomed in the United States. Firms engaged in contract archaeology bid competitively for the privilege of locating, excavating, and reporting on sites affected or destroyed by construction. Hundreds of (mostly small) contract archaeology companies exist.

Cultural Anthropology

Cultural anthropology (also called **ethnology**) is the study of contemporary and historically recent human societies and cultures. As its name suggests, the main focus of this subfield is culture—the customs and beliefs of some human group (the concept of culture is discussed at length in

Peggy/Yoram Kahana/Peter Arnold, Inc.

Anthropologists conduct fieldwork by living among and interacting with living human communities. This fieldworker seems to be helping these two Latin American women with spinning.

Chapter 2). Cultural anthropologists study a huge number of specific subjects, far too many to be listed here. Some of their main interests are:

- studying firsthand and reporting about the ways of life of particular human societies
- comparing diverse cultures to one another to determine if there are any common causes or influences that operate in all cultures
- trying to understand how various aspects of human life—economics, family life, art, religion, communication, and so forth—relate to one another in particular cultures and in cultures generally
- understanding the causes and consequences of cultural change
- making the public at large aware and tolerant of the enormous cultural differences that exist among humankind

This last objective is especially important today, when individuals with different cultural backgrounds increasingly interact with one another as businesspeople, international travelers, students, and migrants. Ethnology helps us to understand cultural differences and to enjoy, celebrate, and even profit from living in an increasingly multicultural world.

To collect information on some group or society, cultural anthropologists conduct firsthand **fieldwork**. Fieldwork ordinarily involves moving into the community under study, communicating in the local language, and living in close contact with the people. Fieldwork provides ethnologists with firsthand experiences that yield insights that could not be gained in any other way. Fieldworkers usually report the findings of their research in books or scholarly journals, where they are available to the general public. A written account of how a single human population lives is called an **ethnography** (which means "writing about a people"). We have more to say about fieldwork in Chapter 4.

Anthropological Linguistics

Defined as the study of human language, linguistics is a field all its own, existing as a separate discipline from anthropology. Linguists describe and analyze the sound patterns and combinations, words, meanings, and sentence structures of human languages. As discussed in Chapter 3, language has some amazing properties, and the fact that humans are able to learn and use language at all is truly remarkable.

Language interests anthropologists for several reasons. The ability to communicate complex messages with great efficiency may be the most important capability of humans that makes us different from primates and other animals. Cultural anthropologists are interested in language mainly because of how the language and culture of a people affect each other. The subfield of **anthropological linguistics** is concerned with the complex relations between language and other aspects of human behavior and thought. For example, anthropological linguists are interested in how language is used in various social contexts: What style of speech must one use with people of high status? What does the way people attach labels to their natural environment tell us about the way they perceive that environment? We return to these and other topics in anthropological linguistics in Chapter 3.

Applied Anthropology

In the past, almost all professional anthropologists spent their careers in some form of educational institution, most commonly in colleges and universities, or in museums. Today, hundreds of anthropologists hold full-time positions that allow them to apply their expertise in governmental agencies, nonprofit groups, private corporations, and international bodies. These institutions and organizations employ anthropologists because they believe that people trained in the discipline will help them in problem solving. In recognition of the growth of noneducational employment opportunities, the American Anthropological Association (the professional organization of anthropologists) now recognizes **applied anthropology** as a separate subfield. In fact, in the 1990s, about half of new anthropology doctorates acquired jobs in some federal, state, or local governmental agency or in the private sector.

Anthropologists who apply their knowledge and research skills to solving human problems are trained in all four of the other subfields. Archaeologists employed as cultural resource managers and physical anthropologists who do

forensic work may be viewed as applied anthropologists, for example. However, most applied anthropologists have their most extensive training in cultural anthropology. A few examples will illustrate some of the ways these anthropologists use their knowledge and research skills in problem solving.

Medical anthropology is one of the fastest growing specializations. Medical anthropologists are trained to investigate the complex interactions among human health, nutrition, social environment, and cultural beliefs and practices. Because the transmission of viruses and bacteria is greatly affected by people's diets, sanitation, sexual habits, and other behaviors, medical anthropologists work with epidemiologists to identify cultural practices that affect the spread of disease. Different cultures have different ideas about the causes and symptoms of disease, how best to treat illnesses, the abilities of traditional healers and doctors, and the importance of community involvement in the healing process. By studying how a human community perceives such things, medical anthropologists can provide information to hospitals and agencies that helps them deliver health care services more effectively.

Development anthropology is another area in which anthropologists apply their expertise to the solution of practical human problems, usually in the Third World. Working both as full-time employees and as consultants, development anthropologists provide information on communities that helps agencies adapt projects to local conditions and needs. Examples of agencies and institutions that employ development anthropologists include the U.S. Agency for International Development, the Rockefeller and Ford foundations, the World Bank, and the United Nations Development Program. Perhaps the most important role of the anthropologist in such institutions is to provide policymakers with knowledge of local-level ecological and cultural conditions, so that projects will avoid unanticipated problems and minimize negative impacts.

Educational anthropology also offers jobs in public agencies and private institutions. Some roles of educational anthropologists include advising in bilingual education, conducting detailed observations of classroom interactions, training personnel in multicultural issues, and adapting teaching styles to local customs and needs. An increasingly important role for North American educational anthropologists is to help teachers understand the learning styles and behavior of children from various ethnic, racial, and national backgrounds.

Recently, enough private corporations have employed anthropologists that we now recognize a specialization in *corporate anthropology*. The growth of overseas business opportunities leads North American companies to hire professionals who can advise executives and sales staff on what to expect and how to speak and act when they conduct business in other countries. Because of their training as acute observers and listeners, anthropologists are employed in the private sector in many other capacities as well.

As these examples show, anthropologists apply their knowledge and skills to the solution of practical human problems in many ways. Speaking very broadly, cultural anthropologists are valuable to agencies, companies, and other organizations because they are trained to do two things very well: first, to observe, record, and analyze human behavior; and, second, to look for and understand the cultural assumptions, values, and beliefs that underlie that behavior.

CULTURAL ANTHROPOLOGY YESTERDAY and TODAY

As the preceding overview of the five subfields shows, anthropology is indeed a broad field of study. Different kinds of anthropologists conduct research on topics and places as diverse as the behavior of African mountain gorillas, the migrations of prehistoric Pacific islanders, modern-day cultures of the Amazon basin, how education in Japan compares to that in North America, and medical clinics in London.

Despite these varied interests, anthropology does have a focus. More so than other fields, an-

thropology's focus is *human diversity*. Humankind is diverse in a multitude of ways, two of which are most important to anthropologists. First, although all modern humans are members of the same species, human populations differ somewhat in their genetic heritage, making humans diverse *biologically*. Second, the customs and beliefs of one society or ethnic group differ from those of other societies or ethnic groups, reflecting the fact that humans are diverse *culturally*. Anthropologists investigate, describe, and try to understand or explain human biological and cultural diversity.

This book's main subject is *human cultural diversity*, which is studied by the subfield known as cultural anthropology. Cultural anthropology itself is an enormously broad specialization, for modern fieldworkers study human communities from all parts of the world, from the Sahara of northern Africa to the Andes of South America, from the streets of Toronto to the high deserts of the American southwest.

In the popular imagination, cultural anthropological fieldworkers go to far-off places and study exotic peoples, or "natives." Except for most stereotypes about the "natives," this image was reasonably accurate until the 1970s. Until then, ethnology differed from sociology and other disciplines that studied living peoples and cultures mainly by the kinds of cultures studied. Anthropologists mainly focused on small-scale, non-Western, preindustrial, subsistence-oriented cultures, whereas sociological studies mainly dealt with large Euro-American, industrial, money-and-market countries. Anthropological fieldworkers themselves often sought out pristine, untouched tribal cultures to study because living among the "primitives" brought prestige and enhanced one's reputation in the discipline.

All this has changed. Contemporary ethnologists study New Jersey fraternities, Swedish churches, the cultural significance of Elvis, Canadian medical clinics, American bodybuilders, British witches' covens, Appalachian towns, and the recent decline of the middle class—to name just a few examples of specific studies recently done by anthropologists in modern industrialized societies. There are many reasons for the trend away from the "far away" in favor of "here-at-home" studies. One is the realization that anthropological concepts and fieldwork methods can yield insights about modern societies that other disciplines miss. Another is that increasing numbers of anthropologists are using their knowledge and training to solve real-world problems. For these and other reasons, more and more North American and European cultural anthropologists today concentrate on their own countries.

Thus, the differences between cultural anthropology and the other disciplines (especially sociology and history) are much less clear-cut than they were just a couple of decades ago. However, anthropology retains its distinctiveness. More than scholars in other fields, anthropologists concentrate on relatively small communities (of a few hundred to a few thousand), in which the researcher can live among the people and participate firsthand in their lives. More than any other single factor, the emphasis on direct contact with people gained from the fieldwork experience distinguishes anthropology from other disciplines concerned with humankind. Also, cultural anthropology remains far more comparative and global in its goals and interests than the other social sciences and humanities.

Finally, it is worth mentioning some of the ways that cultural anthropology overlaps other disciplines. For example, an ethnologist may be interested in agriculture, comparative political and legal systems, or art. He or she will, therefore, become acquainted with the work of economists, political scientists, and art historians—disciplines that specialize in some particular dimensions of human life. Likewise, an ethnologist who specializes in some geographical region (such as West Africa, China, or Brazil) will read the works of historians, sociologists, novelists, and political scientists who also have written about the region. Cultural anthropologists regularly study subjects that are the specializations of other disciplines, as is nicely illustrated by anthropological specializa-

tions in such areas as ethnomusicology, ethnopoetics, ethnobotany, and ethnolinguistics. Cultural anthropology thus cuts across many disciplines, encompassing many of the subjects that other scholars consider their special province—law, religion, literature, music, and so on.

ANTHROPOLOGICAL PERSPECTIVES

Because cultural anthropologists study many of the same kinds of subjects studied by other scholars, obviously it is not what they study that makes the field distinct. The main distinctive feature lies not so much in the kinds of subjects ethnologists investigate as in the approach they take to studying cultures. We believe it is important that cultures and communities be studied holistically, comparatively, and relativistically. It is these perspectives, as much as anything else, that make cultural anthropology distinctive.

Holistic Perspective

To study a subject holistically is to attempt to understand all the factors that influence it and to interpret it in the context of all those factors. With respect to studies of human cultures and societies, the **holistic perspective** means that no single aspect of a community can be understood unless its relations to other aspects of the community's total way of life are explored. Holism requires, for example, that a fieldworker studying the rituals of a people must investigate how those rituals are influenced by family life, economic forces, political leadership, relationships between the sexes, and a host of other factors. Understanding a community's customs, beliefs, values, and so forth holistically is one reason why ethnographic fieldwork takes so much time and involves close contact with people.

Taken literally, a holistic understanding of a people's customs and beliefs is probably not possible because of the complexity of human societies and cultures. But anthropologists have learned that ignoring the interrelations among language, religion, art, economy, family, and other dimensions of life results in distortions and misunderstandings. Although more complicated than this, the essence of the holistic perspective may be stated fairly simply: *Look for connections and interrelations between things, and try to understand parts in the context of the whole.*

Comparative Perspective

As we have already seen, in the early decades of its existence, ethnological research focused mainly on non-Western peoples, many of whom thought and acted quite differently from the citizens of the anthropologist's own (usually European or North American) nation. Anthropologists soon learned that the ideas and concepts that applied to their own societies often did not apply to those of other peoples, whose cultural traditions were vastly different. They learned, for example, to mistrust the claims put forth by French scholars about human nature when the only humans these scholars had ever encountered lived in Western Europe.

More than most people, anthropologists are aware of the enormous diversity of the world's cultures. This diversity means that any general theories or ideas scholars might have about humans—about human nature, sexuality, warfare, family relationships, and so on—must take into account information from a wide range of societies. In other words, general theoretical ideas about humans or human societies or cultures must be tested from a **comparative perspective**. The ways of life of people in different times and places are far too diverse for any theory to be accepted until it has been tested in a range of human populations. We may state the comparative perspective as: *Generalizations about humans must take the full range of cultural diversity into account.*

Relativistic Perspective

Fundamentally, the perspective known as **cultural relativism** means that no culture is inherently superior or inferior to any other. The reason anthropologists adopt this perspective is that concepts such as "superiority" require judgments about the relative worthiness of behaviors, beliefs, and other characteristics of a culture. Most of the time, such judgments are rooted in one's values, and

Cultural anthropologists insist that valid generalizations about humans can be made only after the full range of cultural variability is taken into account. These New Guinea people wear masks to make them into "mud men" for ceremonial purposes.

Christopher Arnesen/Tony Stone Images

one's values, by and large, depend on the culture in which one was raised.

(Incidentally, perhaps you think that surely there are universally valid standards for judging and evaluating cultures. You may well be right. The trouble is, once you get past standards such as "don't take a human life," people don't agree on what they are! And even "do not kill" is not a universal standard, since this injunction must be qualified in various ways.)

To see why approaching the study of cultures relativistically is important, we may contrast cultural relativism with ethnocentrism. **Ethnocentrism** is the belief that the moral standards, manners, attitudes, and so forth of one's own culture are superior to those of other cultures. Most people are ethnocentric, and a certain degree of ethnocentrism probably is essential if people are to be content with their lives and if their culture is to persist. Mild ethnocentrism—meaning that people hold certain values dear but don't insist that everyone else live by those values—is unobjectionable to ethnologists. But extreme ethnocentrism—meaning that people believe that their values are the only correct ones and that all people everywhere should be judged by how closely they live up to those values—breeds attitudes and behaviors of intolerance that are anathema to cultural anthropology.

At the very least, ethnocentric attitudes are detrimental to the objectivity of ethnographic fieldworkers. However difficult to carry out in practice, fieldworkers should try to avoid evaluating the beliefs and behavior of the people being studied according to the standards of the fieldworker's own culture. Like the holistic and comparative perspectives, the essential point of cultural relativism may be stated simply: *In studying another culture, do not evaluate the behavior of its members by the standards and values of your own culture.*

THE VALUE of ANTHROPOLOGY

What insights does anthropology offer about humanity? Plenty, as we shall see in the rest of this book. For now, we simply mention some of the most general ways the field is valuable.

First, because of its broad scope, anthropology gives us the information we need to understand the biological, technological, and cultural development of humankind. Most of the reliable information available about human biological evolution, prehistoric cultures, and non-Western peoples was collected by anthropologists. Because much of this knowledge has become part of our cultural heritage, where it is written about in textbooks and taught in schools, it is easy to forget that someone had to discover and interpret these facts. For example, only in the late nineteenth century did most scientists accept that people are related to apes, and only in the late twentieth century did the closeness of this relation become apparent.

But anthropology has contributed more than just factual material to our understanding of the human condition. Concepts first developed by anthropologists have been incorporated into the thinking of millions of people. For example, in this chapter we have used the term *culture*—a concept that we assume our readers are aware of and a word that is used in everyday life. You may not know that the scientific meaning of this word, as used in the phrase "Japanese culture," is not very old. Into the nineteenth century, people did not fully understand the importance of the distinction between a people's culture (the learned beliefs and habits that made them distinctive) and their biological makeup (their physical characteristics). Patterns of acting, thinking, and feeling often were thought to be rooted in a group's biological makeup—carried in their genes, as we say today. For example, because there often were readily observable differences in the physical appearances of various races, people mistakenly believed that these physical differences accounted for differences in beliefs and habits as well. In other words, differences that we now know are caused largely or entirely by learning and cultural upbringing were confused with differences caused by biological inheritance. Early twentieth-century anthropologists such as Franz Boas marshaled empirical evidence showing that race and culture are independent of each other. As this example shows, anthropologists have added to our understanding of the human condition, although most people are not aware of these contributions.

Another value of anthropology (ethnology, especially) is that it emphasizes the importance of understanding and appreciating cultural diversity; that is, it urges us not to be ethnocentric in our attitudes toward other peoples. The orientation known as cultural relativism is not only important to the objectivity of ethnologists but also is one of the main lessons anthropology offers to the general public. Knowledge of anthropology helps people avoid some of the miscommunication and misunderstandings that commonly arise when people from different parts of the world interact with one another.

As we shall see in future chapters, our upbringing in a particular culture influences us in subtle ways. For instance, Canadians know how to interpret one another's actions on the basis of speech styles or body language, but these cues do not necessarily mean the same thing to people from different cultures. A Canadian salesperson selling products in Turkey may wonder why her host will not cut the small talk and get down to business, whereas the Turk can't figure out why the visitor thinks they can do business before they have become better acquainted. An Anglo American visiting the Navajo reservation in Arizona may misinterpret the Navajos' reticence as unfriendliness or even hostility, when it is just a different way of relating to people.

In short, anthropology teaches people to be aware of and sensitive to cultural differences—people's actions may not mean what we take them to mean, and much misunderstanding can be avoided by taking cultural differences into account in our dealings with other people in the multicultural world of the twenty-first century.

Finally, because of its insistence on studying humanity from a comparative perspective, anthropology helps us to understand both our own individual lives and our societies. By encouraging you to compare and contrast yourself and your ways of thinking, feeling, and acting with those of people living in other times and places, anthropology helps you see new things about yourself. How does your life compare to the lives of other people around the world? Do people in other cultures share the same kinds of problems, hopes, motivations, and feelings as you do? Or are individuals raised in other societies completely different? How does the overall quality of your existence—your sense of well-being and happiness, your self-image, your emotional life, your feeling that life is meaningful—compare with people who live elsewhere? Anthropology offers the chance to compare yourself to other peoples who live in different circumstances.

SUMMARY

1. Defined as the study of humans, anthropology differs from other disciplines in the social sciences and humanities primarily because of its broad scope. The field as a whole is concerned with all human beings of the past and present, and is also interested in all aspects of humanity: biology, language, technology, art, politics, religion, and all other dimensions of human life.

2. As a practical necessity, however, anthropologists must specialize. Traditionally, the field is divided into five subdisciplines. Physical anthropology studies the biological dimensions of human beings, including our evolution, the physical variations between contemporary populations, and the biology and behavior of nonhuman primates. Archaeology uses the material remains of prehistoric and historic cultures to investigate the past, focusing on the long-term technological and social changes that occurred in particular regions of the world. Cultural anthropology, or ethnology, is concerned with the social and cultural life of contemporary and historically recent human societies. By conducting fieldwork in various human communities, cultural anthropologists contribute to the understanding of cultural diversity and to making the general public more aware and tolerant of cultural differences. Anthropological linguistics studies language, concentrating on nonwritten languages and investigating the interrelations between language and other elements of a people's way of life. Finally, applied anthropology uses the concepts, methods, and theories of anthropology to solve real-world problems in such areas as health, development, and education.

3. Until around 1970 cultural anthropology (the main subject of this text) concentrated on human cultures that are popularly known as "tribal," "premodern," or "preindustrial." This is not as true today, when anthropologists often do their research in the complex urbanized and industrialized nations of the developed world. It is increasingly difficult to distinguish ethnology from the kindred disciplines of sociology and history. However, firsthand, extended fieldwork in villages or relatively small towns or neighborhoods continues to be a hallmark of cultural anthropology. Ethnologists also focus on human cultural variation more than other kinds of scholars.

4. Cultural anthropologists also differ from other scholars who study living people by their approach. There are three main characteristics of this approach. Holism is the attempt to understand the interrelations between the customs and beliefs of a particular society. The comparative perspective means that any attempt to understand humanity or explain cultures or behaviors must include information from a wide range of human societies, for anthropologists have learned that most customs and beliefs are products of cultural tradition and social environment, rather than of a universal human nature. The perspective known as cultural relativism refers to fieldworkers' efforts to understand people's behaviors on their own terms, not those of the anthropologist's own

culture. This requires that anthropologists avoid being ethnocentric in their research, for all peoples have their own history and values.

5. Anthropology has made many contributions to our modern understanding of humanity. Only anthropology allows us to see the development of human biology and culture over long time spans. Most of the knowledge we have about human evolution, prehistoric populations, and modern tribal societies was discovered by anthropologists. Early anthropologists were instrumental in popularizing the concept of culture and in showing that cultural differences are not caused by racial differences. The value of inculcating understanding and tolerance among citizens of different nations is another practical lesson of anthropology, one that is increasingly important as nations become more interdependent economically, as international migration increases, and as countries deal with one another on more equal terms. Last, the information that ethnographers have collected about alternative ways of being human allows us to compare our individual lives and our societies with those of people living in different times, places, and circumstances.

KEY TERMS

anthropology
physical (biological) anthropology
paleoanthropology
primatology
human variation
forensic anthropologists
archaeology
prehistoric archaeology
historic archaeology
cultural anthropology (ethnology)
fieldwork
ethnography
anthropological linguistics
applied anthropology
holistic perspective
comparative perspective
cultural relativism
ethnocentrism

SUGGESTED READINGS

Ervin, Alexander M. *Applied Anthropology: Tools and Perspectives for Contemporary Practice.* Boston: Allyn and Bacon, 2000.

Thorough introduction to the subfield of applied anthropology. Covers ethical issues, roles of anthropologists in policy and program assessments, and specific methods.

Fagan, Brian M. *World Prehistory: A Brief Introduction.* 4th ed. New York: Addison-Wesley, 1998.

Covers human prehistory from a global perspective. Prehistory of various continents is presented, with an overview of the development of civilization in different regions.

Farb, Peter. *Word Play: What Happens When People Talk.* New York: Knopf, 1974.

Despite its age, a highly readable introduction to language and how it is used in social life.

Jurmain, Robert, Harry Nelson, Lynn Kilgore, and Wendy Trevathan. *Introduction to Physical Anthropology.* 8th ed. Belmont, CA: Wadsworth, 1999.

Basic and thorough textbook in biological anthropology, covering genetics, human physical variation, primate biology and behavior, and human evolution. Richly illustrated with photos, maps, and charts.

Renfrew, Colin, and Paul Bahn. *Archaeology: Theories, Methods, and Practice.* 3rd ed. London: Thames and Hudson, 2000.

A lengthy and detailed yet readable introduction to archaeological methods, focusing especially on how prehistorians use artifacts to draw conclusions about the past.

The following ethnographies are excellent for introducing the ways of life of various people around the world. All are highly accessible for beginning students.

Balikci, Asen. *The Netsilik Eskimo.* Prospect Heights, IL: Waveland, 1989.

A well-rounded description of an Eskimo people.

Chagnon, Napoleon A. *Yąnomamö: The Last Days of Eden.* San Diego: Harcourt Brace Jovanovich, 1992.

A readable ethnography of an Amazonian people who are threatened by the incursions of missionaries, miners, tourists, and other outsiders.

Farrer, Claire R. *Thunder Rides a Black Horse: Mescalero Apaches and the Mythic Present.* 2nd ed. Prospect Heights, IL: Waveland, 1996.

Concise account of ethnographer's experience with the modern Apache. Focuses on girls' puberty ceremonies, interweaving Apache culture into the account.

Fernea, Elizabeth. *Guests of the Sheik.* Garden City, NY: Anchor, 1969.

A writer, journalist, and academician's account of her experiences in an Iraqi village with her anthropologist husband.

Kraybill, Donald B. *The Puzzles of Amish Life.* Intercourse, PA: Good Books, 1990.

Focuses on how the Amish of Lancaster County, Pennsylvania, have maintained intact communities and their values by selectively using modern technologies.

Shostak, Marjorie. *Nisa: The Life and Words of a !Kung Woman.* New York: Vintage, 1983.

An outstanding biographical account of a San woman.

Turnbull, Colin. *The Forest People.* New York: Simon & Schuster, 1962.

A readable and sympathetic ethnography about the traditional culture of the BaMbuti pygmies of the African rain forest.

chapter 2

CULTURE

Contents

Culture is a word people use almost every day, but few of us think very often about the term or its significance. Sometimes we visit places such as museums or art galleries to broaden our "cultural awareness." Perhaps we go to a symphony or opera to show that we "appreciate culture." Many people think of culture as a quality that some people possess more of than others, as if how "cultured" someone is depends on social class, education, or speech habits. And how often have we heard someone in the "cultural elite" bemoan the deplorable "popular culture" of television sitcoms, violent movies, pierced tongues or navels, and rock or rap music?

All these uses of *culture* are fine, taken in context, but for anthropologists the term has a somewhat different meaning. In anthropological discussions, the distinction between "elite culture" and "popular culture" is largely irrelevant, and it is utterly meaningless to say that one group of people has "more culture" than another. In this chapter we define and discuss the anthropological conception of culture, introducing some new terms and concepts along the way. We shall see how the concept is applied by anthropologists to understand the diverse ways of life of humans in different parts of the world. We show how culture makes human life as we experience it possible.

Anthropologists have defined the term *culture* in hundreds of ways. Virtually all definitions, however, share certain features. There is agreement that culture

- is learned from others while growing up in a particular society or group;
- is widely shared by the members of that society or group;
- so profoundly affects the thoughts, actions, and feelings of people in that group that anthropologists commonly say that "individuals are a product of their culture"; and
- accounts in large part for the differences between groups of people in how they act, think, and feel.

Even given that culture is learned, shared, shapes individuals, and makes human groups different, there is still a lot of room for controversy over the most useful definition. In fact, practically every anthropologist has her or his own favorite definition.

Some prefer a narrow conception of culture. Generally, they think that culture is most usefully conceptualized as a mental phenomenon: Individuals learn culture and carry it in their heads (as the phrase "cultural baggage" implies), much as individuals learn the grammar of their native language. In this view, actual behavior is not *part of* culture, but is a *product of* culture, much as speaking is a product of the knowledge of the grammar of a language. This way of looking at culture is sometimes called the *ideational* conception of culture.

Others think it better to define culture broadly, so that it includes the actual behavior of individuals, as well as the understandings, beliefs, values, and other mental phenomena stored in their heads. In this view, the culture of a human group consists of both mental and behavioral phenomena. Defined this broadly, culture essentially refers to the way of life of some group of people, but especially to how that way of life makes the group distinctive.

When we speak of Chinese culture, for example, we usually mean practically everything about how the Chinese people live—their family life, religion, values, government, and so forth. The word *culture* often is intended to emphasize the unique or most distinctive aspects of a people's customs and beliefs. How the Chinese think and act differs in some ways from how the French, Iranians, Americans, and Japanese think and act, and the phrase *Chinese culture* nicely calls attention to the multitude of differences between the Chinese and other peoples.

So to speak of the culture of a people or human group is to call attention to all the things that make that group different or distinctive from others. When anthropologists use the term, we do not mean that Chinese culture is better or worse than English or Indian culture. We mean only that the three differ in identifiable ways. Anthropologists also do not mean that Chinese, Indian, or English culture is isolated or unchanging. We mean only that each remains distinct in spite of the centuries of contact between them. Finally, anthropologists do not mean that Indian, Chinese, and English cultures are distinctive because of physical (biological) differences among the three peoples. We mean only that English, Indian, and Chinese children are exposed to different ways of thinking and acting as they grow up. They *become* English, Indian, or Chinese because of their exposure to different settings and environments.

A Definition of Culture

If culture is defined broadly, it includes all the things individuals learn while growing up among a particular group: attitudes, standards of morality, rules of etiquette, perceptions of reality, language, notions about the proper way to live, beliefs about how females and males should interact, ideas about how the world works, and so forth. This part of culture is *knowledge*. We all carry such knowledge in our brains, just as we carry the knowledge of our language. Much of it is so ingrained in us that we are hardly aware that we have learned it or that not everyone in the world has learned it.

If we use the broad definition, culture also includes *behavior*: how people act in particular situations (in church, on the job), how they conduct themselves around different people (parents, classmates), what they do when they experience various emotions (anger, sadness), and so forth. Unlike knowledge, behavior can be observed directly. Behavior also varies somewhat between individuals: Not everyone acts the same way when they are angry, even if they are members of the same culture. Anthropologists generally are more interested in *patterns of behavior*—how most people regularly and habitually act in certain situations—than they are in the behavior of individuals as such. For example, even within a single culture, each wedding is different from

other weddings in some ways. But similar kinds of ceremonial procedures are used, people tend to act in much the same way, similar kinds of people attend or contribute, and so forth. Such patterns of behavior at weddings are our main interest.

In this book, we use the broader definition of culture, because it seems to be the one preferred by most contemporary anthropologists. More precisely:

> The **culture** of a group consists of shared, socially learned knowledge and patterns of behavior.

For convenience, we discuss each major component of this definition separately.

Shared . . .

By definition, culture is *collective*—it is shared by some group of people. "Shared by some group of people" is deliberately vague, because the "group" that "shares" culture depends on our interests. The people who share a common cultural tradition may be quite numerous and geographically dispersed, as illustrated by the phrases "Western culture" and "African culture." Although we use such phrases whenever we want to emphasize differences between Africans and Westerners, the peoples to whom they refer are so diverse that the term "group" has little meaning. At the other extreme, the group that shares a common culture may be small. Some Pacific islands or Amazonian tribes, for instance, have only a few hundred members, yet the people speak a unique language and have distinct customs and beliefs.

Despite these and other complexities, when we say people share culture we usually mean at least one of two things. First, the people are capable of communicating and interacting with one another without serious misunderstanding and without needing to explain constantly what their behavior means. Second, people share a common **cultural identity:** They recognize themselves and their culture's traditions as distinct from other people and other traditions. Thus, Africans (or Westerners, or Native Americans) do not share culture by the first criterion, although they do by the second.

People who share a common culture often live in the same **society,** or a territorially defined population most of whose members speak the same language and share a sense of common identity relative to other societies. The identification of a cultural tradition with a single society is sometimes convenient because it allows us to use phrases like "American culture" and "Indian culture." Societies and cultures, however, do not always share the same physical territory. For example, we usually think of a modern nation as a single society, yet many cultural groupings, identities, and traditions coexist within the boundaries of most modern nations.

. . . Socially Learned . . .

To say that culture is *socially learned* is to say that individuals acquire it from others in the process of growing up in a society or some other kind of group. The process by which infants and children socially learn the culture of those around them is called **enculturation** or **socialization.** The learn-

ing of one's culture, of course, happens as a normal part of people's childhood.

To say that culture is *learned* is to deny that culture is transmitted to new generations *genetically*, by biological reproduction. Culture is not part of a particular human group's biological makeup, but is something the people born into that group acquire while growing up among other members. Biological/genetic differences (including "racial" differences) between human populations do not explain the differences in thinking, feeling, and acting between human populations. Africans, East Asians, Europeans, and Native Americans do not differ in their cultures because they differ in their gene frequencies—they do not differ *culturally* because they differ *biologically*. Any human infant is perfectly capable of learning the culture of any human group or biological population, just as any child can learn the language of whatever group she or he happens to have been born into. To state the main point in a few words: *Cultural differences and biological differences are largely independent of one another.*

To say that culture is *socially learned* is to say that the human species does not learn primarily

As children grow up, they learn the culture of their community by observing, interacting with, and communicating with other group members, including their parents. This process of social learning is known as enculturation or socialization.

D. Hardy/Anthro-Photo File

by *trial and error learning*. The main way children learn culture is by observation, imitation, communication, and inference, and not by trial and error. One important way in which humans differ in degree, though not in kind, from other primates is in the ability to learn by imitating and communicating with other humans. For example, I do not have to learn what is good to eat by trying out a variety of foods, rejecting those that taste bad or make me sick, and retaining in my diet only those that are tasty, satisfying, and nourishing. Rather, I can adopt the diet of other members of my family and culture, thus avoiding the costs (and possible danger and pain!) of learning on my own, by trial and error.

Think about the enormous advantages of humans' reliance on social learning rather than trial and error learning. First, anything that one individual learns can be communicated to others in a group, who can take advantage of someone else's experience. A tasty or nourishing new food discovered by someone can be incorporated into an entire group's cuisine. Second, the knowledge and behavior that any generation has acquired is passed down to the next generation, which transmits it to the third generation, and so on. Thus, the knowledge and behavior acquired by one generation is potentially available to future generations (some of it is lost or replaced each generation, of course). By this process of social learning, over many generations knowledge accumulates. Because of this accumulation, people alive today live largely (but not entirely) off the knowledge acquired and transmitted by previous generations. Members of new generations socially learn such knowledge through enculturation and, in modern societies, through formal education in schools and colleges. All this seems commonsensical and not at all remarkable to you—until you try to imagine how life would be different without social learning.

. . . Knowledge . . .

When anthropologists use the phrase *cultural knowledge*, we do not mean that a people's beliefs, perceptions, rules, standards, and so forth are true, in an objective or absolute sense. In our professional role, anthropologists do not judge the accuracy or worthiness of a group's knowledge. Indeed, we recognize that the knowledge of any cultural group differs to a greater or lesser degree from the knowledge of any other group; in fact, such differences are one of the major things we attempt to describe and understand. To anthropologists, what is most important about cultural knowledge is not its Truth Value, but that:

- the members of a culture share enough knowledge to be capable of behaving in ways that are meaningful and acceptable to others, so that they do not constantly misunderstand one another or have to explain what they are doing; and that
- the knowledge leads people to behave in ways that work at least well enough to allow them to survive and reproduce themselves and transmit their culture.

In a few words, cultural knowledge must lead to behavior that is meaningful to others and adaptive to the natural and social environment. We consider some of this knowledge later.

. . . and Patterns of Behavior

The behavior of individual members of a culture is quite variable. In part, people act differently because of the distinctions they make between males and females, old and young, rich and poor, nieces and uncles, plumbers and attorneys, and so forth. Behavior appropriate for women may not be suitable for men, and vice versa. In addition to the distinctions a culture makes between kinds of people are those it makes between kinds of situations or social contexts: A woman acts differently depending on whether she is interacting with her husband, her daughter, her priest, her employee, a clerk, and so forth. Added to this complexity is the fact that each person is unique: One woman's relationship with her husband is not exactly the same as that of another's, even within the same culture.

Despite such complications, within a group that shares culture there are usually behavioral regularities or patterns of behavior. If, for instance, you were to visit the Yąnomamö, an Amazonian rain forest people, you might be shocked by some of the things they do. By most cultures' standards of "normal," the Yąnomamö—called "The Fierce People" by ethnographer Napoleon Chagnon—are unusually demanding and aggressive. Slight insults often meet with violent responses. Quarreling men may duel by engaging in a chest-pounding contest, during which they often put rocks in their hands and take turns beating one another on the chest. Serious quarrels call for clubs, with which men bash one another on the head. Fathers encourage their sons to strike them (and anyone else) by teasing and goading, all the while praising the child for his fierceness.

If, on the other hand, you were to visit the Semai, a people of Malaysia, you might be surprised at their refusal to express anger and hostility. Indeed, according to your culture's standards, they might be too docile. One adult should never strike another—"Suppose he hit you back?" they ask. With this attitude toward violence, murder is extremely rare—so rare, in fact, that there are no

Human groups often differ markedly in their behavioral responses to events. The Yąnomamö, for example, are more prone to react violently than are most other peoples.

penalties for it. The Semai seldom hit their children—"How would you feel if he or she died?" they ask. When children misbehave the worst physical punishment they receive is a pinch on the cheek or a pat on the hand.

A Yąnomamö and a Semai react to similar situations in different ways, with different behaviors. If one Yąnomamö demands something of another—as they often do—and the demand is refused, the asker is likely to fly into a rage and make threats, and may resort to violence. But if a Semai fails to grant the request of another, the person who is refused may experience a psychological state Semai call *punan*. Punan might be translated as "accident proneness" because the Semai think that to make someone unhappy by frustrating their desires increases that person's chances of having an accident. So (and this is perfectly logical, given their beliefs) if you ask me for something and I refuse your request, I have committed an offense against you that could result in your becoming accidentally injured. You, being the victim of the punan caused by my offense, have the right to demand compensation from me.

The contrasting behavioral responses of Yąnomamö and Semai people to requests made by others illustrate an important characteristic of most human behavior: its social nature. Humans are supremely social animals. We seldom do anything alone, and even when we are alone we rely unconsciously on our cultural upbringing to provide us with the knowledge of what to do and how to act. Relationships between people are therefore enormously important in all cultures. Anthropologists pay special heed to the regularities and patterning of these social relationships, including such things as how family members interact, how females and males relate to one another, how political leaders deal with subordinates, what shamans and priests do, and so forth.

The concept of **role** is useful to describe and analyze interactions and relationships in the context of a group. We commonly say that individuals "have a role" in some group. Roles usually carry names or labels. Examples are "mother" in

N. Chagnon/Anthro-Photo File

a nuclear family, "student" in a classroom, "accountant" in a company, and "headman" of a Yąnomamö village. Attached to roles are the group's *expectations* about what people who hold the role should do. Learning to be a member of a group includes learning its expectations. Expectations include rights and duties. The *rights* (or privileges) I have as someone who has a role include the benefits I and other group members agree I should receive as a member. My *duties* (or obligations) as the holder of a role include what I am expected to do for other members or for the group as a whole.

Rights and duties are usually *reciprocal:* My right over you is your duty to me, and vice versa. And my duties to the group as a whole are the group's rights over me, and vice versa. If I adequately perform my duties to the group as a whole, other members reward me, just as I reward them for their own role performance. By occupying and performing a role in a group, I get some of my own wants and needs fulfilled, and I do so by behaving in ways that others find valuable and satisfying. Conversely, failure to live up to the group's expectations of role performance is likely to bring some sort of informal or formal punishment. Among Yąnomamö, young men who refuse to stand up for themselves by fighting are ridiculed and may never amount to anything.

During enculturation into a particular culture, children learn the kinds of roles that exist and the expectations people have about the rights and duties of those roles. The knowledge of roles and expectations that people share is partly responsible for patterns of behavior.

CULTURAL KNOWLEDGE

We have distinguished between cultural knowledge (attitudes, beliefs, assumptions about the world, and other socially learned information stored in our minds) and patterns of behavior (how individuals typically act in various situations and social contexts). In this section we

discuss five specific components of cultural knowledge: norms, values, symbols, classifications of reality, and world views. These are not necessarily more important than other kinds of knowledge, but they do require some discussion because they are not entirely commonsensical.

Norms

A **norm** is a shared ideal (or rule) about how people ought to act in certain situations (occasions, social contexts) or about how particular people should act toward particular other people (depending on their roles). The emphasis here is on the words *ideal, rule, ought,* and *should.* To say that norms exist does not mean everyone follows them all the time; indeed, some norms are violated with great regularity. *Norm* implies, rather, that (1) there is widespread agreement that people ought to adhere to certain standards of behavior, (2) other people judge the behavior of a person according to how closely it adheres to those standards, and (3) people who repeatedly fail to follow the standards face some kind of negative reaction from other members of the group. We are able to make collective judgments about someone's personal morality because we share common norms. Shared expectations about how roles should be performed are one kind of norm. Fieldworkers learn about the norms of other cultures by several methods, including watching how other people react—negatively or positively—to an individual's behavior.

Sometimes people feel norms are irrational rules that stifle their creativity or keep them from doing what they want for no good reason. People may believe that some norms about proper conduct are confining, such as norms about how to dress correctly for special occasions, or about when and to whom we must give gifts, or about fulfilling familial obligations, or about whether we should have tattoos placed on our bodies.

In fact, though, norms are quite useful to us. It is mainly because we share norms that we know how to behave toward others and that we have expectations about how others should act toward us. For example, when you enter a roomful of strangers at a party, you are somewhat uncertain about how to act. But everyone knows how to go about getting acquainted in your cultural tradition, so you soon are introducing yourself and asking the other guests what they do, what they are studying, or—under some circumstances— whether they are married, single, available, or willing. Here, and in many other cases in everyday life, norms serve as useful instructions on how to do something in such a way that others know your intentions.

Values

Values consist of a people's beliefs about the goals or way of life that is desirable for themselves and their society. Values have profound, although partly unconscious, effects on people's behavior. The aims we pursue, as well as our more general ideas about "the good life," are influenced by the values of the culture into which we happen to have been born or raised. Values also are critical to the maintenance of culture as a whole because they represent the qualities that people believe are essential to continuing their way of life. It is useful to think of values as providing the ultimate standards that people believe must be upheld under practically all circumstances.

An excellent example of how values provide ultimate standards is the American emphasis on certain rights of individuals, as embodied in the Bill of Rights to the Constitution. No matter how much some Americans hate what the press prints, what the right or left wing says, or the pro-life or pro-choice movements, few believe that unpopular organizations or speech should be suppressed, so long as they do not engage in or advocate violence. Freedom of the press, of speech, and of religion are ultimate standards that take precedence over the opinions and interests of the moment. People may be deeply attached to their values and, under certain circumstances, some will sacrifice their lives for them.

Symbols

A **symbol** is something that means, stands for, or calls to mind something else. Symbols may be objects (a ring, a flag, a dress pattern, a kind of car), behaviors (an upraised middle finger, a bow, a way of walking, a style of speaking), or events (a ceremony, a celebration, a political convention). Some symbols exist largely or entirely for their symbolic content—there would be no need or use for them at all if they did not carry certain meanings or arouse certain feelings (a flag, a handshake, a wink, many ceremonies). Other symbols also have practical value or functions—in addition to their useful purposes, they convey implicit messages (the kind and age of the car you drive, how you walk or speak, what goes on at political conventions).

Just as we learn norms and values as we grow up, so do we learn the meanings that people in our group attach to symbols. The understandings people share about symbols and their meanings affect the patterns of behavior found in a culture. In fact, unless individuals agree that certain kinds of behavior communicate certain meanings, social interaction would be far more difficult than it usually is, for our shared understandings of what behavior means allows us to interact with one another without the constant need to explain what we are doing.

For the most part, the understandings that people share about the meanings of behaviors, events, and objects are unconscious. It is possible to explain to a stranger the norms and values of our cultural tradition, and to give reasons why we think people ought to act in certain ways or why certain values are important to uphold. We cannot, however, usually explain why a wink, a tone of voice, a way of wearing jewelry, a style of dress, or certain gestures mean what they do. We "just know" because "everyone knows," for such things are "common knowledge."

Two important properties of symbols are that their meanings are usually arbitrary and conventional. *Arbitrary* in this context means that there are no inherent qualities in the symbol itself that lead some human group to attribute one meaning to it, rather than some other meaning. The wink that often means "I'm just kidding" in some cultures is—literally—meaningless in other cultures. *Conventional* refers to the fact that the meanings exist only because people implicitly agree they exist. At an intersection, a red light means "stop," but only because all drivers agree (hopefully!) that it does.

The shared understandings that allow people to correctly interpret the meanings of behaviors is an important part of cultural knowledge, for it is such understandings that make living in social groups possible. To most North Americans, for example, actions such as nodding the head to signal agreement or affirmation, walking hand in hand in public, and embracing a friend or relative seem commonsensical and perhaps "natural." Yet these and other social behaviors do not mean the same thing in all cultures. An important part of enculturation consists of learning how to interpret the behavior of other people and how to adjust our own behavior in accord with their expectations. Culture, in other words, provides us with the common understanding of how to interact with one another appropriately (that is, according to shared expectations) and meaningfully (that is, in such a way that other people usually are able to interpret our intentions).

Nonverbal communication provides a fine example of these common understandings. When you interact with someone face to face, you are engaged in a continual giving and receiving of messages, communicated by both speech and behavior. Spoken messages are intentionally (consciously) sent and received. Other messages— including body language, facial expressions, hand gestures, touching, and the use of physical space—are communicated by nonverbal behavior, much of which is unconscious. Nonverbal messages emphasize, supplement, or complement spoken messages. We are not always conscious of what we are communicating nonverbally, and sometimes our body language even contradicts what we are saying. (Is this how your mother often knew when you were lying?)

The general point is that cultural knowledge conditions social behavior in ways people do not always recognize consciously—at least until someone's behavior violates their common understandings. Furthermore, gestures and other body movements with well-known meanings in one culture have no meaning, or different meanings, in another.

For example, on a Micronesian island where one of the authors lived, people may answer "yes" or show agreement by a sharp intake of breath (a "gasp") or by simply raising the eyebrows. Or one may also answer "yes" by the grunting sound ("uh uh") that carries exactly the opposite meaning to North Americans. Pointing is done with the nose, not the finger. You would signal "I don't know" or "I'm not sure" by wrinkling your nose, rather than shrugging your shoulders. "Come here" or "come closer" is indicated by moving the arm in the direction of the person you are communicating with; this motion is exactly the same one used by North Americans to mean "move further away." For two people of the opposite sex—even spouses or engaged couples—to hold hands in public is offensive and bad manners. However, it is perfectly acceptable for two same-sex friends to walk hand in hand. One should never touch the head of someone else, especially if the person is of similar or higher status. It is rude to walk between two people engaged in conversation; if possible, one walks around them; if not, one says the equivalent of "please excuse me," waits for permission, and then crouches down while passing between them.

Aside from showing the necessity of common understandings for social interaction, these examples show one way misunderstandings occur when individuals with different cultural upbringings interact. Raised in different cultures where gestures and other behaviors carry different meanings, each individual (mis)interprets the behavior of the other based on his or her own culture's understandings, often seeing the other as rude, unfriendly, insensitive, overly familiar, and so forth. Arabs and Iranians often stand "too close" for the Canadian and American comfort zone. Japanese are less likely than North Americans to express definite opinions or preferences, which often comes across to North Americans as uncertainty or tentativeness. The common American tendency to be informal and friendly is viewed as inappropriate in Japan and many other cultural settings, where feelings of warmth and closeness are confined to narrow circles, or where outward manifestations of emotions are held in check.

Classifications of Reality

The members of a cultural tradition share ideas of what kinds of things and people exist. They have similar **classifications of reality,** meaning that the human and natural environments are divided up according to shared and largely unconscious principles. (Some people call these their "cognitive categories.")

For example, people everywhere recognize a category of people who are related to them biologically or through adoption—their relatives, we call them. But the principles by which certain kinds of relatives are placed in cultural categories vary between kinship systems. Thus, English speakers think of the sisters of both our mother and our father as a single kind of relative, and we call them by the same kinship term, *aunt*. But there are some cultural traditions in which the sister of one's mother is considered one kind of relative and the sister of one's father a different kind, and each is called by a separate kinship term.

The same applies to the way people classify their natural environment. Cultural knowledge not only provides the categories by which we classify kinds of people, but also categories by which plants, animals, phases of the moon, seasonal changes, and other natural phenomena are classified into kinds.

For example, on the island of Mindoro in the Philippines live a people known as the Hanunóo, who grow most of their food by a method called shifting cultivation. This method involves farming a plot for one or two years, abandoning it for

a number of years until it has recovered its potential to yield a crop, and then replanting it. The Hanunóo judge whether a plot they abandoned some years previously has recovered enough for replanting by the quantity and kind of natural vegetation that has recolonized the plot. The need to assess the degree of readiness of a plot for recultivation has led the Hanunóo to develop an extremely complex classification of the plants found in their habitat. They are able to identify more than 1,600 "kinds" of plants, which exceeds by more than 400 the number of species that a botanist would distinguish.

Which plant classification is right, that of the Hanunóo or that of the botanist? Both. The point is not that the Hanunóo are right and the botanist wrong, or vice versa. Rather, the botanist uses one set of criteria to decide whether two individual plants belong to the same kind, and these criteria have been adopted because they have proved useful to science. The Hanunóo use a different set of criteria that, over the course of many generations, they have developed for their specific needs. The criteria by which various realms of nature are carved up and assigned to categories are important components of cultural knowledge because they influence the way a people perceive the natural world.

Categories also influence how people use the resources in their environments. Plants and animals are classified not just into various "kinds," but also into various categories of usefulness. What one people consider a "resource" is not necessarily defined as a resource for another people. Muslims and Orthodox Jews consider pig flesh to be unclean. Devout Hindus refuse to consume beef, the flesh of the cattle that are sacred in their religion. The fact that a given animal or plant is edible does not mean that people consider it edible (or else more North Americans would eat dogs, as do many east and southeast Asians, and horses, as do many French).

Finally, people of different cultures differ in their beliefs about the kinds of things that do and do not exist. For instance, some people believe that some individuals (called witches) use malevolent supernatural powers to harm their enemies. Traditional Navajo people believe that witches can change themselves into wolves, bears, and other animals. The Tukano people of the Bolivian rain forest think that a spirit of the forest controls the game animals they depend on for meat. So a Tukano group's shaman periodically makes a supernatural visit to the abode of the forest spirit. He promises to magically kill a certain number of humans and to send their souls to the forest spirit in return for the spirit's releasing the animals so the hunters can find game. In sum, not only do different cultures classify objective reality in different ways, but they differ on what reality is; one culture's definition of reality may not be the same as that of another culture.

World Views

The **world view** of a people is the way they interpret reality and events, including their images of themselves and how they relate to the world around them. World views are affected by how people classify the social and natural world, which we have just discussed. But world views include more than just the way people and nature are carved up by a culture. People have opinions about the nature of the cosmos and how they fit into it. All cultures distinguish physical bodies from spiritual souls and have beliefs about what happens to the latter after the former dies. People have ideas about the meaning of human existence: how we were put on earth, who put us here, and why. They have a notion of what evil is, where it comes from, why it sometimes happens to good people, and how it can be combated. Everywhere we find myths and legends about the origins of living things, objects, and customs.

These examples of various aspects of world view all come from religion. But it is important not to confuse world view and religion, and especially not to think that religion and world view are synonymous. Although religious beliefs do influence the world view of a people, cultural traditions vary in aspects of world view that we do not ordinarily think of as religious.

For instance, the way people view their place in nature is part of their world view: Do they see themselves as the masters and conquerors of nature, or as living in harmony with natural forces? The way people view themselves and other people is part of their world view. Do they see themselves, as many human groups do, as the only true human beings, and all others as essentially animals? Or do they see their way of life as one among many equally human but different ways of life? Most modern scientists share a similar world view: They believe that all things and events in the universe have natural, discoverable causes that we can know through logic supported by certain procedures of observation and experimentation.

A people's conception of time and space is also part of their world view. Westerners are so used to thinking of time in arbitrary units—for our seconds, minutes, and hours are not natural segments of time—that we forget that other people do not share our ideas of how important these units are. Many North Americans frown on "wasting time" and on not "spending time productively," which often means not using time to reach some goal. This view of time as a resource that, like money, can be invested wisely or foolishly is not present in the world view of many other cultures.

CULTURE, BIOLOGY, and HUMAN LIFE

Anthropologists believe that culture is absolutely essential to humans and to human life as it is usually lived—in association with other people, or in groups.

To be sure, living in social groups certainly does not require culture. Many species of termites, bees, ants, and other social insects live in quite complex groups, yet they have no culture. Gorillas, chimpanzees, baboons, macaques, and most other primates also live in groups. Research done by primatologists shows that chimpanzees learn to use simple tools, share food, communi-

Courtesy of Thomas Perry

Culture is essential for human life because it helps people adapt to their surroundings, teaches them how to live with others, and provides interpretations for the world around them. The ceremonial dress of these New Guinea men reminds us that people deal with these problems in a wide variety of ways.

cate well, have intergroup conflicts in which animals are killed, and form relationships in which two individuals who are physically weaker cooperate to overpower a stronger animal. Yet few anthropologists would claim that chimpanzee groups have culture in the same sense as all human groups do. (Some use the term *protoculture* to emphasize that such animal behaviors are learned rather than instinctive.) If other group-living, highly social animals cooperate, communicate, survive, and thrive without culture, why do people need culture at all?

The main reason boils down to the following: The culture of the group into which people are born or raised provides the information ("knowledge," we have called it) they need to survive in

their natural environments and to participate in social life. This knowledge, which infants begin to learn soon after birth, is necessary because humans do not come into the world equipped with a *detailed set of behavioral instructions inherited genetically from their parents*. Rather, people are born with a *propensity to learn the knowledge and behaviors of the group they were born into from observation, interaction, and communication with members of that group*. More than any other animal, humans are, as two biologists have put it, "programmed to learn."

As we have seen, culture is transmitted socially, not genetically, meaning that it is passed on to new generations by socialization, not by reproduction. Just as language provides people with the information they need to communicate thoughts and complex ideas to one another, so does culture provide the knowledge and behaviors that make it possible for them to survive in their environments and live together in groups. Culture is, therefore, necessary for human existence in at least three specific ways:

1. Culture provides the skills needed to adapt to our surroundings. It gives people the knowledge they need to produce the tools, shelter, clothing, and other objects they use to survive in their natural environments. Parents and other adults teach children the techniques they need to acquire food and other essential resources and to protect themselves from nature's elements. As they grow up, children learn the behaviors useful for tracking game, making a garden, herding livestock, or finding a job, depending on how people make their living in a particular society. Since most human populations have lived in the same environment for many generations, if not centuries, the current generation is usually wise to take advantage of the adaptive wisdom learned and passed down by their cultural ancestors.

2. Culture is the basis for human social life. It provides ready-made norms, values, expectations, attitudes, and other knowledge that allow individuals to cooperate with one another, live in families and other kinds of groups, relate to members of their own and the opposite sex, and establish political and legal systems. As they grow up, people learn *social lessons*—what is and is not acceptable behavior, how to win friends, who relatives are, how and whom to court and marry, whether to show glee or sadness, and so forth.

3. Culture affects our views of reality. It provides the categories and beliefs through which people perceive, interpret, analyze, and explain events in the world around them. The culture we acquire while growing up in a given group provides a filter or screen that affects how we perceive the world through our senses. Some objects "out there" in the world are sensed, others are not. Some events are important, others can be ignored. During enculturation, people come to share the categories and beliefs that filter their perceptions of reality and give meaning to things and events. Growing up in a given culture thus leads people to develop shared understandings of the world (keep in mind that "shared understandings" do not imply Truth).

In sum, culture is essential to human life as we know it because it provides us with the means to adapt to our surroundings, form relationships in organized groups, and interpret reality. Adaptation, organization, interpretation—these are three of the main reasons culture is essential to a normal human existence. In future chapters, we look at some of the diverse ways in which various cultures have equipped their members to adapt to their environment, organize their groups, and understand their world.

SUMMARY

1. Culture is the key concept of cultural anthropology. Although the word has been defined in hundreds of ways, it usually is defined broadly as the way of life of some human group. It refers especially to the unique, distinctive aspects of a group's way of life. In this book we define culture as the shared, socially learned knowledge and patterns of behavior characteristic of some group. "Group" may refer to an ethnic group, a society, a tradition, or a subculture, depending on the context of the discussion.

2. Culture is socially learned, meaning that it can be transmitted from one group or individual to another. Cultural knowledge is not true in any objective sense, but it must at least allow a society to persist in its environment and must enable people to interact appropriately and meaningfully.

3. Cultural knowledge has many components, some of which are norms, values, common understandings of symbols, classifications of reality, and world views. Because these and other components of cultural knowledge are products of social learning—not inborn—we must learn them during enculturation, no matter how natural or commonsensical they seem.

4. Culture is essential for human life for three main reasons: (1) Culture provides each generation with the skills and techniques needed to adapt to their natural environment; (2) culture provides each individual with norms, values, expectations, and other information needed to live with others in groups; and (3) culture provides the categories and beliefs by which people sense, screen, interpret, and explain reality.

KEY TERMS

culture	norms
cultural identity	values
society	symbols
enculturation (socialization)	classifications of reality
role	world views

SUGGESTED READINGS

Cronk, Lee. *That Complex Whole: Culture and the Evolution of Human Behavior.* Boulder, CO: Westview, 1999.

A readable yet sophisticated book that addresses issues of relating culture to biology and to "human nature." Author's views are controversial.

Kawagley, Oscar A. *A Yupiaq Worldview: A Pathway to Ecology and Spirit.* Prospect Heights: Waveland, 1995.

The author, himself a Yupiaq of Alaska, describes the world view of his community, which emphasizes ecological balance and spiritual harmony with the natural world. He also covers recent changes and the relationship between Native and American education. Highly readable book for beginning students and those interested in Native Americans.

Middleton, DeWight R. *The Challenge of Human Diversity: Mirrors, Bridges, and Chasms.* Prospect Heights: Waveland, 1998.

A brief (101 pages) discussion of anthropological concepts used to describe and understand cultural diversity. Includes examples of interactions between people of different cultures, including between fieldworkers and local communities.

Norberg-Hodge, Helena. *Ancient Futures: Learning from Ladakh.* San Francisco: Sierra Club Books, 1991.

The author, a linguist, describes all that she admires about a region in Tibet. Includes material on using the land, healing, family, community life, and Buddhism. Also deals with the impact of the West, including tourism and "development."

Spradley, James, and David W. McCurdy, eds. *Conformity and Conflict: Readings in Cultural Anthropology,* 10th ed. Boston: Allyn and Bacon, 2000.

A collection of interesting and informative essays for introductory students.

chapter 3

CULTURE *and* LANGUAGE

Contents

Language is the shared knowledge of sounds, sound combinations, meanings, and rules that allows people to send and receive precise spoken messages. Our ability to communicate complex information is perhaps the main mental capability that makes humankind different from other animals. Language underlies every other aspect of a people's cultural existence—their relations with the natural environment, family life, political organization, world view, and so forth. Practically all of children's socialization depends upon language, which means that language is the main vehicle of cultural transmission from one generation to the next. Some scholars hold that language greatly influences or even largely controls our thinking processes, for the concepts and categories with which we think are derived from the language we learn while growing up in a given community.

We begin this chapter by discussing language in general terms. Then we show how people communicate by following unconscious rules for combining sounds and words in ways that other people recognize as meaningful. We discuss the ways in which the cultural tradition of a people is related to the language they speak. Finally, we introduce how people use language in various social situations.

THE POWER of LANGUAGE

An important point to understand about language is that, like cultural knowledge, speaking and understanding are quite remarkable capabilities of the human mind. Although we speak and listen so often that we consider it routine, our knowledge of how to do so is incredibly complex. To illustrate this complexity, consider the following (very simple) English sentence:

> "My boyfriend and I are flying to his mother's next week."

What do you have to know to understand the precise meaning of this sentence? We cannot begin to list all the linguistic knowledge needed,

but here are a few bits, which we choose because you probably wouldn't think of them on your own:

- Each sound and how it is distinct—for example, "m" is a different sound than "b," and "r" is a different sound than "l" (and, in case you are wondering, "m" and "b" are not different sounds in all the world's 6,000 languages, nor are "r" and "l")
- Each word and its meaning—and the meaning depends on the context (You don't think she means "friend who is a male" or that the couple has wings, right? And "my" doesn't mean she owns him, as it would if she said "my suitcase.")
- Tenses—the flight will happen in the future ("are flying" would usually be interpreted as the present tense, but "next week" tells you she means future; had she said "flew" she would be contradicting herself; had she said "fly" the sentence would be incorrect, though you would understand her meaning)
- That "next" means the week between this week and two weeks from this week (Also, you know that "weeks" run Sunday to Saturday, so if today is Saturday, "next week" could be as early as tomorrow, but if today is Sunday then "next week" could be seven days from today.)
- Implicit meanings: "his mother's" what? ("House" or "home," of course.) Is anyone else going? (Probably not: They're visiting the guy's mother, and couples nearly always do so alone; she knows this just as you do, so if someone else were going, she likely would have mentioned it.) What does the fact that she said "mother's" instead of "parents'" imply?
- Word order—it tells you that her mother is staying while she and her boyfriend are traveling (In another actual language, the same word order means the mom is traveling.)

Notice also that you may be able to say something about the speaker herself from her first four words. (What if she'd said, "Me and my boyfriend . . .")

There is much, much more that you need to know to understand this sentence, as you would easily recognize had we written it in Quechua (a language of the Andes). Our main points, though, are the following. First, even simple messages require an enormous amount of linguistic knowledge to speak and understand. Of course, you can understand messages with far more information than the example sentence. In fact, you can understand an infinite number of messages in English, just as can speakers of any other language.

Second, the knowledge needed for speaking and understanding is largely *unconscious*—can you state the difference between the sounds "m" and "b," or between "r" and "l"? Without linguistic training, chances are you cannot. How many sounds are there in "mother," and what are they? (There are five sounds, and none of them are "t" or "h.")

Third, the knowledge is *intuitive*—in a fraction of a second, you called upon your knowledge of English to decipher the meaning of the sentence. You did not have to think about it, and you understood precisely what the speaker intended—although near-perfect comprehension is not the case for all linguistic messages.

Fourth, the meaning of each individual word is *arbitrary*—words are combinations of sounds that are symbols for meanings, so "week" is *semana* in Spanish, and so on. When you learned English, you learned how to pronounce and how to understand thousands of words and their meanings, which are often multiple and vary with context. In addition to learning the words and meanings, you learned the rules for altering the meaning of certain parts of speech: how to make plurals of nouns, form tenses of verbs, show possessives, and so forth.

Fifth, language is *creative,* meaning that you can say and understand things that no one has ever before said or understood—it is possible that you have heard the example sentence before, but you understand it even if you have not. Suppose I write this completely novel sentence:

"Black holes are red."

You may wonder how I could possibly know, you may think I'm contradicting myself, or you may believe me ignorant since no light escapes from black holes. But you know what I mean.

Sixth, language is made up of *discrete and recombinable elements.* Individual (discrete) sounds make words, and these sounds in different combinations make different words ("m" is in three words, the "y" sound is in "my" and "fly," and so forth). Similarly, words in different combinations make up meaningful sentences, provided, of course, that the words are strung together in accord with the rules of the language.

Finally, language makes it possible to communicate about people, things, and events that are not immediately present, like "mother" and "next week" in the sentence. This property of language, called *displacement,* greatly contributes to the power of language in communication. Language has the displacement property because of the symbolic nature of words and sentences. We can discuss someone who is out of sight because the symbols of language (a name, a title) call the person to mind, allowing us to conceptualize him or her. We can speculate about the future because although its events may never happen, our language includes symbols that stand for future time and more symbols that allow us to form a mental image of events that are only possible. We can learn about past wars in Vietnam and present conflicts in South Asia without experiencing them firsthand. Displacement makes it possible for us to discuss and learn about things that may not even exist, such as ghosts, goblins, and ghouls; in fact, we can give these things detailed characteristics in our mind's eye, even though our real eyes have never seen them. We can tell one another stories about things that never happened, and thus tell lies, create myths, recite folklore, and write literature. I can tell you about the monster that chased me in my dream last night, and from my verbal description of it (knowing that it existed only in my imagination) you can form a mental image of the beast and understand why it woke me up. Obviously, much of cultural knowledge would be impossible without the displacement property of language.

The fact that language uses symbols has another consequence, related to the displacement property. The symbols of language communicate meanings, and because the meanings are arbitrary and conventional (see Chapter 2), they are limited only by the ability of the human mind to comprehend them. Thus, words, phrases, and sentences can be symbols for abstract concepts as well as for concrete persons, places, things, actions, and events. Among these abstractions are *truth, evil, god, masculinity, wealth, values, humanity, infinity, law, democracy, universal, space,* and *hatred.* Humans all understand abstractions comparable to these, although of course these same abstract concepts do not exist in all languages.

Notice also that the process of enculturation would be impossible without language. Language makes it possible for the knowledge in one person's mind to be transmitted into the mind of another person, allowing for social learning. During enculturation, we learn not just "facts" and "lessons" about the world. We hear (or read) stories and myths, whose lessons are only implicit. The world view of a culture is communicated to younger generations by language. And, as we discuss later, the ways in which a people classify reality is encoded in their language.

In brief, language is powerful. It allows people to communicate amazingly complex and precise messages. Because it is creative, it allows us to send and receive an infinite number of novel messages. It allows us to discuss people and things that are out of sight and to conceive of events that might never happen. It makes abstract thought and the discussion of abstract concepts possible. It facilitates the transmission of information from one individual (and one generation) to another. It allows members of our group to discuss plans, contingencies, and possible courses of action, based on our beliefs about what happened in the past and our expectations about what might happen in the future. All these are things we all do so routinely that it is hard to imagine not being able to do them! To appreciate the power of language, try to imagine life without these abilities.

HOW LANGUAGE WORKS

As children learn the language of their community, they master an enormous amount of information about individual sounds, sound combinations, meanings, and rules. The elements (sounds, words) and the rules for combining them make up the total system of linguistic knowledge called a **grammar.** Grammar refers to all the knowledge shared by those who are able to speak and understand a given language: what sounds occur, rules for combining them into sequences, the meanings that are conveyed by these sequences, and how sentences are constructed by stringing words together according to precise rules.

This scientific use of *grammar* differs from the everyday use of the term. In everyday speech we judge people partly on the basis of whether we consider their grammar proper. In the United States there are several dialects (regional or ethnic variants) of English. One, called *Standard American English* (SAE)—the dialect we usually hear in the national news media—is culturally accepted as most correct. Other dialects, especially those spoken by many African Americans and by southern or Appalachian whites, are looked down on by many of those whose dialect is SAE.

But there is no such thing as superior and inferior dialects (or languages) *in the linguistic sense.* (Nor, incidentally, does the phrase "primitive language" apply to any language.) That is, each language, and each dialect, is equally capable of serving as a vehicle for communicating the messages its speakers need to send and receive. So long as a person successfully communicates, there is no such thing as "bad grammar" or people who "don't know proper grammar." The exchange of messages

Merle: I ain't got no computer.
Pearl: I ain't got one either.

is perfectly good English—to members of certain subcultures who speak one English dialect. So long as speakers communicate their intended meaning to listeners, then the words they use or the ways they construct their sentences are as valid *linguistically* as any other. The evaluations we make of someone else's grammar or overall style of speech, then, are cultural evaluations. *Culturally*, people define some dialects as more correct than others. But if the history of the United States had been different, some other dialect of American English might have become standard, and the sentences

Jennifer: I have no computer.
Christopher: Nor do I.

might have become a cultural marker or symbol by which one segment of the population judges another as unsophisticated.

This point is so important that it is worth saying another way. Many languages are not uniform but have variations based on region, class, ethnicity, or some other difference between people. These variations in the grammar of a single language are called **dialects.** The speakers of a language or dialect share a complete knowledge of its grammar. When linguists try to discover this grammar, they call what they are investigating a *descriptive grammar:* They are trying to describe completely and objectively the elements and rules that underlie communication in some particular language or dialect. The descriptive grammar a linguist would write of Black English would differ slightly from that of SAE. But a linguist would never describe the differences between the two dialects in terms of relative superiority, since each dialect is capable of conveying the same messages. So when some speakers of SAE label African American or southern dialects as substandard English, they are basing their judgments on their cultural assumptions about the relative correctness of dialects, but their judgment has no linguistic validity.

With this point about the relativity of languages and dialects in mind, we move on to discuss two aspects of grammar: (1) sounds and their patterning, and (2) sound combinations and their meanings. (A third field studies the rules for combining words into sentences, but this complicated subject is outside the scope of this book.)

Sound Systems

In any act of speaking, what our vocal tract sends out into the world is a string of sounds. Linguists are trained to describe and analyze the nature and patterning of these sounds. The sounds of a language, together with the way these sounds occur in regular and consistent patterns, make up the *phonological system* of the language. The study of this system is called **phonology.**

For example, when you hear the word *debt*, you hear a sequence of sounds that you associate

Erika Stone/Peter Arnold, Inc.

When children master language, they learn the sounds, words, and rules used in their community, as well as how to speak appropriately in given social situations.

with a certain meaning. You do not consciously think, and may even be unable to recognize, that debt consists of three distinguishable sounds, /d/, /ɛ/, and /t/. (The slash marks // denote sounds recognized as distinctive in a single language.) In fact, if someone asked you, "How many sounds are there in 'debt'?" you might say "Four" because you might confuse the sounds in debt with its number of letters in English spelling.

But you do know what the three sounds in *debt* are, although you might not know that you know. You know because you recognize that the word *pet* is a different word than *debt*, although only its initial sound, /p/, is different. You know because you recognize *debt* and *date* as different words, although they differ only in their second sound. And you know because you recognize the profound contrast in meaning between *debt* and *dead*, although this difference is caused by a single sound at the end of the two words. If English speakers did not know, at an unconscious level, that *debt* must be pronounced /dɛt/, rather than /pɛt/, /dayt/, or /dɛd/, they would mispronounce it, and their listeners would be unable to distinguish *debt* from these other words. Conversely, if a listener did not know that /dɛt/ is different from /pɛt/, she or he might expect to receive a cat or dog when the speaker said, "I'm paying my debt to you."

The particular sounds that the speakers of a language recognize as distinct from other sounds are called the **phonemes** of the language. Phonemes are the individual sounds of a language that make a difference in the meanings of its words. For example, we can break up the word *brought* into four phonemes: /b/, /r/, /ɔ/, and /t/. The substitution of any other phoneme for any of the phonemes in the word *brought* would either change the word into another word (e.g., *bright*, in which a different vowel sound, /ay/, is substituted for /ɔ/) or make it unintelligible (e.g., *blought* or *broughk*).

Languages have different phonemes, and various languages' phonological systems are patterned differently. This means that languages recognize and distinguish between sounds based on different sound qualities, and that different

languages may have different logic and consistency in making these distinctions.

As an example of the patterning of the phonological system of one language, compare two phonemes of English: /b/ and /p/. The phoneme /b/ appears in *boy, able, probation,* and *flab*. It is made by putting the lips together and then releasing them while making a slight vibration with the vocal cords. The phoneme /p/ appears in *pat, approach, mop,* and *example*. We make the /p/ sound the same way as /b/, except that we do not vibrate our vocal cords.

You can hear the vibration of your vocal cords in /b/ by placing your hands over your ears while saying the word *bat* slowly and listening for a slight buzz during the pronunciation of /b/. This buzz is the sound your vocal cords make when your lungs force air through them while they are constricted, or tightened, and brought nearly into contact with one another. All sounds in which the vocal cords vibrate are called *voiced*. Examples of other voiced consonants in English are /d/, /z/, and /ǰ/ (/ǰ/ is the first and last sound in *judge*). All vowel sounds also are voiced in English.

Now place your hands over your ears while saying the word *pat*. You will not hear a buzz during the pronunciation of /p/. This is because your vocal cords are completely open, so the flow of air from your lungs is unimpeded and no buzzy sound is created. All sounds in which the vocal cords are open, so that their vibration does not contribute to the sound, are called *voiceless*. Other voiceless phonemes in English are /t/, /s/, and /č/ (/č/ is the first and last sound in *church*).

The only difference between *bat* and *pat* is this first sound, and the significant difference between the sounds /b/ and /p/ is that the vocal cords vibrate during /b/ but are open during /p/. Stated technically, the only difference between the two phonemes is that /b/ is voiced, whereas /p/ is voiceless.

We discussed these two English phonemes in some detail to make a general point: Our understanding of words is based on our shared ability to hear *distinctions* between their constituent sounds and to recognize these distinctions as *significant*. People who speak English have no difficulty hearing the distinctions between the first sounds of *bill* and *pill,* although they do not consciously know what qualities make these sounds different. We also recognize the distinctions between the two sounds as significant—that is, as making a difference in the meanings of the words in which they appear. If the difference between /b/ and /p/ were not significant, we would not recognize any difference between words that differ only in these sounds—*pill* and *bill* would have the same meaning and therefore would be the same word!

Variations in Sound Systems

We have just put into words what every speaker of English unconsciously and intuitively knows: that we detect the difference between sounds such as /t/ and /d/, and /f/ and /v/, and that we recognize this difference as significant. Can't everyone in the world hear this difference, and doesn't everyone recognize this difference as significant?

No, they can't and don't. There are a great many languages in which sounds that differ only in whether they are voiced or voiceless are not recognized as different sounds. In fact, speakers may not be able to hear the difference between such sounds. For instance, in Kosraen, a Micronesian language, the distinctions between the sounds /t/ and /d/, /p/ and /b/, and /k/ and /g/ make no difference in meaning. So the two alternative pronunciations of the following words make no difference in meaning to speakers of Kosraen:

kip and *gip* mean "satiated," "full from eating"
tin and *din* mean "color"
pik and *bik* mean "sand"

It is as if English-speaking people made no distinction between *cot* and *got,* between *tan* and *dan,* and between *pig* and *big.* This does not mean that Kosraen ears are not as sensitive as Canadian, Australian, or English ears. It means only that the Kosraen and English languages do not recognize the same distinctions in similar sounds as making a difference in the meanings of words. In English, /k/ and /g/ are different phonemes; in Kosraen, they are alternative ways of pronouncing the same phoneme.

So differences between sounds that are meaningful in one language's phonological system do not always make a difference in meaning in another's. Conversely, one language may recognize distinctions between similar sounds that the speakers of another language do not detect. For example, we have referred to the English phoneme /p/ as if it is always pronounced the same way. In fact, we use two pronunciations for /p/, depending on the sounds around it. Consider the words *pit* and *spit.* You might think that the only difference between the two is the sound /s/. If so, you are wrong. The /p/ in *pit* is followed by a short puff of air (called aspiration) between it and the vowel; the /p/ in *pit* is said to be aspirated. The /p/ in *spit* is not followed by such a puff; it is unaspirated. (If your native language is English, you cannot hear this difference, but you may be able to feel it: Put your hand immediately in front of your mouth while saying the two words, and you may feel the aspiration after the /p/ in *pit,* but not after the /p/ in *spit.*)

Surely such a slight difference cannot matter, but in many languages it does. In Thai, for example, /p/ and /pʰ/ (the ʰ stands for aspiration) are separate phonemes, which means that those who speak Thai detect the difference between many aspirated and unaspirated sounds and recognize it as changing the meaning of many words. This is seen in the following Thai words:

paa "forest"   *pʰaa* "to split"
tam "to pound"   *tʰam* "to do"
kat "to bite"   *kʰat* "to interrupt"

Note that a difference in sound that is nearly inaudible to a speaker of English changes the meanings of the paired Thai words just listed. Hindi, the language spoken by many Asian Indians, also recognizes the difference between aspirated and unaspirated sounds.

One of the most interesting ways in which languages differ in their phonological systems is the way the pitch of the voice is used to convey meaning. (The pitch of a voice depends on how fast the vocal cords vibrate: The higher the frequency of vibration, the higher the pitch of the voice.) English speakers use pitch to convey different meanings, as you can see by contrasting the following sentences:

She went to class.
She went to class?

The first statement is turned into a question by altering the pitch of the voice. In the question, the pitch rises with the word *class*.

Speakers of English use the changing pitch of their voices over the whole sentence to communicate a message; that is, the voice pitch falls or rises mainly from word to word, rather than within a word. There are many other languages in which a high, medium, or low pitch used within an individual word, or even in a syllable, changes the fundamental meaning of the word.

Languages in which the pitch (or tone) with which a word is said (or changes in the voice pitch during its pronunciation) affects the meaning of a word are known as **tone languages.** Tone languages occur in Africa and in southeastern and eastern Asia. Chinese, Thai, Burmese, and Vietnamese are all tone languages, which is why they have a musical quality to ears accustomed to English. As an example of how pitch can affect meaning, consider these words from Nupe, an African tone language:

bá (high tone) means "to be sour"
bā (mid tone) means "to cut"
bà (low tone) means "to count"

Here, whether the two phonemes in *ba* are pronounced with a high, mid, or low tone changes their meaning. The same principle can apply to syllables within a word—how the pitch of the voice changes between the syllables alters the meaning. This is exemplified by the following Thai words:

nâa (tone of voice falls on second vowel) means "face"
nǎa (tone of voice rises on second vowel) means "thick"

Because the tone with which a word is pronounced, or changes in the tone within the word, can change its meaning, the pitch of the voice is a kind of phoneme in tone languages. It has the same effect as adding /s/ in front of the English word *pot,* which totally alters its meaning to *spot.*

Words and Meanings

Words are combinations of sounds (phonemes) to which people attach standardized, conventional meanings. Any language contains a finite number of words, each matched to one or more meanings. The total inventory of words in a language is called its **lexicon. Morphology** is the study of meaningful sound sequences and the rules by which they are formed.

In studying the meanings of language, morphologists need a more precise concept than *word.* To see why, ask yourself if you know the meaning of the following sound sequences, none of which qualifies as a word:

un	ed
pre	s
non	ing
anti	ist

You do, of course, recognize these sound sequences. Those in the first column are prefixes, which change the meaning of certain words when placed before them. Those in the second column are suffixes, which alter a word's meaning when they follow the word.

Sound sequences such as these are "detachable" from particular words. Take the words *art* and *novel,* for example. By adding the suffix *-ist* to these words, we make new words meaning "a person who creates art" or "one who writes novels." That *-ist* has a similar meaning whenever it is attached to other words is shown by the made-up word *crim*; you don't know what this word means, but by adding *-ist* to it, you instantly know that a *crimist* is "a person who crims." We need a concept that will include prefixes and suffixes such as *uni-*, *-ing*, *-ly*, and so forth to analyze such compound words and their meanings.

Any sequence of phonemes that carries meaning is known as a **morpheme.** There are two kinds of morphemes in all languages. **Free morphemes** are any morphemes that can stand alone as words, for example, *type, walk, woman, establish*. **Bound morphemes** are attached to free morphemes to modify their meanings in predictable ways, for example, *dis-*, *bi-*, *-er*, *-ly*. Thus, by adding suffixes to the example free morphemes, we get:

typist	typed	typing
walked	walking	walks
womanly	womanhood	womanish
established	establishment	establishes

Both prefixes and suffixes—which in English are the two kinds of bound morphemes—can be attached to a free morpheme to change its meaning, as shown in the following examples:

desire	desirable	undesirable
excuse	excusable	inexcusably
possible	impossible	impossibility
health	healthy	unhealthful
complete	completely	incompletely

Note that both free and bound morphemes carry meaning (although the meaning depends on the context in which they are used), unlike most phonemes such as /l/, /g/, /n/, and so on. Just as phonemes are a language's minimal units of sound, morphemes are the minimal units of meaning. Thus, we cannot break down the free morphemes *friend, possible, man,* or *run* into any smaller unit that carries meaning. Nor can we break down the bound morphemes *non-*, *-ish*, *-able*, or *tri-* into any smaller units and still have them mean anything in English.

There is no doubt that the speakers of a language learn its rules for forming compound words by combining free and bound morphemes. That is, people learn how to make new compound words by applying a rule of compound-word

formation, not by learning each compound word separately.

For instance, take the English rule for forming a plural noun from a singular noun. It can be done by adding the bound morpheme /z/, as in: *beads, apples, colors, eggs.* (Incidentally, /z/ represents one of only a few cases in English in which a phoneme is also a morpheme. When used as a bound morpheme at the end of a noun, /z/ usually carries the meaning "more than one.") Children learn the morphological rule for plural formation at an early age, but it takes them a while longer to learn the many exceptions to the rule. They apply the rule consistently to all words, saying "childs," "mans," "foots," "mouses," and so on.

The same is true for the English rule for forming the past tense of a verb. Generally, the bound morpheme /d/ is added as a suffix to the verb, as in *bored, formed, loaded,* and *included.* Again, children learn this rule for past-tense formation early, and they apply it consistently. We hear children say "goed," "runned," "bringed," and "doed."

Thus, one of the many things people unconsciously know when they know a language is its rules for changing the meaning of free morphemes by the addition of bound morphemes. We do not have to learn *tree* and *trees* as separate words. We need only apply a general morphological rule (i.e., add /z/ as a suffix to make a noun plural) to *tree,* or to many other nouns.

LANGUAGE and CULTURE

Often—but not always—the group of people (e.g., a society, an ethnic group) who share a common culture also speak the same language. This fact implies that the language a people speak and the cultural traditions they share have some relationship to one another. What is the nature of this relationship?

There is no consensus on the answer to this question. Three possible relationships are portrayed in the Concept Review. First, a people's language could be one of the subsystems of their culture (example A), just as we say that world view, family, or economy is "part of" culture. In

CONCEPT REVIEW Three Conceptions of the Relationship between Language and Culture

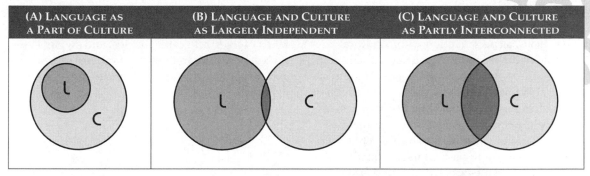

(A) LANGUAGE AS A PART OF CULTURE	(B) LANGUAGE AND CULTURE AS LARGELY INDEPENDENT	(C) LANGUAGE AND CULTURE AS PARTLY INTERCONNECTED

this conception, language is the "part of" culture that allows easy, precise communication among the individuals who share that culture. The problem with such a view, of course, is that all of culture (world view, family, economy, and so on) depends on such communication and, in fact, would probably be impossible without it. This suggests that language is more than "an ordinary component of culture."

Another view is shown in example B. In this conception, language and culture are fairly independent of each other (the fact that the circles in the figure do overlap somewhat reflects the fact that culture and language are not likely to be *entirely* independent phenomena). In favor of this view is the fact that, in a given group, the group's language can and often does remain relatively intact even after most elements of its culture have changed drastically. A people's traditional religion, family life, and economy can practically disappear, yet they often continue to speak their traditional language, with appropriate modifications to their vocabulary. For example, despite the enormous economic and political changes that have swept Asia in the past several decades, Chinese, Japanese, Korean, Hindi, Vietnamese, and other indigenous languages are firmly in place. Problems of communicating with other peoples are solved by bilingualism, in which individuals speak their native or a foreign language, depending on context. Commonly, some language that a great many learn as a second language becomes a

lingua franca. Yet—and this is our main point—the fact that linguistic change or replacement is usually far slower than changes in cultural subsystems suggests that language and culture are not tightly integrated.

Languages sometimes persist even after other traditions have changed because, as we have seen, different languages are to a considerable extent interchangeable in the meanings they can communicate. Given additions to vocabulary, the Navajo language works about as well in Los Angeles as on the reservation, provided, of course, that you are speaking to another Navajo and are willing to add English words like "freeway" to your vocabulary.

But to say—as we did above—that language and culture are "partly independent" or are "not tightly integrated" does not answer our original question of how they are related. Language is in fact closely tied to some elements of culture. A third conception (example C) emphasizes the interconnections, to varying degrees, between language and parts of culture. First, it is clear that language is closely related to cultural classifications of reality (see Chapter 2). Second, many parts of language reflect the social relationships between people and the cultural importance people attach to different things or categories. And third, many scholars believe that language helps to shape the entire world view of a people. Let's look briefly at each of these interconnections between language and culture.

Language and Cultural Classifications of Reality

Cultures differ in how they break up the natural and social world into categories (see Chapter 2). In the 1960s, a specialization within cultural anthropology developed that is usually called cognitive anthropology or ethnoscience. Cognitive anthropologists often study how cultures construct their classifications of reality by perceiving and labeling the world according to different criteria. One conclusion of such research is that classifications are organized in consistent patterns, much like the patterns of sound systems in language.

To see how this organization works, return for a moment to phonology. As we have seen, English recognizes the difference between voiced and voiceless consonants as significant—that is, as making a difference in the meanings of words like *bath* and *path*. On the other hand, many other languages do not recognize this distinction between sounds—meanings of words in these languages are not affected by whether certain consonants are voiced or voiceless. The distinctions between the same sounds are objectively present in all languages, but they are not necessarily perceived and made significant.

Now recall (from Chapter 2) that one difference between cultures is how they classify reality into categories of objects, people, other life forms, and events. This is done by perceiving or not perceiving different features of things, and by recognizing or not recognizing these differences as important (just as the speakers of a language do or do not perceive or recognize differences between sounds). On the basis of these perceptions and recognitions of contrasts and similarities between things, humans define categories of reality. We classify specific objects, people, natural phenomena, and so forth into one or another category, depending on which of their many features we notice and view as significant. Members of different cultural traditions do not necessarily base their categories on the same contrasts and similarities (just as speakers of different languages do not distinguish phonemes based on the same contrasts and similarities).

An example sheds light on how the "cognitive categories" of a people can be built up in much the same way as elements of language. Take three kinds of livestock: cattle, horses, and swine. How do North American livestock farmers categorize and classify these animals? Consider the following list:

Cattle	Horses	Swine
cow	mare	sow
bull	stallion	boar
steer	gelding	barrow
calf	foal	piglet
heifer calf	filly	gilt
bull calf	colt	shoat

(Unless you have a rural background, you may not recognize some of these terms. Farmers need to discuss cattle, horses, and swine more than do suburban or city folk, so they use a rich lexicon to talk about livestock.) Note that the same features are used to contrast the different categories of cattle, horses, and swine. *Cow* and *bull* contrast in the same way as *mare-stallion* and *sow-boar*: the first is female; the second, male. There is a special term for each kind of mature male animal that has been neutered: *steer, gelding*, and *barrow*. There are special terms for newborn animals, regardless of their sex: *calf, foal*, and *piglet*. And there are separate terms for female and male immature animals: *heifer calf* and *bull calf, filly* and *colt, gilt* and *shoat*. Each kind of livestock is then divided into categories based on sex (female, male, and neutered male) and age (adult, immature, and newborn). Each category can be described by the features that distinguish it in the farmers' classification of livestock: a *filly* is an "immature female horse," a *barrow* is a "mature castrated male swine," and so on.

These are the features of animals that farmers find important enough to make the basis of their classification of livestock. Notice that this classification rests on contrasts and similarities between *selected* characteristics of the animals—just as the speakers of a language recognize only *some* features of sounds as significant. Notice also that the classification is patterned: The same contrasts and similarities (sex, age) are used to distinguish kinds of cattle, horses, and swine. Similarly, the phonological rules of a language are patterned: If a feature (e.g., voicing) of one class of sound is recognized as significant for one member of the class, it tends to be recognized as significant for other members of the class as well.

Like the sound systems of languages, the way people classify things is constructed out of selected features of those things, and these same features are the basis for distinguishing other, similar things. Thus, the part of cultural knowledge called *classifications of reality* is organized much like the sound system of language: We perceive only certain differences and similarities as significant and build up our conception of reality from these differences and similarities. Since we generally assigned labels (morphemes) to the resulting categories (and subcategories), language is closely related to a culture's classifications of reality.

Language as a Reflection of Culture

Anthropological fieldworkers try to learn the language of the community they work with, partly because it facilitates interaction, but also because knowing how to speak the language helps fieldworkers understand the local culture. In fact, many aspects of the language a people speak reflect their culture.

For example, a complex lexicon tends to develop around things that are especially important to a community, as we just illustrated with the farmer's classification of livestock. People will assign names or labels to those objects, qualities, and actions that they see as most important, which makes it easier for them to communicate complex information about these subjects.

Examples of how vocabulary reflects people's need to communicate about certain subjects are found among individuals of different subcultural and occupational categories in North American society. Take automobile tools, for example. A pro-

fessional mechanic can identify hundreds of kinds of tools; the Saturday-afternoon home mechanic can identify perhaps several dozen; and the rest of us don't know a compression tester from a feeler gauge. Numerous other examples could be cited to show that a language's lexicon responds to the needs of people to discuss certain topics easily. There are no surprises here.

But not all specialized vocabularies are developed simply to meet the need of the members of some group to converse easily or precisely among themselves. Specialized vocabularies also serve as symbolic markers of status for professions and other groups. Lawyers speak "legalese" only partly because they need to make fine distinctions between points of law that are obscure to the rest of us. Legalese is a secret—as well as a specialized—vocabulary. Entry into the select group of attorneys depends in part on mastery of an esoteric vocabulary with all its nuances. And it is helpful to the profession that the general population cannot understand real estate agreements and other contracts written by attorneys. Most of us are compelled to pay for the specialized knowledge of an attorney to interpret important documents.

In sum, in a diverse and complex society, occupational or other kinds of groups may develop specialized speech to facilitate communication, to mark themselves off from everyone else, to help ensure the continuation of their privileges and rewards, and so on. What about differences *between* whole languages, spoken by members of *different* cultures? Similar ideas apply. To understand them, the concept of **semantic domain** is useful. A semantic domain is a set of words that belongs to an inclusive class. For example, *chair, table, ottoman,* and *china cabinet* belong to the semantic domain of "furniture." "Color" is another semantic domain, with members such as *violet, red,* and *yellow.*

Semantic domains typically have a hierarchical structure, meaning that they have several levels of inclusiveness. For instance, two colors the English language distinguishes can be further broken down:

Blue	Green
aqua	kelly
sky	mint
royal	forest
navy	avocado
teal	lime

We divide the semantic domain of color into specific colors (e.g., blue, green), each of which in turn is divided into "kinds of blue" and "kinds of green," and even into—for some of us—"shades of sky blue" or "tones of forest green."

By now you can see where this discussion is headed: Different languages, spoken by members of different cultures, vary in the semantic domains they identify, in how finely they carve up these domains, and in how they make distinctions between different members of a domain. Some of these differences are rather obvious. For instance, the semantic domain of "fish" is unlikely to be as elaborate among desert dwellers as among coastal or riverine peoples. Tropical lowland peoples are not likely to have the semantic domain we call "snow" in their native language, whereas some Arctic peoples discuss it so much that they have an elaborate vocabulary to facilitate communication about snow conditions. Further, the degree to which some semantic domain has a multilevel hierarchical structure depends on the importance of the objects or actions in people's lives: Island, coastal, or riverine people dependent on fish are likely to have many categories and subcategories of aquatic life, fishing methods, and flood and tide stages, for instance. Can we go beyond such fairly obvious statements?

For some semantic domains we can. There are some things or qualities that seem to be "natural domains," meaning that the differences between their members seem to be obvious to anyone. In fact, they seem to be inherent in the things themselves. We therefore would expect that people everywhere would carve up these domains in similar ways. For instance, color is an inherent (natural) quality of things, which can be measured by instruments that determine the wavelength of light reflected from an object. Surely

anyone can recognize that blue and green are different colors, and surely this recognition is reflected in separate terms for the two colors! Likewise, biological kinship is a natural relationship, in the sense that who an infant's parents are determines who will and will not be his or her closest genetic relatives. What human cannot recognize that his or her aunts and uncles are fundamentally different kinds of relatives than parents?

But although blue and green are objectively different colors, and aunts are objectively different relatives from mothers, people are not obliged to recognize these differences and make them culturally significant. The semantic domains of color and relatives are in fact divided up differently by different cultures, and these divisions are not at all self-evident.

The domain of "relatives" or "kinfolk" is an excellent example of how members of different cultural traditions divide up an apparently natural domain according to different principles. Different cultures do not in fact make the same distinctions between relatives; that is, the way relatives are differentiated is culturally variable.

Consider the relatives that English-speaking people call *aunt*, *first cousin*, and *brother*. An *aunt* is a sister of your mother or father; a *first cousin* is a child of any of your aunts and uncles; and a *brother* is a male child of your parents. These individuals are all biologically related to you differently, so you place them in different categories and call them by different terms.

But notice that other distinctions are possible that you do not recognize as distinctions and that are not reflected in the kinship lexicon of English. Your aunts are not related to you in exactly the same way: One kind is the sister of your mother, another kind is the sister of your father. Why not recognize this distinction between them by giving them different terms? Similarly, your first cousins could be subdivided into finer categories and given special terms, meaning *child of my father's sister, child of my mother's brother,* and so on. And since we distinguish most other categories of relatives by whether they are male or female, (e.g., brother versus sister, aunt versus uncle), why does sex not matter for any of our cousins?

How do we know that the way a culture divides up the semantic domain of relatives into different categories is not entirely natural, or determined by biological relationships? Because different cultures divide up the domain in different ways. People in many societies, for instance, call their mother's sister by one term and their father's sister by another term (although we collapse both into one term, *aunt*). It is also common for people to distinguish between the children of their father's sister and their father's brother, calling the first by a term we might translate as "cousin," the second by the same term as they use for their own brothers and sisters. Even stranger— to those who think that relatives are a purely biological category—are cultures who call the daughters of their maternal uncles by the term "mother" (just like their "real mother"), but not the daughters of the paternal uncles, whom they call "sister"! (These various ways of categorizing kin, by the way, are not random, for anthropologists have discovered that such labels are related to other aspects of a people's kinship system, discussed in Chapter 8.) Obviously, the way various peoples divide up the seemingly "natural domain" of biological relatives is not the same the world over.

Other examples could be cited, but the overall point is clear: Cultures divide up the world differently, forming different categories and classifications of natural and social reality out of the objective properties of things. These differences are reflected in the language of the bearers of the culture.

Language and World Views

As we have just seen, some aspects of a language reflect the culture of the people who speak it. Is the converse also true? Is it possible that knowing a given language predisposes its speakers to view the world in certain ways? Could it be that the categories and rules of their language condition people's perceptions of reality?

Language could shape perceptions and world views both by its lexicon and by its rules for communicating about subjects like time and space. Any language's lexicon assigns labels to only certain things, qualities, and actions. It is easy to see how this might encourage people to perceive the real world selectively. For instance, as we grow up, we learn that some plants are "trees." So we come to think of tree as a real thing, although there are so many kinds of trees that there is no necessary reason to collapse all this variety into a single label. But we might perceive the plants our language calls trees as more similar than do people who speak a language that makes finer distinctions between these plants.

Further, language might force people to communicate about time, space, relations between individuals and between people and nature, and so forth in a certain kind of way. Potentially, this constraint on the way people must speak to be understood by others can shape their views of what the world is like.

The idea that language influences the perceptions and thought patterns of those who speak it, and thus conditions their world view, is known as the **Whorf-Sapir hypothesis,** after two anthropological linguists who proposed it in the 1930s and 1940s. Edward Sapir and Benjamin Whorf believed that language helps define the world view of its speakers. It does so, in part, by providing labels for certain kinds of phenomena (things, qualities, and actions), which different languages define according to different criteria. Some phenomena are therefore made easier to think about than others. The properties that define them as different from other, similar things become more important than other properties. So the lexicon of our language provides a filter that biases our perceptions. Metaphorically, our lexicon digs grooves inside which our thought patterns tend to roll.

But the Whorf-Sapir hypothesis is subtler than this. Whorf suggested that language conditions a people's conceptions of time and space. Whorf noted that English encourages its speakers to think about time in spatial metaphors (e.g., "a long time" and "a long distance"), although time cannot really be "long" or "short" in the same sense as distance. Also, English-speaking people talk about units of time using the same concepts with which they talk about numbers of objects (e.g., "four days" and "four apples"), although it is possible to see four objects at once but not four units of time. Finally, English-speaking people classify events by when they occurred: those that have happened, those that are happening, and those that will happen.

Because they share a certain kind of language, however, Whorf argued that the Native American Hopi must speak about time and events differently. With no tenses exactly equivalent to the English past, present, and future, and no way to express time in terms of spatial metaphors, Hopi speak of events as continuously unfolding, rather than happening in so many days or weeks. Whorf argued that the Hopi language led the Hopi people into a different perception of the passage of time.

What shall we make of the Whorf-Sapir hypothesis? Certainly, none of us as individuals invents the labels our language assigns to reality, nor do we create the limitations our grammar places on the way we talk about time and space. We must adhere to certain rules if we are to be understood. Surely this necessity biases our perceptions to some degree. It is, therefore, likely that language does affect ways of perceiving, thinking about, classifying, and acting in the world. To some degree, then, language does "create" views of reality. The question is, how much? More precisely, how important is language as opposed to other things that also influence perceptions and views of reality?

Although intriguing, the Whorf-Sapir hypothesis is not widely accepted, for several reasons. First, if a language greatly shapes the way its speakers perceive and think about the world, then we would expect a people's world view to change only at a rate roughly comparable to the rate at which their language changes. Yet there is no doubt that world views are capable of changing much more rapidly than language. How else

can we explain the fact that the English language has changed little in the past 150 years compared with the dramatic alteration in the world views of most speakers of English? How else can we explain the spread of religious traditions such as Islam and Christianity out of their original linguistic homes among people with enormously diverse languages?

Second, if language strongly conditions perceptions, thought patterns, and entire world views, we should find that the speakers of languages with a common ancestor show marked cultural similarities. More precisely, we would expect to find the cultural similarities between speakers of related languages to be consistently greater than the cultural similarities between speakers of languages that are less closely related. Sometimes we do find this; unfortunately, we often do not.

For these and other reasons, the Whorf-Sapir hypothesis is not highly regarded today by most scholars. But research on this intriguing idea is continuing, and future results may show some unexpected effects of language on perception, cognition, and world views.

SOCIAL USES of SPEECH

During enculturation, humans learn how to communicate and how to act appropriately in given social situations. They learn that different situations require different verbal and nonverbal behavior, for how one speaks and acts varies with whom one is addressing, who else is present, and the overall situation in which the interaction is occurring.

To speak appropriately, people must take the total context into account. First, they must know the various situations, or social scenes, of their culture: which are solemn, which are celebrations, which are formal and informal, which are argumentative, and so on. Cultural knowledge includes knowing how to alter one's total (including verbal) behavior to fit these situations. Second, individuals must recognize the kinds of interactions they are expected to have with others toward whom they have particular relations: Should they act lovingly, jokingly, contemptuously, or respectfully and deferentially toward someone else? Cultural knowledge thus also includes knowing how to act (including how to speak) toward others with whom an individual has relations of certain kinds.

These two elements—the particular situation and the specific individuals who are parties to the interaction—make up the *context* of verbal and nonverbal behavior. Enough scholars are interested in such topics that a special field of study is devoted to them: **sociolinguistics,** the study of how speech behavior is affected by cultural factors, especially by the social context.

How the speech of the parties to a social interaction reveals and reinforces the nature of their relationship is seen clearly by terms of address. In some parts of the United States, unless instructed otherwise, Americans usually address those of higher social rank with a respect term followed by the last name (e.g., Dr. Smith or Mr. Jones). Those with higher rank are more likely to address those with lower rank by their first name, as among faculty and students. This nonreciprocal use of address terms often not only expresses a social inequality; it also reinforces it each time the individuals address each other. When address terms are used reciprocally—when both individuals call each other by their first names, for example—their relation is likely to be more equal.

Other cultures exhibit customs in speech behavior with which most English-speaking people are unfamiliar. Here are a few examples:

- Some languages accentuate the difference between the sexes far more than English does. In languages such as Gros Ventre (of the northeastern United States) and Yukaghir (of northeastern Asia), men and women pronounced certain phonemes differently, which led to differences in the pronunciation of the words in which these phonemes appeared. In Yana, an extinct language spoken by a people who formerly lived in northern California, many words had two pronunciations, one used by men and one by women. In a few languages, the vocabularies of men and women differ, with men using one word for something and women quite a different word. In a language spoken by the Carib, who formerly inhabited the West Indies, the vocabularies of men and women differed so much that early European explorers claimed (mistakenly) that the sexes spoke different languages! In many languages, the speech of the sexes differs in other respects, such as the degree of forcefulness of their speech, the degree to which they avoid confrontational speech, and the tone of voice.

- In parts of Polynesia and Micronesia there used to be a special language, sometimes called a *respect language,* with which common people had to address members of the noble class. On some islands this was much more than a difference in speech style because different words were used. Often there were severe penalties for commoners who erred in addressing a noble.

- On the Indonesian island of Java, there are distinct "levels" of speech, involving different pronouns, suffixes, and words. A speaker must choose between the three levels—plain, more elegant, and most elegant. The speech style the parties to the interaction use depends on their relative rank and on their degree of familiarity with one another. In choosing which style to use with a specific person, a Javanese thus communicates more than the message encoded in the utterance. He or she also imparts information about the quality of their relationship. Accordingly, changes in the relationship between two individuals are accompanied by changes in speech style.

- In Japanese, a complicated set of contextual norms (called *honorifics*) governs the degree of formality and politeness people normally use to show respect to those of higher social position. For instance, verbs and personal pronouns have several alternative forms that speakers must choose between in addressing others. The main determinant of which forms are used is the relative status of the parties. One form of the verb is used when the speaker is of higher status than the listener, another form when the two are of roughly equal status, and yet another when the speaker is a social inferior. Women, who to some extent even today are considered "beneath" men, would generally be obliged to address men with honorific verb forms that symbolically express the superiority of the addressee. The same applies to personal pronouns (*I, you*), different forms of which are used to reflect the relative status of the parties. In fact, when a social superior is addressing an inferior, he or she often does not use the pronoun *I* as a self-reference but refers to his or her status relative to the person being addressed. For instance, a teacher says to a student, "Look at teacher" instead of "Look at me"; a father says to his son, "Listen to father" instead of "Listen to me"; and so forth. Reciprocally, one usually does not use the pronoun *you* with one of higher status but replaces it with a term denoting the superior's social position. This yields sentences like: "What would teacher like me to do next?" and "Would father like me to visit?" Confused foreigners trying to learn the subtleties of Japanese speech etiquette often are advised to use the honorific forms to avoid giving offense unintentionally. (Fortunately for the rest of us, most Japanese are tolerant of our inability to master the nuances of their honorifics!)

- All societies have customs of taboo, meaning that some behavior is prohibited for religious reasons or because it is culturally regarded as immoral, improper, or offensive. It is fairly common to find taboos applied to language: Some words cannot be uttered by certain people. For instance, the Yąnomamö of the Venezuelan rain forest have a custom known as *name taboo*. It is an insult to utter the names of important people and of deceased relatives in the presence of their living kinfolk. So the Yąnomamö use names such as "toenail of sloth" or "whisker of howler monkey" for people, so that when the person dies they will

not have to watch their language so closely. Other name taboos are enforced only against specific individuals. Among the Zulu of southern Africa, for example, a woman was once forbidden to use the name of her husband's father or any of his brothers, under possible penalty of death.

As these examples show, speech is affected by the social context, including how situations are culturally defined and the particular individuals who are present. Of course, norms partly explain why people's use of language varies with context: You are not expected to act and speak the same way at a party as you do at work or in church, for instance, and you know intuitively and unconsciously how to adjust your behavior to these different social scenes.

The choice of speech style and the use of particular words and phrases are governed by more than just norms, though. People have personal goals, and speaking in a certain way often helps them get what they want. This point is illustrated by political speech.

The Power of Language and the Language of Power

As we have seen, language is an incredibly powerful form of communication—it is efficient, incredibly precise, and creative. Its "power" (effectiveness in communicating messages), though, allows people to use it to enhance their own "power" (influence): By controlling what is said and how it is said, individuals and groups attempt to control public opinions. Those who control the content of messages potentially control the information available to other people. And because human thought processes, emotional reactions, and behavioral responses depend largely on information, language is potentially an instrument of power.

Political speech illustrates how language becomes an instrument of power. Professional consultants and speechwriters advise politicians on what to say (and what not to say) and how to say it to increase political advantage. This happens most obviously during elections. As a rule, candidates use language to cast themselves in a favorable (often moderate) light while making their opponents look bad (most commonly, as left- or right-wing extremists). Political parties choose words that arouse positive emotions and attachments to their programs and candidates.

For example, in the 1994 Congressional elections, the leader of one party advised its candidates to characterize their opponents using words like "pathetic," "corrupt," "waste," "stagnation," "traitors," and "decay." Words used to portray their own party included "moral," "courage," "share," "change," "truth," "duty," and—of course—"family." The memorandum in which this advice was given referred to "Language, a Key Mechanism of Control." The next time you hear a politician give a "speech" (i.e., public address), pay attention to his or her "speech" (i.e., use of words and phrases and overall style). How much do you let your opinions be controlled by these?

Language is a tool of partisan politics in policy debates as well. Some politicians tell Americans that they are "overtaxed" (although American

taxes are among the lowest of all developed nations), so they should get to keep more of their "own money." Such phrases are intended to imply that The American People deserve a "tax break." But you should always ask when you hear this phrase: Which American People are those, exactly? In the summer of 2000, Congress passed a bill that phased out the federal estate tax—the tax levied on the heirs of wealthy individuals and paid out of their estates. To drum up support by making The American People share the pain of the surviving loved ones, the estate tax was called the "death tax." In fact, about 98 percent of all estates owe no tax at all; if you are single, you won't pay the estate tax until you are worth $675,000. Estate taxes also were said to be "destroying small farms and businesses," implying that the heirs would have to sell the property or business to pay the tax. But in 1998, fewer than 50,000 estates paid any tax at all, and of these only 1,200 were mainly farms and small businesses. Had the president not vetoed the bill, some of America's wealthiest families would have saved about $100 billion in estate taxes over the next ten years. This would have been enough to pay for most of the pharmacy bills of the elderly not now paid for by Medicare.

However, we shouldn't be too hard on politicians of either party. We all try to exercise power or influence over other people by using our speech to control how other people think of us. In everyday life we strive to present the image of ourselves that we want someone else to perceive. The opinions that employers, friends, lovers and hoped-for lovers, co-workers, roommates, and even parents have of us depend partly on how we speak—our use of certain words and avoidance of others, the degree of formality of our style, whether we try to hide or to accentuate regional dialects, and so forth. In short, how we speak is an important part of what social scientists call our presentation of self, or how we try to control other people's opinions of us. Like the jewelry we wear and where we wear it; how we sit, stand, and walk; and how we comb our hair or shave our heads, the way we speak is part of the way

Matthew Neal McVay/Tony Stone Images

In public speeches, politicians use language to create favorable impressions of themselves and their policies. This American president truly mastered the language of power.

we tell others what kind of a person we are. Almost without knowing it, we adjust our speech style, mannerisms, and body language to manage the impressions other people have of us. Language can be powerful for all of us, not just for the politicians.

We pointed out earlier that language is composed of symbols that convey conventional meanings. We can now add that the very act of speaking is itself symbolic in another way. Just as the morphemes of language communicate meaning, so do the multitude of ways in which we can say them. Like the foods we eat and the cars we drive, the way we speak is part of the way we present ourselves to the world. Others will interpret not only our words and sentences, but will also read meanings into our speech habits and style. By adjusting our habits and style of speech, we can to some extent control the implicit messages we communicate about ourselves. The act of speaking, then, conveys messages beyond the meanings of the words and sentences themselves. Consciously or unconsciously, every time we speak we tell the world the way we are. What have you told the world today?

SUMMARY

1. Language is one of the most important capabilities of humans that distinguishes us from other animals. Language is an exceedingly precise and efficient form of communication. The knowledge humans possess of language is complex and impressive, although most of us take this knowledge for granted.

2. Grammar refers to the elements of language and the rules for combining these elements to form an infinite number of meaningful sentences. Grammatical knowledge is both unconscious and intuitive. In the linguistic meaning of the word *grammar,* there is no such thing as "bad grammar," nor are some dialects or some languages incorrect or primitive. The study of language is divided into several fields, two of which are phonology and morphology.

3. Phonology is the study of the sounds and sound patterns of language. Only some of the sounds humans are able to make with their vocal tracts are recognized by any specific language. The features of sounds that speakers recognize as significant—that is, as making a difference in the meanings of words in which they occur—vary from language to language. The sounds that speakers recognize as distinct from other sounds are called the phonemes of the language. Among many other differences, languages vary in the way they use voice pitch to convey meanings, as illustrated by tone languages.

4. Morphology studies meaningful sound sequences and the rules by which they are formed. Any sequence of phonemes that conveys a standardized meaning is a morpheme. Free morphemes can stand alone as meaningful sequences, whereas bound morphemes are not used alone but are attached to free morphemes during speech. When people learn a language they learn its free and bound morphemes and their meanings. They also learn the rules by which bound morphemes can be attached to free morphemes.

5. The language a people speak and the culture they share are related. Cognitive anthropologists have illustrated how cultural classifications of reality are built up and organized in the same way as language.

6. Some aspects of language, particularly lexicon, reflect the cultural importance of subjects, people, objects, and natural phenomena. The need to converse easily about some subject leads to the elaboration of semantic domains connected to the subject, as seen in the domain of color. In other domains, such as relatives, anthropologists have discovered surprising diversity in how various peoples divide kin into kinds and give them different labels according to different principles.

7. Some anthropologists have argued that the language a people speak predisposes them to see the world in a certain way by shaping their perceptions of reality. This idea, known as the Whorf-Sapir hypothesis, argues that the lexicon of a language influences perceptions by leading its speakers to filter out certain objective properties of reality in favor of other properties. Other parts of language can also affect perception, and even world view, by forcing people to talk about time and space in a certain way if they are to be understood.

8. Sociolinguistics is the study of how speech is influenced by cultural factors, including culturally defined contexts and situations, the goals of the speaker, the presence of other parties, and so forth. Speech can be used in subtle ways to mark differences in rank and status, as between ethnic groups, classes, and males and females. Public figures such as politicians use language as an instrument of getting and retaining power, both by controlling the images they present and by influencing the content of discussions and debates. Because speech is part of the way we present ourselves to others, control of the way we speak is one way we influence how others perceive us.

KEY TERMS

grammar	morpheme
dialects	free morpheme
phonology	bound morpheme
phonemes	semantic domain
tone languages	Whorf-Sapir hypothesis
lexicon	sociolinguistics
morphology	

SUGGESTED READINGS

Agar, Michael. *Language Shock: Understanding the Culture of Conversation.* New York: William Morrow and Company, 1994.

Enjoyable discussion of the uses of language in society. Lots of illustrative stories and anecdotes.

Farb, Peter. *Word Play.* New York: Knopf, 1974.

Readable, enjoyable introduction to anthropological linguistics.

Fromkin, Victoria, and Robert Rodman. *An Introduction to Language.* 6th ed. San Diego: Harcourt College Publishers, 1998.

Excellent textbook, thorough in its coverage, readily understandable, with many excellent examples.

Lakoff, Robin. *The Language War.* Berkeley: University of California, 2000.

An influential linguist shows how language is used in recent political conflicts and dialogues. Interpretive as well as descriptive.

Below are three popular books by linguist Deborah Tannen that analyze how conversational speech style affects relationships and performance. One focus is on misunderstandings and perceptions based on language use.

Tannen, Deborah. *Gender and Discourse.* New York: Oxford University Press, 1996.

Tannen, Deborah. *Talking from 9 to 5: How Women's and Men's Conversational Styles Affect Who Gets Heard, Who Gets Credit, and What Gets Done at Work.* New York: W. Morrow, 1994.

Tannen, Deborah. *You Just Don't Understand: Women and Men in Conversation.* New York: Ballantine, 1991.

chapter 4

STUDYING CULTURE:
APPROACHES *and* METHODS

Contents

Now that we have covered the essential points about culture and its interrelationships with language, we move on to discuss how anthropologists approach the study of other peoples. The way anthropologists describe and analyze cultures has changed drastically since the nineteenth century, when the field became established. This chapter begins by describing the origins of anthropology. Then we show why some early ideas were discarded by twentieth-century scholars. We cover how each successive approach contributed to the formation of anthropology today, with its emphasis on comparison, relativism, holism, and firsthand fieldwork. Although modern anthropologists agree on certain issues, a major rift exists within the field between those who view the study of culture as a scientific, explanatory enterprise and those who see it as a humanistic, interpretive endeavor. Finally, we discuss ethnographic fieldwork, which is the most important method by which ethnologists describe and attempt to understand other cultures.

NINETEENTH CENTURY: ORIGINS

The discipline we now call anthropology originated as a separate field of scholarly study in the late nineteenth century. By then, most of the world's major geographic regions were known to the Western world. Indeed, much of the non-Western world had become a colony of one or another European power. As a result of centuries of contact and colonization, various Western visitors and colonists had written hundreds of descriptive accounts about the beliefs and customs of the native peoples of the Americas, Africa, Asia, and the islands of the Pacific Ocean. Who were all these people? How were they related to the more "civilized" people of the West? How could Western intellectuals make sense of them and their "savage" ways of life?

Evidence of other, earlier cultures also existed within Europe itself. In the 1800s tools made from stone were discovered in the earth, in clear association with extinct mammals. And in Germany's Neander Valley, a partial skeleton of a human-like creature was unearthed. Who made those ancient stone tools? Could they have been manufactured by the ancestors of modern-day Europeans? Were the Neander bones human and, if so, what did they mean?

Answers to such questions varied, but until the 1800s most explanations of both the prehistoric remains of Europe and of the "savages" of other lands fell within the Biblical interpretation of creation and history. Perhaps savages were the degenerated remnants of one of the lost tribes of Israel, or maybe they were descendants of Noah's errant son, Ham. Whatever the interpretation, the Judeo-Christian world view was adjusted to incorporate these new peoples and cultures.

As the nineteenth century progressed, new theories about the earth and about life itself emerged. In geology, James Hutton and Charles Lyell amassed evidence showing that the earth was many millions of years old (it is even older, we know today), rather than the few thousands of years suggested by the Scriptures. In biology, Charles Darwin's 1859 book *On the Origin of Species* revolutionized theories about life. Rather than each plant and animal being separately made by a Creator and reproducing "after its own kind," Darwin proposed that one species emerged out of another. The great variety of plant and animal life can be explained by a gradual, and entirely natural, process of transformation and diversification. There was great resistance in scholarly as well as religious circles to Darwin's theory of evolution. But by the closing decade of the nineteenth century, it was apparent that evolution explained so much that most scholars accepted it.

Darwin's theory had many implications for Western scientists' understanding of humankind. Darwin himself noted the physical similarities between apes and humans in an 1871 book, arguing that humans likely are related to African apes. Discoveries in Africa in the 1920s confirmed his hypothesis, establishing the field of paleoanthropology as a legitimate science.

But Darwin's ideas also influenced how intellectuals viewed human cultural existence, as well as human biological evolution. To biologists of the 1800s, evolutionary theory suggested that the history of life was progressive: Biologically "lower" and simpler forms gave rise to "higher" and more complex forms. Competition—"survival of the fittest," as it came to be called—was the engine that powered this progress. In the fossil record, it was possible to find evidence of the evolutionary "stages" through which successively more complex forms of life developed. The history of life on earth could be reconstructed by painstaking excavations and meticulous laboratory analysis of fossils.

Many thought that the same notions applied to human cultures. Evolution and progress provided the ideas that suggested how the "savages" of other lands were related to one another, to the early residents of Europe who left behind those mysterious prehistoric tools, and to Western civilization itself. Just as life itself had earlier, simpler forms, so did humankind's various ways of life —that is, cultures. Those prehistoric people of Europe had been living in the early stages of cultural development, just as were the "primitives" of Africa, the Americas, Asia, and the Pacific. By studying these peoples and comparing their customs, scholars could reconstruct the stages of *cultural* progress.

This reconstruction was the main goal of anthropology in the nineteenth century. Western ethnologists tried to use written accounts of the customs and beliefs of non-Western peoples to reconstruct the stages through which human culture progressed on its long road to the pinnacle of human achievement: Western civilization. Evolutionary theory suggested that Polynesians, Africans, Indians, and other representatives of lower stages of cultural evolution are not degenerated folk whose benighted customs prove that they are living under the Devil's iron fist. Instead, nineteenth-century intellectuals reasoned, they are merely "undeveloped." Their thought processes are superstitious (not yet scientific), their technologies are primitive, their manners rude,

Unilineal evolutionists of the late 1800s believed that surviving tribal peoples such as the Tiwi of Australia were living representatives of the earliest stages of cultural evolution. Early twentieth-century anthropologists challenged such notions on the basis of their ethnocentrism and their simplicity.

their morals unenlightened. They are—in a word—precivilized. Therefore, to trace human progress, scholars must study the ancient ancestors of civilization: surviving "primitive" cultures.

To do so, nineteenth-century anthropologists devised an approach that today is known as **unilineal evolution.** Their voluminous writings are highly detailed and complex. But once we understand their assumption that cultural evolution proceeded from simple to complex, with Western civilization at the apex, the essentials of unilineal evolution can be stated fairly simply, as follows. Compile accounts of other cultures written by explorers, settlers, missionaries, traders, and other (mostly Western) observers. From these descriptions, compare all the cultures to determine which are the simplest, the next most simple, . . . somewhat more complex, . . . and the most complex. Classify the cultures into a series of stages of development according to their relative complexity. Label these stages appropriately: "Savagery," "barbarism," and "civilization" were the labels used by the American ethnologist Lewis Henry Morgan. If a new culture (or a new written description of a culture) is found, place it in its appropriate classificatory stage, e.g., the Iroquois of North America belong in the stage of "barbarism." Finally, invent an explanation for why people living at one stage developed into the next stage: Morgan proposed that the invention of pottery propelled some savages into barbarism, whereas some barbarians were launched into civilization once they invented writing. Using these procedures, all cultures can be arranged in a sequence of progressive stages. The "simplest" cultures found on earth today are the surviving representatives of the "earliest stages" of cultural evolution, which of course existed prehistorically.

As an example of this approach, consider E. B. Tylor, whose 1871 book *Primitive Culture* investigated the origins and development of religious beliefs. Tylor argued that religions had passed through three stages. The first was *animism*, defined as the belief that nature is populated by supernatural beings such as ghosts, souls, demons, and nature spirits. How can the origin of such beliefs be explained? Tylor argued that "primitive peoples" sought explanations for their experiences. Two questions puzzled the earliest peoples: (1) What is the difference between a live person and a dead person? (2) What is the origin of the images seen in dreams, trances, and visions? Early humans reasoned (falsely but logically, given their prescientific ways of thinking) that (1) living people have a spiritual essence—a

soul—that gives life to the physical body and causes death when it leaves, and (2) the things people see in their dreams and fantasies actually do exist and are not the products of their imaginations. By this logic, the fact that people sometimes see their deceased relatives in dreams means that souls live on after death. As such beings proliferated, eventually the world was viewed as filled with spirits. The earliest religions were therefore "animistic."

At a later stage of cultural evolution, some of the spirits became elevated to a higher position than others, taking on more prominence in the belief system. They ultimately became gods of the sun, moon, sky, earth, animals, and other elements, thus giving rise to the next stage of religion, *polytheism*, or belief in many gods. Eventually, one god acquired dominance over the others, over time the rest became "false gods," and the final stage of *monotheism* (one god) was born. Religion thus had simple origins in primitives peoples' attempts to explain their experiences, and it evolved into its final—Western—form over many centuries. Or so Tylor believed.

From a modern perspective, the unilineal evolutionists were mistaken, as we shall see. But they did help establish one of the important hallmarks that continues to distinguish ethnology from other fields: the comparative perspective. They recognized that understanding humankind required serious and detailed consideration of peoples and cultures different from themselves. They also had faith that the application of scientific methods and reasoning would lead to the discovery of the natural laws that governed the development of human culture, just as science seemed to be uncovering explanations for natural phenomena. The "history of mankind is part and parcel of the history of nature, . . . our thoughts, wills, and actions accord with laws as definite as those which govern the motion of waves, the combinations of acids and bases, and the growth of plants and animals," wrote Tylor (1871, 2). Many later anthropologists were not sure that such "laws of culture" exist. Still, the search for the general causes of cultural differences and of regularities in culture change remain an interest of many modern scholars.

Another legacy of the nineteenth century is the establishment of anthropology as a separate academic discipline. Scholarly fields that investigate aspects of humankind had long been represented in European and American universities as departments or schools of religion, theology, art, philosophy, classics, history, anatomy, medicine, and so forth. But a discipline whose focus was the physical and cultural diversity of humankind was not established until the last decades of the 1800s. In the United States, the first anthropology course was taught in 1879, at the University of Rochester. In 1886, the first anthropology department was founded at the University of Pennsylvania. It was followed near the turn of the century by university departments at Columbia, Harvard, Chicago, and California (Berkeley).

EARLY TWENTIETH CENTURY: DEVELOPMENT

Nineteenth-century anthropologists established the study of other cultures as a legitimate subject for scholarly research and university education. It was clear that to understand humankind, we must take the great diversity of the world's cultures into account and compare cultures systematically. But by the beginning of the twentieth century, anthropologists on both sides of the Atlantic began to challenge both the methods and the conclusions of the unilineal evolutionists.

American Historical Particularism (ca. 1900–1940)

In the United States, an approach known as **historical particularism** developed. It was "historical" because its main goal was to uncover the past influences on a given culture that shaped its present form. It is called "particularistic" because it emphasized that each people, and each culture, has its own unique past. Each culture, then, is unique and therefore must be studied on its own

terms. More than anyone else, American anthropologist Franz Boas formulated this way of studying and analyzing culture, and his ideas revolutionized the field.

Studying each culture "on its own terms" was not something the evolutionists had done. In their comparisons, they had imposed their own "terms" (e.g., complexity, progress, stages) on other cultures. Take the notion of relative complexity, for example. In the area of technology, perhaps most people will agree that spears as hunting weapons are simpler than bows and arrows, which in turn are simpler than guns and bullets. But what can "complex" mean when applied to other customs and beliefs, such as marriage, political organization, or religion? Does it have any objective meaning to say that animism is "simpler" than monotheism? Boas realized that such features are merely *different* from culture to culture. By any *objective* criterion, one form of marriage or religion does not represent "progress" over another. Only by using ethnocentric assumptions, Boas thought, could one culture be seen as more evolved than another.

This point seemed to mean that the unilineal evolutionists were wrong: Cultures do not develop along a single series of progressive stages, culminating in nineteenth-century European or Canadian or American civilization. Instead, each culture changes along its own path, depending on the particular influences that affect it. To understand a culture, therefore, we must study it *individually*, not as a representative of some hypothetical stage, which it represents only in our minds. Anthropologists must free themselves from preconceived ideas and assumptions and give up speculative schemes of evolution and ethnocentric definitions of progress.

Accompanying Boas' call for less speculation was his demand for more facts. Anthropologists simply did not know enough about human cultural differences to generalize, he felt. What was most urgently needed in his day was more information, which Boas thought could only be obtained from firsthand fieldwork. Anthropologists needed to go out and gather knowledge about

Due to the influence of early twentieth-century anthropologists such as Franz Boas and Bronislaw Malinowski, first-hand fieldwork became essential for the training of new scholars. Here Richard Lee converses with some San people of southern Africa.

experience with it. Anthropologists must therefore immerse themselves in the study of other peoples. They must try to experience their customs and understand their beliefs from an insider's perspective, rather than speculate wildly about cultural progress. And Boas took his own advice. He conducted extensive fieldwork among two Native American peoples, the Eskimo and Kwakiutl, and he sent his many students out to do research on other cultures far from home. The work done on the Polynesian island of Samoa by one of Boas' students, Margaret Mead, became enormously influential in the 1920s and 1930s after the publication of the classic *Coming of Age in Samoa*.

Two other benefits would follow from lengthy, firsthand fieldwork. First, the traditional customs and beliefs of many of the world's peoples already were disappearing rapidly. Boas believed it was the duty of anthropologists to record disappearing traditions before they were gone forever. Many students of Boas did their fieldwork among Native American peoples, whose cultures were believed to be especially endangered.

Second, Boas felt that the main need of the infant field of anthropology was more factual information about other cultures, collected by unbiased fieldworkers. Facts about a given culture should be collected without preconceived notions, for preconceptions are likely to breed inaccuracies. Fieldworkers can only become unbiased by approaching their studies relativistically (see Chapter 1)—not judging another culture's morality by our moral codes, nor evaluating the overall worth of their culture by our own standards of worthiness. More than any other single figure, Boas imparted to anthropology the doctrine of cultural relativism, which requires studying another culture on its own terms. He also did as much as anyone to show that biological differences and cultural differences are largely independent of one another; that is, the culture of a people is entirely learned, not explained by their genetic heritage.

In sum, historical particularism made several enduring contributions to modern anthropology:

other cultures themselves, rather than relying on incomplete and biased accounts written by untrained and often casual observers. This, too, was rare for scholars in the nineteenth century. The unilineal evolutionists have been called "armchair anthropologists" because (with some notable exceptions such as the American Lewis Morgan) they carried out all their research in their offices, using unreliable documentary sources.

Boas was scornful of theories developed in the comfort of an armchair. He believed that to understand another culture, one must have the familiarity that can only come with long personal the debunking of the overly speculative schemes of the unilineal evolutionists, the insistence on fieldwork as the primary means of acquiring reliable information, the imparting of the idea that cultural relativism is essential for maximum understanding of another culture, and the demonstration that cultural differences and biological differences have little to do with one another. These contributions helped to shape modern cultural anthropology.

However, historical particularism has limitations. Consider the claim that each culture is unique. Certainly, if differences between cultures are what we are most interested in, we can always find them. Having discovered them, we can then go on to claim that no two cultures are alike. At some level, the claim that "each culture is unique" is surely correct. So also is the claim that no two individuals brought up within the same culture are exactly alike. Yet they are alike in some ways. So, to some extent, no culture is like any other. But also, in some ways, all cultures do have things in common. There are similarities as well as differences between human ways of life. Historical particularists tended to overlook the similarities and to neglect the investigation of factors that might explain them.

Consider also the statement that, because each culture is the historical product of its particular past, one cannot generalize about the causes of cultural differences. To say (as many particularists do) that adaptation to the environment is most important in culture X, art styles in Y, political rivalries in Z, and so forth, is to say little more than that everything depends on everything else. It is also possible, however, that some influences are more important than other influences in all or most human populations—for example, it is possible that environmental adaptation is generally more important than art or religion in causing a people to live the way they do.

The interests of American anthropologists returned to discovering the general principles of human cultural existence in the 1940s. Meanwhile, another way of studying the cultural and social systems of other peoples developed in Europe.

British Functionalism (ca. 1920–1950)

Around the same time that historical particularism dominated American anthropology, a quite different approach was popular in Great Britain. The basic tenet of **functionalism** was that the cultural features of a people should be explained by the functions they perform. By *functions*, British anthropologists meant how existing ideas and actions contribute to the well-being of individuals and/or to the persistence of the whole group or society.

A leading British functionalist was Bronislaw Malinowski. Malinowski believed that the whole purpose (function) of culture is to serve human biological and psychological needs. These basic, biologically given needs include nutrition, reproduction, shelter, protection from enemies, and maintenance of bodily health. As social animals, people also need affection and emotional security. Unlike other animals, we humans have few inborn drives or instincts that provide behavioral instructions for how to meet our needs. Instead we have culture, which provides the learned behaviors, cooperative patterns, and social institutions (e.g., families, political associations) that make need fulfillment possible. Some parts of culture (e.g., foods, tools used in production) meet our needs directly. Other parts (e.g., family life, educational practices) raise and enculturate new generations of group members. Still other cultural features (e.g., religious practices, art) instill adherence to the common norms and values that make group cooperation possible. These latter features also function to fulfill needs, but they do so indirectly, by helping the society persist over many generations and encouraging individuals to conform.

Malinowski thus considered the biological needs of individuals as the starting point for explaining culture. One cannot argue with the point that culture meets human needs—although it's worth mentioning that living in a given time and place (e.g., modern Los Angeles) also creates additional "needs." But notice that, *by themselves,* the biological needs of individuals cannot explain why cultures differ. All humans everywhere have the same kinds of "needs," yet groups vary in the types of cultures that fulfill these needs. Why do different peoples living in different times, places, and circumstances meet their needs in so many different ways? For example, some people satisfy their need for protein by eating beef, whereas others—such as devout Hindus and Buddhists—not only refuse to consume cattle flesh but maintain a vegetarian diet. So the common human need for protein cannot explain the diverse cultural ways in which protein is acquired. To generalize the point: The basic needs of humans are the same everywhere and can be satisfied in so many different ways that they cannot explain cultural variation. At the least, differences in the natural environment in which people live must be taken into account to explain cultural differences.

A. R. Radcliffe-Brown was another influential British functionalist, but his approach differed greatly from that of Malinowski. Radcliffe-Brown argued that the primary function of different elements of culture is to keep the entire social system in a steady state, or to maintain social equilibrium. He used an analogy to make his point. Society is like a living organism, with individual people analogous to cells and groups of people analogous to organs. In a biological life form, cells and organs are parts of a whole, and each has a function to perform to keep the entire organism alive and reproducing. We study the physiology of the organism by analyzing how all its complementary parts work together to keep the body alive.

Analogously, for Radcliffe-Brown, the functions of the various parts of a cultural system are to maintain the entire "social body." The parts of the culture (*institutions,* as he called them) ordinarily function harmoniously to maintain the entire society or, as we commonly say, "to keep the system going." Occasionally, some part will disrupt the state of equilibrium, but all societies have social mechanisms (e.g., behavioral norms, means of social control) that regulate disruptions and return the social system to a steady state. In studying culture, we need to uncover the func-

tions that different institutions perform and how they relate to one another.

But is the organic analogy valid? Most contemporary scholars would say no. Unlike cells, individual human beings have minds and wills of their own, independent of the requirements of the social system. Also, the emphasis on steady states as the normal condition of society is misguided, many feel. Change—whether at slower or faster rates—is the normal cultural condition, not equilibrium, yet functionalism failed to produce an adequate theory of how and why change occurs. Conflict—violent and otherwise—and disagreements between individuals and groups also is widespread in human communities. We need an approach that explains how and why conflict occurs, not just shows how it is reduced and regulated.

Despite these shortcomings, Radcliffe-Brown's emphasis on how the different aspects of culture relate to one another and to the whole system had at least one enduring impact on how anthropologists study culture today. More than any previous approach, functionalism emphasized the integration of culture: Parts (economy, religion, family, etc.) cannot be understood in isolation from each other or from the whole system. By their insistence that culture forms an integrated system, the British functionalists greatly strengthened the holistic perspective of anthropology (see Chapter 1).

Like their American contemporary Franz Boas, the British functionalists emphasized the necessity for anthropologists to conduct firsthand fieldwork. Malinowski, especially, is well known to all anthropologists because of his ethnographic writings about the Trobriand Islanders of the western Pacific. Not only is fieldwork the best means of obtaining reliable information about a people, but it also is a necessary part of the training of anthropologists, Malinowski believed. We cannot claim to understand people, nor their diverse cultures, until we have immersed ourselves in the experience of some culture other than our own. Further, Malinowski thought the main objective of fieldwork is to see the culture as an insider to the culture sees it. In an often quoted passage from his famous 1922 ethnography of the Tro-brianders, *Argonauts of the Western Pacific,* Mali-nowski (1922, 25) wrote:

> . . . the final goal, of which an Ethnographer [sic] should never lose sight . . . is, briefly, to grasp the native's point of view, his relation to life, to realise *his* vision of *his* world.

Finally, Malinowski thought it essential that field-workers take a holistic view of the culture of the communities they study and live in. In his words:

> . . . the whole area of tribal culture *in all of its aspects* has to be gone over in research. . . . An Ethnographer who sets out to study only reli-gion, or only technology, or only social organi-zation cuts out an artificial field of inquiry, and he will be seriously handicapped in his work. (Malinowski 1922, 11; italics in original)

Although he said it differently, clearly Malinowski was urging fieldworkers to study the interrelation-ships between the various elements of a culture.

Because of the work of early twentieth-century anthropologists like Boas and Malinowski, the fieldwork experience is today an important part of the graduate training of almost all anthropolo-gists. And both relativism and holism are per-spectives that most modern fieldworkers regard as necessary for objectivity and understanding. In fact, many contemporary anthropologists half-jokingly refer to fieldwork as their *rite of passage.* More than other aspects of their training, field-work transforms the anthropologist as a person, giving individual anthropologists a different perspective on themselves and their own culture.

MID-CENTURY EVOLUTIONARY APPROACHES (ca. 1940–1970)

As we have discussed, Boas' attack nearly demol-ished the armchair speculations of the unilineal evolutionists. But one can study a subject without making the same mistakes nineteenth-century intellectuals made. Beginning around 1940, a few anthropologists renewed the study of cultural

evolution shorn, they believed, of the invalid as-sumptions of the unilineal evolutionists. Two such American anthropologists were Leslie White and Julian Steward, whose ideas greatly influ-enced modern thought.

Leslie White believed that the unilineal evolu-tionists had been right about some things. First, the technologies available for harnessing natural resources have, in fact, improved over the cen-turies. White proposed a reasonably objective measure of technological evolution: Since the main function of technology (in preindustrial times, anyway) is to capture the energy locked up in the environment, those technologies that capture the most energy per person are more evolved. Technological progress thus does have an objective meaning and can be measured, at least in a rough way. Second, cultures have, in fact, grown more complex over evolutionary time. And reasonable definitions of cultural com-plexity are possible: Societies with more territory, more occupational specialization, more functional differentiation, and more inequality can be de-fined as "more complex." By these criteria, for example, most hunting-gathering cultures are simple, whereas ancient civilizations such as the Egyptians, the Chinese, and the Inca are complex. The industrial societies of twentieth-century nation-states are still more complex.

Technological progress and cultural complex-ity are, of course, related. In a few words: As technology becomes more productive, societies become larger and more complex. For this reason, White is sometimes called a *technological deter-minist,* meaning that he believed the technology available to a people has enormous impacts on other aspects of their culture. For instance, hunter-gatherers who exploit wild resources must live in small groups and remain mobile according to season. They tend to have few possessions, to share their resources, and to have weak leaders. But people with an agricultural technology are generally more sedentary, live in large villages, accumulate wealth, and develop powerful leaders.

White's contemporary, Julian Steward, agreed that technology was an important part of culture, helping to shape many other aspects of a people's way of life. But Steward felt that the local environment was an important influence on culture. Tools, after all, must be applied to the resources available in the environment to produce food and other necessities. The abundance, seasonal availability, and spatial variability of resources affect how people apply their technology and what and how much they produce. Steward argued that environment and technology together determine the basic form of *adaptation* of a group and that their adaptation in turn shapes the rest of their culture. He therefore is sometimes called a *techno-environmental determinist*.

Despite the fact that they often are labeled as determinists, both Steward and White recognized that some parts of a people's culture are more strongly "determined" by technology and environment than are other parts. The way a people organize their productive and other economic activities is likely to be much more affected by their adaptation than the way they arrange marriages, worship deities, recite myths, or construct art. Even so, aspects of culture that are not directly tied to adaptation may be indirectly tied to it, including marriage (Chapter 7) and religion (Chapter 11).

White and Steward made the investigation of cultural evolution respectable again. Many modern anthropologists specialize in fields such as *human ecology, cultural ecology,* or *cultural evolution,* studying long-term changes in cultures and how people adapt to their environments. Just as importantly, White and Steward felt that anthropology could and should be a science, in the same way that biology or physics are sciences—indeed, White titled one of his books *The Science of Culture* (1949). On this point, a great many contemporary anthropologists disagree, as we shall now see.

ANTHROPOLOGY TODAY: DIVISIONS

Contemporary cultural anthropologists adopt an enormous variety of theoretical perspectives, far

more than we can cover. So we shall focus on one major division within the field today. In part, the modern split is between those who think that ethnology should be a science (like biology) and those who think that ethnology is more of a humanistic field (like literature). Some of the differences between the two perspectives are summarized in the Concept Review.

Those who believe that anthropology is more akin to the sciences tend to believe, like the evolutionists, that cultural differences can mostly be explained by the way human populations relate to their natural and social environments. Like other animals, people have material needs for food and other life-sustaining or life-enhancing resources. Acquiring these needs means that groups have to be organized in certain ways for cooperation or for successful competition with other groups. Many other elements of a people's culture are determined by or are greatly influenced by how people organize their groups and their activities to survive and persist in their environments. Because anthropologists who adopt this view argue that it is the material resources people get out of their environment that shape culture, the approach is often called **materialism.** In essence, materialists think that how a people make their living in their environment is the most important influence on the rest of their cultural existence. (We shall discuss some of these effects in later chapters.)

Those who think that ethnology is a more humanistic field emphasize the uniqueness of each culture, are skeptical of any attempt to generalize about the causes of cultural differences, and hold that cultural anthropology is a descriptive and interpretive field rather than an explanatory one. In these respects, they share many of the beliefs of the historical particularists. They obviously agree that people have material needs. But they think that humans differ from other animals in that these needs can be satisfied in such a multitude of ways that cultural differences cannot possibly be reduced to "need satisfaction." Scholars who follow this line of thinking are often called **idealists** (not to be confused with *idealistic*).

CONCEPT REVIEW Overview of the Scientific and Humanistic Approaches in Cultural Anthropology

SCIENTIFIC APPROACH	HUMANISTIC APPROACH
Main goal is the explanation of cultural differences and similarities, to make generalizations	Main goal is to describe and interpret particular cultures, to achieve an "insider's view"
Humans are part of the natural world, different only in degree from other animals	Humans are unique because they are conscious, cultural beings, different in kind from other animals
Regularities and consistent patterns exist across cultures, discoverable by empirical observation and systematic comparison	Individual cultures are so complex that each culture must be understood on its own terms; comparisons distort the cultures compared
All humans are fundamentally similar, sharing a core of motivations, emotions, behavioral predispositions, and the like	Humans differ profoundly in their motives, emotions, and behavioral tendencies, according to the culture they were raised in
Field methods emphasize observation and quantification of group patterns of behavior; descriptions are objectively attainable in that two trained fieldworkers can discover the same set of facts	Field methods emphasize participation and interaction with individuals; descriptions emerge from interaction of the fieldworker with local people, and two fieldworkers will have different accounts depending on their personal characteristics and these interactions

In essence, idealists deny that culture has any *general* explanation, for they believe that humans and their diverse ways of living are too complex to be reduced to a single formula.

Materialism

Anthropologists who follow the materialist orientation point out that people face the same kinds of imperatives as all mammals: We must receive adequate intakes of food and water, regulate our body temperature (by making shelter, for example), reproduce, cope with the presence of organisms that cause disease, compete successfully, and so forth. Like all animals, human groups must adapt to the conditions in their natural environments. Materialists hold that this imperative is basic and primary.

If one thinks that adaptation to environment and the acquisition of material resources are primary, then those aspects of culture that help people adapt and get resources will strongly affect all other aspects. Humans, more than any

other animal, depend on technology to exploit resources, compete, and cope with other problems of environmental adaptation. Technology includes not just the physical *instruments* (the tools) used to produce food, provide shelter, and generally manipulate the environment. Equally important, technology includes the *knowledge* about the environment, about resources, and about the manufacture and effective use of tools that people socially learn from previous generations (see Chapter 2).

Because humans rely on technology to acquire food and harness other resources, materialists believe that technology is among the most important aspects of culture everywhere, much as White argued back in the 1940s. By "most important," materialists mean that technology strongly affects other cultural aspects, including family life, political organization, values, and even world views. Because the essential purpose of technology is to aid people in making a living in their environments, the environment itself also helps determine culture, just as Steward said. In applying their technology in their environment, over long time periods people discover that certain resources are preferable to others, and that some ways of timing and organizing their labor activities work better than others. For example, those food resources that are most productive and/or nutritious will become culturally preferred and exploited, and the best ways of scheduling and organizing the work to acquire them will become standardized.

In their emphasis on the importance of physical/biological needs, technology, and environment, modern materialists resemble earlier thinkers such as Malinowski, White, and Steward. However, in many ways modern materialists are more sophisticated than their precursors. For example, for the most part earlier theories about causation were *linear,* meaning that one thing makes another thing the way it is; thus, A "causes" B, or A "determines" B. We might see technology and environment as causes, and cultures as effects. But modern materialists are more likely to view technology, environment, and culture as having feedback relationships to one another. That is, as people interact with their environment using their technology, they change the environment, and these changes in turn lead people to alter their technology, which then further alters the environment, and so on. For instance, as people exploit a resource, they often deplete its supply to themselves and future generations. They must then either work harder to acquire the resource in the future, develop a new method of acquiring it, or switch to an alternative resource. Other cultural changes accompany these changes in adaptation.

Following this line of argument, one leading cultural materialist, Marvin Harris, proposes that many important changes in human cultures result from a process known as *intensification.* Although human societies develop various ways of limiting their population growth, over the long term the population in many regions of the world increases. As population grows, people overexploit and deplete resources, which leads to degradation of their environment. This forces them to use their

environment more "intensively": They turn to resources they previously ignored, which requires them to expend more labor in acquiring energy and materials, which leads them to develop new technologies to harvest and process resources. As human numbers continue to increase, people are forced to continually intensify their use of resources. Both population growth and intensification lead to new social relations and organizations, which develop to facilitate the new ways of exploiting nature. In turn, new social arrangements require new world views, values, and norms to reinforce them.

Idealism

A great many (as the twenty-first century begins, probably most) modern ethnologists are skeptical of materialist explanations. They are often called *idealists*—not because they think the world could be a much better place (they are not necessarily idealistic), but because they think that the ideas and beliefs of a culture (its mental components— see Chapter 2) are fundamental in making it the way it is. Most idealists are skeptical of any effort to "explain" culture in the same way that evolutionary theory explains life or that Einstein's relativity theory explains the physical world. People, cultures, and human minds are too complex and unpredictable to be "explained" in the usual scientific sense of the word *explanation*—or so idealists believe.

Idealists believe this for many reasons, but perhaps the most important reason is their insistence on *human uniqueness.* Without denying that humans are animals, they think that humans are such a special kind of animal that special kinds of methods and analysis are required to understand us.

Human uniqueness, as we have seen, consists in our heavy dependence on social learning and in our capacity for complex communication—that is, in both culture and language. In turn, our reliance on culture and capacity for language make it necessary for us to construct our beliefs and orient our behavior by means of symbols. And the meanings of symbols, as we know, are arbitrary and conventional (see Chapter 2), not natural or inevitable. Idealists believe that this has a profound implication for understanding humankind as a whole and for studying particular cultures: Other animals live in the natural world, whereas humans live, in large part, in worlds of their own making and symbolic construction. This means that people manipulate nature (with agriculture, houses, and factories) more than other animals. But more importantly, it means that the way people perceive the natural and social environment, the way they interpret events in that environment, and their view of the world itself depend on their culture.

Consider, for example, the term *resource,* one of the cornerstones of materialist theory about causation. A simple definition might be "something that people use to satisfy their needs or wants." *Resources* thus appear to be "out there," "in nature," available for a people to use or transform into useful products. For materialists, the way people acquire resources is the main factor that shapes other aspects of their culture, and long-term changes in the way populations acquire resources is one of the main things that leads to cultural evolution.

Idealists, though, view resources differently. To them, a *resource* is as much a cultural concept as a material thing. Further, people's "wants" and even what they think they "need" for survival are not fixed and permanent, but variable from group to group. Resources, then, are not in fact "out there" in the environment; rather, they are *culturally defined* or *"culturally constructed,"* as idealists like to say. What one people consider a resource is not defined as a resource for other people. Hindus do not eat cattle; Muslims and orthodox Jews refuse pork and abhor the pig; Americans shun dog meat, insects, and horse flesh; and so on. Some perfectly edible animals and plants are not culturally defined as foods because of a people's world view or classifications of reality. Likewise, wants and needs are not inherent and universal in human nature, but are culturally variable.

A similar contrast applies to the way materialists and idealists view the environment. As we have seen, materialists emphasize the *objective conditions* under which people live and to which their behavior must be adapted. The natural environment is external to the group, and its characteristics are hard realities of nature to which a human group must adjust.

Idealists question whether this reality has very much significance in determining the ways in which any particular people live. They hold that the way a group of people *subjectively perceive* and culturally construct their environment is as important in shaping their adaptation as is the objective environment itself. Material conditions (i.e., technology, environment, and adaptation) do not "determine" the rest of culture, for cultural classifications, definitions, and conceptions shape people's perceptions of the material conditions.

Materialists and idealists also disagree on which needs and wants take priority in human life. Materialists assume that material satisfactions like shelter, nutrition, bodily comforts, wealth items, and so forth are generally the main goals and values in life. The desire for nonmaterial satisfactions are less important or are acted upon only after material needs and wants have been satisfied.

In contrast, idealists think that human-human relationships are at least as important as human-environmental relationships. Humans require more than material satisfactions for a sense of well-being and even for survival. People do not live by wheat and meat (or rice and fish) alone: We need rewarding social relationships, intellectually coherent and emotionally gratifying world views, a sense of who we are, symbols to become attached to, basic values to cling to, and other nonmaterial rewards. In brief, as cultural beings humans seek a meaningful as well as a prosperous existence, and our psychological need for meaning is just as important as our material needs for things. Idealists point out that some people deliberately reject material rewards in the name of cultural preservation or for religious reasons.

Finally, idealists argue that the material conditions people face impose only very broad limits on their behaviors because people can satisfy their needs in a multitude of ways. No human population adapts to its environment in a historical and cultural vacuum. Their history and traditions influence not only how they define *resource* and perceive nature, but also which of the many possible ways of adapting to nature they will adopt. There are many ways to survive and persist in a given environment.

In summary, idealists believe that the human dependence on culture and capacity for symbolic communication make us such unique animals that attempts to explain cultural diversity in scientific terms are likely to be futile. In particular, idealists claim that materialist explanations fail for several reasons:

- Resources, which have such an important role in materialist theory, are culturally constructed, not inherent in nature.
- A people's perceptions of the natural world are as important to their adaptation as are the objective conditions of their environment.
- Unlike other animals, material wants are not paramount among humans, who have a variety of social, emotional, intellectual, and symbolic wants as well.
- Material conditions provide great leeway for any group of people to develop a wide diversity of behaviors and beliefs, based on their particular history and unique traditions.

If all this is true (of course, materialists think they are not true), then how could materialist scholars be so wrong in thinking that environment, resources, technology, and adaptation are the main forces that make cultures the way they are?

Many idealists hold that materialist theories are a product of Western cultural values and beliefs. Because the West places such a high value on material welfare and consumption, materialists mistakenly see these values and beliefs in other cultures. The capitalist economic system requires competition, favors wealth and property accumulation, rewards technological innovation, encourages the transformation of nature, and promotes individualism. Raised and educated in

a social and cultural context in which material values are so important, it is no wonder that so many materialist thinkers see "economic man" in cultures where he does not exist! In brief, many idealists hold that materialist explanations originate from the cultural bias of Western civilization. (We have no space to discuss this here, but some materialists counterargue that some idealists themselves come from a culture that is so privileged that they never have to worry too much about their material wants, so it is they who mistakenly conclude that other peoples don't place priority on such things either. Who then would have the "Western bias," or who would be "ethnocentric"?)

Although in this section we have emphasized the differences between the materialist and idealist approaches, we should note that to some extent these differences result from the different interests of anthropologists. For example, people who study subjects like human adaptation, economic systems, or long-term evolutionary changes in societies are more likely to be materialists. Those who study aspects of culture like mythology, art, oral traditions, or world views are more likely to fall into the idealist camp. Also, in part, the diversity of modern approaches reflects the fact that human beings and their cultures are complex and multidimensional, so the orientation useful to understanding one dimension (e.g., adaptation) may not prove very useful in studying another dimension (e.g., world view).

METHODS of STUDYING a CULTURE: ETHNOGRAPHIC FIELDWORK

Whether they consider themselves humanists or scientists, anthropologists aim to come up with new knowledge. Sometimes the knowledge is about a previously unstudied culture or human community. In other cases, communities are restudied, or some aspect of an already known culture is investigated. Since the early twentieth century, cultural anthropology has relied upon fieldwork as its primary means of acquiring new information about cultures. Fieldwork also is part of the training of anthropologists. Conducting fieldwork, and completing a lengthy dissertation that describes the findings of one's fieldwork, is how graduate students demonstrate that they can "do" anthropology as well as "study" it. In this section, we discuss how fieldwork is conducted and some common problems encountered by fieldworkers.

In the Field: Procedures

Since the days of Boas and Malinowski, ethnographic fieldwork has usually required that researchers live in or close to the community being studied for a long period, usually a year and commonly two or more. Ordinarily, fieldworkers learn the local language and adjust their own behavior—if not always their feelings and thoughts!—to be consistent with local norms and values. Usually, they not only observe but also participate in activities by going to gardens, joining groups, attending weddings and funerals, contributing to feasts, and so forth. All these practices allow the day-to-day observation and interaction essential for adequate understanding of peoples' lives. Many anthropologists are surprised by how much they learn about a community simply by living in it for a prolonged period!

Once in the field, fieldworkers use several methods to acquire specific information. Among these are surveys, interviews, and participant observation.

Surveys are used to gather highly specific information from a lot of individuals or (more often) households quickly. Surveys often occur early during the fieldwork period, because the data desired are—or at least appear to be—relatively easy to obtain. A typical subject for a survey is a census designed to count the total population, find out the age and sex and sex distribution, determine the number of households or families in the community, and discover which family members live together under the same roof. Sometimes all members (or households) in a community will be surveyed, or sometimes only a

sample will be used. The survey may take the form of a written questionnaire delivered and picked up by the researcher. More commonly, the fieldworker visits the people himself or herself, for survey research provides an excellent opportunity to introduce oneself to a lot of people early in the research.

Interviews are another fieldwork method. The fieldworker arranges a time and place to elicit responses to prearranged questions. Interviews may be either structured or unstructured. A *structured interview* usually takes the form of a set of questions with relatively brief and clearcut answers. One major use of structured interviews is to determine the kinship relationships between members of the community, so that genealogies (family trees) can be constructed. This is especially important in groups where kinship relationships are important in determining rights to land or other property, cooperative labor, and/or ritual participation. In such communities, knowing how a person is related to other individuals tells a researcher much more about the person than it would in an industrial society. Structured interviews are used for many other purposes as well, from discovering how people spend their time and money to estimating how often they go to church.

In *unstructured interviews* the fieldworker asks more open-ended questions, hoping that the interviewee will elaborate about the complexities of the answer. The questions often are quite general: "What happens when someone dies?" "How do you decide whom to marry?" "How do you act around your in-laws?" At unstructured interviews, general information about particular subjects is obtained, and possible lines of new investigation are suggested. After many structured and unstructured interviews, fieldworkers begin to have a sense of "how x (and y and z) is done," or of "how people feel about x, y, and z."

Individuals who allow fieldworkers to interview them or observe their activities are called **consultants** or **informants.** Obviously, field research requires the help of many consultants, who nowadays usually are compensated in some way for their time and expertise. Some consultants are enormously helpful, but not all will be familiar with the subjects that interest the fieldworker. Women will know more about some things than men, and vice versa. The elderly often are more knowledgeable about legends, myths, and history. Shamans, priests, or other religious practitioners generally have specialized knowledge that other people do not have—and in fact may not be allowed to have. People in the community whom fieldworkers rely on for their expertise in a particular area, and who spend a large amount of time being interviewed or observed, are called **key consultants** or **key informants.**

Although a great deal of ethnographic information comes from interviews, the method has limitations. At first, the fieldworker may not know what questions to ask, and so the questions themselves may come across as stupid, naive, offensive, or aggressive. (For example, one of the authors asked a Micronesian: "How long do you cook food in the earth oven?" Answer: "Until it's done.") Other questions—although they may interest the anthropologist—may be entirely irrelevant in the local context.

In the late nineteenth and early twentieth centuries, most anthropologists relied mainly on interviews for their information. Most American anthropologists of that time were concerned with collecting information about Native American cultures. Almost all tribes had already been confined to reservations, where maintenance of their traditions was impossible. Their economies, family life, religion, and other cultural elements had drastically changed as a consequence of the white colonization and settlement of their lands. Fieldworkers wanted to record their traditions before they were forgotten. Conducting interviews—usually with elderly people who had grown up in the prereservation period—was often the only way to find out about their traditional cultures. In these decades, anthropologists did collect a lot of information on Native American life.

In the 1920s and 1930s, the interest of anthropologists increasingly shifted from recording rapidly vanishing cultures to understanding the dynamics of present-day cultural systems. Increasingly, fieldworkers wanted to understand how cultures worked, how their parts fit together, how and why they changed, and so forth. In other words, there was more emphasis on understanding cultures as they exist today, rather than on reconstructing their traditional pasts. One of the leaders of this shift in interest was the functionalist Bronislaw Malinowski, who helped popularize another way of gathering information called **participant observation.** This method required fieldworkers to take up residence with the people they were studying and learn their culture by observation of and participation in their daily lives. (Of course, other methods such as surveys and interviews also were employed.)

Participant observation provides researchers with knowledge they cannot gain through either surveys or interviews. Surveys and interviews have inherent limitations. First, people's verbal descriptions of their customs and beliefs are bound to be incomplete, simply because people cannot think of everything and because people are not conscious of all the knowledge their culture has instilled in them.

Crawford/Anthro-Photo File

Participant observation is one of the main ways fieldworkers acquire information from the members of a community. This is David Mayberry-Lewis with the Xavante people of the Brazilian Amazon.

To understand this limitation, consider how you would respond if a fieldworker from another culture asked you to describe a baseball game. How complete and accurate would your description be? Chances are, if you are an avid fan, you could relate enough information for her to gain a basic understanding of the game. You could tell her how many players there are on each side and explain the basic rules about balls, strikes, runs, errors, and innings. From memory alone, it is highly unlikely that you would explain everything that might occur during a particular game. What you probably would give the researcher is an idealized model of a baseball game. Certain facts would be left untold, not because you were hiding them but because they are either so commonplace or unusual that they are not part of your consciousness concerning the game. The same is true of other people's descriptions of their own culture. Interviews alone can give the researcher only a simplified overview of a particular cultural phenomenon, an idealized model.

If a researcher truly wants to understand baseball, she cannot simply talk to someone about it; she needs to at least see a game. In fact, she should observe several games and discuss what occurred with a knowledgeable person. It would be even better to participate, at least in a minor way, in a game. Only by combining interviewing with observing and participating can one begin to understand the rules and dynamics of the game. So it is with the study of other cultural phenomena.

Another limitation of relying on surveys and interviews is that there are always discrepancies between verbal statements and behavior. People don't always actually do what they say they do, and their behavior often diverges from the ideals and norms of behavior. An incident that occurred during Malinowski's fieldwork in the Trobriand Islands illustrates the importance of participant observation in supplementing (and even correcting) interview data. One day Malinowski heard a commotion in the village and discovered that a young boy in a neighboring village had committed suicide by climbing a palm tree and flinging himself onto the beach. In his earlier questioning

of the islanders, Malinowski had been told that sexual relations between a man and his mother's sister's daughters were prohibited. On inquiring into the suicide, he found that the boy had been sexually involved with his mother's sister's daughter, and that in fact such incestuous relationships were not rare. So long as such liaisons were not mentioned in public, they were ignored. In this particular case, the girl's rejected boyfriend had become angry and publicly exposed the transgression. Although everyone in the village already knew of this incestuous relationship, by making it public the ex-boyfriend exposed his rival to ridicule, thus causing him to commit suicide. It is doubtful that such behavior could have been discovered only by interviewing individuals.

In the Field: Problems

Each fieldworker's experience is, in some ways, unique. As individuals, researchers differ in personality, gender, interests, social skills, and other ways. Likewise, host communities vary in their receptivity to and preconceptions about outsiders, past experiences with foreigners, internal political divisions, and other factors that enormously influence the success of the research. While recognizing the uniqueness of each experience, it is useful to discuss some of the common problems encountered by ethnographic fieldworkers.

Stereotyping   In the present context, **stereotypes** are defined as preconceived generalizations about a particular group. Often, we only think of one party to a relationship as having stereotypes about the other, as when we say that one group is the "victim" of stereotyping by another. But stereotyping usually cuts both ways. Hopefully, the fieldworker is trained to be aware of his or her own tendency to stereotype people and can at least partially overcome her or his own preconceptions and cultural biases—although this is far easier said than done! However, members of the community are likely to have their own stereotypes about the cultural or racial group the anthropologist represents. Fieldworkers thus must overcome not only their own stereotypes, but also deal with those of the community.

Most often, fieldworkers are of European or Euro-American ancestry, whereas the host community is not. (Fortunately, this situation is changing today.) Over the history of contact between peoples, the "natives" were generally placed in a subordinate position. No wonder, then, that fieldworkers attempting to gain acceptance so often encounter suspicion and outright hostility! The probing questions about behavior and beliefs asked during interviews naturally arouse further suspicions. Why does this foreigner want to know about our family structure, our political organization, our ritual secrets? What is this person going to do with this information? While the anthropologist is trying to understand the community, its members are attempting to understand what the fieldworker is doing. For example, a minority or tribal group involved in some illegal activity—such as smuggling, poaching, or growing drugs—may fear that the anthropologist will inform government authorities. Members of groups that have more exposure to Western culture often assume that the ethnographer's objective is to make money and that researchers become wealthy by publishing books about them.

In other cases, members of the community may be aware that outsiders do not approve of or believe in certain types of behavior, and few people will disclose information on topics they think will be met with disapproval or scorn. This reticence is particularly evident about certain types of religious beliefs and practices. As a result of Christian missionaries, most non-Western peoples are well aware that Westerners usually deny the validity of witchcraft and the existence of werewolves. Members of societies with these beliefs are understandably reluctant to talk openly about an uncle who they believe can turn himself into a deer or a snake with someone who will probably view what they say as ridiculous. Likewise, they probably would not reveal that their father had been killed by a witch if they thought that the outsider did not believe in witchcraft.

Developing a Role and Rapport   Often against a background of suspicion, distrust, and, in some cases, fear, an anthropologist has to develop a rapport with local people. Rapport means acceptance to the degree that a working relationship is possible, although ethnographers are rarely, if ever, totally accepted by the people among whom they work. However, over a period of time most anthropologists succeed in gaining some degree of trust and friendship, at least with a few members of the group.

The particular role or roles that anthropologists eventually define for themselves within the society vary greatly with circumstances. Depending on the amount and nature of research funding, the fieldworker may be an important economic resource, paying wages to interpreters and assistants or distributing desirable goods as gifts. Anthropologists with a car or truck frequently find themselves providing needed transportation for members of the community. Ethnographers may also provide comic relief by asking silly questions, behaving in a funny manner, making childlike errors in speaking the language, and generally being amusing to have around. They may be a source of information about the outside world, disclosing information to which local people would not otherwise have access. Sometimes community members are as curious about the anthropologist's society as he is about their society. Or the anthropologist may just be considered a harmless nuisance. During the course of research, the typical fieldworker at one time or another adopts all these roles plus many others.

Working with Consultants   As you can imagine, having an anthropologist in your community can be a pain in the neck (or wherever). Most of the time, however, local people are patient and cooperative with fieldworkers and willing to serve as consultants. But sometimes members of the community do not completely understand what the anthropologist is after. Occasionally, people engage in deliberate deception.

For example, collecting genealogies is not always as easy as it might seem because in many societies it is customary not to speak the names of the dead. Among the Yąnomamö of Venezuela and Brazil, not only is it taboo to speak the names of the dead, but it is considered discourteous to speak the names of prominent living men, for whom kinship terms are used whenever possible. When ethnographer Napoleon Chagnon persisted in his attempts to collect genealogies, the Yąnomamö responded by inventing a series of fictitious names for individuals, living and dead, as well as creating fictitious genealogical relationships. Only after five months of intensive research did he discover the hoax. When he mentioned some of the names he had collected during a visit to a neighboring village, the people laughed at him: His informants had made up names such as "hairy rectum" and "eagle shit" to avoid speaking real names.

Ethical Issues Generally speaking, anthropologists do not enter the fieldwork site by invitation of the community, but because of their own research and professional interests. Most often, they are "outsiders" whose cultural upbringing and personal lives differ dramatically from those of the people they are studying. Fieldworkers typically are citizens of wealthier nations than their host communities and therefore have access to more resources than local people. Equally important, members of the local community may *perceive* fieldworkers as richer and perhaps as more powerful than themselves. In the past it was common in European colonies (e.g., in Africa or southeast Asia) for people to worry about "reprisals" from colonial officials should they fail to cooperate with fieldworkers. Such worries are less likely to be so widespread in the twenty-first century, thanks to the spread of formal education and increased contact among peoples of various nations. Still, some people are more likely to defer to the anthropologist because of these perceptions, or to give fieldworkers more of their time than they would otherwise, or to reveal information that they would prefer not to reveal.

For these and other reasons, fieldworkers often face ethical dilemmas, rooted partly in actual or perceived wealth and power differences. Field anthropologists, of course, should never knowingly abuse their privileges or status, but the potential for *unintentional* abuse of consultants is enhanced because local people may *perceive* that there will be costs should they fail to cooperate. Further, occasionally the conduct of the work itself, or the results of the study when published or communicated, has the potential to harm the host community or some members of it. And finally, in the past some anthropologists have been asked not to reveal "secret" information, but have done so anyway, justifying their revelations by their contributions to general knowledge about the human condition.

Because of concern for such ethical issues, in 1971 the American Anthropological Association adopted a code of conduct for fieldworkers and other researchers. The ethical code was revised in 1989 and again in 1998 to reflect new concerns. The entire code is published on the association's web site (www.ameranthassn.org). Like other ethical standards, it is intended to provide guidelines for decision making when potential conflicts of values and goals arise. Briefly, its main provisions include:

- *Not undertaking or not continuing research that will be harmful to the host community.* The primary obligation of fieldworkers is to those they work among, not to the objectives of the research or to the gaining of knowledge. "Harm" includes damage to the safety, dignity, or privacy of consultants and local people generally.
- *Respecting the wishes of individuals regarding their public identification.* Fieldworkers must determine in advance whether key consultants and other people wish to be identified or to remain anonymous in publications. Their wishes are to be honored as much as possible. Sometimes, it is even advisable to disguise the location of the field site.
- *Fieldworkers must obtain the informed consent of people before undertaking work.* People must be told who the anthropologist is and what she or he is studying.

- *Not exploiting individuals or groups for personal gain.* Payment in money or reciprocation in gifts, services, or other forms must be given to consultants.
- *Preserving the integrity of scholarly research and publication.* Specifically, anthropological researchers must be truthful; their actions should be such that future research opportunities remain viable; they should disseminate the results of their work in publications, presentations, classrooms, and other forums; and they should allow others access to the information they obtain.

In short, anthropological fieldworkers should protect the interests of the host community and individual members of it, tell people what they are doing, protect privacy, avoid exploitation, and not misuse the results of their studies.

If all this sounds pretty obvious, remember that ethical codes exist partly because real-life situations are sometimes not at all simple. For example, if a consultant specifically asks that his or her name be used, but the researcher suspects that revealing the identity might prove harmful, what should the anthropologist do? How much payment or reciprocation is "enough" or is "fair"? Should anthropologists avoid work that does not seem to cause harm at present, but that might potentially, someday, be harmful, in some way that cannot be foreseen?

Consider also the attitude of cultural relativism that anthropologists are taught to practice during their fieldwork. In the abstract, relativism is an easy concept (although most will not agree with its more extreme implications). Most students quickly grasp the principle of relativism, but it is more difficult to apply the principle to one's own situation. Sometimes fieldworkers are exposed to certain attitudes and behaviors that are unacceptable in their own value system. For example, some local people may "abuse" family members or certain powerful individuals may "exploit" others. As fieldworkers develop relationships with community members, such "abuse" or "exploitation" becomes personalized.

Under what circumstances, if ever, should a fieldworker intervene—not as an "anthropologist," but as a "fellow human being"? In theory, such intervention is rarely permissible, but the answer is not nearly so clear in real-life situations.

Culture Shock   Many people experience a kind of psychological trauma when surrounded by people speaking a language they cannot fully understand and speak only imperfectly, eating foods that are strange, seeing architecture that is alien, and observing people using gestures and behaving in ways they either do not comprehend or do not approve of. The strange sounds, smells, tastes, sights, and behaviors result in the disorientation of many fieldworkers. Out of their normal cultural context, they do not understand what is happening around them, yet realize that their own actions often are being misunderstood. The symptoms of this **culture shock** are psychological and sometimes even physiological: paranoia, anxiety, a longing for the folks back home, hypochondria, and, sometimes, diarrhea.

The attempts by ethnographers to maintain their relativistic perspective and objectivity in their daily interactions with members of the other society may compound the normal trauma of culture shock. Socially isolated and unable to release their frustrations through conversations with sympathetic others, they often have to cope with their fears and anxieties alone.

For many anthropologists, much of their time in the field is extremely traumatic, which is why many anthropologists view fieldwork as a rite of passage. More than any other aspect of their training, fieldwork transforms the individual from a student of anthropology into a professional anthropologist. Fieldwork is undeniably a significant educational experience. Most individuals return from their fieldwork with a different perspective on themselves and their own culture. Fieldwork often teaches us as much about ourselves as about those we are supposed to be studying.

SUMMARY

1. Anthropology originated as a separate academic discipline in the late nineteenth century, after colonialism intensified contact between peoples of European ancestry and the indigenous peoples of Africa, Asia, the Americas, and the Pacific. Darwin's theory of evolution was one of the main notions that allowed Western intellectuals to make sense of the peoples and cultures of other lands. It seemed to imply that the history of life on earth was progressive, with simpler organisms evolving into more complex ones. Unilineal evolutionists applied this notion to cultures. Using written accounts as their main source of information about non-Western peoples, they arranged cultures into a sequence of progressive stages, from simple to complex, with Western civilization at the pinnacle. Anthropology thus began as the field that studied how humankind had progressed out of rude beginnings into a more "civilized" cultural existence.

2. In the early twentieth century, both American and British anthropologists developed new approaches to studies of other cultures. The American historical particularists, led by Boas, demolished the speculative schemes of the unilineal evolutionists by arguing that concepts such as "complexity" depend on one's point of view and thus have little objective meaning. Boas popularized the notion of cultural relativism that remains a hallmark of ethnology today. In Great Britain, functionalists such as Malinowski and Radcliffe-Brown tried to show how the various parts of a culture and its social system serve to meet the needs of individuals and society. By emphasizing the interrelatedness of cultural systems, functionalism strengthened the holistic perspective. Both the historical particularists and functionalists emphasized the importance of firsthand fieldwork as the surest path to objectivity and as essential for the training of anthropologists.

3. In the middle decades of the twentieth century, scholars like White and Steward returned to cultural evolution, avoiding most of the mistakes of the unilineal evolutionists. White emphasized the importance of technology, Steward of adaptation to the local environment, in making cultures the way they are. Both men thought that how a group acquires resources (energy, food, and so forth) from nature are the main influences on culture. Both also believed that anthropology was a science whose main objective was to explain cultural differences and similarities.

4. Contemporary anthropologists are incredibly diverse in their approaches, but there is a clear and enduring division between those who adopt a scientific versus a humanistic perspective. Materialism is one of the main scientific orientations. Materialists hold that how a people organize their groups and activities to acquire energy and materials from their natural environment is the main explanation for the rest of their culture. In contrast, with their strong belief in human uniqueness, idealists mistrust all such efforts to develop a generalized explanation of cultural phenomena. They favor studying and interpreting each culture individually and are suspicious of most comparative studies.

5. Ethnographic fieldwork is the primary method by which anthropologists acquire new information about a culture. Which specific methods are employed to study a human community varies with the orientation of the fieldworker, the objective of the research, and the nature of the community. Three methods are used by nearly all modern fieldworkers: surveys, interviews, and participant observation. The latter helps to overcome some of the limitations of both surveys and interviews, and is generally regarded as essential for maximum objectivity and understanding.

6. Fieldworkers are faced with numerous obstacles and problems, which vary from experience to experience. Some common problems are overcoming stereotypes, working with consultants (informants), establishing rapport, ethics, and culture shock. Fieldwork not only provides the data that enrich our understanding of human cultural diversity, but it also often affects the anthropologist. It is generally a part of everyone's graduate training.

KEY TERMS

unilineal evolution
historical particularism
functionalism
materialism
idealism
surveys
interviews
consultant (informant)
key consultant (key informant)
participant observation
stereotypes
culture shock

SUGGESTED READINGS

Some volumes on the history of cultural anthropology include:

Bohannan, Paul, and Mark Glazer. *High Points in Anthropology.* 2nd ed. New York: Knopf, 1988.

A reader in the history of anthropological theory, featuring original works by key figures.

Hatch, Elvin. *Theories of Man and Culture.* New York: Columbia, 1973.

Well-written overview of the ideas of leading historical scholars, discussing evolutionism, functionalism, and particularism.

McGee, R. Jon, and Richard L. Warms. *Anthropological Theory: An Introductory History.* 2nd ed. Mountain View, CA: Mayfield, 2000.

A comprehensive volume that includes original articles by leading theorists, from the nineteenth century to the present day.

To understand the contemporary divisions between materialists and idealists, consult some of the following works:

Geertz, Clifford. *The Interpretation of Cultures.* New York: Basic Books, 1973.

Assorted works by an idealist and interpretivist. Good place to start to understand this approach.

Geertz, Clifford. *Negara: The Theatre State in Nineteenth-Century Bali.* Princeton: Princeton University Press, 1980.

Empirical, interpretive study.

Harris, Marvin. *Cannibals and Kings.* New York: Random, 1977.

Intensification hypothesis of cultural evolution is explained and illustrated. Easy reading and an excellent example of materialist thought.

Johnson, Allen W., and Timothy Earle. *The Evolution of Human Societies.* 2nd ed. Stanford: Stanford University Press, 2000.

Outstanding and up-to-date theoretical and factual treatment of cultural evolution. Conceptualizes increasing complexity as shifting from family level through local level to regional level, with examples illustrating the cultures of each level.

Marcus, George E., and Michael M. J. Fischer. *Anthropology as Cultural Critique.* Chicago and London: University of Chicago Press, 1986.

An influential book written from the idealist perspective. Discusses changes in anthropology and ethnography since the 1970s. Argues that the time is right for anthropologists to take on the task of critiquing their own culture.

A number of books deal with the actual experiences of ethnographers in the field. They are valuable for conveying the feeling of fieldwork, of problems ethnographers encounter, of relating to local people, and so forth.

DeVita, Philip R. *The Naked Anthropologist.* Belmont, CA: Wadsworth, 1992.

Collection of twenty-seven articles describing the experiences of fieldworkers. Often humorous.

Dumont, Jean-Paul. *The Headman and I.* Prospect Heights, IL: Waveland Press, 1992.

Account of a fieldworker's relationships with the Panare people of the Venezuelan Amazon.

Golde, Peggy, ed. *Women in the Field: Anthropological Experiences.* Chicago: Aldine, 1970.

Twelve female ethnographers discuss special difficulties they encountered because of their gender.

Hayano, David M. *Road Through the Rain Forest.* Prospect Heights, IL: Waveland Press, 1990.

Describes the fieldwork experiences of Hayano and his wife among the Awa, a people of the highlands of Papua, New Guinea.

Rabinow, Paul. *Reflections on Fieldwork in Morocco.* Berkeley: University of California Press, 1977.

An influential account of the author's experiences in Morocco.

Raybeck, Douglas. *Mad Dogs, Englishmen, and the Errant Anthropologist: Fieldwork in Malaysia.* Prospect Heights, IL: Waveland, 1996.

A fascinating and sometimes humorous book about the author's personal experiences as a fieldworker in Malaysia. Covers topics such as settling in, dealing with people, overcoming local perceptions, having a family along, and so on. An excellent and highly readable account of one ethnographer's experiences.

Ward, Martha C. *Nest in the Wind.* Prospect Heights, IL: Waveland Press, 1989.

Wonderfully readable account of Ward's personal experiences and fieldwork difficulties on the island of Pohnpei, Micronesia.

Many books are written primarily for students new to anthropology, to help them understand the nature of fieldwork and its problems, to teach them methods, and to describe some projects that they can do themselves. Here are some excellent ones:

Agar, Michael. *The Professional Stranger: An Informal Introduction to Ethnography.* New York: Academic, 1980.

Quite good for the beginning student. Tells how ethnographers do their work, with lots of examples taken from the author's own field experiences.

Chiseri-Strater, Elizabeth, and Bonnie Stone Sunstein. *Fieldworking: Reading and Writing Research.* Upper Saddle River, NJ: Prentice-Hall, 1997.

Written for the undergraduate classroom, this book is a guide to student fieldwork. It discusses issues and is rich in examples taken from student projects.

Kutsche, Paul. *Field Ethnography: A Manual for Doing Cultural Anthropology.* Upper Saddle River, NJ: Prentice Hall, 1998.

The author describes the field projects he developed for his introductory students. This book describes his experiences and the student projects themselves. The smaller projects include: mapping a block, describing words students invented, studying body language, and studying a ritual. Students also do a "big ethnography," or a larger scale study of people in a particular setting (e.g., a critical care unit, Denny's restaurant). Examples of student papers on these topics are included.

Spradley, James P. *The Ethnographic Interview.* New York: Holt, Rinehart and Winston, 1979.

Spradley, James P. *Participant Observation.* New York: Holt, Rinehart and Winston, 1980.

Two older but still useful books that complement each other, one focusing on structured interviewing of informants, the other on detailed observation.

chapter 5

ADAPTATION: ENVIRONMENT *and* CULTURES

Contents

We begin our exploration of cultural diversity by discussing adaptation—the main ways in which various human groups relate to their natural environments and how these relationships affect their cultural existence. We begin with adaptation because many anthropologists believe that how a people relate to their environment is the most important influence on their overall way of life. Future chapters deal with cultural diversity in other areas: marriage and family life, kinship and other bases for organizing social life, gender relationships, political organization, religion and world view, and aesthetic expression.

Our focus is the adaptations of preindustrial peoples—that is, those peoples whose traditional economies were based on food production, not on the extraction of resources for factory production. First, we provide some concepts that are useful in studying and comparing systems of adaptation. Then we cover the hunting and gathering adaptation, which nourished humanity for most of our existence as a species. Adaptations in some parts of the world were dramatically altered around 10,000 years ago, when people first domesticated plants and animals. Agriculture and herding imposed new requirements and opened up new opportunities for human groups, resulting in major changes in cultures, as we shall see.

UNDERSTANDING HUMAN ADAPTATION

Adaptation refers to the process by which organisms survive and reproduce in their environment. The environment includes (1) physical features like topography and precipitation, (2) populations of other species like plants and animals, and (3) members of the organism's own species. Living things must cope with all three components of the environment, which nonhuman animals do by means such as genetic changes (evolution) and behavioral alterations (learning).

In studies of human adaptation, it is useful to pay attention to two important features. First, the environment (or *habitat*) includes *natural resources*

that people harness to meet their material needs and wants: food, water, wood and leaves for shelters and fires, stones or metals for tools, and so forth. Second, the environment poses certain *problems* that people must solve or overcome: resource scarcity, excessively high or low temperatures, parasites and diseases, rainfall variability, deficient soils, and so forth. If people are to adapt to conditions in their environments, they must harness resources efficiently and cope with environmental problems effectively.

Like other species, human populations adapt to their environments physiologically and genetically. For example, bacteria, viruses, and parasites kill susceptible individuals, but those who are genetically resistant live and reproduce. By this process of natural selection, over many generations human populations will become more resistant to the microorganisms to which they are exposed. People are part of nature, and natural selection has helped to adapt us to the environments in which we live, just as it has for other organisms.

However, one way in which humankind differs from other species is that we adapt to changes in our environments *mainly*—but not exclusively— by cultural rather than by biological/genetic means. If the climate grows colder or if a group migrates into a colder area, they cope *mainly* by lighting fires, constructing shelters, and making warm clothing, not mainly by evolving physiological adaptations to cold. Humans hunt animals by making weapons and mastering techniques of cooperative stalking and killing, not by biologically evolving the ability to run faster than our game. Group cooperation and technology (including both the tools themselves and the knowledge required to make and use them) allow humans to adapt to a wide range of environments without undergoing major alterations in our genes. Because cultural changes allow us to adapt to varying environments, the human species has colonized every type of terrestrial habitat on earth, from tropical forests to arctic tundra, from the vast grassy plains of central Asia to tiny Pacific islands. The ability to adapt to diverse habitats by means of technology and group living surely is one of the secrets of humanity's success.

People interact with their environments in many ways. One of the most important ways is the harnessing of energy (e.g., food, fuel) and raw materials (e.g., minerals for tools, wood for shelters) from nature. Acquiring energy and materials from an environment is part of *production*, meaning the patterned activities by which people transform natural resources into things (products) that satisfy their material needs and wants. Obviously productive activities are essential for the survival and persistence of both individuals and social groups. Indeed, those anthropologists who follow the materialist orientation (Chapter 4) think that production is so important that many other aspects of a group's culture are shaped by it.

Transforming a natural resource into a useful product ordinarily involves three factors. People (1) expend their own time and energy *(labor, work)*, (2) using the tools and knowledge *(technology)* available to them (3) on the natural *resources* available in their environment. Labor, technology, and resources (called the *factors of production*) are combined in various ways to produce food, shelter, and other material products that people desire.

These concepts are easy to grasp, but there are a few complexities. Many such complications arise from the fact that humans are social animals (see Chapter 2), who live in groups of various sizes and compositions. Because people live together in groups, they have to organize their activities to transform resources into products. Individuals have to know what to do and what to expect others to do, and they have to know when and where to work so they do not come into conflict or violate one another's rights. The *organization of production* solves problems such as who will do what productive tasks, when, where, and how. There are three main factors involved in the organization of production.

First, people usually prefer to spend less rather than more time in work, so they try to use their labor efficiently. Often, people can make most efficient use of their labor by dividing up tasks among themselves according to factors like sex,

age, and skill. For example, young men and young women often have different productive tasks to perform, while children can do some tasks perfectly well. The allocation of productive work to different kinds of people is called the *division of labor*. Ideally, but not always in practice, tasks are allocated according to ability.

Second, to use labor efficiently members of a group often cooperate with one another. For example, several hunters may have a better chance of spotting, tracking, and killing large game, and net fishing may be more productive if people work together. Since cooperation is often more efficient than working alone, a group's *patterns of cooperation* is an important part of how the members organize themselves to produce what they need and want.

Third, humans face the potential problem of conflict over access to natural resources: Which individuals and groups have the right to use a particular resource at a particular time and place? People have to find ways of defining their *rights to resources*. Generally, a given area of land or territory—along with its resources—is allocated to some group. Its members have the right to exploit the area's resources, whereas others are prohibited from doing so, or may do so only with permission.

In modern societies, we solve such problems by defining some people as "owners" of productive property, based in large part on their ability to purchase (or inherit) such property. Preindustrial cultures have property rights also, but they often differ greatly from those of modern industrialized nations. In dealing with preindustrial adaptations, anthropologists have learned that it is essential to distinguish *ownership rights* from *use rights* and *group rights* from *individual rights*. A territory and its resources are most frequently owned by some kind of group—commonly a family unit of some kind or a residential group like a camp or village. The members of this group have collective rights to use the resources. The leader of the group (e.g., the family head, the village chief) allocates the use of the resources among the members. People in the group have the right to use the resources, so long as they do not violate the rights of other group members to use them also. Thus the "property rights" of individuals are always limited by the rights of others.

In sum, production is one important way people interact with their environment. Production involves expending labor and utilizing technology to harness natural resources. Because people live in groups, production is usually a highly organized social activity, involving the division of labor, patterns of cooperation, and the allocation of rights to resources.

Using these concepts, we can describe and compare some of the ways various peoples adapt to their environments. Anthropologists generally divide preindustrial adaptations into three major categories, based largely on how people produce their food supply:

hunting and gathering (also called **foraging**), in which people exploit the wild plants and animals of their territory for food;

agriculture (or **cultivation**), in which people intentionally plant, care for, and harvest crops (domesticated plants) for food and other uses; and

herding (or **pastoralism**), in which people tend, breed, and harvest the products of livestock (domesticated animals) for food, trade, and other uses.

The remainder of this chapter describes these three ways of exploiting the food resources of an environment and discusses some of the main ways that each adaptation affects culture.

HUNTING and GATHERING

Foragers, also called hunter-gatherers, get their food from collecting (gathering) the wild plants and hunting (or fishing for) the animals that live in their regions. By definition, foragers do not attempt to increase the resources found in their environments by growing crops or intentionally breeding livestock for meat and other products. But many foragers do make modest efforts to

Lee/Anthro-Photo File

Hunting and gathering is the oldest form of human adaptation. The !Kung of southern Africa are one foraging people who have been well studied ethnographically. This !Kung woman is bagging mongongo nuts, a nourishing wild food and a staple of the diet.

control or improve the natural resources in their environments in other ways. For example, they may try to increase the supply of edible plants and animals by burning forests and grasslands to attract more grazing animals or to increase the supply of sun-loving edible berries or other plants.

Most physical anthropologists believe that *Homo sapiens* has existed as a species for more than 100,000 years. But there was no farming of crops or herding of livestock anywhere on earth until about 10,000 years ago. The foraging adaptation thus supported humanity for at least the first 90 percent of our existence as a separate species.

However, once plant and animal domestication developed, agricultural and herding peoples began to increase in population and to expand over the landscape. Over the millennia, cultivators and herders pushed many foraging peoples into regions that were not well suited to crops and livestock. As a result, when European contact with people of other continents intensified in the 1700s and 1800s, hunters and gatherers already lived primarily in regions too cold or arid to support agriculture (see Figure 5.1, which shows the main regions where foragers lived at about the time of European contact). By the twentieth century, partly as a result of European colonialism and the geographical expansion of Euro-Americans over most of the New World, foragers had been further forced out of their traditional lands. In many cases, they had died out altogether.

Foraging and Culture

Hunter-gatherers living in different habitats differ in their cultures, partly because environments vary in the kinds and qualities of food resources they contain. Foraging groups of the resource-rich environment of the American Northwest Coast lived a fairly sedentary existence in large permanent settlements, whereas Shoshone of the arid and resource-sparse American Great Basin roamed in small bands or individual families. In spite of environmental differences, most—but not all—foraging groups share certain cultural similarities.

Our main goal in this section is to describe how the adaptive requirements of hunting and gathering affect the cultures of most foraging peoples. A major point to keep in mind is that efficiently acquiring wild food resources from an environment leads foraging peoples to organize their social life in certain patterned ways.

Division of Labor by Age and Gender   The division of labor among foragers is organized largely along the lines of age and gender, although

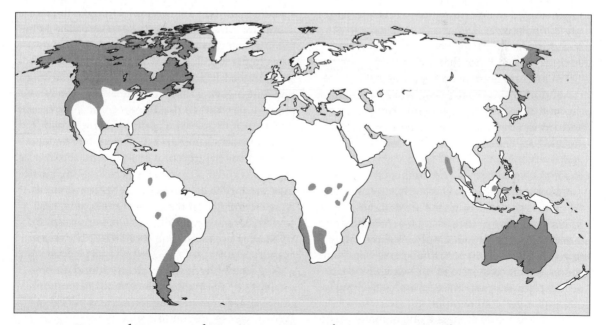

Figure 5.1 Principal Regions of Foragers at Time of First Contact with Europeans

special knowledge and unusual skill also serve as a basis for assigning tasks. Among the great majority of foraging peoples, men do the bulk of the hunting and women most of the gathering of plants. However, it is not unusual for either sex to lend a hand with the activities of the other. For example, among the BaMbuti of the tropical forest of Zaire, the women and children help the men with hunting by driving game animals into nets. But in general, hunting is men's work.

Seasonal Mobility   None of the earth's environments offer the same kinds and quantities of resources year round. There may be seasonal differences in precipitation, and outside the tropics there usually are marked seasonal variations in temperature as well. Ordinarily, game animals are available in some places and not others at different seasons, and nuts and fruits tend to be available only at certain times of the year. For such reasons, most foragers move around according to season.

Foragers migrate to where food or water is most plentiful or easiest to acquire during a given time of year. For example, the Hadza people of Tanzania lived in an arid region with a marked distinction between wet and dry seasons. In rainy months the Hadza dispersed around the many temporary water holes that formed, living on the wild plants and animals in the immediate vicinity. At another time of the year, when these ponds evaporated, they congregated into camps clustered around the few relatively permanent water sources.

Seasonal Congregation and Dispersal   To exploit plants and animals efficiently, most hunters and gatherers also change the sizes of their living groups according to the seasonal availability and abundance of their food supply. At some times of the year, it is most efficient to disperse into small groups, which cooperate in the search for food. During other seasons, these groups will come together in larger congregations.

The Western Shoshone are one of many foraging cultures in which seasonal congregation and

dispersal was advantageous. Until their traditional adaptation was disrupted by white settlers in the nineteenth century, they lived in the arid American Great Basin. Most of their meat came from deer, antelope, and small mammals such as rabbits and squirrels. Plant foods included roots and seasonally available seeds, berries, pine nuts, and other wild products. For most of the year the Shoshone roamed the dry valleys and slopes of the Great Basin in tiny bands consisting of a few nuclear families, or even single families. Families occasionally gathered for cooperative hunting of antelopes and rabbits, which they drove into corrals and nets. But a more permanent aggregation of families was difficult because a local environment did not have enough resources to support large numbers of people for more than a few days.

One critical plant food became available in the fall and in most years was capable of supporting many families throughout the winter. Each year, around October, the cones of the piñon trees on the high mountains would ripen and produce large, nourishing pine nuts. During their travels in late summer, Shoshone families noticed which specific mountain areas seemed to have the most promising pine nut harvest. They would arrange their movements to arrive at these productive areas in the fall. Ten to twenty families would camp in the same region, harvesting and storing pine nuts. During favorable (i.e., rainy) years, the pine nut harvest would support these large camps throughout most of the winter. Spring would find the families splitting up again, to renew the pattern of dispersal into tiny groups until the next fall. No family had exclusive access to any particular territory in any season. Rights to resources were essentially on the basis of first come, first served, here meaning that whichever group arrived at an area first would be free to harvest its plants and animals.

The small group size typically found among peoples like the Western Shoshone is an organizational adaptation to foraging. Over a period of days or weeks (depending mainly on the environment and its resources), groups exhaust the wild resources of a given area and must move into a fresh environment (more accurately, a "recovered" environment). All else equal, the larger the group, the faster it uses up the wild plants and animals of an area and, hence, the more frequently it must relocate. One reason for the small size, then, is that smaller groups do not need to move as often as larger groups.

Bands In most environments, then, efficient foraging requires that people live in small, mobile groups of fifty or less. To distinguish these living groups from the settled villages, towns, and cities found in other adaptations, anthropologists call these mobile living groups **bands.** Band members cooperate in production and usually share rights to harvest the wild resources of a given territory. The size of bands is usually flexible, allowing the number of people living in the band to be adjusted according to the availability of the food supply. Further, individuals are not attached permanently to any band, but have many options about where to live and whom to live with. This way of organizing bands offers many advantages to foraging populations.

The !Kung of southern Africa illustrate these points about band organization. Living in what is now southeast Angola, northeast Namibia, and northwest Botswana, the !Kung are the most thoroughly studied of all surviving hunter-gatherers. The northern part of their environment is an arid tropical savanna, grading into the Kalahari desert toward the south. Until the twentieth century, the !Kung exploited this habitat entirely by foraging. They gathered more than one hundred species of plants and hunted more than fifty kinds of animals, including mammals, birds, and reptiles. Plant foods consisted of nuts, fruits, berries, melons, roots, and greenery. A particularly important and nourishing food was the mongongo nut, which ripens around April and provided about half the people's caloric intake.

Because their habitat received so little rainfall and then only seasonally, the availability of water greatly influenced the rhythm of !Kung life. From

about April to October (winter in the Southern Hemisphere), there was little precipitation, and practically no rain fell between June and September. During this dry season, water for people and animals was available only at a few permanent water holes, around which bands congregated into relatively large settlements of between twenty and fifty individuals. Between November and March—the hot and wet season—temporary water holes formed, and the bands split up to exploit the wild resources around them. But rainfall in this part of the world is not reliable, neither from year to year nor from place to place. In some years, up to forty inches of rain falls during the wet season; in other years, as little as six inches. Drought occurs in about two out of every five years. Precipitation also is spatially unpredictable: One area frequently receives severe thunderstorms, whereas twenty miles away no rain falls.

These characteristics of their physical environment—its aridity, seasonality, and marked temporal and spatial variability in precipitation—influenced the band organization of the !Kung. Because the distribution of wild foods and water was determined by rainfall, the annual cycle of congregation and dispersal of !Kung bands followed the seasonal distinction between wet and dry. During the wet months the bands were spread out among the temporary water holes in camps numbering about ten to thirty. When the bands first moved to a "fresh" water hole, wild resources were relatively plentiful; game was abundant and a wide variety of plant foods were easily available. But the longer a band remained around a water hole, the more the surrounding resources became exhausted. The men had to roam farther afield in their hunting, and the women had to travel longer distances in their plant collecting. After several weeks a camp reached the point at which its members judged that the costs of continuing to forage in the area were not bringing adequate returns in food. They then moved to a new wet-season camp. One ethnographer, Richard Lee, succinctly notes that the !Kung "typically occupy a camp for a period of weeks or months and eat their way out of it" (Lee 1969, 60).

As the dry season approached, !Kung bands made their way back to the area around one of the permanent water holes. These settlements, larger than the wet-season camps, commonly numbered between twenty and fifty and often even more. By the end of the dry season the supply of mongongo nuts and other preferred plant foods was exhausted and the people ate the less tasty bitter melons, roots, and gum. This was considered a relatively hard time of the year, and the !Kung waited in anticipation of the November rains, when they could again disperse into the smaller wet-season camps.

Reciprocal Sharing   It is mutually beneficial for the members of a foraging band to share food and other possessions with one another. The sharing is more or less on the basis of need: Those who have more than they can immediately use share with others. For example, among the !Kung, only some members of a band search for food on a given day. But foods brought back to camp are widely distributed, so even families who did not work that day receive a share.

In many hunting and gathering groups, reciprocal sharing especially applies to meat: Successful hunters returning to camp will share the kill with other families, including those who have not participated in the day's hunt. One reason for the special emphasis on the equitable sharing of meat is the uncertain returns of hunting compared to gathering. Among the !Kung, on most days women return to camp with their carrying bags full of nuts, roots, fruits, and other wild plants. Men's chances of capturing game, however, are smaller: Richard Lee estimates that only about two out of five hunting trips capture animals large enough to take back to camp. Men who are successful one day may be unsuccessful the next, so one reason they give today is so they can receive tomorrow. Reciprocal sharing also is encouraged by the fact that all or most members of a band are close or distant relatives of some kind, and humans generally tend to share with their relatives (see Chapter 6).

Reciprocal sharing usually is *normatively expected behavior,* meaning that people who regularly fail to share are subjected to ridicule or other kinds of social pressures, because they violated shared norms. Going along with the expectation of sharing is a positive cultural value placed on equality of personal possessions (property) and even of social status. Families who attempt to hoard food or other products may be ostracized. Men who try to place themselves above others socially by boasting about their hunting skills or other accomplishments are soon put in their place. The result is that there is both economic and social equality between the families of most hunting and gathering bands.

Rights to Resources   Effective adaptation requires that people have established ways of allocating natural resources between individuals and groups. Many hunters and gatherers are similar in how they determine rights to the resources of their territory: who can harvest which resources, where, and when.

One way to organize rights over a territory and its resources is for each group to establish and maintain exclusive claims to particular territories. Cultural ideas about the relationship between people and territory might be, for example, that this area is *mine* or *ours* and that area is *yours* or *theirs.* In the foraging adaptation, exclusive access would mean that each band has rights to remain in a specific area during a particular season. One benefit would be that the members of each band would know they will be harvesting the foods of particular places at definite times. Another advantage is that bands would not interfere in each other's hunting and gathering activities.

Despite these (apparent) benefits, most foragers organize rights of access in quite a different way. Among the !Kung, for instance, there was a comparatively weak attachment of particular groups of people to specific territories. Particular families tended to return to the same territories year after year, according to season, and over time others came to recognize them as the "owners" of the area. Most often, the more reliable water holes together with the wild resources around them were "owned" jointly by a set of siblings. But by merely asking permission—which was seldom refused—anyone with a kinship relationship to one of the "owners" could come and visit and exploit the area's food and water. Because most !Kung had many relatives who were "owners" of different places, each !Kung had a multitude of options about where and with whom they would live, work, relax, and socialize. As a consequence of multiple options, the composition of a band fluctuated radically, for each band received visiting relatives several times a year. Far from establishing exclusive claims to particular places, !Kung were only loosely attached to territories and for the most part came and went as their preferences and circumstances allowed. Similar patterns were found among most other known hunter-gatherers.

To sum up, most hunter-gatherers develop certain ways of organizing their activities and their groups that facilitate their adaptation:

- a division of labor based mainly on gender and age
- a high degree of mobility, especially from season to season
- congregation and dispersal of groups, largely on a seasonal basis
- living groups consisting of small bands with varying size and flexible composition
- strong norms of reciprocal sharing and value placed on equality in personal possessions and social status
- loose attachment of people to territory and flexible rights to resources

Although these statements describe most gatherer-hunters reasonably well, we must keep in mind that foragers are diverse and exhibit the above six features to greater or lesser degrees.

In fact, in some environments, hunting and gathering peoples lived in quite a different way. Along the Northwest Coast of North America (roughly from Oregon into the Alaskan panhandle), food resources—especially fish—were exceptionally abundant, and the Native Americans who lived there were able to smoke and preserve food for many months. Because of abundance

and storage, there was no need to maintain seasonal mobility or small living groups, so people were essentially sedentary. They lived in large, permanent villages with elaborately decorated plank houses. In addition, wild resources also were more reliable on the Northwest Coast than in most other environments lived in by foragers. Resource abundance and reliability affected property notions along the coast. If a food resource is abundant, and you can usually count on its availability, then it makes sense for you to stay close to it and defend it against other groups that might desire it as well. Northwest Coast people could count on fish being present in their rivers or coastal waters, so they developed more defined property rights. Particular groups were more definitely associated with particular locations than were people such as the Shoshone or !Kung.

DOMESTICATION

Domestication refers to the intentional planting and cultivation of selected plants and the taming and breeding of certain species of animals. It implies that people are making efforts to control the supply and distribution of the domesticated species, in order to increase their usefulness. With respect to plants, in this book we are concerned with *food crops,* or those species that people intentionally select, plant, care for, harvest, and propagate for purposes of eating. People also grow plants for other purposes, such as for fibers (cotton, hemp) or for drugs (tobacco, opium poppy). With animals we are concerned with *livestock,* or those species that people breed, raise, and control for purposes of providing food (meat, dairy products) or other useful things (hides, wool), or for performing work (pulling plows, carrying people and possessions). People keep animals for other reasons also, such as companionship (pets).

The origins of plant and animal domestication are outside the scope of this text. Suffice it to say that in the Old World, domestication occurred by around 10,000 years ago in the Middle East and by about 9,000 years ago in eastern Asia. In the next several thousand years, adaptations based on domesticated plants and/or animals developed in most African, Asian, and European environments that could support farming and/or herding. In the New World, a completely different set of plant species was domesticated in Mexico by about 5,000 years ago, and in northern Peru by 4,000 years ago.

In the Old World, Middle Eastern peoples domesticated several animal species about the same time as plants. In many parts of the Old World, the availability of livestock meant that men in many regions eventually gave up hunting, putting their labor into agriculture, crafts, warfare, and other activities instead. But in the New World, except for residents of the Andes, many peoples who relied on the cultivation of crops for their food got all or most of their meat from deer, antelope, small mammals, fish, and other wild animals. Most New World peoples, then, got the bulk of their meat from wild, not domesticated, animals, even though many of them were farmers.

Plant and animal domestication probably had more long-lasting and dramatic effects on cultures than any other single set of changes in adaptation—except, perhaps, the industrial revolution that began in the late 1700s. For example, once certain plants evolved by human selection into crops, people could produce more food in a given area of land. Increased production allowed them to remain in one place for long periods—over time, groups became more sedentary. They also could live in much larger settlements than the bands of most foragers—groups came to live in villages and, later in some places, in towns and cities.

AGRICULTURE

For tens of thousands of years, the hunting and gathering adaptation worked well. It allowed the total human population to increase to several million. Further, hunting and gathering is a flexible adaptation, meaning that it can be applied to any environment with a sufficient quantity of wild, edible plants and animals. Foraging will work in rain forests, grasslands, tundras, and mountains—given, of course, adequate shelter,

the right kinds of tools and skills, and appropriate ways of organizing production. Given how quickly human groups can adapt, and how quickly new ways of doing things can be communicated and spread if circumstances warrant, one or another hunting and gathering group was able to migrate into all the major continents except Antarctica. By around 10,000 years ago, humans were living on all the major land masses of the earth. Foraging, then, allowed humanity to be a successful species, if we measure success by species numbers and by geographical distribution.

In fact, most modern anthropologists believe that prehistoric hunter-gatherers actually enjoyed a relatively high quality of life. Richard Lee's quantitative studies of the !Kung in the 1960s show that they worked only about two and a half days per week to acquire their food supply. Even adding time spent in other kinds of work, such as making tools and housework, the !Kung worked only around forty-two hours per week. Most modern-day adults would be happy to have such a short work week! Further, the !Kung's relatively modest work efforts were sufficient to keep them well fed most of the time: Adults consumed an average of 2,355 calories and 96 grams of protein per day, more than sufficient for their bodily needs. There are, of course, exceptions, but the bulk of the evidence suggests that hunter-gatherers did not have a particularly hard life.

Why, then, did the foraging adaptation ever change? Why did many groups shift to the agricultural adaptation over the centuries? In fact, agriculture does offer one enormous advantage over hunting and gathering: It can support far more people per unit of territory. Only in favorable environments does the population density of foragers exceed more than one or two per square mile. In contrast, agricultural peoples typically live at densities of dozens or even hundreds per square mile. The ability to support larger numbers of people on a given area of land is probably the main advantage of agriculture over foraging.

Like most benefits, however, the ability to support higher population densities imposes some costs. The creation and maintenance of the artificial community of plants that make up a garden or farm requires labor, time, and energy. First, the plot must be prepared for planting by removing at least some of the vegetation that occurs naturally in the area. In some kinds of agriculture, the landscape itself must be modified by constructing furrows, dikes, ditches, terraces, or other artificial landforms. Second, the crops must be planted, requiring more labor. Third, natural processes destroy the artificial plant community and landscape that people have created: Weeds invade and compete for light and soil nutrients, animal pests are attracted to the densely growing crops, and rainfall and floods may wash away physical improvements. Cultivators, therefore, must "beat back nature" by periodically removing weeds, protecting against pests, rebuilding earthworks, and so forth. Fourth, the act of farming itself reduces the suitability of a site for future harvests, if only by reducing soil fertility. In future years the farmers must somehow restore their plots to a usable condition or their yields will fall. All these necessities require labor and other kinds of energy expenditures.

So farming is a lot of work, and much evidence suggests that people who make their living by

agriculture work at least as long and hard as most foragers. Cultivation also led to other changes—in settlement size and permanence, in ownership of resources, in political organization, and in many other dimensions of life—that culminated in the evolution of whole new forms of culture, as we shall see.

So many ways of farming land exist that we cannot even mention most of them here. Commonly, preindustrial farming systems are divided into two overall forms, based partly on the energy source used in farming and on how often a garden or field is cultivated. They are usually called *horticulture* and *intensive agriculture*. Both have many, many varieties.

Horticulture

In the farming system known as **horticulture,** people use only the energy (power) of their muscles in clearing land, turning over the soil, planting the crops, weeding, and harvesting. Figure 5.2 shows the major regions where horticulture existed at the time of contact by the West. There are no plows pulled by draft animals (such as horses

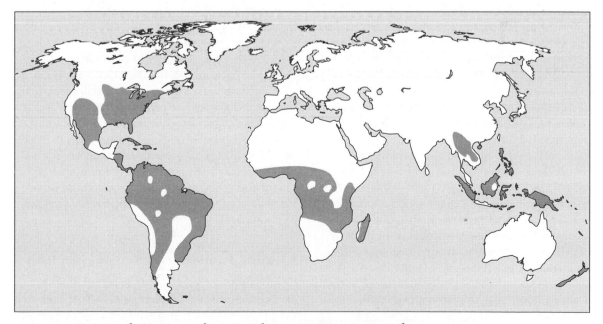

Figure 5.2 Principal Regions of Horticulture at Contact Period

or oxen) to help in preparing the soil for planting. Instead, people use hand tools such as digging sticks and shovels for such tasks. Some horticultural peoples fertilize their gardens with animal or human waste, or with other kinds of organic matter. If irrigation is necessary or useful for higher yields, water is usually hand carried onto the fields from nearby rivers or streams.

One type of horticulture is called *shifting cultivation* (or *slash and burn*). Today, it is practiced largely in the tropical rain forests of Central and South America, southeast Asia, and central Africa. Shifting cultivators farm the forest in a cycle. Using axes, knives, and other hand tools, they first cut down a small area of forest. After allowing the wood and leaves to dry out, they burn the refuse. The ashes often are spread out over the burned area, for they contain useful plant nutrients, and tropical soils are notoriously infertile. Generally, a given garden plot is cultivated for only two or three years before its fertility declines and it is gradually abandoned. Then another area of forest is cleared, and a new garden is prepared, planted, tended, and harvested until it is no longer productive enough. It then is abandoned and its natural vegetation regrows over several years. The land, in other words, is left *fallow* for a long time, during which it gradually recovers its ability to produce an adequate harvest. After many years of regrowth—usually ten or more—a previously abandoned plot is fertile enough to be planted again.

Another example of horticulture is *dry land gardening*. It is defined by the main climatic factor with which cultivators in arid lands have to cope: low, erratic, and unpredictable rainfall. Like all horticulture, it uses no plow, and simple hand tools—hoes, spades, and so forth—powered by human muscles are the characteristic technology. Dry land gardening occurs in the American Southwest, in parts of Mexico, in some of the Middle East, and in much of sub-Saharan Africa. In much of Africa it is supplemented by cattle raising, especially where rainfall is too erratic and unpredictable for people to depend entirely on their crops.

In this type of horticulture, low and highly variable precipitation impedes the growth of crops. Cultivation in arid lands is risky. Even if in most years rainfall and harvests are adequate, there is a good chance that in any given year not enough rain will fall. Therefore, people who cultivate in dry regions have developed various gardening techniques to cope with the possibility of drought.

The Western Pueblo peoples of the North American Southwest illustrate one way to cope with aridity. In this region annual rainfall averages only around ten inches, concentrated in the spring and late summer. Further, in this high country the growing season for corn—the major source of food—is only about five months long. The people are faced with extreme uncertainty: If they plant too early, a spring frost may kill their crops; if they wait too long, they will lose some of the critical moisture from the spring rains.

Over centuries of living in and adapting to their lands, Western Pueblo have learned viable ways to grow their crops. They generally plant corn in lowlands, where rainwater or springs leave the subsoil moist after the spring rains. Yet in some years the rains are so torrential that floods wash away the crops. The people, therefore, diversify both the place and the time of their planting. They sow the seeds of corn, squash, beans, and other crops in several locations, so that no matter what the weather, some fields produce a harvest. Gardens on the flood plains may be lost during an unusually wet year, but upland gardens still yield a crop. Staggering the time of planting likewise lowers the risk of cultivation; by planting crops weeks apart, the risk of losing all of a planting because of an untimely frost is reduced. Thus, by mixing up where and when they plant, the people reduce the risk of cultivation in an arid, highly seasonal environment.

Cultural Consequences of Horticulture

Obviously, shifting cultivation and dry land gardening are quite different varieties of horticulture, practiced in distinct kinds of environments.

But both methods are examples of successful efforts to increase the amount of food that can be produced in an area—the productivity of land is well above what would naturally be available and harvestable by foragers. And even though these kinds of methods are sometimes said to represent "simple" agriculture, both require that people remove most of the natural vegetation from the land so that crops can be planted. Finally, both require that people invest their labor in their gardens or fields (by clearing, planting, and weeding) in expectation of a later return (the harvest). Foragers, as you recall, seldom do such things.

Thus, horticulture improves the productivity of land, modifies the natural environment, and requires people to make a labor investment in their land. These facts alone affect the cultural systems of horticulturalists. How do their cultures differ from those of foragers? Subsequent chapters address this question more thoroughly. For now, we note two of the most important ways in which the horticultural adaptation shapes the cultures of people who live by it.

First, the size and permanence of settlements increase. Rather than living in bands or camps of around twenty to fifty, most horticulturalists aggregate into *villages,* often with hundreds of residents. Rather than moving every few days or weeks, people become more *sedentary,* remaining in the same location for years, decades, or even centuries. Villages are more permanent, both because effective adaptation does not require people to move frequently, and because families who have cleared and planted plots want to stay around at least long enough to recoup their labor investment.

Second, rights to resources differ from those common among most hunter-gatherers. Among horticulturalists, rights to land are better defined, meaning that particular individuals, families, and other groups are more attached to specific places where they or their ancestors have established a claim.

The reason for a more definite claim to resources is as follows. (For now we assume that some kind of family is the group that cooperates in food production.) A horticultural family invests its labor in clearing, planting, and otherwise improving specific and relatively well-defined pieces of land (its plots or fields). This labor investment establishes a family's *claim* to the land. Their claim (their rights over the plot, which includes at least the right to deny other families access to it) arises from the fact that their labor has increased the productivity of the land. Families with claims to specific plots pass their rights along to their children, most of whom will marry and transmit the rights to their own children. In any generation, any given individual or family thus has ownership rights over specific parcels, which usually include the gardens they are actually cultivating. Rights often extend to abandoned plots that they or their ancestors cultivated in the past and to which they or their children may return in future years.

Among horticultural peoples, then, ownership rights over well-defined parcels of land are usually held by families or some other kind of kinship group. In contrast, foragers most commonly have use rights over large territories with only vaguely defined boundaries. Further, horticultural families usually claim ownership over the land itself, because the soil may be made productive by planting crops on it. For foragers, use rights are typically exercised only over the wild resources of a territory, which is valuable mainly because of the wild plants and animals found there.

In sum, two of the major ways the cultures of horticulturalists differ from those of foragers are: (1) living groups (villages) are larger and more permanently settled, and (2) families have more definite rights of ownership over particular pieces of land. These two consequences, in turn, have other effects on cultures. For example, sedentariness means that people can store possessions rather than having to carry them around, raising the potential for wealth accumulation. More definite land rights raises the possibility that some families will inherit or otherwise acquire more productive resources than others. These and other effects are considered in later chapters.

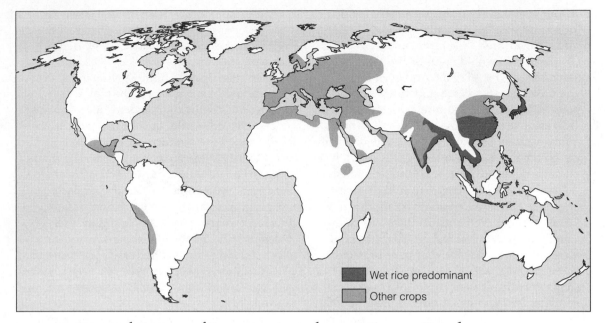

Wet rice predominant

Other crops

Figure 5.3 Principal Regions of Intensive Agriculture at Contact Period

Intensive Agriculture

As we have seen, horticultural peoples use human muscles as the only or main source of power for tools, and they make only modest efforts to improve the soil by fertilization with natural materials. Another characteristic of the horticultural adaptation is that, compared with intensive agriculture, it takes more total land to support a single individual or family of a given size. In shifting cultivation, for every plot of land under cultivation at any given time, several ("abandoned") plots are at various stages of regrowth and recovery. For example, if for every acre of land being cultivated, ten acres are under fallow, then far fewer people could be supported per acre than if only half the land was under fallow at any one time.

Therefore, even though horticulture supports higher population densities than foraging, the number of people it can support is low relative to the farming system known as **intensive agriculture.** (Figure 5.3 shows the major regions where intensive agriculturalists lived at the time of con-

tact with Europeans.) With the latter, fields are farmed more frequently. Indeed, some intensive agriculturalists have their lands under almost continuous cultivation—the same fields are farmed year after year, with only brief fallow. Stated differently, people use their land more *intensively:* To produce higher yields, they work the land harder. This is possible only if people take steps to maintain the long-term productivity of their land. In various regions, such steps include substantial fertilization (generally with the dung of livestock), crop rotation, careful weeding, turning of the soil prior to planting, composting, and other methods. For some of these tasks, a new tool, the plow, and a new source of energy (power), draft animals, are useful. Using plows pulled by horses, oxen, water buffalo, or other draft animals, a farmer can more quickly prepare the soil. In addition to traction for the plow, livestock provide many other useful products: meat, milk and other dairy products, manure, hides, and transportation. After harvest, livestock are turned loose to graze on the unharvested stubble, fertilizing fields in the process. In some regions,

Ahmed/David R. Frazier Photolibrary

animal muscle is used to power the mechanical pumps that carry irrigation water to the fields. Livestock also perform other kinds of work, such as turning the heavy stone wheels used to grind grains into flour.

For all these reasons, intensive agriculture is substantially more productive than horticulture. An acre of land produces greater yields and, hence, is capable of supporting far more people—five, ten, and even twenty times the number per unit of land than most horticultural adaptations. Supporting more people is probably the main advantage of intensive agriculture over horticulture.

In the Old World, especially in parts of Asia and Europe, intensive agriculture involved the use of the plow. But before the coming of Europeans, New World peoples had no domesticated animals suitable for pulling plows. Indeed, outside the Andes of South America, the only animals domesticated by Native Americans were dogs, turkeys, and Muscovy ducks. Andean people also had llamas and alpacas, but these were not used in plow agriculture. Despite this limitation, Native American civilizations in places such as the valley of Mexico (Aztec, for example) and the Andes found ways of increasing the yields of their lands by intensifying their produc-

tion systems. In the valley of Mexico, for example, natural swamps were reclaimed by filling in earth and constructing raised fields that were planted with crops like tomatoes, squash, and corn. By continually adding new nutrients from organic matter to these gardens, the people could keep them under almost continuous cultivation. In the Andes, stepped terraces were constructed to reduce erosion and an incredible variety of sweet potatoes and other crops were grown during the summer.

Another method of increasing yields, practiced by many intensive cultivators, is the use of irrigation to cope with natural rainfall deficiencies. Various irrigation methods are used around the world. Sometimes streams are dammed to conserve runoff, and ditches are dug to transport water to the fields. In some Asian river valleys, channels are dug to transport water and fertile silt to fields during the annual monsoons, when the rivers overrun their banks. In many mountainous regions of Southeast Asia, the level of water in hillside rice fields is controlled with an elaborate system of diked terraces.

In sum, compared with horticulture, intensive agriculture is more productive per unit of land. Its high productivity is due to factors such as shortened fallow periods (or having no fallow at all), preparing land more thoroughly prior to planting, removing weeds, adding manure and other organic matter to preserve fertility, and manipulating the supply of water. These (and other) inputs give people greater control over conditions in their fields, leading to higher yields per unit of land.

Cultural Consequences of Intensive Agriculture

The development of intensive methods of farming the land eventually had dramatic cultural consequences in many regions. Some of the most important effects of this form of adaptation result from its relatively high productivity. A single farm family using intensive methods can usually feed many more people than just its own members. Far more than either foragers or horticulturalists, intensive farmers can produce a **surplus** over and above their own subsistence (food) requirements. This surplus can be used to feed other people, families, and other kinds of groups, who no longer need to produce their own food.

What happens to this surplus? Many things, depending on circumstances. Excess food can be traded for other useful products like pottery, tools, wood, and clothing. If the community uses money (see Chapter 6), families may produce surplus food for sale, and the money they earn is used to buy other goods. If the village or other settlement has a strong political leader, such as a chief, he can collect the surplus from his subjects and use the food to pay laborers who work on public projects such as trails, temples, and irrigation works. If the community is part of a larger, more encompassing political system, with a ruler and a governmental bureaucracy, then the government will collect part of the surplus as a tax, which it uses for public purposes (e.g., support of armies, the judiciary, and the religious hierarchy) or to further its own political interests.

All these possibilities illustrate a central fact about most peoples who depend on intensive agriculture: Most are not politically independent and economically self-sufficient communities, but

These peasants in Thailand are working in their wet rice fields. Peasants both work for their own subsistence and produce cash crops and other products to sell to town and city dwellers.

are incorporated into some kind of larger organization. The villages in which most of them live are part of a more inclusive political system that dominates or rules them in some way. The surplus production of intensive farmers is traded, sold, or taxed (or all three) and supports people who do not themselves do farm work, such as rulers, aristocracies, bureaucracies, priests, armies, merchants, and craft specialists.

Intensive agriculture, then, is strongly associated with large-scale political and economic organization. Farm villages produce food and other products for people who live elsewhere and, in turn, receive things (products, services) from the larger system. The association of intensive agriculture with large-scale political organization is ancient, going back 5,000 years in parts of the Old World and more than 2,000 years in two large regions of the New World.

In prehistoric times intensive agricultural peoples were incorporated into the four major civilizations of the ancient Old World: the valley formed by the Tigris and Euphrates rivers of Mesopotamia, the Nile valley of Egypt, the Indus

River valley of Pakistan, and the Shang cities of China. The food supply of these civilizations was produced by intensive agriculturalists, who paid tribute or taxes to support the rulers, priests, armies, and officials who ran the government apparatus. In the New World, too, agricultural peoples were part of large-scale political units, such as the Mayans, Toltecs, and Aztecs of Mesoamerica, and the Incas of the Andean coast and highlands (Figure 5.4).

In these parts of the world, within a few centuries or millennia after the development of intensive agriculture, the socially and politically complex organization we call **civilization** (or "living in cities") emerged. All civilizations have a formal, specialized form of government known as the *state* (discussed further in Chapter 10). States are large-scale political units featuring a ruler, a governing bureaucracy, class distinctions between the elite and common people, and methods of extracting labor and surplus products from those who are responsible for farming the land. All these ancient civilizations were supported by

intensive agriculture, and all involved large-scale irrigation and water control. Certainly, it appears from current evidence that intensive agriculture is virtually a prerequisite for civilization. No known civilization ever developed out of a foraging or horticultural adaptation. (The Mayan civilization was once thought to have been an exception, but recent evidence shows that the Mayans, too, used intensive methods.)

In the modern world most people are incorporated into large-scale political units, namely, into nations. In most industrial nations, however, intensive agriculture has been largely replaced by mechanized agriculture based on energy derived from electricity and fossil fuels rather than from humans and animals. Today, most intensive agriculture occurs in the less developed countries of southern Asia and Southeast Asia, Latin America, and Africa. Intensive agriculturalists typically fit into these nations economically as peasants.

Peasants are rural people who are integrated into a larger society politically (i.e., they are subject to laws and governments imposed from outside

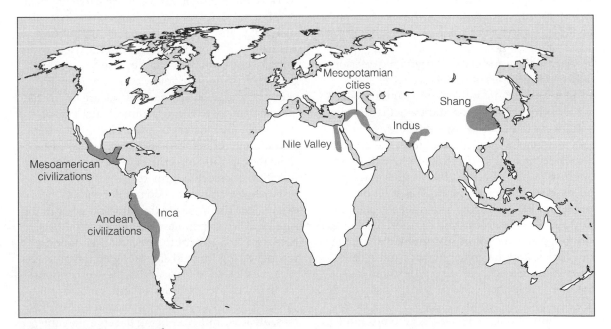

Figure 5.4 Ancient Civilizations

their communities) and economically (i.e., they exchange products of their own labor for products produced elsewhere). In many Third World countries, peasants make up the bulk of the population and produce much of the food consumed by town and city dwellers. Peasants typically subsist mainly from foods they grow themselves, although many also produce nonagricultural products for market sale. Peasant households produce goods that are sold for money, traded or bartered for goods produced by other people, paid to a landlord as rent, or rendered to a central government as taxes.

The peasantry first arose in the ancient civilizations just mentioned. The agricultural labor of prehistoric peasants fed the craft workers, the merchants, the state-sponsored priesthoods, the political elite, the warriors, and the builders. The tribute (usually paid in food, labor, or both) rendered by peasants was extracted from them by armed force or threat of force. This rendering of goods and labor by peasants to members of a more powerful social category continued into historic and modern times. The peasantry of medieval Europe, for example, eked out a meager living, paying a substantial portion of their annual harvest to their lords or working many days a year on their lord's estate.

Given the vast social and economic division between categories of people we term "elites" and "peasants," or "nobles" and "commoners," some anthropologists question whether the development of intensive agriculture was a curse or a blessing for most of humanity. There is little doubt that it is a blessing to those who throughout history have received the surplus made possible by intensive methods. And most scholars agree that the productivity of intensive agriculture allowed the specialized division of labor that led to writing, metallurgy, monumental architecture, cities, and the great religious and artistic traditions we associate with civilization. Indeed, the word *civilization* (referring to living in cities) itself has positive connotations for most people.

But how about the peasants, who produced the food that made all this "progress" possible?

For them, writing meant that more accurate accounts could be kept of their tribute payments or of the number of days they worked for overlords. Iron and other metals meant that peasants had better agricultural tools; yet for the most part they were not allowed to use them to ease their own labor, but only to produce more surplus for others to consume. Metal also meant that weapons became more effective, so that the citizens of one state could slaughter the citizens of another state more effectively. Most peasant families continued to live in hovels, even while great palaces, religious structures, and walled cities and towns were constructed and the workers fed by the peasants' agricultural labor. Both prehistorically and historically, peasants around the world have been denied many of the benefits offered by technological progress and artistic achievements, although their agricultural labor has made much of this progress and achievement possible.

PASTORALISM

Most farming people keep domesticated animals. Southeast Asian and Pacific horticulturalists raise many pigs and chickens. Intensive agriculturalists maintain livestock such as horses, oxen, water buffalo, and cattle, which they use to pull their plows, fertilize their fields, and provide dairy products and meat. These livestock are not merely supplementary to the agricultural adaptation; because of the meat, eggs, milk, hides, wool, transportation, fertilizer, and horsepower they provide, they usually are critical to the survival and nutrition of assorted farmers.

However, cultivators do not depend on their domesticated animals to the same extent or in the same way as do peoples known as pastoralists, or herders. Herders acquire much of their food by raising, caring for, and subsisting on the products of domesticated animals. With a few exceptions, the livestock are gregarious (herd) animals, with cattle, camels, sheep, goats, reindeer, horses, llamas, alpacas, and yaks being the common animals kept in various parts of the world.

Agriculture and pastoralism are not necessarily mutually exclusive adaptations, for a great many pastoral peoples also farm the land. When we characterize a people as "pastoral," we mean that the needs of their animals for naturally occurring food and water profoundly influence the seasonal rhythms of their lives. The key phrase here is "naturally occurring." Most farmers raise crops that they feed to their livestock or maintain fields in which their animals graze. In general, pastoralists do neither of these. Their herds graze on natural forage and therefore must be moved to where the forage naturally occurs. Some or all of the pastoral community must take their livestock to wherever the grasses or other forage are available in a given season. This high degree of mobility, known as **nomadism,** characterizes the pastoral adaptation. Most commonly, pastoralists are seasonally nomadic—they do not wander aimlessly. Their migrations often are "vertical," meaning that animals are taken to highland areas to graze during the hottest season of the year.

Advantages of Herding

Although people who herd animals are found on all continents, for the most part herders live in only certain kinds of environments (see Figure 5.5, which shows the main areas where pastoralists lived prior to European expansion). The pastoral adaptation occurs mainly in deserts, grasslands, savannas, mountains, and the tundra. These environments obviously are diverse, but they do share a common feature: Cultivation is impossible, extremely difficult, or highly risky because of inadequate or great yearly fluctuations in rainfall (as in deserts or savannas) or very short growing seasons (as in mountains and tundras). As always, there are exceptions to our generalizations, but most pastoralists live in regions that are not well suited to cultivation using preindustrial technologies.

In such arid or cold environments, the herding of livestock offers several advantages over the planting of crops. First, most of the vegetation of grasslands and arid savannas (grasses and shrubs)

The Maasai of Kenya and Tanzania adapt by herding cattle and other livestock. Pastoralism offers important advantages in arid or cold environments not well suited to agriculture.

Adrian Arbib/Anthro-Photo File

and of tundras (lichens, willows, and sedges) is indigestible by humans. Livestock such as cattle, sheep, and reindeer are able to eat this vegetation and transform it into milk, blood, fat, and muscle, all of which are drunk or eaten by various pastoral peoples. Thus, in some areas livestock allow people to exploit indirectly certain wild plant resources not directly available to them.

Another advantage of herding may be called *subsistence risk reduction.* Under preindustrial conditions in areas of low and unreliable rainfall, crops often fail because of drought. Livestock provide an insurance against these periodic, unpredictable droughts and accompanying crop failures. Not only do they store meat "on the hoof," but they also can be traded or sold to neighboring peoples for cultivated foods.

Finally, a big advantage of keeping livestock is their mobility: Herds can be moved to the areas of freshest or lushest pasture, to sources of water,

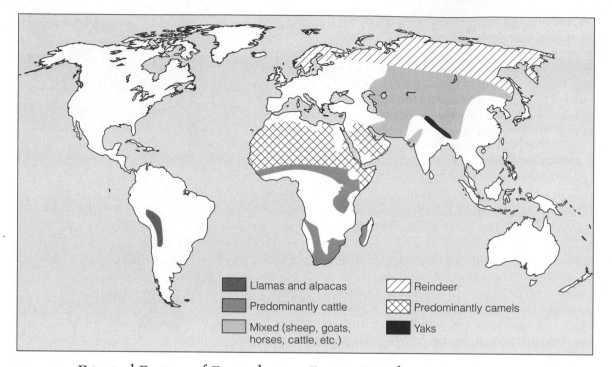

Figure 5.5 Principal Regions of Pastoralism at Contact Period

away from neighbors who have grown too aggressive, or out of easy range of tax-seeking governments that often want the nomads to settle down so they can be better controlled.

With advantages like these you may well wonder why pastoralism was not more widespread in the preindustrial world. Why did the herding adaptation not spread to areas where cultivators lived? Part of the reason is that environmental conditions are not always conducive. For example, until recently pastoralism seldom was found in tropical forests, largely because of lack of forage. (Today, enormous tracts of tropical forest in Central and South America are cleared and replanted in grasses suitable for cattle grazing.) Livestock diseases also limit the distribution of pastoralists. For example, much of eastern and southern Africa is occupied by cattle herders (most of whom also farm, however). Herders would presumably be even more widespread on the continent were it not for the limitations imposed by the presence of the

tsetse fly, which transmits the debilitating disease sleeping sickness to cattle.

But perhaps the main factor limiting the distribution of pastoralism is that herding is not the most productive way of using resources in those areas in which agriculture can be carried out reliably. The best way to understand why is to apply the ecologists' "10 percent rule." The food energy produced by photosynthetic plants lies at the base of any ecosystem except the deep oceans. In the presence of sufficient water, carbon dioxide, and minerals, plants convert the energy of sunlight into simple sugars. Herbivores (plant-eating animals) consume the vegetation and use it to maintain their own bodies and produce offspring. Carnivores (animal-eating animals) in turn feed on herbivores. At each of these levels of the food chain, most of the energy is lost as it is carried to the next level. Thus, herbivores transform only about 10 percent of the plant energy they consume into their own flesh and blood.

Carnivores transform only around 10 percent of the energy they acquire by eating herbivores into their own bodies. At each trophic level, 90 percent of the energy consumed is lost to respiration, waste production, and other processes. The 10 percent rule says that only 10 percent of the energy locked up in living matter at one trophic level is available to the next level.

Now we can see why herding is not as efficient a way of exploiting an environment as agriculture: Overall, pastoralists eat higher on the food chain. More total food energy can be obtained from an environment by farming because much more energy can be gained from (cultivated) plants than from (herded) animals. People did not necessarily figure out that they could most productively exploit an environment by growing crops rather than raising animals, and then opt for cultivation. More likely, cultivation won out over herding—in areas that are suitable for both—because of its greater labor productivity. Further, the 10 percent rule also translates into higher potential (and actual) population densities for cultivators, who in the past may have outcompeted pastoralists for those territories that both could exploit.

Aridity, temperature, short growing seasons, and other ecological and climatic factors do not totally explain the distribution of the pastoral adaptation, however. Some pastoralists live in areas where crops could be grown, and they certainly know how to cultivate, but they consciously choose not to grow crops. The cattle-herding Maasai of Kenya and Tanzania are an example. In some parts of the Maasai territory cultivation is possible, and in fact most neighboring tribes combine cattle herding with cultivation of sorghum and other crops. The proud Maasai, however, look down on cultivation because their herds represent wealth and are the main symbol of their cultural identity relative to their neighbors. Maasai, therefore, live largely off the products of their cattle—blood, milk, meat, curds—and trade with their neighbors for the cultivated foods they do eat. The reasons they continue their pastoral adaptation are, therefore, as much "cultural" as "ecological."

The Karimojong: An Example from East Africa

One people who illustrate many of the above points about the pastoral adaptation are the Karimojong, who live in the modern nation of Uganda. Living on an arid savanna with marked seasonal differences in rainfall, traditionally they subsisted by a combination of horticulture and cattle herding. The 60,000 Karimojong are a fairly representative example of a cultural area known to anthropologists as the "East African cattle complex." In this complex, found throughout the East African savannas, cattle are more than an ordinary source of food. The East African man loves his cattle like some North Americans love their sports utility vehicles. Cattle represent wealth and manliness. They are the source of prestige, influence in tribal affairs, and wives (for an East African man must transfer cattle to his wife's relatives to marry her, a practice we discuss in Chapter 7). When sacrificed ritually cattle are religious symbols and are the source of blessings from the ancestors and gods. Underlying all these cultural elements of the cattle complex, according to Rada and Neville Dyson-Hudson, who studied the Karimojong, is the important role of cattle in subsistence: "First, last and always the role of cattle in Karimojong life is to transform the energy stored in the grasses, herbs and shrubs of the tribal area into a form easily available to the people" (Dyson-Hudson and Dyson-Hudson 1969, 4).

This transformation is not mainly achieved by eating the animals' flesh, as Westerners might expect. Rather, the Karimojong—and most other East Africans—consume the products of living cattle: milk and blood. Lactating cows are milked twice daily. Every three to five months, several pints of blood are taken from the jugular of some animals and drunk, usually immediately. Cattle meat is consumed mainly on religious occasions; the meat is shared among all participants.

There is a marked sexual division of labor in Karimojong subsistence activities. The central portion of the tribal territory is crossed by several rivers and hence is relatively well watered during the rainy season. Here the women live in permanent settlements, where they cultivate sorghum (an African grain) and a few other crops. The central area, however, produces good grasses for the herds only during the rainy season, so for most of the year the cattle must be taken to greener pastures, often miles away from the settlements. The Karimojong therefore have another kind of settlement, the mobile "cattle camps" that are run by males, especially by young men. Rainfall is quite unpredictable, especially during the driest half of the year. But localized storms do occur, and for many days afterward grass grows well in restricted areas. The men of the cattle camps—accompanied by the cattle—move frequently in search of pasture. While living in the cattle camps, men live largely from the milk and blood of their animals, supplemented by the beer made from sorghum that the women sometimes bring when they visit.

Both cultivated crops and livestock are necessary foods for the Karimojong. Even a short three-week drought during the sorghum-growing season will seriously reduce the harvest, but the mobility of the livestock allows them to be taken to places where there is sufficient forage. Cattle thus provide an insurance against climatic and other forces that make cultivation too risky to rely on. They also allow the Karimojong to make use of those parts of their territory that are too dry to support cultivation. The cattle transform vegetation indigestible to humans into milk, blood, and meat, which eventually are eaten by the people.

CONCEPT REVIEW Major Forms of Adaptation and Their Cultural Consequences

FORM OF ADAPTATION	FOOD ACQUIRED BY MEANS OF	BASIC ORGANIZATION OF COMMUNITIES	RIGHTS TO RESOURCES	INTERNAL DIFFERENTIATION
Hunting/ Gathering	Collection/ gathering of wild plants; hunting of animals; sometimes fishing	Small, mobile bands numbering between about 10–50, usually varying seasonally	Flexible access to resources over large territories	Division of labor based on sex and age; equality based on sharing
Horticulture	Cultivation of crops using hand tools, with or without livestock	Scattered hamlets or villages of 100 or more, largely but variably sedentary	Ownership of land and productive resources by kin groups and/or residential groups	Variable, but little specialization and inequality
Intensive Agriculture	Cultivation of crops with animal-powered plows or other means of using land intensively	Central administrative places with cities and towns surrounded by rural "peasant" communities	Vested in or controlled by multilevel administrative officials responsible to the "state"	Craft and service specialization with social distinctions and major inequalities
Pastoralism	Livestock provide products (meat, milk, hides, wool) to eat, trade, and sell	Seasonally nomadic living units of varying size and composition	Grazing rights based on membership in families, kin groups, or the tribe itself	Variably complex; based on age, sex, and often hereditary distinctions

Conclusion: Adaptation and Culture

This chapter has synthesized an enormous amount of information on human adaptation and some of the main ways it affects cultural systems. The factual data we have covered have been collected and compared over many decades by hundreds of anthropologists. It is worth noting that many complications have not been discussed for lack of space, and many exceptions to our generalizations have been ignored in the interest of tracing broad patterns. With these warnings about the hazards of simplification in mind, the main ideas of this chapter are further condensed in the Concept Review. It summarizes how people who live by each form of adaptation acquire their food supply and how adaptation *broadly* affects the organization of human communities, rights to natural resources (property ownership), and the internal differentiation of society (the kinds of social and economic distinctions that exist within a given community). In future chapters, we discuss other dimensions of cultures.

Summary

1. Adaptation refers to how organisms interact with their environments, acquiring characteristics that lead to their survival and reproduction. One important feature of human adaptation is that it is carried out primarily—but not exclusively—by cultural changes: Humans adapt to new habitats by means of cultural changes in technology and organization, not mainly by alteration in their genes. One of the most important ways in which human populations interact with their environments is by production, which requires labor, technology, and natural resources. To produce a product efficiently, human groups organize themselves by the division of labor, patterns of cooperation, and defining rights to natural resources.

2. The earliest form of human adaptation was hunting and gathering, or foraging. Foragers live nearly exclusively from the wild plants and animals available in their habitats. All human groups acquired their food from hunting and gathering until around 10,000 years ago, when plants and animals were first domesticated. Over the next several millenia, farmers and herders grew in numbers and expanded into regions previously occupied by foragers. Only a few foraging cultures survived into the twentieth century.

3. The adaptive requirements of living from only wild plants and animals greatly affected the cultures of most foraging peoples. People had to organize their activities so that at the proper season, they could be at the places where wild foods were naturally available. Accordingly, the majority of foraging cultures studied by anthropologists exhibited the following characteristics: (1) a division of labor based mainly on sex and age, (2) high mobility, (3) congregation and dispersal of groups, usually based on seasonal changes, (4) small living and cooperative groups called bands, (5) reciprocal sharing, and (6) loose and flexible rights to the resources of a given territory. These features are well illustrated by cultures such as the Hadza, Shoshone, and !Kung. However, in especially resource-rich environments such as the Northwest Coast of North America, the great abundance and high reliability of natural resources allowed people to settle in large, nearly permanent villages, and to develop well-defined rights to territory.

4. Domestication is the attempt to increase the productivity of an environment by planting and cultivating certain plants (crops) and taming and breeding certain animals (livestock). Domestication first arose 10,000 years ago in the Old World and around 5,000 years ago in the New World. As plant and animal domestication spread into new regions over several millenia, this new way of adapting to nature greatly affected human cultures. Most modern scholars believe that the main advantage of domestication over hunting and gathering is its ability to support far greater numbers of people per unit of land.

5. One of many forms of agriculture is called horticulture. Horticulturalists use only hand tools in planting, cultivating, and harvesting their plots or gardens, as illustrated by shifting cultivation and dry land gardening. Like other forms of cultivation, horticulture produces more food per acre than foraging, and it requires that people make a labor investment in particular pieces of land (their plots). Increased productivity and labor investments alone had two important consequences for cultures: (1) People remained in one place for a long time (sedentism), and the size of their settlements increased (villages), and (2) particular families established their own claims to particular pieces of land, producing cultural beliefs that land is defined as the property of specific groups.

6. As populations grew in certain regions, horticultural methods were no longer sufficient to produce enough food, so land had to be worked more intensively. Intensive agriculturalists use various methods to keep yields high, including keeping a single field under production longer, with little or no fallow. In the Old World, livestock were harnessed to plows to till the fields, whereas New World intensive agriculturalists used other methods. Fertilization with animal manure and other organic matter and irrigation are common among intensive agriculturalists. These and other methods eventually raised productivity enough that a single farm family was able to produce a surplus over and above its own food needs. Out of this surplus potential, a new form of culture, called civilization, arose in several favorable regions of both the Old World and the New World. Always supported by intensive agriculture, civilization and city life changed human life profoundly, leading to new develop-

ments such as writing, specialization, huge architectural structures, roads, and familiar artistic traditions. But whether the class of peasants enjoyed very many of these benefits is questionable.

7. The pastoral adaptation usually occurs in regions that are unsuitable for agriculture due to aridity, cold temperatures, or inadequate growing seasons for crops. In these kinds of habitats, herding offers several advantages. It allows people to convert, through their livestock, indigestible grasses and other vegetation into edible flesh and dairy products. It reduces the risk of living in an unreliable environment, both because livestock provide a way of storing food on the hoof and because the food supply (herds) can be moved to more favorable places when times are hard. Although herding improves humans' ability to live in cold or arid habitats, agriculture is capable of producing far more total food than herding in favorable regions. This is probably why people usually farm the land where it is possible to do so, with some exceptions such as the Maasai. The Karimojong of Uganda illustrate many of these points about the herding adaptation.

Key Terms

adaptation	horticulture
hunting and gathering (foraging)	intensive agriculture
	surplus
agriculture (cultivation)	civilization
herding (pastoralism)	peasants
band	nomadism
domestication	

Suggested Readings

The following books are readable factual and/or theoretical overviews of preindustrial human adaptations:

Bates, Daniel G. *Human Adaptive Strategies: Ecology, Culture, and Politics.* Boston: Allyn and Bacon, 1998.

An introduction to adaptations based on foraging, subsistence-based agriculture, pastoralism, and modern mechanized agriculture. Overviews the impacts of different forms of adaptation on cultural, and especially political, systems.

Campbell, Bernard. *Human Ecology.* 2nd ed. New York: Aldine, 1995.

Describes how humans have adapted to various environments, both prehistorically and today.

Kelly, Robert L. *The Foraging Spectrum: Diversity in Hunter-Gatherer Lifeways.* Washington, DC: Smithsonian Institution Press, 1995.

An overview of hunter-gatherers. Excellent reference source.

Two recent books by respected authors describe the effects of environmental factors on cultures and history:

Diamond, Jared. *Guns, Germs, and Steel: The Fates of Human Societies.* New York: Norton, 1997.

Discusses the effects of differences in natural environments on cultures and their evolution. Argues that environmental factors are the main causal agents in long-term cultural changes, and largely explains why some societies are more successful than others.

Fagan, Brian. *Floods, Famines and Emperors: El Niño and the Fate of Civilizations.* New York: Basic, 1999.

Readable book arguing that periodic shifts in rainfall and climate over large regions of the earth help to account for the rise and fall of complex societies.

Readable case studies of particular hunting and gathering peoples include:

Balikci, Asen. *The Netsilik Eskimo.* Prospect Heights, IL: Waveland Press, 1989.

A study of Netsilik adaptation, technology, kinship, marriage, and religion.

Hoebel, E. Adamson. *The Cheyenne.* New York: Holt, Rinehart and Winston, 1978.

A reconstruction of Cheyenne life during the mid-nineteenth century.

Lee, Richard B. *The Dobe Ju/'hoansi.* 2nd ed. Fort Worth: Harcourt Brace College Publishers, 1993.

A brief but reasonably comprehensive overview of the Dobe, a local population of !Kung (Ju/'hoansi) of southern Africa.

Thomas, Elizabeth Marshall. *The Harmless People.* Rev. ed. New York: Vintage, 1989.

A readable account of the !Kung written from a personal perspective.

Turnbull, Colin. *The Forest People.* New York: Simon and Schuster, 1962.

An ethnography of the BaMbuti (pygmies) of Zaire. Good description of their hunting and organization.

Ethnographies of agricultural and pastoral adaptations include:

Barth, Fredrik. *Nomads of South Persia.* Prospect Heights, IL: Waveland Press, 1986.

A study examining the culture of the Basseri, a pastoral, sheep- and goat-herding society of southern Iran.

Critchfield, Richard. *Villages.* New York: Anchor, 1983.

Basically a travelog of the author's visits to peasant villages on every continent, this book gives a sense of the tone and quality of peasant lives.

Critchfield, Richard. *Villagers: Changed Values, Altered Lives.* New York: Anchor, 1994.

Similar in style to the author's 1983 book, but deals more with recent changes resulting from integration of peasants into national and global economic systems.

Geertz, Clifford. *Agricultural Involution.* Berkeley: University of California Press, 1963.

A case study of agricultural intensification of wet rice in Indonesia caused by population growth and Dutch colonial policy.

Lansing, Stephen J. *The Balinese.* Fort Worth: Harcourt Brace Jovanovich, 1995.

Describes Balinese culture and the intricate relationship between Hindu temple rituals and the irrigation of wet rice fields.

Netting, Robert McC. *Smallholders, Householders: Farm Families and the Ecology of Intensive, Sustainable Agriculture.* Stanford: Stanford University Press, 1993.

Breathtaking in geographical scope. Discusses relationships among population, land use, work, cultivation methods, productivity, ownership patterns, and household organization.

chapter 6

EXCHANGE *and* ECONOMIC SYSTEMS

Contents

The previous chapter covered the major types of preindustrial adaptations and discussed some of the most important ways adaptation affects cultures. How people produce the food and other products they need and desire is part of what is commonly called their *economic system.* Producing things, though, is usually only the first step toward the final use *(consumption)* of the product. Commonly, products are *exchanged* between individuals and groups between the time they are produced and consumed. In fact, in some economic systems, things are produced explicitly for exchange, and once the value acquired from the exchange has been gained, the producer has little further interest in the product.

Among peoples who produce most or all of their own food, it might seem that they have few reasons to exchange products—when you and your family produce most of what you consume and consume most of what you produce, one might think that the exchange ("trade") of products would be minimal. But this view assumes that the purpose of exchange is mutual need for the material products that are exchanged. Sometimes this is the case. More commonly, however, exchange in preindustrial societies is oriented as much toward social and/or political goals, rather than narrow economic purposes. For example, individuals and groups exchange objects to create and sustain warm social relationships, to create or pay off social debts, to create and recreate political alliances, and to provide assistance to those in need. Material products (objects) flow back and forth between individuals and groups, but the acquisition of material products or the pursuit of profit is not the main purpose of the exchange.

Depending on other aspects of their adaptation and overall culture, different societies organize the exchange of products (or goods) in different ways. Economic anthropologists, who specialize in the comparative study of economic systems, often classify exchanges into three major modes, or types:

- **Reciprocity,** in which two individuals or groups pass objects back and forth, with the aim of (1) helping someone in need by sharing goods with him or her, (2) creating, maintaining, or strengthening social relationships, or (3) obtaining the objects for oneself.
- **Redistribution,** in which the members of an organized group contribute products or money into a common pool or fund; a central authority usually has the privilege and responsibility to make decisions about how the products or money later will be reallocated among the group as a whole.
- **Market,** in which products or objects are sold for money, which in turn is used to purchase other products or objects, with the ultimate goal of acquiring more money, which can be spent on more products or objects.

Most products change hands through market exchange in modern industrial capitalist economies, but enormous quantities of products and objects also are transacted through reciprocity and redistribution. Examples of reciprocity are various gifts we give and receive on holidays, birthdays, weddings, baby showers, and other culturally special occasions. If you are employed, every pay period you participate in redistribution, for federal, state, and city governments collect a portion of your wage or salary as taxes, which they expend on public purposes or transfer to other members of society.

Although all these exchange forms exist in modern societies, not all preindustrial cultures have all three. Some kind of reciprocity occurs in all human populations, at least in the form of gifts. But redistribution implies the existence of a central authority to organize the collection of products from the group and to make decisions about how they will be reallocated. Redistribution, therefore, is an insignificant exchange mode in societies that lack strong leaders who make decisions on behalf of the group. The market mode of exchange requires money, private property, and certain other features that are absent in many preindustrial populations. The Concept Review shows the three exchange forms graphically.

RECIPROCITY

Reciprocity refers to the giving and taking of objects without the use of money or other media of exchange. It can take the form of sharing, hospitality, gift giving, or barter. To cover these varieties, anthropologists identify three forms of reciprocity.

Generalized Reciprocity

The defining feature of **generalized reciprocity** is that those who give do not expect the recipient to make a return at any definite time in the future. Generalized reciprocity occurs between individuals who are (or who are culturally expected to be) emotionally attached to one another and, therefore, have an obligation to help one another on the basis of relative need. In North America, parents who provide their children with shelter, food, vehicles, college educations, and interest-free loans are practicing generalized reciprocity. Giving without expectation of quick and equivalent

return should occur between parties to certain other kinds of social relations, such as wives and husbands, siblings, and sometimes close friends.

Reciprocity occurs in all human populations. Among some peoples it is the dominant form of exchange, meaning that more goods are passed around using this form than any other. For example, most foragers expect band mates to share food and be generous with their possessions. (This fits with the fact that most or all members of a small hunting and gathering band are relatives of some kind.) Among the !Kung (see Chapter 5), the band or camp itself is a social group within which food sharing is culturally expected, and those who are stingy with possessions or who fail to share food with band mates are subjected to ridicule (or worse). Broadly speaking, generalized reciprocity is the dominant mode of exchange in very small human groups in which all or most members are relatives.

Balanced Reciprocity

In **balanced reciprocity,** products are transferred to someone and the donor expects a return in products of roughly equal value (i.e., the exchanges should "balance"). The return may be expected immediately, or whenever the donor

CONCEPT REVIEW Three Forms of Exchange in Economic Systems

RECIPROCITY	REDISTRIBUTION	MARKET
Back and forth exchange of products, gifts, and objects, symbolic of relationships as well as satisfying material needs and wants	Collection of products and valuables by a central authority, followed by distribution according to some normative or legal principle	Free exchange of products (P_1, P_2) or services (S_1, S_2) for money ($\$$) at prices determined by impersonal forces of supply and demand

In preindustrial societies, balanced reciprocity often creates and sustains important relationships. Reciprocal invitations to feasts are a common form of balanced reciprocity, as illustrated by the killing of a pig on the island of Tanna in the nation of Vanuatu.

Courtesy of Lamont Lindstrom

demands it, or by some specified time in the future. With generalized reciprocity, the giver continues to provide material assistance even though the receiver does not return anything for a long time. With balanced reciprocity, the giver refuses to continue to transfer objects to the receiver if the latter does not reciprocate within the appropriate time period. Donors may merely be angry if the receivers fail to reciprocate, may complain or gossip to others, may try to force reciprocation, or may suspend all relations until objects of equal value are returned.

Although the value of the objects exchanged is supposed to be equal (at least roughly), balanced reciprocity is characterized by the absence of bargaining between parties. In some preindustrial economies, the exchange of goods without having to negotiate for each transaction (How much of A will you give me for my B?) frequently is organized by a special relationship between two individuals known as a *trade partnership*. Individuals of one tribe or village pair off with specific individuals (their "partners") from other regions with whom they establish long-lasting trade relationships.

For instance, in the Trobriand Islands off the eastern tip of the island of New Guinea there was a form of balanced reciprocity called *wasi*. Residents of coastal villages traded fish for yams and other garden crops produced in the mountainous interior. The *wasi* was formalized: A coastal village paired off with an interior village, and within each village individuals formed trade partnerships. The rates at which garden produce was exchanged for fish were established by custom, so there was no haggling at any particular transaction.

In *wasi*, each trade partner received foods not readily available locally, so parties to the transaction gained material benefit. In many other cases, balanced reciprocity takes the form of mutual exchanges of gifts or invitations for social and political purposes. That is, the exchange is not motivated primarily by the desire of the parties for the objects, but by their desire to establish and maintain good relations with one another. Gifts are a material symbol of good relations. They sustain relations of friendship and mutual aid between individuals and groups. This is why, cross-culturally, gift-giving ceremonies frequently are part of diplomacy and peacemaking between formerly hostile groups; the gifts symbolize the beginning of a new period of peaceful coexistence.

Thus, on your friend's birthday, instead of giving her a CD in exchange for a gift of about equal value on your own birthday, you both could save the cost of wrapping paper and cards by buying the objects for yourselves. But then the social value of the gift—expressing and strengthening your friendly relationship—would not be attained. Friendships are created and maintained by such exchanges, as you know if you have ever been a party in a relationship in which the exchanges remain "unbalanced" for a long time.

In fact, most of us have experienced the anger or disappointment at not having our gifts or invitations reciprocated. Many of us also know the embarrassment of being unable to return a gift of equal value to a gift we have received. If you are thoughtful, perhaps you have given only a small gift to a friend who has less money than you do, to spare your friend the awkwardness of being unable to reciprocate.

So the back-and-forth flow of tangible objects often symbolizes warm personal feelings about a relationship. Exchange communicates feelings perhaps even better than words, both because "talk is cheap" and because some of us never seem to know the right words to say. On the other hand, failing to present objects of appropriate value on certain occasions also symbolizes one's personal feeling, although in a less "warm" way (and, no, "forgetting" is not acceptable!).

But we also are familiar with another side of balanced reciprocity: the use of gift giving for social and political goals. Gifts not only are material symbols of existing social relations; they can also be used to create social bonds that are useful to the giver, and to obligate people from whom the giver wants something. Gift giving makes someone indebted to you, and therefore can be used to create an obligation to return a favor. Political lobbyists and sales representatives know this use of balanced reciprocity.

For an example of how balanced reciprocity helps to create and sustain political alliances, we turn to the Maring of highland Papua New Guinea. These people live by a combination of shifting cultivation, pig keeping, and hunting. Each Maring settlement is engaged in periodic warfare with some of its neighbors. Unless a settlement is unusually large, its members form a political alliance with one or more nearby settlements. When warfare occurs, the warriors of each settlement rely on their allies for military support and, in the case of defeat, for refuge. Most Maring settlements must establish and sustain military alliances if they are not to be defeated in warfare.

An important expression of continued goodwill between allied groups is periodic invitations to feasts and exchanges of wealth objects and other valuables. Every few years, whenever they accumulate sufficient pigs, the members of a settlement invite their allies to an enormous feast, appropriately called a *pig feast*. At the pig feast, which is attended by hundreds of people, allies bring large quantities of wealth objects to exchange and pay off debts; they consume enormous quantities of pork provided by their hosts; they are on the lookout for potential spouses and sexual partners; and they aid the host community in the ceremonial dancing that the Maring believe is ritually necessary for success in the fighting that will soon occur. The host group uses the occasion of their pig feast to gauge the amount of military support they can expect from their allies: The more people who attend the feast, the more warriors the host settlement will be able to put on the battleground. Later, the guests will have accumulated enough pigs to reciprocate by hosting a pig feast for their allies, who come with wealth objects and pledge their military support by helping the host group in their ceremonial dancing.

The Maring pig feast, with its reciprocal exchanges between the hosts and guests from allied groups, is an important event in maintaining good relations between allies. A group sponsors a pig feast to compensate their allies for their previous military aid as well as to reciprocate previous pig feasts they have attended. The failure to organize a pig feast large enough to compensate one's allies can result in the weakening and sometimes even termination of an alliance.

Thus, balanced invitations to feasts are critical to the military success and continued survival of a Maring community.

Negative Reciprocity

The distinguishing characteristic of the third kind of reciprocity—known as **negative reciprocity**—is that both parties attempt to gain all they can from the exchange while giving up as little as possible. Negative reciprocity usually is motivated largely by the desire to obtain material goods at minimal cost.

Insofar as it is motivated mainly by the desire for material products, negative reciprocity is like market exchange; it is different mainly because no money changes hands between the participants. In economies that use money to purchase goods and services, market exchange partly or largely replaces negative reciprocity.

But in economies with no money, negative reciprocity is an important way for individuals and groups to acquire things that they do not produce themselves. Few populations are entirely self-sufficient: Some foods they like to eat do not occur where they live; some materials they need to make tools are not found locally; or they lack the skill to produce some of the objects they use. To acquire these products, people produce other products to exchange for "imports."

Negative reciprocity in the preindustrial world often takes the form of *barter*. In the interior highland of Papua New Guinea, many indigenous peoples manufactured money or wealth objects by stringing shells together into long chains or belts. Because these shells did not occur naturally in the interior, they were traded from people to people until they reached their final destination. Salt also was a trade object because it occurred in only a few areas.

In western North America, the obsidian (volcanic glass) used to make stone tools occurred in only a few areas; other peoples acquired it through trade. In some cases these trade routes stretched for hundreds of miles, with the obsidian passing through the hands of numerous middlemen before finally being made into a tool.

Reciprocity and Social Distance

Each of the three types of reciprocity tends to be associated with certain kinds of social relationships. As Marshall Sahlins, who first distinguished the three varieties, noted, the kind of reciprocity that occurs between individuals or groups depends on the social distance between them. By **social distance** is meant the degree to which cultural norms specify they should be intimate with or emotionally attached to one another.

This is seen clearly in North American cultural norms of reciprocity. We expect an individual to practice generalized reciprocity with his or her children and perhaps with siblings and elderly parents; in fact, given our norms about family obligations, we judge people as uncaring or selfish if they do not. But if a middle-income person repeatedly lends money to a cousin or puts a niece through college, we are likely to regard him or her as either unusually generous or a bit foolish. He or she has extended generalized reciprocity beyond the range of relatives to whom we culturally consider it appropriate.

A normative association between exchange form and social relationship also applies to market transactions. In market exchange, individuals are supposed to be "looking out for their own private interests," "trying to get the most for their money," and so forth. We regard this as fine—in fact, as smart shopping—with transactions between strangers in a department store or car lot. But when the seller and buyer are friends or relatives, it is difficult for them to disentangle their economic transaction from their personal feelings for each other. Kinship and friendship cannot easily be mixed with market exchange, because kinship and friendship are supposed to have an element of selflessness, whereas buying and selling are assumed to have selfish motives. Therefore, although I may buy my friend's used car, I feel uneasy about the transaction: What will I do if the car is a lemon?

Note also that as our social relations with other people change, so does the kind of reciprocity we practice with them. Most adults have experienced one way in which this occurs: As we grow up, our increasing independence from our parents is manifested by a change in the way we exchange goods with them. We go from being the recipients of generalized reciprocity to more of a balanced reciprocity as we become more independent, and finally—at least until the advent of Social Security—to being the provider of generalized reciprocity.

Finally, changing one form of reciprocity into another can be used as a way of changing the nature of a social relationship. Because the form of reciprocity practiced between two individuals is related to the degree of social distance between them, the social distance can be decreased or increased by one party beginning to initiate a new form of exchange. Or someone can signal his or her wish to draw another person close (reduce the social distance between them) by tentatively initiating a relationship of balanced reciprocity. Reciprocity has social uses in our culture, just as it has among preindustrial peoples such as the Maring.

Thus, I can let you know of my desire to become your friend by giving you an unexpected gift or invitation to dinner. In turn, you tell whether you share my feelings by whether you return my gift on an appropriate occasion, repeatedly find reasons to refuse my dinner invitation, or come to dinner several times at my place without reciprocating. If we both use this "strategy of reciprocity," neither of us needs to be put in an embarrassing position of verbalizing our feelings. I signal my wish by my initial gift or invitation, and you decline or accept my offer of friendship by your response.

In sum, forms of reciprocity tend to be associated with types of social relations, so the reciprocity practiced between people changes as their relationship changes. We can use reciprocity to achieve social goals: Reciprocating or refusing to reciprocate gifts or invitations sends messages that are too embarrassing to say outright.

REDISTRIBUTION

The major difference between reciprocity and redistribution—the second major mode of exchange—is the way the transfer of products is organized.

With reciprocity, products pass back and forth between two participants, with no third party to act as intermediary. With redistribution, products, objects, or money collected from many individuals or groups are taken to a central place or put into a common pool or fund. Some overarching authority (empowered to make decisions on behalf of those who contributed) later draws from this pool or fund in returning public goods and services that allegedly benefit the group as a whole.

In modern nations, redistribution takes the form of taxes on wages, profits, retail sales, property, inheritance, and other income and assets. To understand redistribution, think about how our tax system is supposed to operate. Federal tax revenues, for example, are used for two main purposes. First, they are expended in such a way as to benefit the whole country. The citizens receive law enforcement, national defense, infrastructure (e.g., dams, roads, airports), parks, regulation of polluting industries, and so forth. Resources collected from the citizenry are expended on public goods and services. Second, taxes are used to provide assistance for individuals in need. These are "transfer payments" in the form of social welfare, Social Security, Medicaid and Medicare, disaster relief, and so forth. Such public expenditures are based on moral norms and cultural values about social justice, equal opportunity, and helping those in need. Redistribution systems around the world are used for similar purposes: to provide public goods and services and to provide assistance to individuals and groups in need.

But there is another side to systems of redistribution, a side with which we also are familiar. First, there often is conflict over who should provide the public resources, how the resources should be expended, and how much of a share of them should be given to those who collect and distribute them. People disagree over redistribution: When many individuals have contributed to the public pool or fund, not everyone is likely to agree on how the "public resources" should be spent for the "public good." Much of the conflict between political parties in modern industrial democracies is rooted in disagreements over who should be taxed and how much, and over how government revenues should be spent. Parties and various interest groups are, in many cases, quarreling over redistribution: Who pays? Who gets what? And how much?

Second, those who make decisions about redistribution frequently use public resources for their own pleasures or ambitions, rather than to benefit the entire population. In modern democratic nations, for instance, officeholders make deals to allocate federal tax dollars to finance highway construction in their districts. Commute times may be lowered in the short term, but the real purpose is to provide jobs for their constituencies or to serve special interest groups who help with their reelection. More generally, political considerations frequently enter into decision making about redistribution: Whom shall we help? What will we get in return?

A common form of redistribution in the preindustrial world is known as **tribute.** The subjects of a chief or other title-holder contribute products (usually including food) into a common pool under the control of the chief, who acts as the central authority. Often the tribute is culturally viewed as a material symbol showing that the subjects continue to acknowledge the chief's sacred authority. Some of the accumulated products are consumed by the central authorities and their relatives, some are distributed to support the work of crafts specialists (e.g., potters, weavers), and some are redistributed to the whole population at public feasts, celebrations, and ceremonies.

Examples of redistribution systems using tribute payments exist on many of the islands of Polynesia and Micronesia in the Pacific. On many islands, the entire population was divided traditionally into two ranks or classes, noble and commoner (see chapter 10 for more about rank and class). Members of the nobility did little agricultural or other manual work, but instead managed the political systems and organized religious ceremonies. Commoners produced the food and other forms of tribute, which fed the nobility and their families and which supported other kinds of specialists. On some islands, the tribute rendered by commoners was used mainly for public pur-

poses, such as feeding people who worked on trails and public buildings, providing relief from temporary food shortages, and publicly celebrating special events. On other islands, the nobles were sufficiently powerful to use the tribute to make themselves materially wealthy: They lived in the best houses, slept on the softest woven mats, wore special clothing, had numerous servants, and ate only the finest foods.

MARKET EXCHANGE

To say that objects or services are exchanged "on the market" means that they are bought and sold at a price measured in money. Person A possesses goods that person B wants to acquire; B acquires the goods by giving A some quantity of money that both A and B agree on; A then uses the money to acquire goods from other people. Market exchange thus requires (1) some object used as a medium of exchange, that is, *money*; (2) a rate at which goods exchange for money, that is, *prices*; and (3) parties to exchanges who have alternative buyers or sellers and are free to make the best deal they can, that is, prices determined by *supply and demand*. On the third point, markets imply the absence of physical coercion: If prices are set by supply and demand, neither party to a transaction can be forced to buy or sell from the other party. This is what we mean by a "free" market—no third party (a government or a monopoly, for example) sets prices or forces anyone to buy or sell from anyone else, and no single supplier of a product controls enough of the market to force people to buy from him, her, or it (in the case of firms).

Because markets (as we define them in this text) require the presence of money, we begin by discussing some of the diversity in money objects and money uses.

Money

Money consists of objects that serve as *media of exchange* in a wide range of transactions of goods, services, or both. This facilitation of exchange is the main function of money. If an economy uses money, individual A can acquire something from individual B without having to return an object desired by B; money can be given instead, and B can then use the money to buy an object or a service of her or his choice.

Other characteristics of money derive from its function as a medium of exchange. For example, money serves as a *standard of value:* The value of the goods and services that can be exchanged for money can be compared with one another because money serves as a common measure of how much things are worth. Money also is a *store of value:* Because it can be used to purchase various goods, it represents wealth or purchasing power in a portable form.

Although those of us who live in market economies seldom think about them, money has some interesting properties. For example, notice that if one individual, A, sells something (including labor as well as objects) to B in return for money, then A has (as we say) "made money" off the sale. Individual A may think he or she has made a good deal, but B may turn around and sell the product to someone else, C, in return for more money than was paid to A for it. B has also made money—sometimes big money! This is the simplest form of *profit,* and profit making is greatly facilitated by the use of money.

Notice also that, in our example, individual B has not produced anything tangible, but has merely sold a product to C that was bought from A, the producer. If B does this often enough, so long as C wants the product and is willing to pay B more than B paid A for it, then B can grow very wealthy, for money serves as a store of wealth. *Wealth accumulation,* therefore, is facilitated by markets and money, although it also exists in some economies with neither markets nor money.

Not just any object is suitable to be used as money. Money objects must be *durable,* or the value they store deteriorates over time. The supply of the money object must *limited,* because if people can get all they want of it, its value inflates and it becomes worthless as an exchange medium. The monetary supply can be controlled by a government, which manufactures the only "legal

tender" in the society; or the supply can be controlled by using only imported or rare objects as money. Imported shells are especially common in preindustrial economies, partly because of their durability. The supply also can be controlled by having the money require a lot of labor to manufacture: Money remains scarce because it takes time to make it.

An enormous variety of objects serve as money in one or another region of the world. We already are familiar with currencies of modern nations, issued by governments that control the money supply. In preindustrial economies, the kinds of objects that take on the characteristics of money are quite diverse. In Africa, for example, the following objects served as money in one or another part of the continent: iron, salt, beads, cowrie shells, cloth, gin, gold dust, metal rods, brass bracelets, and livestock. In Melanesia the list of money objects is also diverse: assorted shells (often modified in some way and sewn into fibers to form long belts), salt, the red feathers of a certain bird (also woven into belts), and pigs.

There are nonmonetary economies, in which all exchanges are based on one of the three forms of reciprocity. But even in economies that do have an exchange medium, the range of goods that can be acquired with money varies greatly. In some the range is broad. Many kinds of resources and goods can be bought and sold, including labor, land, tools, and sometimes even people (slaves). In these systems, money serves as a generalized medium of exchange; that is, it can be used to acquire many kinds of goods and services, including land and labor. Some anthropologists call this **multipurpose money.**

Money is multipurpose in modern North America. In principle, money can buy privately owned natural resources, labor, and goods. Even money itself can be sold for price (interest). Some preindustrial peoples also have multipurpose money. For example, the Kapauku people of Irian Jaya, which is now part of Indonesia, used imported cowrie shells and two types of necklaces as currency. Kapauku money could be used to purchase almost anything, including land, labor, crops, pigs, tools, and medical services.

Leopold Pospisil (1978), the ethnographer, writes:

> Among the Kapauku an overwhelming amount of goods is exchanged through sales. . . . In their selling and buying most of the Kapauku are strictly profit motivated. Often they invest money in pigs, chickens, large woti (bailer shell), inner bark, or animal teeth, for the purpose of breeding the animals for profit, speculating on sales of the bailer shell, or for making artifacts for sale. . . . Besides the necessity of having to buy with money such commodities as land, manufactured products, labor, and services such as surgery, curing, and midwifery, the Kapauku have to pay for favors and acts for which even in our capitalistic society there is no charge. For example, one pays a bride price for a wife, the services of a foster father have to be paid for by the grown boy, a grief expressed by strangers or distantly related people over the death of a close relative has to be recompensed in money, and almost all crimes can be settled through a proper transfer of shell currency. (21–22)

Kapauku sales occurred on a daily basis, much as we make purchases of one or another item regularly. Periodically, however, Kapauku leaders organized enormous ceremonies attended by hundreds of people who came to sell and buy and to make and pay off loans.

The Kapauku represent an extreme in the range of uses to which money can be put, as well as in their intense desire to accumulate wealth. Often we find the range of money uses in preindustrial economies to be narrow; only a few categories of goods are purchased with money. For example, it may be possible to buy food, clothing, and a few other goods, but land is not available for sale at any price, and labor is almost never sold. Here, money is called **limited-purpose money.**

A famous example of limited-purpose money comes from among the Tiv of Nigeria, studied by Paul Bohannan. Tiv money consisted of metal rods, but the rods could not be used as an exchange medium for all other objects or products. For one thing, land could not be sold, and labor was exchanged among relatives on the principle of generalized reciprocity, and not bought and sold. For another thing, among these people objects circulated in different exchange spheres. Certain kinds of objects could only be transacted for certain other kinds of objects. In other words, objects were culturally classified into categories, within which they were freely exchangeable, but between which exchange was difficult.

The "subsistence sphere" category included cultivated crops, chickens and goats, and some tools and household goods. Goods within this sphere were exchangeable by means of barter. The "prestige sphere" included slaves, cattle, a special kind of white cloth, and metal rods. Within the prestige sphere, metal rods functioned as an exchange medium: One could sell cattle for metal rods and then use the rods to acquire white cloth or slaves, for example, but the monetary function of metal rods normally was limited to the prestige sphere.

However, it was possible to acquire subsistence goods in exchange for metal rods. But these transactions were rare, for two reasons. First, few people were willing to trade their metal rods for subsistence goods. This is because goods that circulated in the prestige sphere had much greater cultural value to Tiv than subsistence goods. Second, metal rods were worth an enormous amount of subsistence goods. Yet the metal rods had no denominations; that is, unlike dollars and cents, they were not divisible into fractions. So for a Tiv to try to exchange one metal rod for subsistence goods would be like an American taking a thousand-dollar bill into a grocery store to buy food, with the clerk unable to make change. As a result of these two factors, Tiv metal rods were largely limited-purpose money.

The Tiv example serves to remind us that just because we find it convenient to call some object "money" does not mean that it has all the characteristics of our own currency. Indeed, some anthropologists believe that money objects are lacking in preindustrial economies, and that money is a Western concept that we should not attempt to apply to other cultures. This problem is mainly semantic, however: If we define money simply as a medium of exchange, it is found in many other economies. To avoid confusion and false impressions, we do need always to specify its uses and its cultural meaning to the local people.

As we discuss next, we also need to be careful with how we use the term *market*, because many non-Western markets do not work the same way as ours.

Marketplaces

Those of us who live in industrialized economies are accustomed to purchasing most of what we need and want in restaurants, car lots, supermarkets, and shopping malls. That is, we rely on the market to satisfy our desires—we earn money from our jobs and spend the money on goods and services. In the process, we depend on other organizations (companies) to produce and sell the products we wish to buy.

Even in the modern world, millions of rural peasants are not nearly so dependent on market forces. Rather than selling their labor to others in return for a wage, they work the land and fish the waters to supply food for their families directly. Rather than producing goods to sell at a price to others, they consume most of what they produce themselves. There are places in most peasant communities where goods are bought and sold—there are *marketplaces*. But people do not rely on marketplaces for most of what they consume, nor do they spend most of their working hours producing goods to sell at the marketplace.

Such peasant marketplaces are common in West Africa, southern and Southeast Asia, the Caribbean, and Central and South America. Peasant vendors sell food, cloth and clothing, leather products, livestock, and other goods produced by their families. Traveling merchants (middlemen) bring commodities imported from the developed world or from elsewhere in the region to sell to local people at the marketplace.

Although much buying and selling occurs, peasant marketplaces are not the same as modern shopping malls or department stores. There are several differences between peasant marketplaces and the markets with which people of urbanized,

Courtesy of Garrick Bailey

At peasant marketplaces like this one in Guatemala, many vendors produce or make their wares themselves, and most buyers do not rely on purchased products for all their needs.

industrialized societies are familiar. First, the categories of products sold at the marketplace are limited, and in fact, most people produce most of their own subsistence using family labor. Most people do not acquire their livelihood from selling their labor for a wage. Rather, they rely on the marketplace only for certain categories of goods that they cannot produce for themselves efficiently. Most people are not making their living by selling something (objects, labor) on the market.

Second, producing and marketing goods for monetary profit are part-time activities for many vendors. Many marketplaces are staffed mainly by peasants, who sell small quantities of food, pottery, furniture, fibers, crafts, or other objects they have produced with family labor. Indeed, marketplaces frequently are periodic, meaning that they do not open every day, but only for a day or two a week. Peasant vendors sell their products on whatever days the market is open in their region. Traveling merchants typically visit several markets in different regions in a single week, often buying products for sale at one market and reselling them at a distant market a day or two later.

Third, peasant vendors usually sell products that they or their family members, rather than hired laborers, produce. This means that the kinds and quantities of goods offered for sale by any single vendor usually are small. Most marketplaces also feature products sold by people who specialize in buying them wholesale and selling them retail. Such people are dependent on the market—with all its insecurities and risks—for their livelihood. They therefore have developed various marketing strategies to reduce the risks they face. We conclude this section by considering some of these strategies.

When we who live in a market economy visit a marketplace—a store or car lot, for instance—we normally buy goods from strangers. We do not expect any special treatment. We pay the same price as everyone else. If we need credit, we expect to pay the market rate of interest. We expect sellers to be looking out for themselves, just as sellers expect us to be trying to get the most for our money. This characteristic of our market exchanges is referred to as the "impersonality of the marketplace." This impersonality is expressed nicely by the old saying that "one person's money is as green as anyone else's."

Marketplace vendors in many peasant communities frequently develop more personal relations with their customers. In the Caribbean nation of Haiti, for example, sellers and buyers may establish long-lasting special relationships with one another. The market middleman (although most are women in Haiti) purchases food and other good wholesale from several farmers for transport and retail sale at a marketplace. She establishes a special relation, known as *pratik,* with many of her suppliers and customers. *Pratik* involves certain concessions. For instance, when a middleman buys produce from a farmer, she may pay a little more than the market rate or give the

producer a loan against a future crop. A market vendor gives special treatment to some of her best customers as well. When a *pratik* partner approaches her stall, she quotes the going price for the product on that particular day; but when the transaction is consummated, the seller throws in a few extra items of produce.

According to Sidney Mintz, who studied Haitian marketplaces, *pratik* relationships are beneficial because they increase the economic security of vendors, who sacrifice short-term gains for long-term reliability of suppliers and customers. Because they themselves usually are poor and because competition between them is severe, vendors seek to maintain long-term relationships by granting better deals to their *pratik* than the current market prices. This allows them to develop a steady clientele who return to them again and again, thus reducing their risks.

The same kinds of relations are reported for a marketplace in a Philippine town studied by William Davis. Here, also, sellers attempt to reduce their risks by gradually building up a steady, large clientele of customers, rather than by squeezing all the money they can from a single transaction. Each vendor maintains "special customer" relationships (called *suki*) with numerous people who regularly buy his wares. The customer receives credit, favorable prices, extra quantities of goods at a given price, the best quality goods his *suki* partner has to offer on a particular day, and certain services. The vendors benefit as well: Their *suki* customers are expected not to patronize any other suppliers of goods they carry. This is a great advantage in calculating the minimum quantities of goods they will be able to sell and, hence, helps to keep them from unintentionally stocking more of some categories of goods than they can sell.

In both Haiti and the Philippines, the impersonality of the marketplace is modified by the formation of personal ties between sellers and buyers. Both *pratik* and *suki* increase the security of marketplace trade for vendors, their suppliers, and their customers.

SUMMARY

1. This chapter covers exchange, or the patterned ways in which products are transferred between the time they are produced and the time they are consumed. Economic anthropologists find it convenient to classify the variety of exchanges that exist in human economies into three major modes, or types: reciprocity, redistribution, and market.

2. Reciprocity is the giving and receiving of objects without the transfer of money. Generalized reciprocity usually occurs between parties who are culturally obliged to assist one another in times of need, as among relatives and sometimes close friends. With balanced reciprocity, a return of an object of equivalent value is expected. The goal of balanced reciprocity may be the acquisition of goods for their utility, as in the Trobriand *wasi.* More often it is motivated by the desire to create or sustain good relations between individuals (as in gift giving) or political alliances between groups (as with the Maring pig feast). Negative reciprocity is characterized by the desire of both parties to acquire as many goods as possible while giving up as few as possible, as in barter.

3. The variety of reciprocity that is likely to characterize transactions between individuals and groups depends on the normative degree of social distance between them. This implies that exchange relations alter if social relationships change. Conversely, one party can initiate an attempt to alter a relationship by an offer of a good, and the other party can signal acceptance or rejection by his or her response. Therefore, varying the type of reciprocity can be used to draw people closer together or to push them further apart. In effect, a reciprocal exchange of goods (and services) can also serve as an exchange of messages about feelings and relationships.

4. In redistribution, the members of a group contribute goods or money into a pool or fund, and a central authority reallocates or uses them for public purposes. Taxes in modern nations and tribute in chiefdoms are examples. Normatively, redistribution is supposed to provide resources to increase public welfare, either to provide public goods or to support those in need. In fact, there is much conflict over collection and allocation, and those officials who do the collecting and allocating frequently use their authority for private ambitions rather than public interest.

5. Market exchange involves the buying and selling of goods; it therefore requires money and prices determined by supply and demand. Money makes the exchange of goods and services more convenient and also facilitates the making of profit and the accumulation of wealth. Money functions as a medium of exchange, a standard of value, and a store of value. These functions mean that money objects must be durable, and their supply must be limited or controlled in some way. The range of goods and services that can be bought with money varies between economies. Money types can be characterized as multipurpose (like modern currencies) or limited-purpose (like Tiv metal rods).

6. The affluent citizens of most modern urbanized, industrialized countries make their living by selling their labor on the market and purchasing commodities at stores and other retail establishments. Rural peasants of many countries are not so reliant on markets, for they produce most of their food themselves and shop at local marketplaces for only some of their needs and wants. In peasant marketplaces, most vendors are small-scale and part-time. In many regions they develop special relationships with sellers to reduce their risks, as illustrated by *pratik* in Haiti and *suki* in the Philippines.

KEY TERMS

reciprocity	negative reciprocity
redistribution	social distance
market	tribute
generalized reciprocity	multipurpose money
balanced reciprocity	limited-purpose money

SUGGESTED READINGS

Douglas, Mary, and Baron Isherwood. *The World of Goods: Toward an Anthropology of Consumption.* New York: W. W. Norton, 1979.

An examination of cultural theories of consumption.

Gowdy, John, ed. *Limited Wants, Unlimited Means: A Reader on Hunter-Gatherer Economics and the Environment.* Washington, DC: Island Press, 1998.

A recent collection of twelve important articles dealing with foragers.

Neale, Walter C. *Monies in Societies.* San Francisco: Chandler and Sharp, 1976.

A brief book about the uses, forms, and functions of money in a variety of economies.

Plattner, Stuart, ed. *Economic Anthropology.* Stanford: Stanford University Press, 1989.

A collection of recent articles on economic systems.

Sahlins, Marshall. *Stone Age Economics.* New York: Aldine, 1972.

This influential "classic" deals with the organization of production and modes of exchange in preindustrial economies.

Wilk, Richard R. *Economies & Cultures: Foundations of Economic Anthropology.* Boulder: Westview Press, 1996.

A readable and thoughtful overview of the field of economic anthropology, focusing on major issues and debates.

chapter 7

DOMESTIC LIFE

Contents

Families are one of the central institutions of all societies. Some kind of family is usually the group that nourishes and enculturates children, and a child's early family experiences greatly influence the kind of adult he or she will become. Families are also the basis of households, which not only live together but often work together, own property together, play together, and worship together. In this chapter, we look at some of the ways in which cultures differ in their family and household organization.

DEFINITIONS

Kin group refers to people who view themselves as relatives, who share a common identity based on their kin ties, and who cooperate in certain kinds of activities. **Domestic group** refers to individuals who live together in a single household. Because the residents of a household usually are also relatives, a domestic group is one type (but only one type) of kin group. Other kinds of kin groups (much larger than domestic groups) also exist, as we shall see in Chapter 8.

Anthropologists use the term **consanguines** to refer to "blood" relatives—people related by birth. The term **affines** is used to refer to "in-laws"—people related by marriage. So a person's consanguineal relatives are all of her or his blood relatives, and one's affinal relatives are all of one's relatives by marriage. Your parents, siblings, grandparents, parents' siblings, and cousins are examples of your consanguines. Your sister's husband, wife's mother, and father's sister's husband are some of your affines.

Societies everywhere have domestic groups and kin groups, and all peoples distinguish between consanguineal and affinal relatives. But the nature of these groups and relations between kin are highly variable cross-culturally. In North America and most other highly industrialized, urbanized societies, the most important domestic unit is made up of a married couple and any unmarried children they may have. We call this the **nuclear family,** and this kind of group is what

Canadians and Americans ordinarily mean when they say "my family." In many other societies, nuclear families are embedded in and merged into much larger kin groups, some consisting of hundreds of members. We discuss these larger kin groups in the next chapter. Here we deal with the major types of domestic groups that exist in the world's cultures and the ways in which they are formed.

MARRIAGE: DEFINITIONS and FUNCTIONS

If a North American were asked for a definition of marriage, she or he might offer something like the following:

> Marriage is a relationship between a woman and a man involving romantic love, sex, cohabitation, reproduction and childrearing, and the sharing of the joys and burdens of life.

People trained in law might also note that marriage has legal aspects, such as joint property rights. Religious people would add that marriage is a relationship sanctioned by God that should last until the parties are separated by death.

This definition is fairly serviceable in North America, but it is not broad enough to encompass all the diversity that anthropologists have found. In many cultures, marriage is much more likely to be a public matter that concerns a broad range of relatives who must consent to—and often even arrange—the marriage of a couple. Also, cohabitation in the same house is by no means universal: In many villages in Melanesia, Southeast Asia, and Africa, the men sleep and spend much of their time in a communal house (called, appropriately, the men's house), while their wives and young children live and sleep in a separate dwelling.

Similarly, romantic love between the couple is often not considered necessary for marriage, and sometimes it is not very relevant to the relationship. For example, in China and Japan a man and woman seldom had a chance to fall in love before they married because often they had not even

Western assumptions about marriage often do not apply to other cultural traditions. In this Taiwanese wedding procession, the bride is ceremonially taken to her husband's home.

Martha Cooper/Peter Arnold, Inc.

met. Sometimes boys and girls were betrothed at birth or as children. In both Japan and China, even when couples were married as adults, the marriage was arranged by their parents with the aid of a matchmaker, usually a female relative of the groom's family or a woman hired by them. The matchmaker tried to find a woman of suitable age, wealth, status, and disposition for the young man, and "matched" not only the couple to each other, but also the woman to the husband's parents. After marriage, the wife was incorporated into her husband's family; her labor would be very much under the control of her husband's parents, especially her mother-in-law; she worshiped the ancestors of her husband's family, not those of her own parents; her behavior would be closely watched lest she disgrace her in-laws; and her children became members of her husband's kin group, not her own.

There are many other examples of cultural diversity in marriage. Sex is not always confined to the marriage bed (or mat). A formal ceremony (wedding) recognizing or validating a new marriage is not universal. The marital tie may be fragile or temporary, with individuals expecting to have several spouses during the course of their lives. Or the tie may be so strong that even death does not end it. In traditional India a widow was forbidden to remarry, and often threw herself onto her husband's cremation fire (a practice now illegal). There are culturally legitimate marital relationships that are not between a man and a woman. Among the Nuer of the southern Sudan, an older, well-off woman sometimes pays the bridewealth needed to marry a girl. The girl takes male lovers and bears children, who are incorporated into the kin group of the older woman.

Formulating a definition of marriage that encompasses all the cross-cultural variations in the relationship is a difficult task, because somewhere there is a society that does not fit the definition. Numerous definitions have been offered, but there is no agreement on the "best" one. Most anthropologists agree, however, that marriage ordinarily involves

- a culturally defined relationship between a man and woman from different families, which regulates sexual intercourse and provides for reproduction;

- a set of rights the couple and their families obtain over each other, including rights over the couple's children;
- an assignment of responsibility for enculturation to the spouses or to one or both sets of their relatives; and
- a division of labor in the domestic group.

This conception of marriage is useful because it emphasizes the functions that marriage performs in almost all communities. Three functions are among the most important:

1. Marriage forms the social bonds and creates the social relationships that provide for the material needs, social support, and enculturation of children. Until they reach ten or more years of age, human children are totally or largely dependent on adults for food, shelter, protection, and other bodily needs. Equally important, children require the presence of adults for the social learning crucial to complete their psychological and cultural development. It is theoretically possible that only one adult, the mother, is required; but almost everywhere, marriage helps to create and expand the relationships through which children receive the material support and enculturation necessary for their immediate survival, future maturity, and eventual reproduction.

2. Marriage defines the rights and obligations the couple have toward each other and toward other people. Some rights and obligations, of course, concern sex. The marriage bond reduces (but does not eliminate) potential conflicts over sexual access by defining and limiting adult sexual access to certain individuals (normatively or legally, at any rate). Extramarital sex is not, of course, prohibited to the same degree in all cultures, but there are always limitations placed on it, and usually it is punished formally or informally. Other rights and duties concern the allocation of work and other activities. Marriage helps to define these rights and duties ("a good husband should . . .") and establishes the household within which family members do things for one another.

3. Marriage creates new relationships between families and other kinds of kin groups. In a few societies nuclear families are able to produce what they need to survive by themselves. But in no society are the members of the same nuclear family allowed to have sex, marry, and produce children. Sexual relations between parents and children and between sisters and brothers are defined as incestuous and are prohibited normatively or legally. Violators of this prohibition—known as the **incest taboo**—usually are punished, sometimes by death. Except in a few cultures in which members of royal families had sexual relations to produce an heir of highest possible rank, the incest taboo applies to members of one's own nuclear family. It usually is further extended to prohibit sex between some cousins, uncles and nieces, aunts and nephews, and other relatives that a culture defines as close. The near universal prohibition on sexual activity with close family members forces individuals to marry someone other than their immediate relatives. Every marriage creates a potential new (affinal) relationship between the relatives of the couple. The importance attached to these affinal relationships varies cross-culturally. At the very least, the families of the wife and husband will have an interest in the children. In addition, many societies use the relationships created by intermarriage to establish important trade relationships or political alliances, as we will see later in this chapter.

Because marriage is useful to individuals and to societies, marriage and family are nearly universal among the world's cultures. However, no particular form of marriage or type of family is universal. Cultures evolved various marriage and family systems to perform these functions. One of the most unusual (now extinct) systems was that of the Nayar of southern India.

Nayar "Marriage"

Before Great Britain assumed colonial control over part of India in 1792, the Nayar were a caste (see Chapter 10) whose men specialized in warfare.

Many Nayar men were away from their villages much of the time because they served as soldiers for several surrounding kingdoms and in other parts of India. Nayar women were required to confine their sexual activity to men of their own or a higher subcaste. They suffered severe penalties—death or ostracism—if they violated this norm. Among the Nayar no nuclear families existed, and in fact the Nayar had no marriage as the term is used in this book.

Nayar villages were composed of a number of kin groups. Children joined the kin group of their mothers. Each group was linked for certain ceremonial purposes to several other groups: some from the home village and others from neighboring villages. Any Nayar caught having sexual relations with anyone in his or her own kin group was put to death; intragroup intercourse was regarded as incestuous. Every few years, all the prepubescent girls of a kin group gathered for a large ceremony. People from the linked kin groups also attended, for the purpose of the event was to ceremonially "marry" these girls to selected men from the linked kin groups. At the ceremony, each "groom" tied a gold ornament around the neck of his "bride," and each couple retired to a secluded place for three days. After this period all the "grooms" left the village, and each had no further responsibilities to his "bride"; indeed, he might never even see her again. For her part, the "bride" and the children she would later bear had only to perform a certain ritual for her "husband" when he died. The ritual tying of the ornament by a man of a linked kin group did, however, establish a girl as an adult, able to have sexual liaisons with other men when she reached sexual maturity.

After her "marriage," each girl continued to live with her own kin group. When she reached sexual maturity, she began to receive nighttime male visitors from other kin groups. She established long-lasting sexual relations with some of her partners, who were expected to give her small luxury gifts periodically. Later, when she bore a child, the infant was believed to be the product of a legitimate union if one of its mother's partners paid the birth fees. Her child then became a member of the kin group of herself, her sisters, and her brothers, who gave the child material and social support. If none of her partners did so, it was assumed that she had had sexual intercourse with someone of a lower caste, and she, and sometimes her child, would be expelled from her kin group or killed.

MARRIAGE: A CROSS-CULTURAL PERSPECTIVE

The relationship we call marriage varies enormously cross-culturally. Most cultures allow multiple spouses. And the nature of the marital relationship—living arrangements, expectations of spouses, who decides who marries whom, authority patterns, how the relatives of the couple relate to one another, and so forth—differs from people to people.

Marriage Rules

Everywhere, the choice of a spouse is governed by norms that identify members of some social groups or categories as potential spouses and specify members of other groups or categories as not eligible for marriage. One set of rules is called **exogamous rules.** Exogamy ("outmarriage") means that an individual is prohibited from marrying within her or his own family or other kin group or, less often, village or settlement. Because the incest taboo applies to those people whom the local culture defines as close relatives, members of one's own nuclear family and other close kin are almost everywhere prohibited as spouses. Note that the incest taboo prohibits sex, whereas rules of exogamy forbid intermarriage.

Other kinds of marriage rules are known as **endogamous rules.** Endogamy ("inmarriage") means that an individual must marry someone in his or her own social group. The classic example of endogamous groups is the caste in traditional Hindu India (see Chapter 10). Other kinds of endogamous categories are orthodox Jews, races in the American South during slavery and, more recently, in South Africa, and noble classes in many ancient civilizations and states.

The purpose of endogamous rules most often is to maintain social barriers between groups of people of different social rank. Rules of endogamy maintain the exclusiveness of the endogamous group in two ways. First, they reduce the social contacts and interactions between individuals of different ranks. Intermarriage creates new relationships between the families of the wife and husband and potentially is a means of raising the rank of oneself or one's offspring. Endogamy has the effect of keeping affinal relationships within the caste, class, ethnic group, race, or whatever; this reinforces ties within the endogamous groups and decreases interactions between the groups. Second, endogamy symbolically expresses and strengthens the exclusiveness of the endogamous group by preventing its "contamination" by outsiders. This is most apparent with Indian castes because the cultural rationale for caste endogamy is to avoid ritual pollution: The Hindu religion holds that physical contact with members of lower castes places high-caste individuals in a state of spiritual danger, precluding the possibility of marriage between them.

Technically, the term *endogamy* applies only to cultural rules (or even laws) about confining marriage to those within one's own group. But it is important to note the existence of de facto endogamy, meaning that although no formal rules or laws prohibit outmarriage, most people marry those they consider to be like themselves. De facto racial and social class endogamy exists in most modern nations, including North America. This is partly because opportunities for members of different classes to get to know one another often are limited. De facto endogamy also exists because of powerful norms against marrying outside one's own "kind." Members of elite classes (and parents and other relatives of young people) may worry that would-be spouses of lower-class standing would not fit in with their social circle (to put their objection politely). Likewise, interracial couples are warned about the social stigma attached to their relationship and about the "problems" they and their children will encounter—problems that exist largely because many people think interracial marriages are themselves problematic!

How Many Spouses?

Cultures vary in the number of spouses an individual is allowed to have at a time. There are four possibilities:

- **Monogamy,** in which every individual is allowed only one spouse.
- **Polygyny,** in which one man is allowed multiple wives.
- **Polyandry,** in which one woman is allowed multiple husbands.
- **Group marriage,** in which several women and men are allowed to be married simultaneously to one another.

The last three possibilities are all varieties of **polygamy**—meaning "plural spouses." Notice that the three types of polygamy refer to the number of spouses *allowed* to a person, not necessarily to how many spouses most people have.

It may surprise members of monogamous societies to learn that most of the world's cultures allow polygamy. The most common form of plural marriage is polygyny, which is allowed in most societies of the world. Polyandry, on the other hand, is rare. There are less than a dozen societies in which it is documented—less than 1 percent of the world's cultures. Group marriage, so far as we know, has never been a characteristic form of marriage of a whole human society. Indeed, most anthropologists believe that group marriage, where it has occurred, has been a short-lived phenomenon brought about by highly unusual circumstances.

Comparisons of frequencies such as those just mentioned pose difficulties in assigning a particular people unambiguously to one of these four categories. (To appreciate this problem, answer the following question: Did the Nayar have polyandry, group marriage, or no marriage at all?) But they do give an accurate impression of how common or rare each form of marriage is in the human species.

Many Westerners misunderstand the nature of polygamous marriages, seeing them mainly as attempts, usually by men, to get access to more sexual partners. We fail to recognize the social and economic conditions that make these forms of marriage advantageous.

Polygyny   Even though most cultures allow polygynous marriage, only a minority of men in these societies actually have more than one wife. Thus, polygyny exists as an alternative form of marriage, rather than as the predominant (most common) form. But in those societies that allow it, polygyny ordinarily is the preferred form of marriage. Men, in particular, desire to have multiple spouses, although most men are unable to achieve their goal.

Even with only a minority of men married polygynously, an obvious problem exists for other men. If some men have two or more wives, this reduces the number of marriageable females so that some men cannot marry. This is, in fact, often the case. But in other cases this problem is not as acute as one might think, because in many populations there are more marriageable women than men at any one time. In some cultures more males than females die prematurely because they engage in hazardous activities, such as warfare and hunting, thus increasing the number of men who are able to find wives, even though some men are polygynous.

Polygyny assures that virtually all women find husbands. This is important for a woman's welfare because marriage legitimizes her children, and in many cultures children are her main or only source of social security—they are the people she depends on for support in old age. There is another reason why a woman wants to marry in polygynous societies: to ensure that her children are well provided for. In the majority of polygynous societies, inheritance of land, livestock, and other wealth and productive property passes from fathers to sons. A woman need not marry to bear children, but she does want a husband to assure that her sons have an adequate inheritance; her married daughters usually acquire their rights to resources from their husbands.

For their part, most men prefer to have two or more wives. Men usually have both social and economic incentives for marrying several women. Socially, a man's status is directly related to the size of his family and, hence, to the number of his wives and children. Also, when a man marries more than one woman, he acquires a new set of affines—fathers- and brothers-in-law whom he can call on for support, trade, or political alliances. Economically, there are also short- and long-term benefits, especially in horticultural and pastoral adaptations where a woman's labor is important in providing food and wealth to her family. The more wives and children a man has, the larger the work force available to his household. In pastoral societies in Africa and elsewhere, polygyny enables a man to increase the size of his herds, since he has more herders (wives and children) to tend livestock. Similarly, in those farming societies in which female labor is important, a polygynous man has more family members to tend fields and harvest crops. As he grows older he will have more children and grandchildren to look after his herds or work his fields and care for him. Thus, as long as he has the resources to support them, a man usually tries to acquire additional wives.

Usually only well-to-do men are able to afford more than one wife. "Afford," however, does not mean what North Americans might think; it is often as much a matter of being able to acquire additional wives than of being able to support them. Most polygynous peoples have the custom of bridewealth (discussed later), which requires a prospective groom and his relatives to give livestock, money, or other wealth objects to the kin of the bride. Although fathers and other relatives typically are obliged to help a young man raise bridewealth for one wife, only a minority of men can get together sufficient resources to provide bridewealth for additional wives.

There may be social and economic advantages for the co-wives of a polygynous man. Many North Americans think that no woman would want to be part of a "harem." But the most prestigious marriages for a woman are to husbands of wealth and status—the very men who are most likely to have married other women. Not only will the woman herself be better provided for, but her children may also receive larger inheritances of land, livestock, wealth, or other property. In addition, co-wives may lighten a woman's workload. Co-wives usually work together and cooperate on chores such as producing, processing, and preparing food; tending livestock; and caring for children. Thus, it is not unusual for a wife to encourage her husband to take additional wives to assist her in her chores.

Polygynous marriages also have inherent problems. A frequent problem is rivalry between co-wives and favoritism by husbands. Several strategies are used in polygynous societies to minimize friction. One strategy is for a man to marry women who are sisters, a widespread practice known as *sororal polygyny*. The rationale for sororal polygyny is that sisters are used to working together, have preexisting emotional bonds, and are likely to be less jealous of one another. Sisters are, therefore, likely to be more compatible than unrelated wives. In most cultures in which a man marries a number of women who are unrelated, each wife usually has a separate dwelling, which helps to minimize conflict with her co-wives. Also, co-wives usually are allocated different livestock to care for and have separate gardens to tend and harvest. The effect of such practices is that each wife, together with her children, is semi-independent from the other wives. Despite such practices, rivalry and jealousy among co-wives is a problem in many polygynous marriages.

Polyandry   Polyandry, the marriage of one woman simultaneously to two or more men, is a documented practice in only about a dozen societies. Much has been written about this unusual form of marriage, but ethnologists have not yet satisfactorily explained it. Some believe that female infanticide is partly responsible, arguing that the death of large numbers of girls would produce a shortage of adult women. Female infanticide does have the effect of decreasing the number of marriageable women, but far more human groups allow many of their female infants to die than practice polyandry. Female infanticide is not a general explanation for polyandry.

Wherever polyandry exists, it does so as an alternative form of marriage. Like polygyny, polyandry is allowed, but it is not the predominant form of marriage; most couples are monogamous even where polyandry is allowed. Therefore, to understand the reasons for polyandry, we indicate some of the special conditions that lead some people to choose to join in a polyandrous marriage.

The insufficiency of a family's land to support all of its heirs is one such condition. All available farmland is already owned by another family or by a landlord. Many European peasants faced this problem during the Middle Ages and even into the nineteenth century. In Ireland and some other parts of Europe, one solution was *primogeniture,* under which the oldest son inherited the farm and most of its property and the younger sons had to find other ways of supporting themselves. Younger sons served in the army or became priests or found some other occupation. Daughters who did not marry usually either remained at home or joined a nunnery. After the Industrial Revolution in the late 1700s, many migrated to cities and went to work in factories.

Some peoples of the Himalayas developed another solution—polyandry. The rugged topography and high altitude of Tibet and Nepal sharply limit the supply of farmland. Traditionally, all sons, regardless of age, have an equal claim on Tibetan family property. A farm may be adequate to support only a single family, but a couple may have three or more sons. If the sons divided their inheritance by each taking his own wife, the land would become so fragmented that the brothers' families would be impoverished. To solve this problem, sometimes all the sons marry one woman. This form of polyandry, called *fraternal polyandry,* helps to keep the farm and family intact and limits the number of children in the family. Although the oldest son usually assumes primary responsibility for the wife and children, he is not supposed to be shown sexual favoritism by the wife, who has sexual relations with all her husbands. When children are born, ideally each brother treats them as if they were his own, even if he knows that a particular child was fathered by one of his brothers. To the brothers, the advantage is that polyandry preserves the family property, keeping the land, the livestock, the house, and other wealth together. Also, one brother can stay in the village and work the family land during the summer, while another brother takes the livestock to high mountain pastures and a third brother (if present) visits towns in the lowlands to sell the family's products. This system also has advantages for the wife, who has multiple husbands to work for and help support her and her children. Her life usually is less physically strenuous and she usually has a higher standard of living than a woman married to only one man.

Although Himalayan polyandry has economic advantages, sometimes problems arise. A younger brother can at any time decide to end the arrangement, claim his portion of the family property, marry another woman, and establish his own family. The oldest brother does not have this option because as head of the family he bears primary responsibility for supporting their wife and children.

Marriage Alliances

Cultures vary in the importance they attach to the bond between wives and husbands. In some, there is no formal wedding ceremony. Instead, a couple is recognized as "married" when they regularly live together and as "divorced" when one of them moves away (or gets thrown out!). Each partner retains her or his own separate property, so the separation or divorce is not very "messy." In the contemporary United States, the wedding ceremony is often an expensive affair, marriages are supposed to endure, and couples usually own houses, furniture, and other property jointly. Yet more than half of all American

marriages will end in divorce, made "messy" because of conflicts over property and custody of the children. For many Americans, monogamy is *serial monogamy*, meaning only one legal spouse at a time.

Some cultures consider the marital relationship to be so important that young people cannot be trusted to choose their spouses wisely. Marriage is seen to establish lasting social relationships and bonds not only between the couple but also between their families and other relatives.

The affinal ties between kin groups created by marriage have social, economic, political, and, often, ritual importance. Marriage establishes an alliance between the members of two kin groups, and in many cultures **marriage alliances** are critical for the well-being and even survival of the intermarried groups.

The Yąnomamö, a horticultural and hunting tribe of the Amazon rain forest of South America, provide a good example of how intermarriage creates and maintains ties between kin groups. Every Yąnomamö village was constantly under threat of attack, so each had to be prepared to defend itself; likewise, the men of each village periodically went on raids intended to capture the women and resources of its enemies. It was, therefore, advantageous for villages to establish and maintain military alliances for mutual defense and offense. The smaller villages were obliged to enter into military alliances or they soon would be raided by their more numerous enemies. Having allies also was helpful in case of military defeat: A defeated group could take refuge with an allied village, whose members would feed and protect the refugees until they could establish producing gardens in a new location.

Marriage was a key strategy in creating and maintaining these alliances. When the men of a Yąnomamö village wanted to make an alliance with another village, they began by trading. For instance, one village might tell the other it needed clay pots and would be willing to trade its bows for them; or it might say that it needed hallucinogenic drugs used in shamanistic curing and would trade its hammocks for them. The people of each village were capable of making all these products for themselves; trade provided the excuse that villages used to visit one another to begin alliance formation. If no trouble broke out during the trading—for a Yąnomamö village did not even trust its longtime allies, much less its prospective allies—mutual invitations to feasts would follow. If the feasts did not turn violent, the men of the two villages would agree to give some of their "sisters" (female consanguines) to one another. This was considered the final stage of alliance formation; once the villages had exchanged women, the alliance was—by Yąnomamö standards—secure.

The Yąnomamö illustrate how intermarriage creates bonds and establishes important political relations between villages. In many cultures, these bonds and relations are important to families or entire settlements. If marriages are a means of establishing ties that are critical to a group's material well-being or survival, then the choice of which group to marry into may be too important to be left entirely up to the woman and man whose marriage creates the relationship. Older, wiser, and more responsible people should be making such critical decisions. This helps to explain one widespread custom—arranged marriages—that many Westerners view as an infringement on individual freedom.

The importance of the ties between kin groups created by intermarriage is also revealed by two other widespread customs. In the **levirate,** if a woman's husband dies, she marries one of his close kinsmen (usually a brother). The relations between the intermarried kin groups are considered too valuable to risk. Because both her dead and her new husband belong to the same kin group, the affinal relationship remains intact. The converse custom, the **sororate,** also preserves the affinal ties between kin groups even beyond the death of a spouse. With the sororate, if a woman dies, her kin group is obliged to replace her with another woman, for which no additional bride-wealth need be transferred. The Zulu of southern Africa, as well as many other African peoples,

practiced both the levirate and the sororate. In societies with these customs, marriages—and the affinal ties they create—endure even beyond death.

Marital Exchanges

In most cultures, the marriage of a man and a woman is accompanied by some kind of transfer of goods or services. These *marital exchanges* take numerous forms, including the North American custom of wedding showers and wedding gifts. In these, the presents given by relatives and friends supposedly help the newlyweds establish an independent household. We give things that are useful to the couple jointly, with food-preparation and other household utensils easily the most common type of gift. Many couples even register at stores so that their relatives and friends will provide the items they want.

From a cross-cultural perspective, the most unusual feature of North American marital exchanges is that nothing is transferred between the relatives of the groom and bride: The couple treats the gifts as their private property. Like most of our other customs, this seems natural to us. Of course the gifts go to the couple—what else could happen to them?

The fact that the couple gets the gifts meshes with several other features of Euro-American marriage. First, it usually is the bond through which new independent households are started, so the husband and wife "need their own stuff." If, in contrast, the newlyweds moved in with one of their relatives, they would not have as great a need for their own silverware, wine glasses, and other possessions. Second, our marriage-gift customs fit with the importance our culture gives to the privacy of the marital relationship: It is a personal matter between the husband and wife, and their relatives should keep their noses out. If the in-laws like each other and socialize together, well and good, but our marriages generally do not create strong bonds between the families of the bride and groom. (In fact, the two families often compete for the visits and attention of the couple and their offspring.) As we saw in Chapter 6, gifts make friends and vice versa; the fact that the affines do not exchange gifts with each other is a manifestation of the absence of a necessary relation between them after the wedding. If, in contrast, the marriage created an alliance between the two sets of relatives, some kind of an exchange would probably occur between them to symbolize and cement their new relations. Third, the gifts are presented to the couple, not to the husband or wife as individuals, and are considered to belong equally and jointly to both partners. But there are marriage systems in which the property of the wife is separate from that of her husband; if divorce should occur, there is no squabbling over who gets what.

With this background in mind, what kinds of marital exchanges occur in other cultures?

Bridewealth   **Bridewealth** is the widespread custom that requires a man and his relatives to transfer wealth to the relatives of his bride. It is the most common of all marital exchanges, found in more than one-half the world's cultures. The term *bridewealth* is well chosen because the goods transferred usually are among the most valuable symbols of wealth in the local culture. In sub-Saharan Africa, cattle and sometimes other livestock are the most common goods used for bridewealth. Peoples of the Pacific Islands and Southeast Asia usually pay their bridewealth in pigs or shell money and ornaments.

One of the most common rights a man and his relatives acquire when they transfer bridewealth to his wife's family is rights over the woman's children. Reciprocally, one of a wife's most important obligations is to bear children for her husband. This is well exemplified by the Swazi, a traditional kingdom of southern Africa. A Swazi marriage is a union between two families as well as between the bride and groom. The payment of bridewealth—in cattle and other valuables—to a woman's relatives establishes the husband's rights over his wife. A woman's main duty to her husband is to provide him with children. If she is unable to do so, her relatives must either return the bridewealth they received for her or provide a second wife to the husband, for which he need

pay no extra bridewealth. Reciprocally, a man must pay bridewealth to gain rights of fatherhood over the child of a woman, even though everyone knows he is the child's biological father. If he does not do so, the woman's relatives will keep the child; if the woman herself is later married to another man, her new husband will not receive rights over the child unless he pays bridewealth.

Brideservice   As the term implies, **brideservice** is the custom whereby a husband is required to spend a period of time working for the family of his bride. A Yanomamö son-in-law is expected to live with his wife's parents, hunting and gardening for them until they finally release control over their daughter. Among some !Kung bands (Chapter 5), a man proves his ability as a provider by living with and hunting for his wife's parents for three to ten years, after which the couple is free to camp elsewhere.

Brideservice is the second most common form of marital exchange; it is the usual compensation given to the family of a bride in roughly one-eighth of the world's cultures. However, sometimes it occurs alongside other forms of marital exchange and occasionally can be used to reduce the amount of bridewealth owed.

Dowry   In cultures that have the custom of **dowry** the family of a woman transfers a portion of their own wealth or other property to their daughter and her husband. Dowry is ordinarily the share of a woman's inheritance that she is allowed to take into her marriage for the use of her new family, although her parents are still alive. The woman and her family do not acquire marital rights over her husband when they provide a dowry; rather, the bride and her husband receive property when they marry, rather than when the bride's parents die. By doing so, parents give their female children extra years of use of the property and also publicly demonstrate their wealth.

Dowry transfers largely are confined to Europe, southern Asia, and the Middle East. Most peoples that have it are intensive agriculturalists and have significant inequalities in wealth. It is a relatively rare form of marital exchange, occurring in only about 5 percent of the societies recorded by anthropologists.

Dowry is common in parts of India, where it includes jewelry, household utensils, women's clothing, and money. Much of the dowry is presented to the bride on her wedding day, but her parents and maternal uncle often provide gifts periodically throughout her marriage. Dowry, then, is not always a one-time expense for a family but may represent a continual drain on their resources.

KINSHIP DIAGRAMS

At this point we need to introduce a set of notational symbols that will be useful in the remainder of this chapter and the next. This notation allows us to express diagrammatically how any two persons are (or believe themselves to be) related by bonds of kinship. The symbols appear in Figure 7.1, along with an example of how they would be used to show a married couple with five children. By stringing a number of symbols together, it is possible to make a complete chart—called a *genealogy*—that shows all the relatives of a given individual and how they are related to that individual. In these charts, or kinship diagrams, it is useful to have a reference individual, or a person to whom everyone on the chart is related. It is customary to call this reference individual "ego." In Figure 7.1 ego is symbolized by a square to show that his or her gender is irrelevant for the purposes of the genealogy. (If ego's gender mattered, we would symbolize him or her with either a triangle or a circle.)

POSTMARITAL RESIDENCE PATTERNS

In modern Euro-American societies a newly married couple usually establish a new domestic group (household) in their own apartment, condo, or house. Couples do not always set up a new

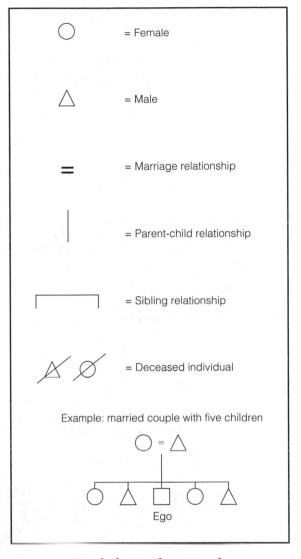

Figure 7.1 Symbols Used on Kinship Diagrams

household in many other cultures. They often move into an existing household, either that of the husband or that of the wife. Where most new couples in a society establish their residence is known as the **postmarital residence pattern.** Cross-cultural research shows that our own pattern, in which couples form new households separate from their parents, is uncommon; in fact, it occurs in only about 5 percent of the world's cultures.

What are the other common patterns? It is possible to identify a dozen patterns, but here we present only four. In order of most frequent to least frequent, they are as follows:

Patrilocal: Couples live with or near the parents of the husband.
Matrilocal: Couples live with or near the wife's parents.
Bilocal: Postmarital residence is optional between either the wife's or the husband's kin; roughly one-half of all couples choose each.
Neolocal: Couples live apart from both parents, establishing a separate dwelling and independent household.

Approximately 70 percent of all societies have patrilocal residence as the predominant pattern. Thirteen percent have matrilocal residence. Bilocality is characteristic of 8 percent, and neolocality of 5 percent. Other forms account for the remaining 4 percent.

What kinds of factors affect postmarital residence patterns? What determines whether newly married couples live separately or move in with their relatives? There is no simple answer, but property rights and inheritance forms are important influences on postmarital residence patterns. In societies in which the most important productive property is held by men, and in which inheritance passes from fathers to sons, brothers will have good reasons to join their fathers (and each other) in a common household to cooperate and protect their interest in land, livestock, or other wealth. When the sons of most families in a society bring their wives and children into their father's existing household, this results in the residence pattern anthropologists call patrilocal. Where important resources are controlled or owned by women, and if female labor is also important in supplying food for their families, then sisters tend to live and work together, and matrilocal residence is most likely to develop.

Neolocal or bilocal patterns are most often found in societies in which inheritance of important resources passes through both sexes, rights to resources are flexible or ill defined, or most people rely on wage labor for their livelihood. This may be why both foragers and modern industrialized countries are usually neolocal or bilocal. Among foragers, people need to maintain access to several territories, so rights to critical

In Iran, traditionally most couples lived in or near the family of the husband's father, a pattern known as patrilocal residence. This Iranian extended family is enjoying a feast together.

Courtesy of Akbar Mahdi

resources are loose and flexible (as explained in Chapter 5). Nuclear families may move between the husband's and wife's bands, depending on sentimental ties or short- or long-term availability of resources.

Modern industrialized nations usually are neolocal for two major reasons. First, job availability forces many couples to move away from their home towns. This is especially true for "upwardly mobile" couples seeking increased income, better opportunities, and a more affluent lifestyle. Second, in industrialized countries most workers do not rely on their family connections for access to their livelihood but sell their labor on an impersonal market to an employer they have never met. In other words, most ordinary citizens do not inherit much productive property from their parents and do not rely on their parents for their livelihood, so they establish independent households free from parental control and interference. The result is neolocal residence and an emphasis on nuclear family ties.

Although control over resources and form of inheritance are important overall influences, no single factor "determines" postmarital residence. For instance, if most couples rely on the wife's family for access to the resources they need to survive and raise children, then most couples will live with the wife's family and matrilocal residence will be predominant in the society. But a multitude of other factors also affects residence choices. In fact, in some societies even though women have much control over land, residence is not matrilocal because these other factors are locally more important than keeping sisters together in a common household. The same complexities apply to the other residence patterns, so there is no single explanation.

FAMILY and HOUSEHOLD FORMS

Residence patterns affect all kinds of family relationships in a human community. Postmarital residence places a new nuclear family, which is created by a new marriage, with one set of relatives rather than the other set. In turn, whom a newly married couple lives with influences whom they will cooperate with, share property with, and so forth. If postmarital residence is patrilocal, for instance, then the husband lives with and works with his own consanguines (his father and brothers). The wife is likely to cooperate in household chores, gathering, gardening, and other tasks with members of her husband's family, more than with her own.

Postmarital residence also determines which relatives will share strong emotional bonds with the children of the couple. If residence is matrilocal, then the children of sisters (who are "cousins") live together in a single household (much like "sisters" and "brothers"), and are likely to view their relationship as being like "real" siblings. The children of brothers, on the other hand, will live in different households and are likely to view themselves as more distantly related.

The prevailing form of residence also affects the kinds of household and family units that exist among a people. Consider neolocal residence. If all or most newlyweds set up their own households, separate from and independent of that of either set of parents, then a new household and family unit is established with each new marriage. This emphasizes the social and economic importance and independence of nuclear families because mothers and fathers—and not more distant relatives—are most likely to be the main teachers of children and "breadwinners" for the household. The couple maintains relations with their parents, siblings, and other relatives, of course, but neolocal residence tends to lead to an emphasis on nuclear families as the most culturally important and stable family unit.

Other kinds of households and family groupings exist among the world's peoples, some much larger in size than nuclear families. These units—known as **extended families**—are made up of related nuclear families. Because the related nuclear families usually live in a single household, here we use *extended family* and *extended household* as synonyms. Extended households typically include three and often four generations of family members. Figure 7.2 provides some of the most common forms.

Many anthropologists think that the form of family (household) that is prevalent in a society depends on its postmarital residence pattern. For example, with patrilocal residence the married sons of an older couple remain in the household of their parents (or, often each son builds his own house on his parents' land, near their dwelling). As they grow up and marry, the daughters go to live with their husbands' parents. If all the sons and daughters of a couple do this, the resulting household is of a type called *patrilocally extended*— brothers live in a single household with their own nuclear families and parents (see Figure 7.2a). If all families in the village, town, or other settlement follow this pattern, then the settlement consists of patrilocally extended households. Notice that the residents of each household are related to one another through males. The married women of the community live scattered in the households of their husbands, or perhaps many of them have married out of the community altogether.

The converse occurs with matrilocal residence. The mature sons leave as they marry, and the daughters bring their husbands to live with them in or near their parents' households. The house-hold type formed by the co-residence of daughters and sisters with their parents is called the *matrilocally extended* household (see Figure 7.2b). The sons of an elderly couple are scattered in the households of the women they have married, either in their own home community or in another community. If most people follow this residence pattern, then the community consists of numerous households made up of women related through females, plus their husbands and children.

The same relationship between residence and prevalent household form applies to the other residence patterns. With bilocal residence there is no consistency in whether households are made up of people related through males or females: Some couples live with the husband's family, others with that of the wife. The household type is *bilocally* (or *bilaterally*) *extended* (see Figure 7.2c). The community's households are a mixture of people related through both sexes in roughly equal frequency. With neolocal residence the settlement—be it village or modern suburb— consists of relatively small domestic units made up of nuclear families.

We can now see one reason why postmarital residence patterns are important: They give rise

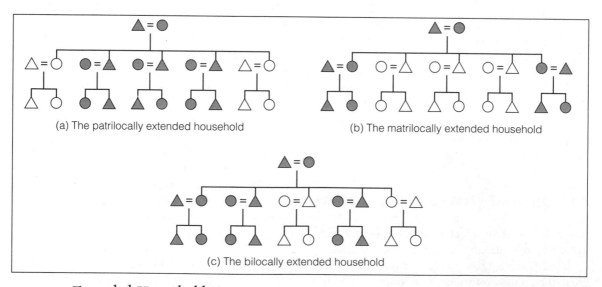

(a) The patrilocally extended household

(b) The matrilocally extended household

(c) The bilocally extended household

Figure 7.2 Extended Household Forms

to various household and family forms. The kinds of family and domestic groups found among a people result from where newly formed nuclear families go to live. And who lives with whom—the household type—is important, since households so often hold property in common, cooperate in production and other economic activities, enculturate children together, and sometimes even worship the same ancestral spirits.

If this book were concerned solely with industrial societies, our discussion of groupings formed on the basis of kinship relations would probably end at this point. In industrialized societies, other kinds of relations and groupings—economic, educational, political, religious, and so on—are organized by relationships other than kinship—by specialized firms, schools, parties, governments, churches, and so on. But, as we discuss in the next chapter, many preindustrial cultures use kinship principles to form much larger kin groups that organize and perform a range of other activities.

SUMMARY

1. All human populations have some kind of family groupings to organize and facilitate childrearing and other essential domestic activities. New nuclear families are formed by marriage, which forms social bonds that provide for children, establishes new relations between intermarrying families, and involves the exchange of goods and services between husbands and wives. Although a relationship like marriage is universal in human societies, the form of marriage, the rights and duties it establishes, and many other aspects of the marital relationship vary. The Nayar illustrate an unusual form of marriage, if it is marriage at all.

2. Marriage is everywhere governed by rules of exogamy and/or endogamy. Marriage systems commonly are classified by the number of spouses an individual is allowed: polygyny, monogamy, polyandry, and group marriage. In preindustrial societies, marriage often is the cornerstone of alliance relations between families or larger kin groups. The Yąnomamö illustrate the use of strategic marriages to create and sustain military alliances, a practice quite common in the preindustrial world. The levirate and sororate are customs that preserve affinal relationships even after the death of a spouse.

3. New marriages ordinarily are accompanied by the exchange of goods or services between the spouses and the families of the bride and groom. The most common forms of marital exchange are bridewealth, brideservice, and dowry. These exchanges are used to create affinal relationships, compensate a family or larger kin group for the loss of one of its members, provide for the new couple's support, or provide a daughter with an inheritance that attracts a husband.

4. Postmarital residence patterns determine where newly married couples establish their residence. In order of most common to least common, four of the patterns are patrilocal, matrilocal, bilocal, and neolocal. Many factors, including inheritance patterns and economic forces, influence which form will predominate in a given community. No single factor can adequately explain the cross-cultural variation in residence patterns.

5. Anthropologists are interested in postmarital residence patterns mainly because a newly married couple's residence influences which kinship relationships will be most emphasized in a society. In particular, the prevalent forms of family and domestic groups in a community arise out of many couples living with one or another set of relatives. Patrilocally, matrilocally, and bilocally extended families often are interpreted as the crystallization of postmarital residence patterns.

KEY TERMS

kin group
domestic group
consanguines
affines
nuclear family
incest taboo
exogamous rules
endogamous rules
monogamy
polygyny
polyandry
group marriage
polygamy

marriage alliances
levirate
sororate
bridewealth
brideservice
dowry
postmarital residence
    pattern
patrilocal residence
matrilocal residence
bilocal residence
neolocal residence
extended families

SUGGESTED READINGS

Collier, Jane F. *Marriage and Inequality in Classless Societies.* Stanford: Stanford University Press, 1988.

Compares marriage systems and marriage exchanges in small-scale societies from a theoretical perspective, discussing their impact on male-female relationships.

Goody, Jack, and S. J. Tambiah, eds. *Bridewealth and Dowry.* Cambridge: Cambridge University Press, 1973.

A collection of papers examining the causes and consequences of bridewealth and dowry.

Suggs, David N., and Andrew W. Miracle, eds. *Culture and Human Sexuality: A Reader.* Pacific Grove, CA: Brooks/Cole, 1993.

An outstanding collection of articles dealing with sexuality and related topics from a cross-cultural perspective. Includes both case studies and theoretical articles.

Most ethnographies contain a description of the domestic life of the people studied. The following are a few ethnographies specifically focused on domestic life.

Hart, C. W. M., and Arnold R. Pilling. *The Tiwi of North Australia.* New York: Holt, Rinehart and Winston, 1979.

A brief ethnographic study of an Australian culture with a most unusual marriage system.

Levine, Nancy. *The Dynamics of Polyandry: Kinship, Domesticity, and Population in the Tibetan Border.* Chicago: University of Chicago Press, 1988.

Case study of fraternal polyandry in the Himalayas.

Malinowski, Bronislaw. *The Sexual Life of Savages.* New York: Harcourt Brace Jovanovich, 1929.

Not what you may think from its title. An ethnography that describes courtship, sexual norms, marriage, domestic relations, and love magic in the Trobriand Islands.

Pasternak, Burton. *Kinship and Community in Two Chinese Villages.* Stanford: Stanford University Press, 1972.

Empirical study of Chinese kinship at the local level.

Stack, Carol B. *All Our Kin: Strategies for Survival in a Black Community.* New York: Harper and Row, 1974.

An outstanding ethnography that shows how African Americans in a midwestern city use family ties to cope with poverty.

Turnbull, Colin M. *The Mountain People.* New York: Simon and Schuster, 1972.

A very well-written and readable account of the Ik of East Africa. The study is disturbing because it shows the deterioration of the family under extreme economic pressures.

Wolf, Margery. *The House of Lim.* Englewood Cliffs, N.J.: Prentice-Hall, 1968.

A very readable study of family life in a Taiwanese farm family.

chapter 8

KINSHIP

Contents

Humans are social animals. We are born, live, and die as members of groups. We rely on cooperation with others for survival and for economic and emotional well-being.

The most basic organized cooperative groups are those based on kinship or biological ties. Within these groups, the relationships individuals have with one another depend largely on what kinds of relatives they are. However, societies differ as to which categories of relatives are the most important.

This chapter discusses the ways in which principles of kinship are used to create groupings and to organize social relationships.

KINSHIP

Beliefs about biological relationships are culturally determined, and such ideas vary from people to people. In the United States, for example, the children of one's parents' siblings are all considered to be the same kind of relative: first cousin. *Cousin* seems like a natural (i.e., biologically given) category of kinship. In actuality, the people you call *first cousins* are related to you differently. Some are your mother's sisters' children, some your mother's brothers' children, some your father's brothers' children, and the rest your father's sisters' children. If you reply, "Yes, but they all are the children of my aunts and uncles," then someone with another kinship system might ask, "But what makes you think that both your father's sister and your mother's sister are the same kind of relative (aunt)? After all, you call your mother and your father by different terms because of their gender; why then do you ignore the gender of your parent when you call the sisters of both your parents *aunt*?" You might ask in frustration, "How else would you do it?"

In fact, there are several other ways to do it. There are human kinship systems in which the brothers of your father are not culturally categorized as the same kind of male relative as the brothers of your mother. In some of these, the brothers of your father are called *father* (like your biological father), whereas the brothers of your mother are

called by a kinship term that translates roughly as *male mother*. There are kinship systems in which your relatives through your mother are considered to be different kinds of kin to you than your relatives through your father. In its kinship systems, humanity is surprisingly diverse. Various populations view the biological connections between relatives differently and make use of them differently in forming groups, allocating roles to people, culturally classifying kin, and establishing norms of proper behavior between relatives.

Why have anthropologists devoted so much attention to kinship?

Significance of Kinship

In industrialized nations there are thousands of kinds of economic, social, political, and religious groups that organize different aspects of our lives. Each individual participates in the activities of a number of formal and informal groups. We might belong to formal groups such as a labor union, the Audubon Society, the Republican party, and the United Methodist Church, and also take part in many informal gatherings with our co-workers, neighbors, and friends.

These groups share two important characteristics: (1) They are *voluntary:* if individuals' interests change, or if they find some other group of people who better meet their goals, they are free to change jobs, churches, neighborhoods, and friends, and (2) for the most part, they have *nonoverlapping membership;* we cooperate and interact with different individuals in the various groups to which we belong. Members of each of these groups have varying and sometimes contradictory expectations about how we should behave because we perform different roles in each of the groups. Behavior often is modified according to the context of the particular group of people we are associating with at the moment—we act one way at home, another at church, and yet another at work.

In contrast, among most preindustrial peoples, one lives with, works with, socializes with, and often worships with the same people, most of whom are relatives. Kin groups and kin relationships are *multifunctional,* meaning that they organize many kinds of activities. Most of the activities organized by the companies, schools, governments, churches, and other specialized groups in our own society are not organized by one or another kind of kin group. Kinship relations are far more important to the organization of these preindustrial societies than they are to our own. Thus, to understand these societies we must study their kinship systems.

Cultures vary in kinship in significant ways.

Forms of Kin Groups   A person belongs to a **kin group** because he or she is a relative (usually a child) of other members of the group. In the American kinship system, people become members of the family groups of both their mothers and their fathers. There is no systematic society-wide pattern of cooperating with relatives through one's mother or father, although particular individuals may develop closer ties with one or another side of their family.

In contrast, many other cultures place primary importance on one side of the family—either the paternal or the maternal side—in preference to the other. For example, in many cultures most individuals become members of their father's kin group. They might live with their father's relatives, inherit property from their fathers but not their mothers, and worship their paternal but not their maternal ancestors. In such systems, relatives through one's mother usually are recognized as kin, but kin of a fundamentally different and less important kind than paternal relatives. There are also systems in which kin groups are organized around maternal relationships, and paternal kin are culturally deemphasized.

Normative Expectations of Kin Relationships
In each society, people expect certain kinds of social relations with individuals related to them in a certain way. These expectations are part of the norms of a kinship system. Cross-culturally, these norms are surprisingly variable. There are systems in which husbands and wives do not sleep and eat in the same dwelling; in which brothers must rigidly avoid their sisters after puberty; in which sons-in-law are not supposed

Kinship relations are important partly because they organize cooperative activities of many kinds. Here a Spanish family cooperates in the harvest.

Robert Frerck/Tony Stone Images

to speak directly to their mothers-in-law; in which a boy is allowed to appropriate the property of his maternal uncle but must show utmost restraint and respect toward his paternal uncle; and in which people are expected to marry one kind of cousin but are absolutely forbidden to marry another kind of cousin. In sum, many patterns of behavior toward relatives that members of one culture regard as normal are absent in other cultures.

Cultural Classifications of Relatives   Kinship relationships are created through biological reproduction. When a woman gives birth, her relatives and those of her mate become the biological relatives of the child. Thus, the kinship relationship between any two people depends on how these individuals are related biologically. Yet anthropologists claim that kinship is a cultural, rather than a biologically determined, phenomenon. We make this claim because societies differ in their use of the biological facts of kinship to create groups, allocate roles, and classify the domain of relatives. In our kinship system, for example, whether a woman is our maternal or paternal aunt makes no difference: We still call her *aunt* and think of both our maternal and paternal aunts as the same kind of relative. But side of the family makes a difference in some kinship systems: father's sisters and mother's sisters are completely different kinds of relatives and are called by different terms.

FORM of DESCENT

Consider the ways people know how individual relatives are related to them. In our society people are your biological relatives because of a shared common ancestor in some previous generation. Your sister is the female child of your parents; your aunts and uncles are children of your grandparents; your first cousins are the grandchildren of your grandparents; and you share a common set of great-grandparents with your second cousins.

Thus you have an enormous number of living biological relatives. You have or had two parents, four grandparents, eight great-grandparents, and sixteen great-great-grandparents. All the people descended from your sixteen great-great-grandparents are your relatives (third cousins). Going back in time, the number of your ancestors doubles every generation. Assuming twenty-five years between generations, twenty generations ago (about the year 1500) you had more than one million ancestors, and all the descendants of these ancestors are biologically related to you, however remotely.

From the total range of potential biological kin, all cultures consider some kinds of relatives as more important than others. The reduction in the number of important relatives is accomplished in two main ways: (1) forgetting or ignoring the remoter kinship relationships, and (2) emphasizing some kinds of kinship relationships and deemphasizing others. In North America we use mainly the first method: Most people forget who their kin are beyond the range of second cousin because they have little incentive to keep track of their more distant relatives.

Many cultures—especially preindustrial ones—use the second method: They consider that some kinds of relatives are more important than others. The most common means of making some relatives more important than others is to use the sex of connecting relatives as the basis for defining which kin are close. For example, if people consider that kin relationships traced through males are most important, then individuals will think that their father's relatives are more important than their mother's relatives—for some purposes, at least. Relationships through females will be deemphasized and perhaps forgotten in two or three generations. If you lived in such a culture, some of your second cousins on your father's side would be quite important relatives, but you might not consider your second cousins through your mother as relatives at all.

Kinship relationships, then, are defined by how people trace their descent from previous generations. How people in a given culture trace their descent is called their **form of descent.** Descent can be traced through males, females, or both genders.

CONCEPT REVIEW Forms of Descent

FORMS	CHARACTERISTICS	ASSOCIATED KIN GROUPS
Unilineal a) Patrilineal b) Matrilineal	through male line through female line	(patri)lineages and (patri)clans (matri)lineages and (matri)clans
Cognatic	through either male or female line	cognatic descent groups
Bilateral	equally through both male and female lines	kindred

UNILINEAL DESCENT

In many cultures, relationships traced through only one gender are considered most important. Anthropologists say that such cultures have **unilineal descent,** a term that refers to the fact that people place importance on either their mother's ancestral line or their father's ancestral line, but not both. Depending on which gender is the most important for tracing kinship relationships, two categories of unilineal descent are most common: **patrilineal descent** (through the male line) and **matrilineal descent** (through the female line). Patrilineal is more common. There are about three times as many patrilineal as matrilineal cultures.

In Figure 8.1, the patrilineal relatives of the person labeled *ego* are shaded in. The kinship diagram shows that ego's patrilineal kin include only those relatives related to ego through males. For instance, ego's father's brother's children are related to ego through two males, whereas ego's other first cousins are not.

Looking at patrilineal descent another way, ego's patrilineal kin include all the people descended through males from the man labeled founder in Figure 8.1. In fact, any two individuals shaded in the diagram are related to one another through males. This includes women as well as men, but the children of these women are not related through males and, therefore, are not patri-

lineal kin. The children of the women have their own set of patrilineal relatives, which they take from their fathers.

How does patrilineal descent affect behavior toward different relatives? Probably the most widespread effect is in the inheritance of property. In patrilineal societies, property is passed down through the male line from fathers to sons. In contrast, most people in North America today trace their kinship relationships through both genders. You probably do not distinguish between your two grandfathers but think of yourself as related in the same way to both, and you may potentially inherit from both. But in a patrilineal society, your father's father would play a far more significant role in your life, and it would be from him that you would expect to inherit wealth or receive land rights. Your mother's father would pass his property on to his sons and sons' sons— not to you because you are related to him through your mother, not your father. Likewise paternal uncles are far more important, as are cousins related to you through the male line. These people would be primarily responsible for your economic and social welfare, and you would probably cooperate and associate with them and your own siblings.

Your matrilineal kin are related to you through female links. They include your mother, mother's mother, mother's mother's mother (if she is alive),

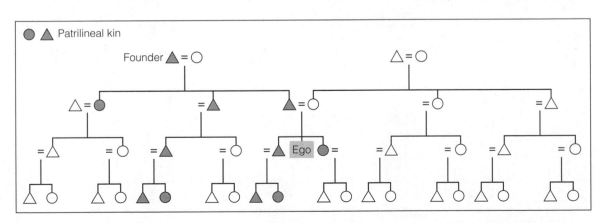

Figure 8.1 Patrilineal Descent

plus the daughters of all these women and their children. The sons and brothers of these women are your matrilineal kin, but their children are not. In Figure 8.2, we have shaded the people who are ego's matrilineal relatives. Note that only one set of cousins—ego's mother's sisters' children—are shaded in the diagram. They are the individuals who are related to ego through female links, and therefore, ego is likely to have closer relationships with them than with other cousins. Property is most likely to be inherited from one's mother and maternal grandmother and from the brothers of these women. In matrilineal societies, men usually leave most of their property to their sister's children. As a result, maternal uncles (mother's brothers) are important figures in one's life, and in some respects they assume the role we usually associate with fathers.

In unilineal descent systems some cousins, in particular, will be more important relatives than other cousins: father's brothers' children in patrilineal systems, mother's sisters' children in matrilineal systems. Recognition of the fact that not all cousins are "alike" in unilineal societies has led anthropologists to distinguish between *parallel cousins* and *cross cousins*. Two sets of cousins are parallel cousins if their parents are of the same sex, so your parallel cousins are your mother's sisters' children and your father's brothers' children. People are cross cousins if their parents are siblings of the opposite sex, so your cross cousins

are your father's sisters' children and your mother's brothers' children. The significance of this distinction is that in unilineal descent systems, one set of parallel cousins always belongs to the same kin group as ego, as you can see by contrasting the cousins shaded in Figures 8.1 and 8.2. On the other hand, no cross cousin is ever in ego's kin group in a society with a unilineal descent form.

Unilineal Descent Groups

Larger kin groups of people—known as **descent groups**—can be established on the basis of kinship ties. A **unilineal descent group** is a grouping of relatives, all of whom are related through only one sex. A matrilineal descent group is a group whose members are (or consider themselves to be) related through females, or who trace their descent through female links from a common ancestress. A *patrilineal descent group* comprises people who trace their descent through males from a common male ancestor.

A *matrilineal descent group* exists when people descended from the same woman through females recognize their group identity and cooperate for some purposes. When a matrilineal rule of descent establishes a group of people all related to one another through females, we say that the group is created using the *matrilineal principle*. The matrilineal principle is "Everyone joins the

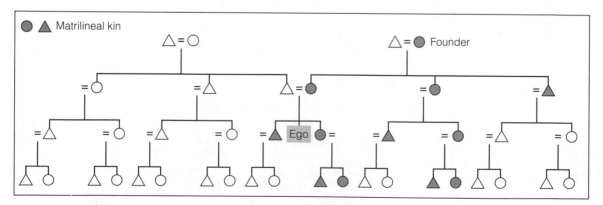

Figure 8.2 Matrilineal Descent

descent group of his or her mother" or "Only the children of the female members of a group become members." Looking back to Figure 8.2, all the individuals on the diagram are members of a single descent group. Only the female members pass their membership in the group along to their offspring. The children of the group's men join the descent groups of their mothers, which usually are a different group because of incest and exogamy rules.

Groups also can develop by repeated application of the *patrilineal principle*. In any given generation, only males transmit their membership in the group to their offspring. The result of applying this principle for several generations is a group of people related to one another through males. In Figure 8.1, all the shaded individuals are in the same descent group, and all joined the group of their father.

Using either of the unilineal descent principles, groups of various sizes can be formed in such a way that smaller groups are nested inside larger groups. A nuclear family can be made part—or a "segment"—of a unilineally extended family. The unilineally extended family is a segment of a somewhat larger group, which in turn is a segment of a still larger unilineal group. This segmentation of unilineal groups can continue until groups with thousands of members are formed. It is not even necessary that members of the larger and more inclusive groups know exactly how they are related. If the descent principle is patrilineal, for example, everyone only need remember to which group their fathers belong. So long as only the males of the group transmit this membership to their offspring, everyone whose fathers were members will know that they, too, are members of the same patrilineal descent group and, therefore, are somehow related through males.

Unilineal descent groups can be small or enormous, depending on the fertility of members of previous generations and on the genealogical depth of the group—that is, on how far back in time any two members of the group must go to trace their relationship to each other. Genealogical

depth provides a convenient way to classify the kinds of unilineal descent groups that are most common cross-culturally. From "shallowest" to "deepest," they are unilineally extended families (Chapter 7), lineages, and clans.

Lineages A **lineage** is a unilineal group composed of several extended families whose members are able to trace their descent through males or females from a common ancestor or ancestress. The extended families that make up the group must be able to state how they are related to one another for anthropologists to call the group a lineage. Lineages may be either patrilineal (patrilineages) or matrilineal (matrilineages), depending on the form of descent prevalent among a people.

Clans **Clans** are unilineal descent groups whose members are descended from a common ancestor through the male line (patriclans) or a common ancestress through the female line (matriclans). The major difference between a clan and a lineage is generational depth. The common ancestor or ancestress of the clan lived so far in the past that not all members of the clan can explain precisely how they are related to one another. Like lineages, clans usually are exogamous. Members of the clan think of themselves as relatives and frequently refer to one another as "clan brother" or "clan sister." In many societies, clans own or control land and other forms of property. Most clans are totemic; their members are symbolically identified with certain supernatural powers associated with particular animals, plants, and natural forces such as lightning, the sun, and the moon. Clans commonly take the name of their primary totemic symbol, and thus are called the bear clan, the sun clan, and the eagle clan. The association with particular supernatural powers gives specific clans control over particular religious rituals. Although the function of clans varies from one society to another, they usually are among the most significant economic, social, and political units in the society.

Whereas lineages may exist without being aggregated into clans, clans are almost always subdivided into lineages, which are, in turn, subdivided into extended families (Figure 8.3).

Descent Groups in Action

Two examples illustrate how unilineal descent principles organize cooperative activities: (1) the Tikopia, a patrilineal people who live on a Pacific island, and (2) the Hopi, a matrilineal Native American people of the Southwest.

Tikopia: A Patrilineal Society   Tikopia is a western Pacific island covering about six square miles. In the late 1920s, when it was studied by Raymond Firth, Tikopia had a population of about 1,200. Tikopians traced their descent patrilineally and used this principle to establish groupings of people related through males. They viewed their society as composed of four patriclans, each with a name that passed from fathers to sons. Each patriclan was subdivided into several patrilineages, averaging about thirty to forty members. The members of each patrilineage traced their descent in the male line back to a common ancestor—the founder of the patrilineage—who lived four to six generations ago. Each patrilineage ordinarily considered the oldest male descendant of this founder to be its head. The women of a lineage married men of other lineages, so the children of the lineage's women did not become members of it.

The lineage controlled rights over land and certain other kinds of property. Each lineage owned several parcels of land on which yams, taro, coconut, and breadfruit were planted. The families of the lineage had the right to plant and harvest crops on lineage land; once they had planted a parcel, they had the right to continue to use it. They could not, however, sell, trade, or give the land away to members of other lineages. The same rights applied to the parcels of land on which a family established their dwellings: They could live on one of the lineage's house sites but could not dispose of it to outsiders.

Ordinarily, each nuclear family cultivated the lineage land of its husband-father. In Tikopia, the female members of a patrilineage retained their use rights to lineage land even after they married. When a woman married, a parcel of the land of her lineage was provided for her own and her husband's and children's use. A woman could not, however, pass any of her rights to this land to her children; when she died, the use of the parcel reverted to her patrilineage. Her children received use rights to land from their own fathers' lineage.

The social rank of individuals was also determined largely by their kin group and their status within it. One lineage of each clan was considered the senior lineage. Because its living members were believed to be directly descended (through males) from the founder of the clan, it was the highest ranking lineage of that clan. They received certain kinds of respect from their clanmates and had the right to select a male member to serve as the clan chief. Just as the lineages were ranked on the basis of genealogical closeness to the senior lineage, so families within a single lineage were ranked by their closeness to the head of the lineage.

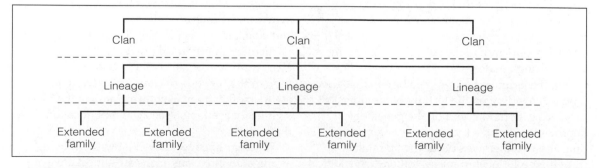

Figure 8.3 Typology of Unilineal Kinship Groups

Each descent group was allocated ritual duties to perform. Each of the four clan chiefs served as the religious leader and organizer of certain religious ceremonies. Each clan had its own ancestral spirits, which were the deceased former chiefs of the clan. Each clan also had its own deities, with whom its chief acted as intermediary.

Each clan was responsible for carrying out rituals that ensured the availability of food. Each of the four major subsistence crops was spiritually associated with a particular clan, and the gods of this clan were believed to control the crop. The chief of the clan performed important rituals that ensured the continued supply and fertility of whichever crop "listened to" (as the Tikopia phrased it) the gods of his clan. Thus, each clan—in the person of its chief—had ritual responsibilities toward the other three clans.

Like clans, Tikopian patrilineages also cooperated in religious contexts. Although the members of a single patrilineage usually lived scattered among several settlements, each patrilineage had a house that its scattered members regarded as sacred because it was believed to be the ancestral home of the entire lineage. The members of a lineage periodically held religious ceremonies at this house to honor the deceased ancestors of their kin group.

Hopi: A Matrilineal Society The Hopi of Arizona divide themselves into about fifty exogamous matriclans (some of which are now extinct). Clans are not residential groups, for most have members who live in more than one of the Hopi's nine villages. Each clan is subdivided into several matrilineages. The female members of a Hopi matrilineage usually live in adjoining houses within the village.

The Hopi postmarital residence pattern is matrilocal; after marriage a man usually joins his wife, her sisters, and her other matrilineal relatives to form a matrilocally extended household. Most Hopi extended families consist of one or more older women, their daughters and husbands, and sometimes even their granddaughters and their husbands. Because of lineage and clan exogamy and matrilocal residence, husbands are

outsiders, and their real home is with their mothers' extended family. The residential core of a matrilineage thus consists of its women, who live close to one another throughout most of their lives. The married men of the lineage are scattered among the households of their wives, although they frequently return to their matrilineal home for rituals and other responsibilities or in case of divorce.

Most property, secular and ceremonial, is inherited matrilineally. Living space is passed from mother to daughter. Farmland, on which the Hopi formerly depended for more of their subsistence, is owned by a clan, with each lineage having use rights over particular parcels at any one time. The husbands of the lineage's women do most of the farming to support their families, although they themselves do not own the land.

Membership in a matriclan also establishes one's relationships with the supernatural world. Each clan is mystically associated with a number of supernatural powers called *wuya*. Clans usually take their name after their principal *wuya*, such as bear, rabbit, corn, snake, cloud, sun, and reed. The members of a matriclan pray to their *wuya*, asking them for protection and for bountiful harvests.

Hopi religion features a ritual calendar that includes a large number of required ceremonies. In most cases, each ceremony is "owned" by the members of a certain clan; this clan has primary responsibility for ensuring that the ceremony is performed on time and in the proper manner. Every clan represented in a village has a clanhouse in which the masks, fetishes, and other sacred items used in the ceremonies it owns are stored. The clanhouse usually consists of a room adjoining the dwelling of the senior female member of the clan. This woman, known as the *clan mother*, is in charge of storing ritual paraphernalia and ensuring their proper respect. The position of clan mother is passed down by a woman to either her younger sister or her daughter, depending on age and personal qualities. There is also a male head of each clan who is in charge of the performance of ceremonies owned by his clan. A male clan head passes his position and the requisite ritual knowledge to either his younger brother or his sister's son. In this way, culturally important ritual knowledge is kept within the clan.

Among the Hopi, as in most other matrilineal systems, the roles of father and husband differ from those in patrilineal systems. When a husband moves in with his wife and her relatives after marriage, he brings only clothing and a few personal items. Nor does he accumulate much property because the house, its furnishings, the food stored there, and other goods remain the property of his wife's family. Although a man provides food for himself and his family by working in the fields of his wife, the products of his garden labor belong to his wife. The children similarly are viewed primarily as members of their mother's lineage and clan, and indeed they have no rights to use land or any claim to ritual knowledge or property of their father's kin group.

Neither the Tikopia nor the Hopi "typifies" patrilineal and matrilineal kinship. There is considerable diversity in patrilineal and matrilineal systems. The Tikopia and Hopi do illustrate some of the differences between patrilineal and matrilineal peoples with respect to recruitment into groups, allocation of roles, nature of sentimental attachment, and organization of common activities. As in many other preindustrial societies, their kin groups carry out most of the cooperative activities that more specialized groups perform in industrialized nations.

Cognatic descent

Cultures with **cognatic descent** have no formal rule about whether individuals join the groups of their mothers or fathers. A **cognatic descent group** consists of all the individuals who can trace their descent back to the common ancestor (or founder) of the group, through both female and male links.

In cognatic descent, people make choices about the groups they want to join. The choice commonly is based on factors such as one's chances of inheriting rights to land use or other forms of

property or wealth; the desire to associate with a relative of high status or rank; childhood residence; and emotional ties. For example, in a cognatic system you might decide to reside and cooperate with your mother's relatives if her kin group has a lot more land available for you to cultivate than does your father's group. Or if a coveted political office or honorific title is about to become vacant in your father's group, you might decide to try to acquire it by moving in and working with his relatives.

Cognatic descent is found on all continents, but it is especially prevalent among Polynesians, including the Samoans, Hawaiians, and Tahitians. The residents of these islands and most other Polynesian islands were divided into numerous cognatic kinship groups, the membership of which sometimes numbered in the thousands. Details varied from island to island, but generally speaking, a person could join any cognatic group or groups to which he or she could trace ancestry. Membership in the descent group bestowed rights to agricultural land, house sites, and some other kinds of property.

In cognatic descent, everyone potentially belongs to several groups because everyone has the opportunity to join all the groups to which their parents belong, and each parent probably is a member of at least two groups. If the kin groups intermarry, everyone potentially will belong to a great many groups—perhaps even to most of the groups that exist in their society.

Unlike unilineal systems, cognatic descent groups have overlapping membership. This potentially poses a problem for access to land and other culturally valued things. For example, if all members of a group have rights to the land collectively owned by this group, and if half or more of the entire population potentially has such rights, then the "right" does not mean much.

The problem of overlapping membership may be solved in several ways. Effective membership commonly is restricted only or largely to those individuals who reside on or use the group's land. Among the Maoris of New Zealand, the

In Samoa, cognatic descent relationships make people eligible to acquire titles that bestow prestige and leadership. This is a Samoan "talking chief" making a speech.

Don Smetzer/Tony Stone Images

hapu (kin group) potentially consisted of everyone who could trace their ancestry back to its founder. However, only people who lived on the land and participated in the daily life of the *hapu* were effective members. More often than not, a couple would live with the *hapu* of the husband's parents. The husband's and wife's connections and membership in other *hapu* would be remembered, but the claim of their children and grandchildren to membership in these *hapu* might be forgotten.

In some Polynesian cultures, people keep up their membership in several groups by contributing labor and foods to feasts sponsored by the groups and generally showing their interest in and commitment to the groups. The islands of Samoa provide an example. Each Samoan village has a council that plans public activities, levies fines, and performs other functions for the whole community. Each village is composed of several cognatic kin groups known as *'aiga*. Although each *'aiga* has branches represented in several villages, every *'aiga* has an ancestral homeland village. In its homeland village, each *'aiga* has the right to select one or more of its men to hold

titles, or *matai*, and it is these titleholders who serve as the *'aiga*'s representatives to the village council. Acquisition of a *matai* carries great honor, as well as authority to regulate use of the *'aiga*'s land, resolve disputes among the *'aiga*'s members, organize feasts and ceremonial gifts, and assess the members for contributions to marriages, funerals, and other events.

When a title becomes vacant because of death or some other reason, all members of the entire *'aiga* have a voice in choosing the new *matai*. Because people belong to several (often six or more) *'aiga* simultaneously, they have a voice in choosing the new *matai* for several groups, although they may not exercise their rights in all the *'aiga* to which they belong. Because men belong to several groups, they have the right to compete for and gain a title in these groups.

The Maori *hapu* and the Samoan *'aiga* illustrate some of the common functions of cognatic kin groups: They hold property and regulate access to land, organize cooperative activities, and serve as the structural basis for acquiring honored and authoritative political roles. In these respects they are similar to the lineages and clans of unilineal systems. But in cognatic systems the range of individual choice about group membership is much wider.

BILATERAL DESCENT

In **bilateral** (two-sided) descent systems, kinship relationships are traced through both genders. Relatives through both parents are regarded as equal in importance; cousins are seen as the same kind of relative, for instance, whether they are related to ego through the mother or the father.

Bilateral kinship exists in most contemporary Western countries, but it is also common in other parts of the world. No large, well-defined, property-holding groups exist in bilateral systems in contrast to unilineal and cognatic systems. The tracing of kinship relationships bilaterally produces associations of relatives known as the **kindred.** A kindred consists of all the people that a specific person recognizes as bilaterally related to himself or herself.

To understand bilateral kinship and the kindred, imagine a Canadian or an American woman named Liz. Liz recognizes her relatives through her father and mother as equivalent and interacts with them in much the same way (unless she has established strong bonds with someone because they live close by or for some other reason). The more distant the relationship, the less likely Liz is to interact with or even know who her relatives are. She is likely to see many of her kindred in the same place only at such events as weddings, funerals, and family reunions. Many of Liz's relatives do not know one another (her cousins on her mother's side are unlikely to know her cousins through her father). All the members of her kindred do not consider themselves relatives, and they certainly do not own any common property.

As this hypothetical example shows, a kindred is *ego-focused*; each individual is the center of his or her own set of relatives. Only you and your siblings share the same kindred; your mother has a different kindred, as do your father and all your cousins. Unilineal and cognatic descent groups

are *ancestor-focused*; people are members of a descent group because they recognize descent from a common ancestor.

INFLUENCES on KINSHIP SYSTEMS

There are a number of factors that seem to *influence* (as opposed to *cause*) which form of kinship a people will have.

One of the most important influences is the primary mode of adaptation (see Chapter 5) of a people. About 60 percent of all foraging societies are bilateral or cognatic, according to a cross-cultural study by David Aberle. Bilateral and cognatic descent allow individuals considerable choice in selecting which groups to affiliate with. In foraging cultures individuals and families can maintain relationships with many bands and move to and harvest the resources of any band to which they trace a kinship relationship. Since hunters and gatherers encounter seasonal, annual, and spatial fluctuations in wild food availability, keeping territorial options open is advantageous.

Other descent forms are also affected by adaptation. About three-fourths of pastoral societies have patrilineal descent. According to one hypothesis, the association between nomadic herding and patrilineal descent exists because livestock most often are owned and managed by men. To conserve labor devoted to protecting and moving animals to seasonally available pastures, a group of brothers often combines their animals into a single herd. Brothers tend to stay together to cooperate in herd management and look after their inheritance; therefore, they will reside patrilocally. Patrilocal residence associates male relatives together in a single location, whereas it disperses females. Descent through males develops as a consequence. Also, inheritance of animals typically passes from fathers to sons.

Patrilineal descent also has been interpreted as a way to improve success in intergroup warfare. It keeps a group of related males together and thereby increases their willingness to cooperate in battles.

Matrilineal descent is more likely to be found among horticultural peoples (see Chapter 5) than it is with any other adaptation; nearly 60 percent of matrilineal cultures are horticultural. This association is probably because women perform so much of the daily subsistence work in most horticultural populations. Yet most horticultural societies have patrilineal descent. Thus, no single determinant can explain all cases of matrilineality, or for that matter the other forms of kinship. Possibly cross-cultural variations in kinship are influenced by so many complex factors that no generalized explanation is possible.

KINSHIP TERMINOLOGY

In Chapter 2 we noted that one of the major components of cultural knowledge is the way a people classify natural and social reality. Kinship relationships and kinship groups are a major part of social reality in human cultures. Just as cultures differ in the ways they trace their descent and form social groupings of relatives, they also differ in the way they classify types of relatives, or labeled categories. The labeled categories are called **kin terms,** and the way in which a people classify their relatives into these categories is called their **kinship terminology.** For instance, *aunt* is an English kin term, and the fact that most native English speakers consider all the sisters of both their parents as the same type of relative is part of the English kinship terminological system.

Most people think that the kin terms they use to refer to different relatives reflect the way those relatives are related to them biologically (genetically). In fact, this is true for some English kin terms: *mother, father, sister, brother, son,* and *daughter* all define individuals related to you in distinct biological ways (setting aside considerations of adoption, foster parenting, or step relatives).

However, there are other English kin terms that do not perfectly reflect genetic relatedness. Consider the terms *uncle* and *aunt.* They refer to siblings of your parents, and they differ only by their gender. But the individuals you call *aunt*

and *uncle* are related to you in four different ways: your father's siblings, your mother's siblings, your father's siblings' spouses, and your mother's siblings' spouses. Note that both consanguineal and affinal relatives are included in the English terms *uncle* and *aunt.* The same idea applies to some other terms: A particular term groups together several individuals related to you in different ways. Thus, *grandfather* includes mother's father and father's father; *grandmother* is used for mother's mother and father's mother; and *first cousin* refers to a wide range of people who have quite different biological connections to you.

A people's kinship terminology only partly reflects the biological relationships between individuals. More fundamentally, it reflects the various norms, rights and duties, and behavioral patterns that characterize social relationships between kinfolk. Using a single term for relatives of different kinds reflects the cultural fact that people think of them as the same kind of relative; in turn, people consider them as the same kind of relative because they have similar kinds of relations with them. Thus, the men we call *uncle* have the same general kinds of social relationships with us regardless of whether they are our mother's or our father's brothers.

No matter how strange some kinship terminology systems may appear to us, all are logically constructed. For one thing, every term has a reciprocal term. For example, the reciprocal of *grandfather* is either *granddaughter* or *grandson.* If you call a woman *mother,* she will call you *son* or *daughter.*

Kinship terminologies are constructed using several criteria. Three of the most important criteria are (1) gender of referent, (2) generation, and (3) side of the family. In the following discussion, *ego* refers to the person using the given kin term.

The gender of the individual to whom the term refers (the referent) usually is a relevant criterion for the kin term used. In English, gender matters for terms like *brother* and *sister, uncle* and *aunt,* and *grandfather* and *grandmother.* Indeed, gender is the only criterion that distinguishes the relatives just mentioned from one another. Gender is irrelevant, however, for another of our kin terms, *cousin.*

Kinship terms usually reflect whether the individual referred to is of the same or a different generation than ego's. In English, specific terms are used for relatives in ego's own generation (*cousin*), in ego's parents' generation (*aunt*), and in ego's children's generation (*niece*). In describing kinship terminologies we call ego's parents' generation the *first ascending generation* and ego's children's generation the *first descending generation.* Although the terms used in most kinship terminologies reflect generational differences, two systems of terminology use terms that transcend generations.

Side of ego's family is a third criterion by which kin terminologies are constructed. In English, side of the family is irrelevant: Relatives through the mother receive the same terms as relatives through the father. Many other cultures place special emphasis on relationships through females (mothers) or males (fathers), and this emphasis is reflected in their terminological systems.

Varieties of Kinship Terminology

Only the five most common types of kinship terminology, Eskimo, Hawaiian, Iroquois, Omaha, and Crow, will be discussed. Do not be misled by the names of these systems. Lewis Henry Morgan, the American anthropologist mentioned in Chapter 4, developed the basic classification system for kinship terminology in 1871. He named each system after the first people he discovered using it. Although four terminologies are named after Native American groups, they are found throughout the world. To simplify our discussion, only the terms used for biological relatives in ego's generation and in ego's first ascending (parental) generation will be discussed. To make these systems easier to understand, the terms are translated into their closest English equivalents. These translations are, however, only rough approximations; some terms have no exact English equivalents.

Eskimo   **Eskimo kinship terminology** is the easiest for English speakers to understand because this is the system we use (see Figure 8.4). In this system, ego's biological mother is called *mother* and ego's biological father is called *father.* These are the only two persons to whom these terms apply. The term *aunt* is used both for ego's father's sister and ego's mother's sister, and the term *uncle* is used for father's brother and mother's brother. The terms *brother* and *sister* are used only for the children of ego's mother and father. The term *cousin* is used for all children of ego's uncles and aunts.

Hawaiian   **Hawaiian kinship terminology** is the simplest because it uses the fewest terms (see Figure 8.5). All relatives in ego's first ascending generation are called either *mother* or *father.* The term *mother* is extended to include ego's mother's sister and ego's father's sister, and *father* is extended to include father's brother and mother's brother. In ego's own generation, everyone is called either *brother* or *sister.* Thus, Hawaiian terminology includes no terms equivalent to the English terms *uncle, aunt,* or *cousin.* Although the Hawaiian system extends the terms *mother* and

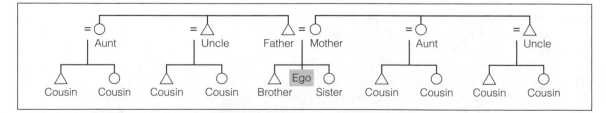

Figure 8.4 Eskimo Kinship Terminology

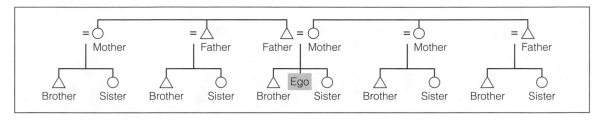

Figure 8.5 Hawaiian Kinship Terminology

father, this does not mean that individuals are unable to distinguish their biological parents from their other relatives of the parental generation.

Hawaiian often is called a generational system because only the generation of the term's referent is relevant.

Iroquois   Iroquois kinship terminology categorizes relatives very differently from either the Hawaiian or the Eskimo systems (Figure 8.6). The term *father* includes father's brother but not mother's brother. *Mother* includes mother's sister but not father's sister. The term *uncle* is used only for mother's brother; *aunt* is used only for father's sister. If we look at ego's generation, we also see a difference. The children of father's brother and mother's sister are called *brother* and *sister.* The term *cousin* is used only for the children of mother's brother and father's sister. Thus, in the Iroquois system, ego differentiates cousins. Although this distinction may seem unusual to us, it also exists in the Omaha and Crow systems, so we need to understand the logic behind it.

The Iroquois system distinguishes between parallel and cross cousins. Parallel cousins are terminologically classified with ego's own brothers and sisters. Cross cousins are distinguished from parallel cousins and called by a term that we would probably translate as *cousin.* To understand the logic behind calling parallel cousins *brother* and *sister* and cross cousins *cousin,* we have to go back to the terms used for ego's parents' siblings. Ego's father's brother and mother's sister are called *father* and *mother,* respectively. Thus, it is logical to call their children *brother* and *sister* (what do you call the children of the people you call mother and father?). Ego calls his father's sister *aunt* and his mother's brother *uncle,* so it is logical to call their children (ego's cross cousins) by a term we would translate as *cousin.*

Omaha   Omaha kinship terminology is difficult for English speakers to understand (see Figure 8.7). The terms used in the first ascending generation are identical to the Iroquois system. Also, as in the Iroquois system, parallel cousins are called *brother* and *sister.* The only difference between Iroquois and Omaha is how cross cousins are treated. Omaha terminology has no equivalent to the English term *cousin.* In addition, in Omaha terminology a distinction is made between cross cousins on the mother's side (the children of

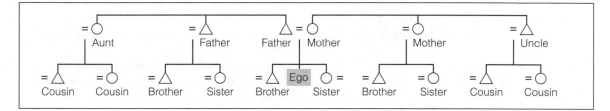

Figure 8.6 Iroquois Kinship Terminology

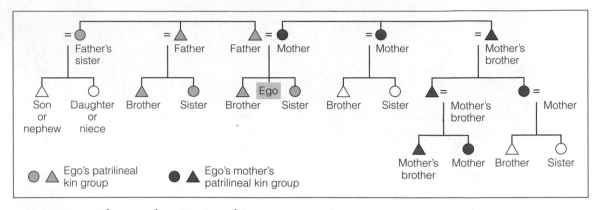

Figure 8.7 Omaha Kinship Terminology

mother's brother) and cross cousins on the father's side (the children of father's sister). Mother's brothers' daughters are called *mother*, and mother's brothers' sons are called *mother's brother* (or *uncle*). Thus, ego's maternal cross cousins are grouped with individuals in ego's parents' generation. The situation appears even more confused for ego's paternal cross cousins, since the term used depends on ego's sex. If ego is a male, he calls his father's sisters' children *niece* and *nephew*. If ego is a female, she calls her father's sisters' children *son* and *daughter*.

Why are there two separate terms for father's sisters' children, depending on the sex of ego? This distinction is perfectly logical. Remember that kinship terms are reciprocal and that we have only indicated the terms used by ego. To understand why the sex of ego is important in this relationship, we must ask: What would father's sisters' children call ego? In Figure 8.7, you can see that ego is their mother's brother's child. Thus, if ego is female, they would call her *mother*, and she would reciprocate by calling them *son* or *daughter*. If ego is male, they would call him *uncle*, and therefore he would call them *niece* or *nephew*.

Crow Crow kinship terminology is said to be the mirror image or reverse of Omaha (see Figure 8.8). First ascending generation terms are the same as in the Omaha and Iroquois systems. As in the Omaha and Iroquois systems, parallel cousins are

called *brother* and *sister*. Once again the difference is in the terms used for cross cousins. In the Crow systems, father's sisters' children are called *father* and *father's sister* or *aunt*. Using the same logic discussed for the Omaha system, in the Crow system mother's brothers' children are called *son* or *daughter* if ego is male and *niece* or *nephew* if ego is female.

Determinants of Kinship Terminology

In previous chapters we have emphasized that cultures are integrated: One aspect "fits" with others and sometimes makes sense only when understood in context. Kin terminology systems constitute a prime example of this integration.

The five terminologies just described can be separated into two types. Among the peoples who use the Eskimo or Hawaiian system, the distinction between mother's and father's kin is not recognized. Among the many cultures that use the Iroquois, Crow, or Omaha system, the logical principle of distinguishing relatives according to family side is relevant. Why does the side of the family matter in some terminological systems but not in others?

The side of the family matters in some terminologies because some people trace their descent through only one of their parents. The side of the family makes no difference in other systems because these populations trace their kin connec-

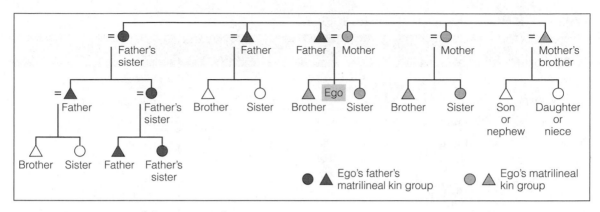

Figure 8.8 Crow Kinship Terminology

tions equally through both parents. The prevalent rule of descent and the relationships between kin are the most important "other aspects" of a people's cultural system that influence the way they culturally classify their relatives. In general, the way a people trace their descent affects the relationships between kin, which affects how relatives are placed into cultural categories, which affects the terms used to refer to various kin. However, the correlations between types of kinship terminologies and forms of descent are far from perfect.

Because the Eskimo classification is most familiar, we begin with it. If we compare it with the other terminologies, it differs in two main ways: (1) It makes no distinctions between ego's father's and mother's relatives, and (2) no other relatives of any kind are lumped together with nuclear family relatives. Assume that these two features reflect people's ideas about how various kin are related. We might conclude that people think (1) that both sides of the family are of equal importance to an individual (or, rather, there is no systematic pattern of importance through one side over the other), and (2) that nuclear family relatives are somehow special and thought of differently from other kinds of relatives. In the case of the contemporary United States, we happen to be right. Our surnames are inherited mainly through males, but other than this, we are no more likely to have special relationships with

our kin through our fathers than through our mothers. And, generally, the members of our nuclear families are special: We do not expect to inherit much, if anything, from other relatives; we usually do not live in extended households; we do not have any ancestors to worship as a large kin group; kin groups larger than the nuclear family usually do not own property in common; and so on. The hypothesis that the prevalent forms of descent, groupings, and relationships are reflected in kin terminology seems to account nicely for why the Eskimo system developed among ourselves.

More generally, we ought to expect the Eskimo classification of relatives to be associated with cognatic or bilateral kinship. And usually it is: About 80 percent of all societies that use the Eskimo terminological system have either bilateral or cognatic kinship. This is because neither side of any given ego's family is consistently emphasized, nor does ego consistently join the kin group of her or his mother or father. Ego, therefore, does not think of his or her mother's or father's relatives as being any different. The absence of a special relation with kin through either parent is reflected in the terminological system.

What about the Hawaiian system? As in the Eskimo system, family side is irrelevant. Logically, it ought, then, to be associated consistently with cognatic or bilateral kinship. Ego should have important relations with the siblings of his

CONCEPT REVIEW Kinship Terminologies

TERMINOLOGY	PARALLEL COUSIN TERMS	CROSS COUSIN TERMS	ASSOCIATED FORM OF DESCENT
Eskimo	cousin	cousin	bilateral or cognatic 80%
Hawaiian	brother or sister	brother or sister	bilateral or cognatic 60%
Iroquois	brother or sister	cousin	unilineal 80%
Omaha	brother or sister	mother or mother's brother niece/nephew or Son/daughter	patrilineal 90%
Crow	brother or sister	father or father's sister niece/nephew or son/daughter	matrilineal 70%

or her parents and with their children. Despite this logic, the Hawaiian terminology is not as consistently associated with cognatic or bilateral kinship as is the Eskimo terminology; in fact, about 40 percent of societies that use the Hawaiian classification are patrilineal or matrilineal.

And the Iroquois system? Ego's father and father's brother are assigned a single term, which is different from mother's brother. Mother and mother's sister are given the same term, which is not the same term ego uses for father's sister. Thus, ego distinguishes between maternal and paternal aunts and uncles in the first ascending generation. The fact that the side of the family matters in this generation seems to imply unilineal descent. And in fact the Iroquois system usually is found among peoples who trace their descent unilineally: Around 80 percent of all Iroquois terminologies occur in unilineal descent forms.

The Omaha system also distinguishes between sides of the family, like the Iroquois system. In fact, it carries the distinctions between the mother's and father's side "down" into ego's own generation. If you look back to Figure 8.7, you will see that the Omaha system differs from the Iroquois system by its splitting of cross cousins according to whether they are related to ego through ego's mother or father. Mother, mother's sister, and mother's brother's daughter are lumped together, although they are members of different generations. Mother's brother and

mother's brother's son likewise are lumped together under a single term.

What can explain this way of classifying relatives? The fact that these relatives are all related to ego through ego's mother must mean something; and the fact that they are classified together and distinguished only by their gender must be significant. Indeed, these features are clues to the logic behind the Omaha terminology. It is found among peoples with patrilineal kin groups.

How does patrilineal descent make sense of the Omaha system? In Figure 8.7 all relatives in the diagram who belong to ego's own patrilineal group are colored in. Notice that the cousins in ego's group are called *brother* and *sister*, to reflect the fact that they are in ego's own lineage. We have used a different color for those relatives who are members of ego's mother's patrilineal group. Notice that all the members of this latter group are assigned only two terms—one for the male members of the group and one for the female members of the group. Their common social characteristic as members of ego's mother's kin group overrides the biological fact that they are members of three generations. The Omaha system makes perfect sense, provided it is associated with patrilineal descent forms. And, indeed, more than 90 percent of all cultures that use the Omaha terminological system are patrilineal.

Because the Crow system is the mirror image of the Omaha system, we can make sense of it by showing how it reflects kinship relationships among matrilineal peoples. Go back to Figure 8.8 and look at the colors used for members of ego's own matrilineal descent group and for the matrilineal group of ego's father. You will see that all the male members of ego's father's group are called by the same term, as are all the female members of the same group. The underlying logic of the Crow terms is apparent, given matrilineal descent: Ego lumps together relatives who belong to the same descent group as his or her father. More than 70 percent of all people who use the Crow terms are also matrilineal.

The Hawaiian, Iroquois, Omaha, and Crow terminological systems make sense once we understand that they reflect the prevalent relationships and groupings of kin produced by various ways of tracing kinship connections.

SUMMARY

1. Relationships and groups based on kinship are an especially important component of the social organization of preindustrial peoples. Although kinship is based on biological relatedness, societies vary in their kinship systems.

2. One way cultures vary is in how people trace their relationships back to previous generations— in how they trace their descent. The most common forms of descent are patrilineal, matrilineal, and cognatic. All three kinds of descent principles place people in kinship groups and assign roles to them. In preindustrial cultures, groupings established on the basis of kinship usually are more important than in industrialized nations.

3. Matrilineal and patrilineal descent are both unilineal forms of descent, meaning that a person traces his or her descent through either females or males, but not through both sexes. Unilineal descent groups may be formed using the matrilineal or patrilineal principle, yielding kin groups composed of people related through females and males, respectively. The main kinds of descent groups are extended families, lineages, and clans. All may be based on either the matrilineal or patrilineal principle.

4. In cognatic descent, people trace their ancestry through both males and females, depending on choice and circumstance. Kin groups whose members have use rights to common property or resources and who cooperate socially, economically, politically, and ritually are found in many parts of the world.

5. Peoples who trace their kinship relationships bilaterally have no true kin groups larger than extended families, because the kindreds of different people overlap so much. In most industrialized nations, kinship is bilateral, and large numbers of an individual's relatives are likely to congregate only on certain occasions such as weddings, funerals, and family reunions.

6. One important influence on the kinship systems of a culture is its economy. Cognatic descent and bilateral kinship are common among foragers, who find it beneficial to maximize social contacts and access to diverse territories. Nomadic pastoralists usually are patrilineal, which is probably related to the tendency for males to own and manage herds. Patrilineal descent also is likely to be found among peoples who are heavily engaged in warfare with close neighbors. Matrilineality is most likely to occur among populations who are horticultural. These general associations have been supported by cross-cultural studies, but so many forces influence descent forms that no single explanation suffices to account for their occurrence.

7. People group their relatives into labeled categories by recognizing some differences between relatives and ignoring others. Five systems of kin terminology are: Eskimo, Hawaiian, Iroquois, Omaha, and Crow.

KEY TERMS

kin group	cognatic descent group
form of descent	bilateral
unilineal descent	kindred
patrilineal descent	kin terms
matrilineal descent	kinship terminology
descent groups	Eskimo
unilineal descent group	Hawaiian
lineage	Iroquois
clan	Omaha
cognatic descent	Crow

SUGGESTED READINGS

There are a number of excellent texts and collections of readings on kinship, descent groups, and the classification of relatives. The following is a list of such books.

Collier, Jane F., and J. Yanagisako, eds. *Gender and Kinship: Essays Toward a Unified Analysis.* Stanford, CA: Stanford University Press, 1987.

Collection of recent articles focusing on relationships between the sexes and kinship.

Fox, Robin. *Kinship and Marriage: An Anthropological Perspective.* New York: Cambridge University Press, 1984.

Excellent comparative introduction to marriage forms, kinship systems, and their causes and consequences.

Keesing, Roger M. *Kin Groups and Social Structure.* New York: Holt, Rinehart and Winston, 1971.

An introduction to the theory of kinship, but can be difficult reading for undergraduate students.

Pasternak, Burton. *Introduction to Kinship and Social Organization.* Englewood Cliffs, NJ: Prentice-Hall, 1976.

A short, introductory text with a cross-cultural orientation.

Schneider, David M. *American Kinship: A Cultural Account.* 2nd ed. Chicago: University of Chicago Press, 1980.

A symbolic account of American kinship written by a leading idealist.

Schneider, David M., and Kathleen Gough, eds. *Matrilineal Kinship.* Berkeley: University of California Press, 1961.

Contains a description of nine matrilineal systems and an analysis of some dimensions of variation in matrilineal societies. Introductory essay by Schneider is a good overview.

van den Berghe, Pierre L. *Human Family Systems: An Evolutionary View.* Rev. ed. Prospect Heights, IL: Waveland, 1990.

Analyzes marriage, family, and kinship systems from an evolutionary outlook. Author believes families are vehicles for increasing biological fitness.

The following classic ethnographies include excellent descriptions of specific kinship systems.

Eggan, Fred. *Social Organization of the Western Pueblos.* Chicago: University of Chicago Press, 1950.

The author describes and compares the social organization of the Hopi, Hano, Zuni, Acoma, and Laguna pueblos.

Evans-Pritchard, E. E. *The Nuer.* Oxford: Clarendon, 1940.

An ethnography of an African society, long considered one of the classic studies of social organization.

Firth, Raymond. *We, the Tikopia.* Boston: Beacon Press, 1936.

An ethnographic study of domestic life, kin relationships, descent groups, and marriage on a tiny Polynesian island.

chapter 9

GENDER

Contents

A long with kinship and age, gender is a universal basis for organizing group activities and allocating roles to individuals. Everywhere, your identity as a male or female matters: It makes a difference in who you are, what you have, how you interact, and what you can become. But anthropologists have found that in different cultures, gender matters to different degrees and in different ways. These cultural variations and the factors that affect them are the subjects of this chapter.

The field of gender studies is so vast that we must focus our coverage on only four of the main issues to which anthropologists have made important contributions: (1) the cultural construction of gender, (2) multiple (as opposed to "dual") genders, (3) the sexual division of labor, and (4) gender stratification. Where relevant, we suggest specific ways to use anthropological findings and perspectives for understanding gender in contemporary societies.

In any society, gender is a key feature of a person's *social identity:* How other people perceive you, feel about you, and relate to you is influenced by the gender to which they assign you and by how your culture defines gender differences. Less obviously, an individual's *self-identity* is affected by cultural beliefs and ideas: Your conception of yourself depends partly on how your culture distinguishes masculinity and femininity, attaches roles to one or the other sex, and uses symbols (such as dress, behavior, speech style, and sexual preferences and practices) to help define differences between females and males.

The importance of a person's self-identity as a member of a particular sex is most apparent in social relationships. Certainly, you are aware of how important your sexual identity is when you interact with someone of the opposite sex. But even in same-sex interactions, your social behavior is affected by your culture's norms, categories, world views, symbols, and other ideas and beliefs that influence your group's conceptions about gender. Cultural conceptions of "masculinity" and "femininity" matter just as much in same-sex as in opposite-sex interactions.

Finally, just as sexual identity affects interactions between individuals, so do beliefs about gender affect behavior in a variety of social settings and contexts: in the workplace, home, school, church, political arenas, to name a few. Our culture's ideas about males and females—and about masculinity and femininity—permeate most of our personal relationships and our society's institutions, whether or not we are consciously aware of it.

Cultural Construction of Gender

Ideas about gender itself and differences between the sexes vary from people to people. Societies and other social groups differ in how much importance they attach to whether a person is female or male and in what specific behaviors they expect from females and males. To emphasize such cultural variations, anthropologists make a conceptual distinction between *sex* and *gender.*

An individual's sex is determined by her or his biological inheritance—your genitals, associated hormonal frequencies, and secondary sexual characteristics (breasts, body size and musculature, and the like) are greatly affected by your sex chromosomes and other aspects of your genetic makeup.

In contrast, gender is culturally defined, not strictly biologically determined. How males and females perceive and define themselves and each other, what it means to be a woman or a man, what roles are seen as appropriate for men and women—these and many other dimensions of femaleness and maleness are learned during socialization rather than fixed at birth. They are culturally variable, not universal to the human species or constant across all cultures. Anthropologists use the phrase **cultural construction of gender** to emphasize that different cultures have distinctive ideas about males and females and use these ideas to define manhood/masculinity and womanhood/femininity.

The notion that gender is culturally constructed is too easily and too often misunderstood. Some scholars (especially biologists) mistakenly believe that anthropologists claim that genetic (physical) differences between the sexes do not matter because differences in male and female behaviors are determined by culture, not genes.

Some anthropologists do claim this, of course. But most accept that biological differences between females and males "matter"—that is, are relevant for both ideas and behaviors—in all cultures. However, because of our comparative perspective, we also are aware that diverse human groups have used these differences in a multitude of ways. In symbols, diverse groups have attached meanings to female-male differences that go beyond the biological/anatomical distinctions. In cultural classifications, male-female differences are minimized in some cultures, maximized in others. In values, "patriarchy" crudely describes some groups, "sexual equality" others. In behavioral patterns, some groups fairly rigidly differentiate between female and male activities and roles, others allow both sexes to participate in similar kinds of activities according to individual preferences and circumstances. Anthropologists are most fascinated by such variations between human communities. But this fascination does not imply that we do not recognize similarities or deny biological realities.

One implication of the cultural construction of gender is that no single culture's constructions are entirely based on the biological differences between the sexes. In other words, there are no cultures that are in a "state of nature" with respect to their conceptions of gender. We cannot find a people whose women or men act exactly as their genes dictate, or whose conceptions of femininity or masculinity are based entirely on biological factors. This fact makes it very difficult to determine the impact of biological (sexual) differences on the behaviors of females or males, for everywhere cultural (gender) constructions obscure and complicate the impacts of genes. (Notice, though, that this does not mean that genetic differences are not important, but only that their effects are hard to determine.)

The Hua of Papua New Guinea

One people whose cultural construction of gender differs markedly from that familiar to most of our readers is the Hua, who live in the interior mountains of Papua New Guinea. Studied by Anna Meigs in the 1970s, the Hua are a patrilineal, horticultural people who live in villages of around 100 to 300 people. As we shall see, Hua culture constructs gender on the basis of female-male differences that are not recognized by people outside of Papua New Guinea. And because of this construction, Hua believe that later in life each gender can become like the other in certain respects.

Each Hua village contains one or more large men's houses, occupied by initiated people who belong to the patrilineages of the village. Initiated people include mainly adult men, but also some older women who have become "like men" (as discussed later). Uninitiated people—including young women, girls, and boys who have not yet been through the male initiation ceremonies—live in separate houses.

In Hua culture, gender is constructed in the following way. Hua believe that bodies contain a life-giving substance (like a vital essence) that they call *nu*. *Nu* is thought of as a real, physical substance—not a mystical or magical thing—that can be transferred from one person to another and gained and lost in various ways. Female bodies contain an excess of *nu*, which in Hua thought makes women grow faster and age more slowly than men but also makes them unattractively moist. On the other hand, men naturally contain a smaller amount of *nu,* so they have difficulty with growth and maintenance of vitality later in life, but they are attractively dry and hard. Hua explain many of the differences between men and women by the amount of *nu:* Men are stronger and fiercer because they are dry, for example.

Nu takes several forms. It is both gaseous (breath) and liquid (blood, sweat, semen, female sexual secretions). A transfer of *nu* between individuals may be either harmful or helpful, depending on the nature of the relationship between the giver and the recipient. Transfer of *nu* may occur during eating, sexual intercourse, and other kinds of direct and indirect contact. For example, a woman transfers her *nu* to people when she serves food to them. *Nu* from her bodily secretions and under her fingernails adheres to the food and gets ingested by her children or her husband. A woman also transfers *nu* to her husband when she has intercourse with him. But the giving of feminine *nu* to a man in the act of intercourse is harmful to the man because it pollutes and debilitates him. Intercourse is also damaging to a man because he contributes his scarce *nu* (in the form of breath and semen) to a woman during sex, so she gains strength and vitality at his expense.

The amount of *nu* one has can be regulated by one's activities and by the kinds of food one eats. Various events in people's lives require regulation of the amount of *nu* they should have. Women need extra *nu* during pregnancy, so they eat lots of foods that are considered rich in *nu*. (Broadly speaking, these are fast-growing foods with high moisture content.) During menstruation women have too much *nu*, so they avoid the same kinds of food. For their part, men do not have enough *nu* for full growth and maturation, so during certain periods of boyhood they are encouraged to eat foods with lots of *nu*. At other times, when they are undergoing the initiation ceremonies that make them into strong men able to fight to defend the village, they are supposed to rigorously avoid *nu*-rich foods because such foods will weaken and pollute them. In fact, during initiation ceremonies there are strict taboos not only on the eating of these foods but also on eating foods from gardens tended by women or foods prepared by women. These taboos exist to keep the boys free of the pollution caused by contact with women.

Nu is what makes women polluting to males, and the greater the difference in *nu* between a woman and a man, the more dangerous that woman is to the man. But both men and women can and do lose or gain *nu*, depending on their activities, their diet, and how old they are. After decades of engaging in sexual intercourse with

and eating foods touched by their wives and other women, middle-aged and elderly men have picked up lots of *nu*. They become invulnerable to further contamination by contact with females and therefore may eat *nu*-rich foods and participate in sexual intercourse with less anxiety than younger men. Gaining *nu* over the years makes them become "like women."

Women lose *nu* whenever they menstruate, handle and prepare food, and have babies. Their *nu* is transferred to others by these activities and events. Over their life course women thus are drained of *nu*, and this draining means that they become less and less dangerous to males as they grow older. Women who have given birth to more than two children are considered to have lost enough *nu* so that they are no longer polluting. They therefore have become "like men," Hua say.

In these ways Hua culture constructs gender categories on the basis of beliefs about quantity of *nu* as influenced by a person's stage in the life cycle. Women normally possess more *nu*. In fact, women at the height of their procreative years—when they are menstruating, sexually active, giving birth, and nursing infants—generally need and have the most *nu* of all. Men most of the time have much less *nu*. Most women lose *nu* as they age, so become more "like men," whereas older men pick up *nu* from a lifetime of relations with women, so become more "like women."

Constructing gender classifications on the basis of the quantity of *nu* allows for more than two gender categories. Indeed, Hua culture recognizes gender distinctions based on a person's genitals (in which case one is either male or female) and distinctions based on the quantity of *nu*. The latter criterion gives rise to two additional nondiscrete (more/less) gender categories that the Hua call *figapa* and *kakora*. Although the *figapa/kakora* distinction is relevant only in certain ritual contexts, it is significant that people who are genitally male or female can be classified with the opposite gender for certain purposes.

Figapa, which Anna Meigs translates as "uninitiated person," are people whose bodies contain lots of substances associated with femininity (e.g., menstrual blood, vaginal secretions, fluids associated with childbirth). *Figapa* include the following kinds of people:

• children of both sexes because they have recently been in intimate contact with a woman, their mother;
• women in their child-bearing years because they are the essence of femininity and their bodies contain maximum amounts of feminine substances;
• postmenopausal women who have not had at least three children because their bodies are not sufficiently drained of feminine substances; and
• elderly men because female *nu* has been transmitted to them by their lifetime of activities that exposed them to contact with women.

These people—whether or not their genitals are female—are all "like women" because their bodies contain lots of substances symbolically considered feminine.

Kakora, translated by Meigs as "initiated person," consists of

• males in their early teens through the prime years who have been initiated (except elderly men) because during the initiation procedures they have rigorously avoided female foods and contact with women and so have minimal quantities of *nu;* and
• postmenopausal women with more than two children because three or more childbirths have drained them of most feminine substances, so they are no longer a source of danger to males.

People who are *kakora* are eligible to live in the men's house and to obtain the secret "male" knowledge gained during initiation ceremonies. As Meigs (1990, 109) puts it, the feminine substances in such older women's bodies have been "massively cleaned out three or more times," and without these substances culturally associated with femininity they are "like men." Therefore, they may live in the men's house.

This example is presented in such detail because the Hua so clearly illustrate the cultural construction of gender. The objective physical distinctions between the sexes—genitals, beards, breasts, and so on—are differences that are recognized and relevant for behavior in all known cultures. But, as the Hua show, cultures use the raw material (to speak metaphorically) of these differences to construct varying beliefs about the ways in which females and males differ. (Thus, Hua believe that men and women differ not only in the usual physical ways but also in the quantity of *nu* each has.) These beliefs in turn affect the attitudes each sex holds about the other and the behavior each sex adopts toward the other. (Thus, Hua men in some contexts and at some ages are fearful about the possibility of feminine pollution and therefore try to minimize their contact with women, their intake of food prepared by women, and their sexual relations with women.)

The more different some culture's beliefs are from one's own, the more obvious it is that those beliefs are a cultural construct rather than a biological imperative. Therefore, because Hua beliefs pertaining to male-female relationships seem exotic to most Westerners, the fact that gender is culturally constructed among these people is readily apparent. However, all people's ideas about gender are culturally constructed. To stimulate thought, we very briefly present some ideas on the construction of gender in Euro-American culture.

Speaking generally, many Americans see females as caring of others, emotional, socially skilled, physically fragile, family oriented, and patient. Males are taken to be more selfish, rational, tolerant of physical discomfort ("tough"), coordinated, and individualistic.

Now consider the possible effects of these cultural conceptions on the uneven distribution of occupational roles between women and men in the modern American economy. The predominant pattern is for members of each sex to move into jobs for which they are held to be best suited, given American cultural conceptions of gender. This happens for at least two reasons. First, individual men and women more often seek those jobs that they find appropriate for their sex or believe they have the best chance of getting or succeeding in; people apply for certain kinds of jobs according to their preferences, based in part on their beliefs about "sex roles." Second, employers tend to hire people according to their own cultural conceptions of which sex is likely to do well in a particular job; the employment market itself allocates men and women into certain kinds of jobs.

This is changing rapidly today, but many jobs remain disproportionately female or male. Thus, women predominate in jobs that involve nurturing (e.g., nursing, day care, teaching elementary students, pediatric medicine), routine interactions with the public (e.g., receptionists, store clerks, restaurant waiters), repetitive and patient use of fine motor skills (word processing, sewing and stitching), and cleaning and housekeeping. A few of the jobs in which men predominate are those involving outdoor activity (equipment operation, driving, carpentry and construction), high-level decision making (management, administration), and knowledge of mathematical principles (science, engineering, computer programming). How much of the occupational difference between the sexes results from the American cultural construction of gender, which defines females as having certain inherent characteristics, males as having a contrasting set?

To say that gender is culturally constructed is not equivalent to saying that physical differences between males and females are irrelevant. In fact, such differences are everywhere relevant in many ways, including the allocation of work activities. But, as discussed in the next section, biological differences between the sexes are relevant in diverse ways and to varying degrees in the world's cultures.

GENDER CROSSING and MULTIPLE GENDER IDENTITIES

The Hua are only one of hundreds of examples that illustrate how a particular culture may construct gender in a way that is unfamiliar (and even may seem strange) to other peoples. Along with many other peoples in Papua New Guinea and elsewhere, the Hua show how biological differences between the sexes matter in social life in all cultures, but that they matter in diverse and sometimes unexpected ways.

Anthropologists have learned that there are a great many peoples in the world who tolerate and even institutionalize gender diversity *within* their own communities and societies. Biologically male or female individuals who, for one reason or another, wish to adopt aspects of the role or behavior of the other sex are allowed to do so, with little or no social stigma or formal punishment. A boy who shows that he does not wish to participate in manly behaviors is not forced to conform or ostracized, but is allowed to act like a woman in certain respects or contexts. Conversely, a girl who shows an affinity for male activities is allowed to participate in manly roles when she becomes an adult. In short, people can adopt the behaviors and roles typical of the other sex, in features such as clothing, work, and sexual preference, without experiencing social or legal punishment from other members of their communities.

These practices or customs often are called **gender crossing,** for obvious reasons. It is important to realize that, in many cultures, gender crossing is or was *institutionalized.* It is expected that a certain number of people are born who will, when they mature into adulthood, become like the other sex in some ways. Rather than stigmatizing such persons or trying to force them to uphold the group's standards of femininity or masculinity, they are accommodated and integrated into social life.

Most North Americans will interpret "institutionalized gender crossing" as meaning that some cultures tolerate or accommodate lesbians, gays, and bisexuals. This interpretation is generally correct, but in fact there is much more to gender crossing than sexual orientation, as we shall see. First, let's consider briefly how anthropological thinking about gender crossing has changed recently.

Until the 1970s or 1980s most anthropologists viewed gender crossing in the following way. In any society, a few individuals are born who do not fit into the existing social roles defined as "male" or "female." There will always be some boys who do not want to go to war, hunt, or compete in politics, but prefer to play with girls, do domestic work, tan skins, or otherwise act in ways culturally considered feminine. Likewise, some girls display behavior culturally associated with masculinity, preferring to play boy games, use weapons, dress like males, or whatever. In many human societies, such persons eventually learned to outwardly conform with the normal sex roles, or they were considered deviant and punished or stigmatized throughout their lives. In some societies, though, a legitimate and institutionalized role existed that allowed them to satisfy their natural inclinations while serving the group in various ways. Institutionalized gender crossing thus was interpreted as a cultural mechanism that provides a legitimate outlet for people who otherwise might be unhappy or cause problems in the social life of the community. Physically weak men could serve the group in ways other than warfare or hunting, for example, and women with manly traits contributed in other ways.

Certainly, this interpretation presents a somewhat favorable image of cultures that allow gender crossing. Some human groups do not insist on rigid conformity to their sexual stereotype, but allow diversity, in contrast to chauvinistic cultures like the anthropologists' own. Unlike "us," "they" normalize individual variation in aspects such as dress style, sexual orientation, work activities, mannerisms, and the like, rather than insisting on uniformity. And unlike many of "us"—who view men who act like women and women who act like men as morally degenerate, dangerous to society, or genetically abnormal—"they" did not despise or ostracize such individuals, but provided them with legitimate roles in the community's social life. The usual lessons were: (1) "We" ought to be more like "them" by tolerating variation and accepting people as individuals whom we value and who can contribute in various ways, and (2) not all peoples in the world require conformity to their society's normal sex roles, so

there is no reason to think that our "intolerance" is universal and, therefore, inevitable. These two lessons are worth learning or, at least, pondering.

Still, some anthropologists today feel that this view disparages gender-crossed individuals, because it assumes that they cannot live up to the expectations of their "real sex," so they are allowed to "change their sex." Further, it assumes that, in all cultures, people classify individuals as belonging to one of only two genders (female and male), so that a woman who doesn't want to be completely a woman must become partly like a man, and vice-versa. In fact, the term "gender crossing" itself implies that there are only two alternative genders.

In contrast, some contemporary anthropologists argue that many societies have more than two gender identities. Rather than dual genders, they say, such cultures are culturally constructing **multiple gender identities.** They define a third or even a fourth gender of "man-woman" or "woman-man" (or "not woman–not man," or "half man–half woman," as some indigenous terms often translate). These third or fourth gender identities go well beyond Euro-American definitions of homoeroticism, transvestism, transsexualism, or other concepts familiar in the Western cultural tradition.

Multiple gender identities are well documented for many Native American peoples. In his 1998 book *Changing Ones,* Will Roscoe reports that more than 150 Native American cultures had institutionalized multiple gender identities for either males, females, or both sexes. Males adopted the dress, tasks, family roles, or other aspects of womanhood. Females took on activities usually associated with manhood, such as warfare or hunting. When they did so, they did not become the opposite sex, but took on alternative third or fourth gender identities. Far from being ridiculed, ostracized, despised, or otherwise socially stigmatized, such individuals in most cases were treated with respect and valued for their contributions to their families or group.

Among the Navajo of the Southwest, for example, third gender persons generally were welcomed by their families and local groups. An anthropologist in the 1930s quoted a Navajo elder:

> If there were no *nadle* [men-women], the country would change. They are responsible for all the wealth in the country. If there were no more left, the horses, sheep, and Navaho would all go. They are leaders just like President Roosevelt. (Quoted in Roscoe 1998, 43)

The elder surely exaggerated, but his statement shows the Navajo's recognition of the contributions of men-women. They often managed their family's property, supervised work, and became medicine men or took on other ritual responsibilities.

People who were biologically female could adopt alternative roles as well, which also were valued in many Indian communities. A girl who came to be known as Woman Chief was adopted by a Crow family during the nineteenth century. Like boys, she hunted deer and bighorn sheep while growing up. When the man who raised her was killed, she took responsibility for the family, acting as both father and mother. Later in life, she helped save her camp from an attack by the Blackfoot and went on horse raiding parties. Eventually Woman Chief took four wives and participated in council deliberations in her band, a role usually reserved for men.

Most Native tribes had a special word for such roles in their language, but gender identities varied so much from people to people that applying a single English word is problematic. To refer to males assuming an alternative gender, most anthropologists use the term *berdache*, taken from a term used by early French explorers of the Southeast. Some Natives and scholars today find this term inaccurate and offensive because the original Arabic term meant "male prostitute." But the original meaning of *berdache* is not popularly known, so we continue to use it here, along with *man-woman, woman-man,* or *third or fourth gender identity,* depending on context.

As you might expect, most early Anglo observers of Native American men-women or women-men misunderstood these individuals and their roles in society. They overemphasized the sexual orientation of the person, whereas in fact their sexual behavior varied from tribe to tribe and from individual to individual within the same tribe. In most cases, even though *berdache* were homosexual, sexual behavior usually was not the aspect of the role that was considered the most important element by the people themselves. Further, male *berdache* rarely engaged in homosexual activity with *one another.* Where homosexuality was an aspect of the role, the men with whom relations occurred were not considered homosexuals at all.

Another common feature wrongly believed to define the role is transvestism, which, although common, was not found in all cultures. Sometimes men-women dressed like men, sometimes like women, and sometimes their choice of clothing depended on the situation. Among the Navajo, some *nadleehi* (men-women) wore women's clothing, others did not or only sometimes did so. Woman Chief, the adopted Crow woman, did not wear men's clothes, although she adopted many other aspects of the male role.

A truly complete portrayal of third and fourth genders defines the roles as multidimensional, thus recognizing that practices varied not only from tribe to tribe, but from individual to individual within the same tribe. Nonetheless, certain patterns are apparent. Serena Nanda identifies several features of gender variants that were widespread (but not universal) among Native American peoples. Four of the main characteristics are:

1. Cross-gender occupation or work activities— a preference for the work of the opposite sex and/or for work set aside for their third or fourth gender identity.

2. Transvestism—in most cultures third and fourth gender individuals were distinguished from men and women in their dress style. Most commonly, they cross-dressed, but sometimes they wore a combination of female and male garments.

3. Associations with spiritual power or a spiritual sanction—possession of special powers derived from spiritual forces, usually combined with a personal experience interpreted by the group as a calling.

4. Same-sex relations—the formation of sexual and emotional bonds with members of the same sex, who were not themselves men-women or women-men.

These four widespread characteristics of third and fourth gender identities provide a convenient way to organize our discussion, but the variability of the role must always be kept in mind. No single dimension is "typical."

Cross-Gender Occupation or Work Roles

Adopting the work roles of the opposite sex was a widespread feature of men-women or women-men. This aspect often received special attention in various Native communities. Probably more than any other single dimension, occupation/work best defines the role. A famous Navajo *nadleehi* who died in the 1930s was unusually skilled in weaving blankets, a typically female task. In many tribes, individuals who performed the tasks of the opposite sex often excelled at the work, in the opinions of their communities. Sioux *berdache* (called *winkte*) dressed like women and lived in their own tipis at the edges of camps. The quill- and bead-works of a Sioux *winkte* were often highly valued because of their fine quality. Among the matrilineal, matrilocal Zuni of the American Southwest, a *lhamana* (man-woman) was looked upon favorably by the women of his family, for it meant he would stay with the household of his birth rather than leave upon marriage. Matilda Cox Stevenson, a nineteenth-century ethnographer, wrote that Zuni *lhamana* would do almost double the work of a woman, for they were not burdened by childbirth or the heaviest duties of child care. In spite of such examples, to say that all gender variants exhibited "sex role reversal" in work performance is simplistic, for the most famous Zuni man-woman was We'wha, who participated in both female and male tasks.

Commonly, a child who showed an inclination for the work of the opposite sex was considered by others to be suited for an alternative gender role. For example, girls who acted as though they wanted to go hunting or use weapons were seen as potential women-men. A Mohave adult told a 1930s ethnographer that "[adults] may insist on giving the child the toys and garments of its true sex, but the child will throw them away" (Roscoe, 1998, 139). A child could not control such behavior, in the Mohave view, for the kinds of dreams a child had affected whether the child would become a man, a woman, a man-woman, or a woman-man. Among the Zuni, as children grow up they experience several rites of passage that initiate them into various specialized ceremonial groups and also instruct them in the ceremonial and work duties appropriate for their sex. While a child, one Zuni man-woman underwent the first male initiation ceremony but not the second, making him an "unfinished male" (Roscoe 1991, 144), who could participate in some male activities but not others, such as warfare and hunting.

Transvestism

Transvestism was one of the most common ways in which alternative genders expressed their identity. Wearing the clothing of the opposite sex was especially common and culturally significant among the tribes of the Great Plains, including the Arapaho, Arikara, Blackfoot, Cheyenne, Crow, Gros Ventre, Hidatsa, Iowa, Kansa, Mandan, Omaha, Osage, Oto, Pawnee, Ponca, and speakers of the Siouxan language. After whites began settling the West, most regarded men-women (which many simplistically categorized as "sodomites") as disgusting or sinful. Because it was a visible manifestation of the *berdache* role, transvestism was especially abhorrent to Anglo government officials, missionaries, educators, and settlers. Due to formal punishments and white ridicule, this symbol of alternative gender identity had largely disappeared by the early twentieth century.

Associations with Spiritual Powers

Usually, communities perceived men-women and women-men as having some sort of unusual powers or abilities derived from spiritual sources.

Among the Cheyenne of the Great Plains, *berdache* were known by a term that translates as "halfman-halfwoman." They served as masters of ceremony for the important Scalp Dance that followed a successful raid by a war party. They also possessed powerful love medicines, so their services were sought after by young men and women who wanted to attract heterosexual partners. Lakota believed that *winkte* could predict future events and could bestow lucky names on children. Osh-Tisch (whose name translated as "Finds Them and Kills Them"), of the Crow tribe, had a vision as a youth and became a powerful medicine person. One Navajo man-woman memorized numerous curing chants and learned to construct dozens of the intricate sandpaintings used in curing rituals (see Chapter 12). He was widely credited with near-miraculous healing powers.

Same-Sex Relations

The sexual orientation of Native American *berdaches* varied from people to people (and even from person to person within a single tribe). Understandably, reliable information on the sexual orientation of third and fourth gendered persons is rare. Some seem to have refrained from sex altogether. But the most common pattern was for men-women to be sexually active with men and sometimes women, but not with other men-women. These relations (most Anglo-Americans or Canadians would culturally categorize them as "homosexual relations") in most cases were an expected aspect of the third or fourth gender role. Thus, a (genitally) male *berdache* would engage in sex with men of his group, without stigma or punishment for either party. The man would not be considered homosexual, for he had not had relations with another man, but with a man-woman. In some tribes, a man would take a man-woman as a second "wife"—again apparently without stigma.

Even less is known about the sexual practices of women-men, and often early observers just stated that they were women who avoided marriage, or refused to marry. It appears, though,

that they most commonly had relations with females. The complications of characterizing a person's sexual orientation are shown by a Mohave woman-man, who had three wives (sequentially). All three eventually left her, and later in life the woman-man became very active sexually with men.

After contact with Euro-Americans, multiple gender identities were suppressed in most regions where Native Americans still lived, especially after the confinement of so many Natives to reservations in the 1800s. The majority of whites—settlers, traders, government agents, missionaries, and others—found the existence of a *legitimate* role such as man-woman or woman-man abhorrent. Because most viewed the custom as sinful, as harmful to Indian character, or as an obstacle to Native assimilation into Anglo society, they often imposed legal or social punishments for third and fourth genders. For example, in the 1920s, large numbers of Indian children were taken away from their families and communities—by force when necessary—and placed in on- or off-reservation government-run boarding schools. In these Indian Schools (as they are known today), the explicit goal was to socialize and educate Indian children into Anglo culture. By separating Native children from their families and traditions, the theory was, they could be more quickly and thoroughly assimilated into white society. Of course, young people who showed signs of assuming alternative gender identities were punished.

Through such educational and legal mechanisms, multiple gender identities were suppressed. Even some tribes that had once accepted third and fourth genders came to reject such persons. For instance, in the 1940s, some Winnebago told an ethnographer that "the berdache was at one time a highly honored and respected person, but that the Winnebago had become ashamed of the custom because the white people thought it was amusing or evil" (quoted in Roscoe 1991, 201).

In North American society generally, popular ideas about gender-crossing and homosexuality changed dramatically in the late twentieth century. Polls done in 2000 show that most United States citizens favor giving spousal benefits such as medical care and life insurance to same-sex domestic partners. But the vast majority oppose same-sex marriage, which is not now legally recognized in any state. General Motors and other American automakers now provide spousal benefits such as health insurance for domestic partners of either sex, partly reflecting the modern realities of the labor market and partly reflecting changes in society's attitudes about sexual preference. Despite such changes in attitudes, most North Americans still regard cross-dressing, transsexuality, and homoeroticism as deviant behaviors. Most conservative religious people view them as sinful, and even some Protestant denominations generally considered fairly liberal do not allow ordination of gays and lesbians.

Cultures such as the Native American examples mentioned above show that attitudes of fear, hatred, and intolerance of transsexuals and homosexuals are not universal. Indeed, acceptance and even appreciation of alternative genders is fairly common among Native peoples. Perhaps the knowledge that there are lots of cultures in which alternative genders are accepted is relevant for our attitudes about diversity in sexual orientation and other gender-related issues in twenty-first-century societies. Knowledge of such cultures must, however, be balanced by noting that there are a great many other peoples whose attitudes towards homoeroticism are highly negative.

THE SEXUAL DIVISION of LABOR

The **sexual division of labor** refers to the patterned ways in which productive and other economic tasks are allocated to men and women. It implies, necessarily, that males and females share or pool some of the products of their work. Each sex has access to the products and/or services produced by the other, so that the tasks of males and females are, to some extent, complementary. Some kind of division of labor on the basis of sex

is found in all cultures, although the specific tasks performed by the two sexes vary.

In North America the sexual division of labor, and indeed the roles of males and females in general, is rapidly changing: Males are performing tasks and holding occupational roles that twenty or thirty years ago were associated with females, and vice versa. In many other societies, however, the social roles of females and males are more sharply divided and the sexual division of labor is more clearly defined.

Many ethnographic studies provide all the information needed to demolish one common ideal of this topic: that it is only natural for men to be the breadwinners and for women to be the caretakers of the family. Breadwinning—that is, producing the supply of food and other material needs and wants of domestic groups—is definitely not an activity of men exclusively, or even largely. As we shall see, in many societies men produce most of the good, but in others women's contribution to daily subsistence equals or exceeds that of men.

This finding contradicts the opinion of those who think that the widespread domination of men over women is rooted in the "fact" that men's labor is more important to physical survival and material well-being than women's labor. Those who hold this view argue that women are everywhere economically dependent on men, which in turn makes women everywhere subordinate to men. But where females are subordinate to males, it is not simply because the things men do are somehow more important to family and group survival than the things women do. (What could be more important to group survival than bearing children?) This ethnocentric idea probably comes from the way most modern industrial economies worked in the mid-twentieth century: By and large, men earned the money that allowed their families to purchase the goods they needed to survive. It is falsely concluded that the same economic dependence of wives on husbands characterized other peoples.

This is the anthropologist's usual warning about confusing the beliefs and practices of one's own culture with those of all humans. Most people's ideas about what is and is not "natural" for humans to think and do are products of a specific culture at a particular time. Unless we become educated about the cultural diversity of humanity, we consistently—and usually mistakenly—conclude that the ideas and practices of our own society are universal or even inherent in human nature.

So Man the Breadwinner and Woman the Homemaker do not accurately describe the sexual division of labor in other cultures. Humankind is too diverse for that. But despite cultural variation, there are some cross-cultural regularities and patterns in the sexual division of labor. What are these patterns, and how can they be explained?

Understanding Major Patterns

Table 9.1 summarizes a vast amount of comparative work on the sexual division of labor. It lists some specific tasks and whether they are more likely to be performed by females or males. Those tasks toward the left of the table are more likely to be performed by males; those to the right are more likely to be done by females. The nearer an activity is to the left, the more likely it is to be performed by males, and vice versa for females.

A few comments are needed to clarify Table 9.1. First, the table does not portray the sexual division of labor in any specific society. Rather, it represents a kind of composite or aggregate of information drawn from hundreds of societies in various parts of the world. For example, the tasks listed as "Predominantly Females" should be interpreted as those that are done by women in most societies, although in many specific societies (which are "exceptions") one or another of the tasks are performed mainly by men. Tasks listed as "Exclusively Males" are accomplished by men in all or almost all societies, with very few exceptions.

Also, Table 9.1 includes only those activities that produce some kind of material product. Left out of the table are other activities that are predominantly or exclusively male, such as holding political office and fighting wars. Also omitted are some activities, such as caring for infants, that are predominantly or exclusively women's work in all cultures. Of course, there is a sense in which all activities are "productive" (of social order or of children, for example), but here our discussion is limited to activities usually considered to be "economic tasks."

Two patterns are revealed by Table 9.1. First, the table shows that all human groups divide *some* kinds of labor by sex in similar ways. Some tasks are done mainly or nearly exclusively by one sex in most societies. For instance, hunting, land clearing, soil preparation, working with hard materials, and cutting wood are exclusively or predominantly men's work in just about all cultures. Gathering wild plants, processing plant foods, and cooking are mainly the work of females in most cultures. In short, although cultures certainly vary in the kinds of tasks allocated to women and men, there are widespread (although not universal) patterns; consistently, some tasks are likely to be done by men, others by women. The first thing to explain is: Why are some tasks done mostly by women, whereas others are done mainly or entirely by men?

Second, notice the tasks listed under the column labeled "Either or Both Sexes." These tasks are not sex-specific—that is, they are about equally likely to be performed by men or women, depending on the particular society. Members of either sex may do them, or both may work together on them. For example, whether men or women plant crops, milk animals, or work with skins or leather varies from people to people, with no clear pattern apparent. In sum, which sex performs these kinds of tasks is so culturally variable that we cannot generalize about who will do them; whether they are done by women, men, or both depends largely on local circumstances. The second thing to explain is: What determines the cultural variability in the sexual division of labor? Why are women more heavily involved in agriculture (planting, tending, and harvesting crops) in some societies than in others, for example?

Table 9.1 Patterns in the Sexual Division of Labor

	TASKS PERFORMED BY GENDER				
	EXCLUSIVELY MALES	PREDOMINANTLY MALES	EITHER OR BOTH SEXES	PREDOMINANTLY FEMALES	
Extracting food and other products	Hunting Trapping	Fishing	Gathering small land animals	Gathering shellfish, mollusks	Gathering wild plant foods
		Clearing land Preparing soil	Planting crops Tending crops Harvesting crops		
		Tending large animals	Milking animals	Tending small animals	
	Woodworking Mining Lumbering			Gathering fuel	Fetching water
Manufacturing, processing, and preparing goods for consumption	Butchering				Processing plant foods Cooking
	Boat building Working with stone, horn, bone, shell	House building Making rope, cordage, nets	Preparing skins Making leather products	Making clothing Matmaking	
				Loom weaving	
	Smelting ore Metalworking			Making pottery	

Source: Adapted from Murdock and Provost (1973).

This section focuses on hypotheses that deal with the first question. We put off discussion of the second question until the next section.

What can explain why some tasks are nearly always done by men, whereas others are performed by women in most cultures? Biological differences between the sexes provide one possible explanation. Perhaps tasks are assigned in such a way that the members of each sex do what they are physically able to do best.

This notion may sound like biological determinism. If stated carefully, though, it is not. Physical differences between men and women are only *relevant* in explaining the sexual division, not *determinative*. To say that biological differences alone account for ("determine") similarities would be outrageously wrong. The sexual division of labor *varies* cross-culturally, whereas the

biological differences between females and males are *similar* everywhere. You cannot explain something that varies by something that is the same everywhere.

To say that physical differences between the sexes are relevant is to say something like the following: Because of biological differences, men can perform certain kinds of tasks more efficiently than women, and vice versa, and these differences are reflected in the widespread cross-cultural similarities in the sexual division of labor.

Consider an example. Anthropologists used to say that there was at least one task that was everywhere done by men: hunting. Hunting seems to require certain biological capabilities—such as speed, strength, and endurance—that men have more of than women. Hunting also was thought to be incompatible with certain responsibilities universally borne by women for biological reason: pregnancy, lactation (breastfeeding), and child care. Pregnant women would have a hard time chasing game; lactating mothers would have to quit the hunt several times a day to nurse their infants; and the risk of injury to both mother and young child would be high. Because men could hunt more effectively than women, in foraging populations men hunted. In contrast, gathering required less strength and endurance. Since men had to spend so much of their time hunting, which women couldn't do as effectively, gathering became largely women's work.

These arguments are partly valid, but female and male biological differences do not make it physically mandatory that males are the hunters and females are the gatherers in foraging populations. For one thing, not all kinds of hunting, and not all tasks connected to hunting, require superior strength, speed, and endurance. For another, there are questions about whether males typically have more endurance than females. Finally, there is no necessary biological reason why a woman could not give up hunting only during her pregnancy and lactation and leave her older children in camp under the care of someone else.

And in fact, it is just not true that hunting is *universally* a male activity. When BaMbuti pygmies of the Zaire rain forest hunt animals with nets, the women help by driving game into the nets held by men. In another part of the world, Agnes Estioko-Griffin has reported on hunting by women among the Agta, a mountain tribe of the Philippines who live on the island of Luzon. Agta men do most of the hunting, but women often accompany them in teamwork efforts, and women frequently hunt together without the company of men. Interestingly, sometimes women take their infants with them on the hunt, carrying the children on their backs. There are some differences between the methods used and types of game hunted by women versus men. Still, cases such as the Agta and BaMbuti show that the "man the hunter" image is oversimplified.

But this does not make it entirely wrong. The great majority of cultures in which hunting is a significant means of acquiring food are foragers or horticulturalists. There is no question that in most of these cultures women do most of the gathering of wild plants or the planting, weeding, and harvesting of cultivated plants, whereas men hunt to provide meat. The male hunting/female gathering pattern is not quite universal, but it is common enough that many anthropologists believe that there must be some physical differences between men and women that are relevant to the division of labor.

The three female/male biological differences that most significantly affect the sexual division of labor are summarized in the Concept Review. They are: (1) the relative overall strength of the two sexes, (2) the possibility that regular heavy exercise depresses female fertility, and (3) the biological fact that only women give birth to and nurse infants and young children. The three factors interact, but we discuss each separately.

CONCEPT REVIEW Factors Affecting the Major Patterns in the Sexual Division of Labor

Physical Strength	Most men are stronger than most women, so work tasks requiring greater strength generally are performed by males
Fertility Maintenance	Heavy, prolonged physical exercise leads to hormonal changes that depress female fertility, so most strenuous tasks are done by males
Child Care Compatibility	Women are everywhere the bearers and primary caregivers for infants and young children, so they tend to perform those tasks that can be combined efficiently with child care

Relative Strength One biological difference is the average difference in strength between men and women, which allows men to perform tasks requiring great strength more efficiently. In Table 9.1, superior average male strength is *relevant*—again, no anthropologists claim it is all-important—in many tasks under the heading "Exclusively Males" and in some of the tasks labeled "Predominantly Males," such as clearing land and preparing soil. On the other hand, male strength has no obvious relation to other exclusively or predominantly male tasks, such as trapping, butchering, and working with fibers. Also, note that women often do tasks that require significant strength, such as gathering fuel and fetching water. So relative strength does influence patterns in the sexual division of labor, but other factors must also matter.

Fertility Maintenance Women have another physical characteristic that might explain why some activities are allocated to males. Modern female athletes—especially long-distance runners—often do not menstruate and ovulate monthly. Apparently, this is because of a low ratio of body fat and complex hormonal changes in women who engage in prolonged physical exercise. It has been suggested that productive activities that require comparable exertion—notably hunting—would depress a woman's fertility, and thus help to explain why most hunting is done by men. Possibly female reproduction would be so decreased by the strenuous exercise involved in activities such as hunting that the population might not be able to maintain its numbers over the course of many generations. However, it is difficult to know whether fertility reduction accounts for why women so rarely hunt or cut down trees. For instance, we do not know how much (or even if) the exertion involved in hunting would affect women's ability to bear children. Before we could know, we must study several cases of women hunting in the same way as men to measure hunting's effect on female fertility. No one has yet done so.

Compatibility with Child Care A third biologically based difference is that women are the bearers, nursers, and primary caretakers of infants and young children. This reproductive fact means that women are best suited to perform those tasks that can be combined with child care. Back in 1970, Judith Brown argued that such tasks have several characteristics:

- They are fairly routine and repetitive, so they do not require much concentration.
- They can be interrupted and resumed without significantly lowering their efficient performance.

United Nations

Many tasks commonly performed by women are compatible with bearing, nursing, and caring for infants and highly dependent children. This African woman can process grain and care for her child at the same time, for example.

- They do not place the children who accompany their mothers to the site of the task in potential danger.
- They do not require women and children to travel very far away from home.

The gathering of various products and the domestic work listed in Table 9.1 are highly compatible with child care. In addition, among horticultural peoples, garden tasks such as planting, weeding and tending crops, and harvesting usually are done by women; these activities, too, seem to be highly compatible with caring for children.

In sum, biological factors like strength, fertility maintenance, and child care requirements interact to affect the patterns of preindustrial societies shown on the far left and far right sides of Table 9.1. Notice, though, that even if all three factors in combination "explain" the widespread patterns in the sexual division of labor (which they do not), none of them can explain the *differences.* In fact, no biological difference between males and females alone can explain the cross-cultural diversity in the sexual division of labor. The biological differences between the sexes in strength, reproductive physiology, and ability to care for infants are constant in all human populations. But a condition that is constant in all groups cannot, by itself, account for things that vary between the groups. Constants cannot explain variability and diversity. We need other hypotheses to account for the cultural variability in the sexual division of labor.

Understanding Variability

We cannot discuss all the variability, so we focus on only one subject. Lots of comparative studies reveal a fairly consistent difference in the degree of women's versus men's involvement in certain agricultural tasks, specifically in those tasks labeled "Either or Both Sexes" in the middle column of Table 9.1. In most horticultural groups, much—and in some societies nearly all—of the everyday garden work is carried out by women. For example, in parts of the Pacific, the Amazon basin, tropical Africa, and North America, women do most of the planting, weeding, tending, and harvesting of crops, although men do participate in clearing new land and preparing the plots or fields for planting. However, in groups that rely more heavily on intensive agriculture, women's work in the fields and women's contribution to the food supply is less important. (See Chapter 5 for the distinction between horticulture and intensive agriculture.) To phrase the relationship in a few words: Women are far more likely to be involved in direct food production in horticultural than in intensive agricultural communities.

There seem to be several reasons for this general pattern. First, in the New World horticultural Native Americans had few or no domesticated animals, so men's contribution to the food supply centered around hunting. This left routine garden work to women. In contrast, virtually all intensive agriculturalists relied on livestock for meat, dairy products, hides, wool, and other products, so men spent relatively little time in hunting. Also, in Europe and Asia, nearly all intensive agriculturalists used the animal-powered plow to turn the earth prior to planting. Some researchers have suggested that most women are not strong enough to perform the heavy work of plowing efficiently. (You might remember, though, that draft animals provide most of the muscle power for plow agriculture, which makes this suggestion difficult to evaluate. You might also remember that men are stronger than women only "on average.")

There is a second reason why women are less involved in direct cultivation in intensive agricultural societies. In Europe and Asia the horticultural and intensive agricultural adaptations tend to involve the farming of different kind of crops. Roughly half of horticultural societies grow *root crops* like yams, sweet potatoes, manioc (cassava), or taro. In contrast, about 90 percent of intensive agriculturalists rely on *cereal crops* like rice, wheat, corn, barley, and millet.

This difference in crop type affects the sexual division of labor. Root crops can be stored in the ground for long periods after they first become ready to eat, so they typically are harvested continuously during the growing season (think of familiar crops like carrots or potatoes, which you pull or dig up as needed). Either daily or a few times weekly, a woman goes to the garden and returns with root crops for herself, her children, and her husband. In contrast, cereals (because they are the seeds of plants) tend to ripen at about the same time each year, usually near the end of the growing season. They have to be harvested in a short period of time, dried and processed, and stored for the rest of the year.

How does crop type affect the tasks of men and women? Cereal crops generally require a lot of labor to process (e.g., winnowing, drying, grinding) before cooking. This labor is considered women's work in most cultures (see Table 9.1). Further, people who rely on wheat, rice, barley, or other grains usually face periods of intense labor requirements: At the beginning of the growing season and at harvest time, there is a need for laborers who can do a lot of hot, heavy work in a short period that cannot be interrupted by other tasks. Such work is generally done by men (see the previous section). In contrast, root-growing horticulturists tend to spread cultivation tasks out more evenly over the entire year, making gardening a day-in, day-out, repetitive task that requires less strength and that is more compatible with child care.

A third influence is warfare. Men in most horticultural communities were responsible for defending the local village, neighborhood, or kin group from their enemies. In regions such as highland New Guinea and parts of the Amazon, group survival depended on the ability to defend land and resources from attack. Community welfare often was improved by taking over the land of enemy neighbors, so offensive as well as defensive warfare was common. Men were not actually fighting their enemies most of the time, of course, but maintaining community defenses and guarding against surprise raids did require significant amounts of time.

For most peoples, the odds of success in warfare were increased by making alliances with other groups, which required a lot of politicking, mutual visiting, and exchanges, further consuming male time and energy. Also, male solidarity

("male bonding") was advantageous, so in many groups where warfare was prevalent there were elaborate male-only rituals or social events that strengthened ties between men and helped socialize boys into manhood and the warrior role. All these pressures connected to defensive and offensive warfare led men to concentrate much of their time and resources in fighting, preparing to fight, or maintaining political relations needed for success in fights. Routine garden tasks were left to women, partly by default.

To summarize, comparative research indicates that women are less involved in direct food production in intensive agricultural systems than in horticultural systems. Three of the most important factors that influence female involvement in cultivation tasks are:

- In horticultural adaptations, more of men's time is spent in hunting than in intensive agricultural adaptations, so men have less time for producing plant foods.
- Compared to horticultural communities, intensive agriculturalists are more likely to grow cereal crops, which makes it more likely that men will concentrate more on farm work, women more on domestic work.
- Horticultural peoples tend to be subjected to pressure from hostile neighbors, so men are more busy fighting, guarding, politicking, exchanging, and creating bonds and relationships among themselves.

In brief, as agricultural systems grow more intensive, other factors change that usually lead to reduced women's involvement in direct food production.

It is important to emphasize that these relationships are *generalized*, meaning that they may not hold for any particular human group. Horticultural peoples "tend to" be more affected by warfare pressures, intensive agriculturalists are "more likely to" grow cereals than roots, and so forth. Obviously, there are many exceptions to the general patterns.

Consider the Kofyar of Nigeria, for example. They construct terraces, spread goat manure over their fields, use compost, and practice other methods of increasing yields that observing anthropologists call "intensive." Yet quantitative studies in the 1990s reveal that Kofyar women work about as much as men in agriculture. The Kofyar and many other peoples do not have the relationship between cultivation intensity and male labor that comparative research says they "ought to have" or "predicts they will have."

The Kofyar and other exceptions to the general pattern illustrate two other points. First, the existence of a general relationship established by comparative research does not tell us what any particular group of people are doing or thinking. The culture of any people is a product of a complex interaction among their history, adaptation, beliefs, and other factors. In any particular group, factors *unique* to that group may be more important than factors that are *generally* important. Thus, the fact that Kofyar women work the land about as much as men, even though the Kofyar farm the land intensively, does not "disprove" the general point that women's labor becomes less important as land use becomes more intensive.

Second, just because there are exceptions does not invalidate a generalization provided, of course, that the general pattern is well established. If we are interested in the factors that influence the cultural variations in the sexual division of labor, then we must do comparative work to look for general patterns. The fact that particular cultures do not fit the pattern does not invalidate the generalization—at least not until the number of exceptions becomes large enough to make us suspicious of the existence of the general pattern!

At any rate, the preceding discussion represents an excellent example of the materialist theory of culture, discussed in Chapter 4. It assumes that the way a population exploits its habitat (by horticulture or more intensive methods) greatly affects the kinds of tasks women and men do (given the physical differences between the sexes and given the biological fact that women give birth to and nurse children). So the material conditions of life in a certain kind of adaptation interact with biological differences between women and men to produce an overall pattern of the division of labor along gender lines. That, at least, is the argument.

GENDER STRATIFICATION

A fourth main issue in the anthropological study of gender is **gender stratification,** or the degree to which groups of people allocate material and social rewards to women and men *based on their gender.* Other sources of unequal rewards include class, caste, family origins, and race (as discussed in the next chapter). Here we discuss only rewards based on whether one is a male or a female. We ignore such complications as third or fourth gender identities.

Gender stratification is also often referred to as "the status of women," with the implied phrase "relative to men." Whatever we call it, gender stratification is difficult to define, for it includes many components that interact in complex ways. Here are some of these components, including for each component a question whose answer would indicate high, moderate, low, or nonexistent gender stratification for some culture:

- The kinds of social roles men and women perform: Are some roles limited to males only or to females only? If so, which roles and how are they valued?
- The cultural value attached to women's and men's contributions to their families and other groups: Are men's contributions overvalued relative to women's?
- Female deference to males: Do women defer socially to their husbands or male relatives? How much and in what contexts?
- Access to positions of power and influence: Do women hold offices in the political arena? Can and do women control family or household members and domestic tasks?
- Control over personal decision making: Do women control their own lives by making marital, sexual, childbearing, work, leisure, and other important decisions for themselves?

- General beliefs and ideas about the sexes: Are men considered to be superior to women intellectually, psychologically, and/or physically?

These are some of the main dimensions that should be considered in evaluating the degree of gender stratification in particular cultures. Think of the list as some of the main features that constitute the overall "status of women" in particular cultures. Obviously, gender stratification is multidimensional, which makes it difficult to categorize it as "high" or "low" even within a single culture. Why is it so difficult?

For one thing, some of the components are not consistent with other components. For example, studies of family life often report that women have a great deal of control in making decisions about childrearing and about the allocation of domestic resources, even though they have little independence outside the domestic context. In two Andalusian towns of south Spain, David Gilmore's fieldwork showed that wives have great autonomy in managing household affairs. He believes this is because many women are able to live near their own mothers, so that wives and their mothers frequently "gang up" on a husband. Even in male-dominated societies like traditional Japan and China, the eldest female in a household usually had the right to manage household affairs with a fair degree of autonomy. Yet in China, Japan, and many other societies, women were not allowed to participate in public affairs, had hardly any property of their own, had little say over whom they married, and were clearly subordinate to their fathers and husbands socially and even legally.

Added to the fact that specific aspects of women's status vary according to social context and situation is the fact that distinctions of rank or class (considered in Chapter 10) or of ethnic affiliation (Chapter 13) often override male-female distinctions. In modern North America, most professional white women enjoy higher living standards and achieve more of what their culture values than do working-class black men—what shall we say about stratification based on gender versus class?

A final factor complicating the concept of gender stratification is that in most cultures, a woman's status changes over the course of her life. For example, most scholars agree that "the status of women" was comparatively low in traditional China, Japan, and India. In all three regions, most families were patrilocally extended (Chapter 7), so when women married they left their own families and moved into or near the house of their husband's parents. A young wife was subjected to the authority of her husband's mother and was duty-bound to work extremely hard. But as a woman settled into the household, had a son, and aged, her status improved and she gradually took over control from her mother-in-law. When the latter died, she became the everyday manager of the household and became an authority figure over her own daughters-in-law after her sons married. The same pattern of women's status improving with age appears in numerous other cultures.

So we must avoid thinking of gender stratification as a unitary phenomenon. Like other social relations, male-female relations are complex. This is not surprising. Concepts like "the status of women" or "gender stratification" are concepts used by contemporary social scientists, not universal concepts. The people whose lives and cultures anthropologists study may not have such concepts at all! Nor are women's and men's lives in any community so simple that anthropologists (or for that matter, anyone else) can categorize them unambiguously by statements like "women have low status in culture X." (This point—that simple categorizations are misleading—is one you might remember when a friend bemoans how some region, or country, or religion, "puts women down.")

In spite of the complications, there are significant cross-cultural variations in gender stratification. Few anthropologists would deny that there is much less gender stratification among the Native American Hopi and Iroquois than among the Kapauku and Imbonggu of New Guinea. Gender stratification is meaningful in comparing cultures, especially if we are interested in questions such as whether women are subordinate to men in all human societies—which we are!

Universal Subordination?

A question asked by anthropologists interested in gender is whether females are everywhere subordinate to male. Are there societies in which women and men are equal? Are there societies in which women dominate men?

The answer to the second question is no. Despite the stories we sometimes read or the occasional old adventure movie in which the hero is captured by "amazons," not a single instance of clear female domination over men has ever been found by ethnographers. Matriarchy—rule by women over men—does not exist, nor has it ever existed, to the best of our knowledge. Clearly there have been and are individual women who hold great power, control great wealth, and are held in high esteem. Certainly there are queens, female chiefs, and individual *matriarchs* of families and kin groups. But no instance of *matriarchy*—women as a social category holding power over men as a social category—has been documented.

The first question, of whether cultures exist in which men and women are equal, has a more uncertain and complex answer. Even anthropologists who have devoted their careers to studying gender cannot agree. On the one hand, some scholars believe that women are never considered to be fully equal to men. They interpret the ethnographic record as showing that an asymmetry always exists between the sexes in one or more areas of life.

Those who believe that male dominance/female subordination is a cultural universal point to two fairly well established ethnographic generalizations. One applies to political institutions. In political life, sexual asymmetry always exists. In no known society are the primary political authority roles restricted to females. But in many societies all women are denied the right to succeed to political offices. In the majority of cases even kin-group leadership roles are dominated by men. Male elders of the lineage or clan decide how the group's land and other resources are to

be used and allocated, how the group's wealth objects are to be disposed of, whether the group is to engage in a battle to avenge a wrong, and so on. (But as we shall soon see, women often do have significant influence over these matters, especially in matrilineal societies.)

The other realm of life in which sexual asymmetry is found is religion. In many societies women are excluded from performing major religious leadership roles and are forbidden to participate in the most important rituals.

According to some anthropologists, then, the activities of males are everywhere regarded as more important than those of females. Women are universally subordinate to men.

But the ethnographic record can be interpreted differently. Some ethnologists who have looked at the same kinds of "ethnographic facts" have found examples of what they consider sexual equality.

The Iroquois, a matrilineal and matrilocal people of northeastern North America, are the most famous ethnographic example of women achieving full equality (or is it only relative equality?) with men. Iroquois women produced the corn and other cultivated foods, put them in storage, and largely controlled how they were distributed from the storehouses. Iroquois men were away from their apartments in the longhouse much of the time, engaged in warfare or cooperative hunting expeditions. After the introduction of the fur trade into northeastern North America in the seventeenth century, men were away searching for beaver pelts or raiding their neighbors for pelts. The matrilineally related women of a longhouse influenced their inmarried husbands' behavior by withholding provision from their hunting trips and war parties. Only men had the right to hold the most powerful political leadership offices because only males could be elected to the great council of chiefs. But representatives to the council were selected by the older women of the various matrilineages, and these women also had the right to remove and replace men who did not adequately represent the group's interests. Also, women had a voice in the deliberations of the council itself. They could veto declarations of war and introduce peace-making resolutions.

Among the Iroquois of north-east North America, there was minimal gender stratification. One reason for the "high status" of Iroquois women is that they controlled most of the production and distribution of cultivated foods, giving them influence over the activities of men. Matrilineal descent and matrilocal residence also affected sexual equality, for it allowed groups of related women to live together or near one another.

© 1992 Stock Montage

So who is right? Are women subordinate to men in all societies or not? Certainly, the Iroquois and other peoples demonstrate that women in some cultures have achieved considerable control over their own lives and over public decision making—but do such cases represent *full equality* of males and females? Indeed, would we know "total equality" if we saw it in a society? What would it look like? Would men and women have to carry out the same kinds of economic tasks before we could say they are equal? Is monogamy necessary, or can a society be polygynous and still qualify? Shall we require that women occupy 50 percent of all leadership roles before we say they have equal rights and equal control?

Obviously, many questions must be answered before we can say whether women are everywhere subordinate—not the least of which is how we would know complete gender equality if we were to encounter it somewhere! A more answerable question, though, is: What influences the degree of gender stratification in a society?

Influences on Gender Stratification

Women's status is affected by a multitude of factors. So far no one has shown that any small number of forces are the primary determinants of

women's status in all times and places. Here we discuss only a few hypotheses that point to the kinds of influences that are most widespread and important.

Women's Contributions to Material Welfare

Many people argue that women's role in production strongly influences their property rights, their role in public affairs, their degree of personal freedom, and other dimensions of their overall status. One idea is that where women produce a sizable proportion of the food, shelter, clothing, and other necessities of existence, their contributions will be recognized and rewarded with influence, property, prestige, dignity, and other benefits. In other words, the sexual division of labor, together with the proportion of valued goods women produce, are strong influences on women's overall status.

Such ideas might apply to some foraging and horticultural peoples, among whom women's gathering or gardening contributes a sizable amount of resources to their domestic groups. Women's productive labor might give them a status that is closer to equality with men than they have in other forms of adaptation in which their subsistence contributions are not as great. For example, among the BaMbuti and Aka, two foraging groups of the central African rain forest, women's labor is critical for success in net hunting, and ethnographic reports on both these "pygmy" peoples report male-female equality or near equality.

But everyone's status is "closer to equality" in most hunter-gatherer and many horticultural populations (see Chapters 5 and 10). So perhaps the relative lack of gender stratification in these adaptations results not from women's importance as food providers but from something else that "levels out" social inequalities of all kinds.

Women's Control over Key Resources   A more complex proposal is that women's contribution to production, by itself, is not enough to "earn" them relative equality. It is *necessary* for women to contribute heavily to material welfare to gain resources, rights, and respect, but this alone is not *sufficient*. One specific hypothesis is that women must also own productive resources (land, tools), or have considerable control over the distribution of the products of their labor, or both. If women own productive resources and have a great deal of say over what happens to the goods they produce, then they can have some influence on the activities of men. Overall, this gives them more equality. Peggy Sanday found some support for this hypothesis in a cross-cultural study (1973).

This hypothesis seems to account reasonably well for some specific cases. For instance, Iro-quois women controlled the production and distribution of important resources. They used this control to nominate their kinsmen to chiefly positions and to influence the public decision making from which they were formally excluded. Likewise, Hopi (see Chapter 8) women owned land and had considerable control over the distribution of its products. Women had relatively high status in both these societies, as they did among many other Native American peoples.

Along the same lines, in many West African and Caribbean societies, women are more active than men in market trade in foodstuffs, handicrafts, textiles, and other goods produced by themselves. Sometimes market-trading women are able to transform their independent control over exchangeable resources into more equitable relations with men. Wives commonly maintain separate income from their husband, which they are free to spend on themselves and their children. Among the Yoruba of Nigeria, women are active in market trade and in craft production, which gives them access to income and economic security independent of their husbands and other men. Many women purchase houses in urban areas and use the rent to improve their own and their children's economic well-being and social autonomy. According to Sandra Barnes (1990, 275):

> Property frees the owner from subordinating herself to the authority of another person in domestic matters. It places her in a position of authority over others and in a position to form

Concept Review   Influences on Gender Stratification

Contribution to Material Welfare	The greater the contributions women make to the material (food, clothing, wealth, etc.) welfare of the group, the higher the general status of women in the group.
Control over Key Resources	Ownership of productive resources (land and tools) and/or the degree of control women have over the distribution of the products of their labor, influences their status in the group.
Descent and Postmarital Residence	In matrilinial (see Chapter 8) and/or matrilocal (see Chapter 7) societies, women have relatively higher status than in those societies with other forms of descent and postmarital residence.

R. Krubner/H. Armstrong Roberts

Where women commonly earn income for themselves by marketing food, crafts, and other products, as in this peasant marketplace in Jamaica, their overall status tends to be relatively high.

social relationships in the wider community that are politically significant. Property owning legitimates her entry into the public domain.

The economic independence that some Yoruba women are able to acquire translates into increased participation in neighborhood associations and other public affairs and allows them much freedom from male authority.

Thus, many ethnographic and comparative studies suggest that controlling resources is one way for women to get respect and independence from their husbands, brothers, and other men. This ability to acquire some measure of control over family resources helps to account for why many late-twentieth-century North American wives demanded and received more help from their husbands in housework and child care. Beginning in the 1950s, more and more married women left hearth and home for wage employ-

ment. Increased female employment stems from many factors, including widespread cultural desires for an ever-increasing living standard, increasing worries about divorce, and economic changes in which most people now work in services rather than in farms and factories. In the twenty-first century, not only do working wives have psychological ammunition against their husbands' domestic incompetence or laziness—they've put in eight- or ten-hour days on the job just like their husbands—but increasingly, women have the resources to back up their demand—they don't really need the loser, anyway.

Descent and Postmarital Residence The form of descent and postmarital residence also influences the degree of gender stratification. Many anthropologists have noted that women in matrilineal and matrilocal societies have greater equality in many areas of life. What is it, specifically, about matrilineality and matrilocality that gives relatively high status to females? It is not that "women rule" in these societies. Generally speaking, men hold positions of both political and domestic authority in matrilineal societies (see Chapter 8). The main difference is whom among their relatives men have authority *over:* their sisters and sisters' children in matrilineal systems, versus their sons, unmarried daughters, and sons' children in patrilineal systems.

But other elements of matrilineality and matrilocality benefit women. In a cross-cultural study Martin Whyte found that women enjoy more authority in domestic matters, have more sexual freedom, and have more worth placed on their lives in these societies. Two factors contribute to their equality. First, because husbands live with the families of their wives, sisters remain with or close to one another throughout their lives. A typical wife thus has her mother, sisters, and perhaps other female relatives around to support her in domestic quarrels. Second, in many matrilineal and matrilocal societies, domestic authority over a married woman is divided between her husband and her brother. Alice Schlegel suggests that this arrangement increases her freedom because each man acts as a check on the other's attempts to dominate her.

Contrast this situation to patrilineal and patrilocal China before the mid-twentieth century. When a Chinese woman married she was incorporated as a member of her husband's household. This was symbolized by the fact that she began to pay homage to his deceased patrilineal ancestors rather than to her own. A woman's relationships with her own parents and siblings were sharply curtailed when she married. Her main duties were to work for her husband and his parents, to obey them in all things, and to bear them male heirs. In many respects a new wife was treated as a domestic servant to her father- and mother-in-law: She was given arduous household tasks to perform for most of her waking hours, and she could be berated and even beaten with impunity. Only when she herself bore sons and heirs to her husband's family did her status improve, and

only when she herself became a mother-in-law to her sons' wives could she relax a bit. The Confucian social and moral philosophy, which held that women must always be submissive to men, affected the way wives and daughters-in-law were treated. But also important were the social facts that wives were fully incorporated into the households of their husbands' parents, and the lines of authority over them were clearly and legally redrawn on their marriage. A Chinese wife had few viable alternatives to submission to her husband's family and few sources of social support when she was treated poorly. In contrast, in most matrilocal and matrilineal cultures women do have alternatives to suffering the dominance of their husbands, and they likewise receive support from their own relatives.

Gender Stratification in Industrial Societies

We conclude by bringing together some of the information and ideas covered in this chapter and briefly suggesting how they might be relevant to women living in industrialized, modernized nations.

First, notice that anthropological research on gender stratification provides women everywhere with a hope and a warning. Part of the hope derives from the fact that women's roles and rights, and the restrictions placed upon them, vary from place to place and from time to time. Although it may be very difficult or impossible to say whether women and men have "totally equal status" in any culture, we certainly know that sexual equality varies—and varies significantly. So there is reason to think that modern societies can move further toward eliminating barriers to female opportunity and achievement.

The other hope? Some of the factors we have covered here suggests that any change that improves women's independent access to material resources and to social support will have positive impacts on their status in other realms of life. If married women have their own source of income independent of their husbands, then they are better able to become empowered within their families and to escape relationships with men who are physically or psychologically abusive. If, as in matrilineal and matrilocal societies, women are able to maintain relationships of "sisterhood" (i.e., support from other women), and/or of extended family ties (i.e., aid from their own relatives), then they can mobilize these supportive relationships in times of hardship. If women have legal recourse to sue discriminating employers and would-be employers, then their opportunities and compensation on the job will be improved by the threat of monetary damages.

The warning? Cross-cultural studies have not yet discovered the key that unlocks the door leading to "total equality" (whatever that might look like) between the sexes. Comparative anthropological work—like most work dealing with

human behavior and beliefs—is highly suggestive, but it is not conclusive. Thus far we cannot identify the one or two or three things that women can do that will lead to equal treatment in the workplace, in the household, in the bedroom, and in the political arena. No one or two or three male-dominated institutions could be changed that will radically improve the position of women in various realms of their lives, for example, outlawing sexual discrimination in the workplace and making comparable pay for comparable work legally mandatory might not be realized in greater female-male equality in other contexts such as family life or politics. Even a female CEO can be abused by her husband. Therefore, feminists— of both sexes—need to continue to work on a broad front to achieve their objectives.

SUMMARY

1. Physical differences between females and males are recognized and relevant to social behavior in all known cultures. Although whether one is a male or female matters to all peoples, it matters in different ways and to different degrees.

2. A person's sex is determined biologically, by her or his genes, but gender is a cultural construct. The cultural construction of gender means that cultures vary in how they perceive the physical differences between the sexes, in the significance they attribute to those differences, and in the way those differences are made relevant for self-identity, task and role allocation, access to property and power, and so forth. The Hua illustrate the cultural construction of gender.

3. Human groups vary in their tolerance of individual variations in gender identities. Many peoples allow gender crossing, in which males are allowed to enact female roles and vice-versa. Still others recognize multiple sexual identities, in

which there are not only two, but three or four genders roughly corresponding to man-woman or woman-man. Native American peoples seem especially tolerant of gender crossing and to allow for multiple gender identities.

4. The sexual division of labor varies cross-culturally. Sexual stereotypes holding that men are breadwinners and women are caretakers are not true. Male domination is not rooted in men's supplying the material necessities of existence because women's labor frequently produces much or most of the food supply. There are certain widespread patterns in the sexual division of labor. Three factors that influence the broad cross-cultural similarities in the sexual division of labor are: superior male strength; the depression of fertility that seems to occur when a woman engages in heavy exercise; and the compatibility of a task with the care of infants and young children. But no *biological* difference between the sexes can account for the cross-cultural variations in the sexual division of labor. It is pretty well established that female labor is more important in subsistence tasks in horticultural populations compared with intensive agriculturalists. Reasons for these differences are related to the types of crops grown (root crops versus cereal grains), the amount of time spent in food processing, and the greater prevalence of warfare in horticultural groups.

5. A fourth issue in gender studies is the causes of cultural diversity in sexual stratification. Even specialists in this subject cannot agree whether ethnographic studies reveal that females are universally subordinate to males. This is mainly because no explicit criteria can be used to judge whether there are populations in which males and females are fully equal. It does seem to be true that females as a social category are never dominant over males as a social category.

6. A multitude of forces influence women's overall "status" in a culture, including their relative contributions to subsistence, their control over key resources, and the prevalent pattern of descent and postmarital residence. These conclusions have relevance for women in twenty-first-century societies.

KEY TERMS

cultural construction of gender
gender crossing
multiple gender identities
sexual division of labor
gender stratification

SUGGESTED READINGS

Books that are excellent brief introductions to the anthropological study of gender include:

Friedl, Ernestine. *Women and Men: An Anthropologist's View.* New York: Hold, Rinehart and Winston, 1975.
Gilmore, David D. *Manhood in the Making: Cultural Concepts of Masculinity.* New Haven, Conn.: Yale University Press, 1990.

Nanda, Serena. *Gender Diversity: Crosscultural Variations.* Prospect Heights, IL: Waveland Press, 2000.
Roscoe, Will. *Changing Ones.* New York: St. Martin's Press, 1998.

The following books investigate gender from a comparative perspective:

Buckley, Thomas, and Alma Gottlieb, eds. *Blood Magic: The Anthropology of Menstruation.* Berkeley: University of California Press, 1988.
Dahlberg, F., ed. *Woman the Gatherer.* New Haven, CT: Yale University Press, 1981.
Martin, M. K., and B. Voorhies. *Female of the Species.* New York: Columbia University Press, 1975.
Sanday, Peggy R. *Female Power and Male Dominance.* Cambridge: Cambridge University Press, 1981.

Some useful edited volumes include:

Cohen, Theodore, ed. *Men and Masculinity: A Text Reader.* Belmont, CA: Wadsworth/Thomson Learning, 2001.
di Leonardo, Micaela, ed. *Gender at the Crossroads of Knowledge: Feminist Anthropology in the Postmodern Era.* Berkeley: University of California Press, 1991.
Morgen, Sandra, ed. *Gender and Anthropology: Critical Reviews for Research and Teaching.* Washington, DC: American Anthropological Association, 1989.
Ortner, Sherry B., and Harriet Whitehead, eds. *Sexual Meanings: The Cultural Construction of Gender and Sexuality.* Cambridge: Cambridge University Press, 1981.
Rosaldo, M. Z., and Louise Lamphere, eds. *Women, Culture, and Society.* Stanford, CA: Stanford University Press, 1974.
Sanday, Peggy Reeves, and Ruth Gallagher Goodenough, eds. *Beyond the Second Sex: New Directions in the Anthropology of Gender.* Philadelphia: University of Pennsylvania Press, 1990.

chapter 10

POLITICS *and* SOCIAL INEQUALITY

Contents

Every society has both formal and informal means to organize and control the actions of its members through systems of individual rewards and punishments. This chapter discusses the various mechanisms by which societies direct and channel individual social behavior through systems of equality and inequality, political organization, and social control.

SYSTEMS of EQUALITY and INEQUALITY

Inequality is the extent to which culturally valued material and social rewards are allocated disproportionately to individuals, families, and other groups.

There are three categories of rewards. The most tangible reward is *wealth,* or ownership of valued material goods. Another kind of reward is *power,* or the ability to make others do what you want based on coercion or legitimate authority. A final type of reward is *prestige,* or the respect, esteem, and overt approval granted by others to individuals they consider meritorious. Prestige (or *honor*) is a social reward, based on judgments about an individual's personal worthiness or the contributions the individual makes to others in the group.

The distribution of each kind of reward varies between societies. Some groups allow ambitious individuals to acquire wealth, power, and prestige, whereas others make it difficult for anyone to accumulate possessions, gain control over others, or put themselves above their peers socially. For instance, many North Americans admire "self-made men" who have earned higher income (wealth) than other people by their own talents and efforts. Such men would be looked down on as self-centered and ungenerous in many other cultures.

Societies can be classified by "how much" inequality they exhibit with respect to wealth, power, and prestige. Imagine a continuum. At one end there are societies that feature only slight differences between individuals and groups in access to these rewards. At the other end are societies with marked contrasts in access to rewards. In the middle there are a myriad of societies that

are intermediate between the two extremes: Some have contrasts in prestige but lack significant differences in wealth, for example.

Morton Fried formulated a threefold classification of the kinds and degree of inequality found in human cultures. He labeled the three basic types **egalitarian, ranked,** and **stratified**.

Fried's three categories have little to do with access to rewards based on sex or age. When we call a society egalitarian, for example, we do not mean that females and males receive equal or nearly equal rewards, or that elderly people and young people are economically or socially equal. Even in egalitarian societies there are social distinctions based on sex and age (see Chapter 5). Essentially, egalitarian means that there are few differences in access to rewards between families or other kinds of kin groups within a society. At the other end of the continuum, in societies we call stratified, there are major differences in access to rewards between families and/or kin groups, in addition to any distinctions based on sex or age.

It is also important to understand that these categories are merely points along a continuous spectrum of systems of inequality. It is impossible to pigeonhole all human societies into one of these types because most fit somewhere in between the three categories. The terms *egalitarian, ranked,* and *stratified* are useful mainly as short descriptions of the kinds and range of variation in inequality found cross-culturally.

Egalitarian-ranked-stratified is the temporal order in which the three forms developed. Until about 10,000 years ago, most people on earth lived in egalitarian societies. Ranked societies developed in a few areas about then, and a few thousand years later stratification developed in the great civilizations (see Chapter 5). Over the next 4,000 to 5,000 years, stratified societies spread throughout most of the world, as some peoples and nations conquered and ruled over others.

Egalitarian Societies

Egalitarian societies are at the low end of the inequality continuum. Setting aside distinctions based on sex and age, there is little noticeable difference in received rewards between individuals and families. People who work hard, or who have attractive personalities or valuable skills, may be rewarded with respect and prestige from other members of their group. But egalitarian groups have various cultural mechanisms to prevent any individual from becoming too "big." And even people who are respected rarely have more possessions or power than others.

Mobile foragers such as the Inuit, !Kung, BaMbuti, and Aka are egalitarian. James Woodburn identified several reasons why access to rewards is evenly distributed among such foragers. First, and most obviously, frequent seasonal movements of the band or camp are necessary for effective adaptation. Mobility makes it difficult to transport possessions, and hence to accumulate wealth.

Second, the cultural value placed on reciprocal sharing (see Chapter 5) helps prevent individuals or family groups from becoming wealthier than their band mates. It is difficult to accumulate wealth because other people demand their share, and failure to share is socially punished.

Third, among mobile foragers, families are not tied to specific territories but have the right to visit and exploit the resources of many areas, often due to bilateral kinship relations (Chapter 8). If someone tries to give orders or exercise control over others, people have enough options so that they are free to leave and live elsewhere.

If people move around in their environments a lot, are required to share food and other possessions, and have a range of options about where to live and whom to live with, then inequality in wealth and power does not have much chance of developing. If it should develop, it does not have much chance of persisting for very long.

Ranked Societies

In ranked societies there are a limited number of high-ranking social positions, usually titles or some kind of formal, named offices. The titles confer high honor on people who hold them. In most cases, the privilege of holding a title or occupying an office is largely or entirely hereditary

within certain families, lineages, clans, or other kin groups.

In one of the most common types of ranked societies, all kin groups are ranked relative to one another. Within each kin group, each member is ranked relative to all others, usually on the principle of genealogical seniority (elders being superior in rank to younger people). The most valued positions that bring the highest rewards in prestige, wealth, and power are held by the highest ranking individuals of the highest ranking kin group. This way of ranking individuals and kin groups is most well documented for several ancient Polynesian chiefdoms.

An excellent example of such a ranked society is Tikopia, a tiny Pacific island whose kinship

Political authority is frequently indicated by differences in dress, as in the case of American Indian peoples on the northwest coast of North America.

system is described in Chapter 8. When studied by Raymond Firth in the 1920s, Tikopia's 1,200 persons were divided into four patrilineal clans, each with its own chief who exercised authority over his clanmates. Each clan in turn was divided into several patrilineages. Every Tikopian patrilineage had a head, who was believed to be the oldest living male descendant of the man who founded the lineage about four to six generations ago. Alongside this ranking of individuals within a single lineage, the various lineages of a single clan were ranked relative to one another. One lineage of each clan, supposedly the original, "senior" lineage from which the "junior" lineages had budded off, was considered the noble lineage. Members of other lineages of the clan had to defer socially to members of the noble lineage, according to Tikopian standards of etiquette. In addition, the noble lineage of each clan selected one of its members to be the chief of the whole clan.

Chiefs and other members of the noble Tikopia lineages had little more wealth than anyone else. The nobility did receive tribute from other lineages of their clan, but they gave away most of it in the many public activities that they organized and financed through redistribution (see Chapter 6). The chief and nobility of each clan had no way to deny access to land and ocean resources to members of other lineages, for each lineage was considered to have inalienable rights to certain pieces of land. The Tikopia nobility, then, received much prestige and token tribute from other islanders, but they did not use this tribute to enrich themselves, and their sphere of power was limited. They were honored, but their wealth and power were not great. It is mainly in this respect that ranked societies contrast with stratified societies.

Stratified Societies

Stratified societies are at the high end of the inequality continuum. A society is said to be stratified if

- there are marked inequalities in access to all three kinds of rewards: wealth, power, and prestige;

- this inequality is based primarily on unequal access to productive resources such as the land and tools people need to make their living; that is, a few people control access to the resources others need to survive at culturally acceptable levels;
- unequal access to rewards has a strong tendency to be heritable throughout the generations, regardless of the personal qualities or aptitudes of individuals. Most individuals (and families) do not move very far up or down the social ladder during their lifetimes.

Stratified societies vary in the cultural ideas they have about the possibilities of social mobility. In some, such as North America, upward or downward mobility is considered possible, although numerous studies have shown it to be uncommon. In many others, especially in preindustrial societies, one's position is considered fixed, often because of beliefs that existing inequalities are hereditary or ordained by supernatural beings.

In stratified societies individuals, families, and other groups are differentiated on the basis of their relative access to rewards. A social group whose members share about the same degree of access to rewards is called a *social stratum*. The two major kinds of strata are **classes** and **castes.**

There are two major differences between class and caste systems. First, by definition, castes are endogamous groups: They have cultural norms or laws that require individuals to marry within their caste. As discussed in Chapter 7, rules that mandate marriage within one's own group have the effect of maintaining the distinctiveness of the group relative to other groups. There is no possibility of upward mobility through intercaste marriage, and there are no children who have potentially anomalous group membership. One is born into the caste of one's parents, one marries someone in the same caste, and one's children are likewise born into and remain members of one's own caste. In contrast, class societies allow people to marry someone of a different class; in fact, intermarriage between classes commonly is an avenue of social mobility.

CONCEPT REVIEW Systems of Equality and Inequality

FORM	CHARACTERISTICS	ASSOCIATED ECONOMIC FACTORS
Egalitarian	Equal access to rewards. Productive resources open to all; little wealth difference. Influence based on personal qualities. Prestige based on personal achievements.	Common among foraging peoples (involved in hunting and gathering) and horticultural societies. Economic exchange based on reciprocity.
Ranked	Access to rewards limited by kinship. Productive resources held in common by kin group. Wealth differences between members of kin group. A limited number of formal positions with authority, which is inherited and/or achieved within kin group. Significant differences in prestige. Inherited and/or achieved within kin group.	With some foraging peoples involved in fishing and with some horticultural and intensive agricultural peoples. Economic exchange based on redistribution.
Stratified (a) Caste	Formal, named, hierarchically ranked groups. Membership determined at birth. Endogamous. Productive resources individually owned. Economic activities limited by caste. Tremendous wealth differences based on inherited wealth and caste. Formal positions with authority. Access limited by inheritance and determined by caste membership. Tremendous differences in prestige. Limited by inheritance and determined by caste.	Found with intensive agricultural peoples. Economic exchange based on market economy.
(b) Class	Informal, named, hierarchically ranked groups. Group boundaries ambiguous, with membership determined by personal achievements and/or inheritance. Productive resources individually owned. Access is based on achievement and/or inheritance. Tremendous wealth differences. Formal positions with authority. Access determined by achievements and/or inheritance. Tremendous differences in prestige. Access determined by achievements and/or inheritance.	Found among both intensive agricultural and industrial peoples. Economic exchange based on market economy.

Second, caste systems have some kind of prohibition against contact between members of different castes. High-caste members, for example, sometimes believe that they will be spiritually polluted if they come into contact with members of other castes. Thus castes have more permanent membership and more rigid social boundaries than classes.

❋ CASTES in TRADITIONAL INDIA

The best-known caste system is that of India. India's caste system is complex and varies from region to region. The following description is generalized. There are four main caste categories, or *varnas*. (A *varna* is not itself a caste.) Each *varna* is ranked relative to the others in honor and degree of ritual purity, and each is broadly associated with certain kinds of occupations.

The highest *varna* is the Brahmins, or priests and scholars; next is the *varna* of nobles and warriors, the Kshatriyas; third are the Vaishas, or merchants and artisans; and ranked lowest are the Shudras, or farmers, craftspeople, and certain other laborers. A fifth category—outside and ranked below the *varnas* —are the untouchables, to whom falls work considered polluting to the *varnas.*

The *varnas* are large, inclusive categories into which specific castes are placed. The villages in which most people live are divided into much smaller and specific groupings called *jati* (castes, as the term usually is used). For example, in a particular village the Shudra *varna* might be represented by several *jati* with names such as weaver, potter, and tailor. There are thousands of these castes in India, distributed among the many thousands of villages. Each village contains a number of castes, most of which are named according to the occupation traditionally performed by their members. Thus, a village might include castes of priests, merchants, blacksmiths, potters, tailors, farmers, weavers, carpenters, washers, barbers, leather workers, and "sweepers" (the last refers to those who remove human waste matter from people's houses).

India's traditional caste hierarchy is so intimately tied up with Hindu doctrines that the two are almost inseparable. Hindu religion holds that spiritual souls are reborn into different physical bodies at various stages of their existence—this is the doctrine of reincarnation. Souls ultimately desire an end to the cycle of earthly birth, death, and rebirth, but to achieve this end each soul must be reborn many times into many bodies, both animal and human. Souls attempt to move up the "ladder" of reincarnation, from lower forms of life to higher ones; from animals to humans (of various ranked castes) to gods.

The particular body (be it human or animal) that a soul is born into depends on how closely that soul adhered to proper standards of behavior in previous lifetimes. For souls that had made it up to human forms in their previous incarnation, these standards include avoidance of activities that Hindus believe are polluting. Among the most polluting activities are handling and working with animal carcasses or the bodies of deceased humans; touching excrement and other waste materials; dealing with childbirth; and eating meat. People who regularly perform these activities are not only polluted themselves, but anyone of a higher caste who comes into physical contact with them likewise becomes polluted and must bathe ritually to cleanse himself or herself. One's present place in society—one's "station in life"—varies with the degree to which one is associated with pure and impure activities. In turn, because of reincarnation, whether one is associated with pure or impure activities depends on one's behavior in previous lives—such as the degree to which one has allowed oneself to become polluted or failed to cleanse oneself.

People are low caste either because their soul has not yet been through enough lifetimes to have reached a higher form, or because their sins in a previous lifetime merit reincarnation into a low caste. In the present life, people have what they deserve. Thus, all "men" were not created equal, in the Hindu world view; it is legitimate that some castes have more power and privilege and more status and wealth than others.

In Hindu beliefs, one's soul is reincarnated into a higher or lower form partly according to how well one fulfills the obligations of one's caste in the present life. Leather workers, for instance, cannot do much to improve their lot in this life; but by faithfully fulfilling their obligations to members of higher castes, their souls will receive higher reincarnations in future bodies.

Working with animal carcasses is polluting, so leather working is a defiling occupation and leather workers are so polluting as to be untouchable. The same applies to sweeping: People who remove human wastes from houses or spread excrement over village fields are polluted, and their touch pollutes those of higher castes. Therefore, members of the leather working, sweeping, and other castes associated with defiling occupations were traditionally untouchable. (Discrimination against people of untouchable ancestry is illegal in modern India, although it still occurs.) Untouchables usually live in their own special section of the village, separate from members of higher castes. Because they contaminate temples by their entry, they cannot go inside a temple. Their touch contaminates water, so they have to use separate wells. These and other restrictions on their behavior sometimes are extreme.

However, members of high-ranking castes, such as priests, landowners, warriors, and merchants, need the services of low-ranking castes. Again, this is because Hinduism defines some activities that are essential for life as polluting, so castes who would be defiled by these activities need lower castes to perform these services for them. The bullocks essential for farming die, so someone has to remove dead cattle from the village. Brahmin women give birth just as other women do, so the women of some low-ranking caste have to serve as midwives, since other Brahmin women would become polluted by so serving. Everyone passes bodily wastes, so someone must remove these wastes from the houses of high-caste members lest they pollute their occupants. Accordingly, each caste has its proper role and function in the economic, social, and religious life of the village.

CLASSES in INDUSTRIAL SOCIETIES: The UNITED STATES

Class societies have strata—the classes—that have different degrees of ownership of productive property and material goods; that have different degrees of political influence; and that are ranked in the respect or esteem accorded their position in the class hierarchy.

There are no occasions on which the members of a given class come together for discussion or common action (unlike, say, an extended family or lineage). Indeed, members of a single class do not necessarily believe they have much in common with one another (unlike the members of a labor union). Many people cannot identify the class to which they belong (unlike Indian *jati* or *varna*); more than four-fifths of Americans refer to themselves as "middle class." People cannot say how many classes exist in their societies. In fact, there is considerable debate within the social sciences over what the term *class* means, or if it has anything other than the vaguest meaning.

Yet there are enormous differences in wealth, power, and prestige that exist in many societies. The term *class* refers to all the people in a given society who receive comparable rewards. Members of different classes have different access to the material resources (income, wealth), influential relationships (social contacts), and cultural knowledge (education, "social graces") that are valued in the culture. Unlike caste membership, people can move up or down in a class system during their lives through interclass marriage, personal talent, hard work and effort, or good luck. More commonly, being born into a given class puts one so far ahead or behind others that relatively few people rise or fall very far in the hierarchy during their lifetimes.

This section concentrates on the class structure of one industrialized society, the United States. In this country, the kind of work one does often is assumed to be the best single overall indicator of class membership. ("What kind of work do you do?" or "Where do you work?" is one of the first questions American adults ask of new acquaintances, the answer to which gives a lot of information about a person very quickly.) Occupation is generally the best determinant of income, and one's income influences so much else: overall lifestyle, access of one's children to education, the kinds of people with whom one associates socially, the kind of church or club to which one belongs, and so on.

Unfortunately for our desire to make societies neat and orderly, there are problems with defining a class on the basis of occupation or any other single criterion. For one thing, different criteria used to define class membership do not always agree. For instance, people do not agree on the prestige of many occupations—attorneys are despised by some but granted high prestige by others, for example. The same applies to politicians, physicians, academicians, police, and numerous other professionals. Further, the degree to which some occupation is respected by the population at large does not always reflect the relative wealth and/or access to power of those who practice it.

So it often is difficult to decide to which class an individual belongs. One approach, favored by some sociologists, is to separate the three kinds of rewards from one another and define a separate class ranking for each reward. Classes defined on the basis of prestige (*status groups*, as some call them) can be distinguished from classes based on income or wealth (*economic classes*), for instance. The definitions and methods used for ranking the classes depend, to some extent, on the interest of the social scientist, as well as on the nature of the society under study.

In the United States, probably the most widely accepted approach to stratification uses the concept of economic class. Individuals and families are placed in classes based on their wealth. Using wealth as the primary basis of class ranking has four major advantages. First, it is more measurable than other indications of class membership.

Second, wealth is the best single indication of the overall benefits individuals and families are receiving from their citizenship in the nation.

Third, exceptional wealth is generally correlated with ownership of productive resources such as factories, financial institutions, and income-producing real estate. By and large, the very wealthy people in the country own the nation's large businesses. They either built their companies themselves, or their ancestors made fortunes through business activity and passed ownership along to the current generation.

Fourth, wealth levels broadly determine people's access to political power. Through campaign contributions, the wealthy exercise a greater voice in choosing who is nominated and elected to important offices. Through lobbying efforts, the rich enjoy greater influence on the laws and policies of the nation than their numbers warrant. By providing much of the funding for think tanks and other public advisory groups, the wealthy subsidize the expertise of many economists, political scientists, sociologists, and other social scientists who advise government. Many appointed officials in the executive branch of the federal government are members of the elite. Some appointees move back and forth between business and government service regularly.

The distribution of wealth in the United States is closely tied to class inequalities. The distribution of annual income is summarized for the year 1995 in Table 10.1. In the table, American families are divided into fifths based on their 1995 cash income. For example, the richest one-fifth (or the wealthiest 20 percent) of American families earned

Table 10.1 Distribution of Family Annual Income in the United States, 1995

PERCENTAGE OF INCOME EARNED BY		AMOUNT EARNED, 1995
Poorest fifth	4.4	Less than $19,070
Second fifth	10.1	Between $19,070 and $32,984
Third fifth	15.8	Between $32,985 and $48,984
Fourth fifth	23.2	Between $48,985 and $72,259
Richest fifth	46.5	Over $72,260
Richest 5%	20.0	Over $123,656

Source: U.S. Department of Commerce (1997, Table No. 725).

46.5 percent of the total income earned by all American families in 1995. The poorest one-fifth of families earned only 4.4 percent of all family income. The table also shows that the richest 5 percent of American families earned 20 percent of the total family income.

The distribution of income does not fully reflect the extent of economic inequality in the United States, because figures on annual *income* do not show how much *wealth* is owned by families of different classes. In fact, yearly income figures such as those given in Table 10.1 greatly underestimate the degree of economic inequality in the United States. If we consider the distribution of wealth, we see that middle-income families, and even families who are generally considered affluent, own little in comparison with the truly wealthy.

People's material standards of living are not determined in any simple way by their income, nor is their influence over local, state, and national political decision making. Living standards and political influence are more greatly determined by a person's or family's net worth, that is, by all assets (property) minus all indebtedness. There are two kinds of assets: financial assets such as savings and checking accounts, stocks, bonds, money-market funds, and trusts; and tangible assets such as real estate, houses, automobiles, and other personal property. The assets a particular family owns are a better measure of its wealth than its annual income. Tangible assets directly affect material standards of living, and both tangible and financial assets represent stored-up purchasing power, since by selling them families can acquire additional money.

The Economic Policy Institute, a private think tank, published a 1994 study titled *The State of Working America: 1994–5,* written by Lawrence Mishel and Jared Bernstein. The following data are taken from this 1994 report, which summarizes the latest available figures on the distribution of wealth (net worth) for the year 1989.

To summarize the information in the report, we divide American families into one of three categories:

- Very rich: the richest 1 percent of American families.
- Rich: the next richest 9 percent of American families.
- Everyone else: the rest of America's families, or 90 percent of all families.

How much of the nation's privately owned wealth is owned by these three categories of families?

- The very rich families own 39 percent of all assets.
- The rich families own 33 percent of all assets.
- Everyone else (the "bottom" 90 percent) owns 28 percent of all assets.

Together, the very rich and rich families (the wealthiest 10 percent) own 72 percent of all personal wealth. Obviously, the distribution of wealth in 1989 was much more concentrated than the distribution of annual income. Thus, the United States serves as an example of the extent of economic inequality that sometimes develops in stratified societies.

FORMS of POLITICAL ORGANIZATION

The boundaries of a *polity,* or politically organized unit, may or may not correspond with the boundaries of a particular way of life. For example, the Comanches of the Great Plains shared a common language, customs, and ethnic identity, yet politically, they were never organized above the local group. Thus, the term *Comanche* refers to a people with a common language and culture who never united to carry out common political activities.

At the other extreme we find highly centralized polities that incorporate several culturally distinct peoples. In these instances, the political boundary is suprasocietal and multicultural. The United States is unusual in this regard only in the degree of cultural heterogeneity that exists in the population. France, although predominantly "French," also includes Bretons and Basques. India has several hundred different ethnic groups.

Russia, China, Indonesia, and the Philippines also integrate highly diversified populations into a single polity. In fact, every large and most small countries in the world today politically integrate several ethnic groups (see Chapter 13).

Political organization of preindustrial societies takes four basic forms. From the least to the most complex, these forms are **bands** (**simple** and **composite**), **tribes, chiefdoms,** and **states.** Today, few societies exist that are not integrated into state-level political systems. Thus, to understand societies organized at less complex levels, we have to reconstruct the structure of such societies at an earlier period.

Bands

As the least complex form, bands were probably the earliest form of human political structure (see Chapter 5). As more complex political systems developed, band-level societies were unable to compete for resources. Thus, bands survived until the modern period only in regions of the world with limited natural resources. Most known band-level societies were found in the deserts and grasslands of Australia, Africa, and the Americas. A few others lived in the tropical forests of Africa, Asia, and South America and in the boreal forest and tundra regions of North America and Asia.

Bands consist of a number of families living together and cooperating in economic activities throughout the year. Band-level organization most frequently was found among peoples with foraging economies, which usually dictated low population densities and high seasonal mobility. As a result, only a relatively small number of people could stay together throughout the year. Bands ranged in size from only a dozen to several hundred individuals. The adaptive significance of the band's size and seasonal mobility is described in Chapter 5. This chapter is concerned with leadership statuses and political organization of bands.

The smallest bands, called *simple bands,* usually were no larger than an extended family and were structured as such. Leadership was informal, with the oldest or one of the older male members

of the family serving as leader. Decision making was reached through consensus and involved both adult males and adult females; simple bands operated as families. Because all members of the band were related either through descent or by marriage, they were exogamous units, and members of the band had to seek spouses from other bands. Thus, although an autonomous economic and political unit, every band was, by social necessity, allied through intermarriage with other bands, usually territorially adjacent ones. Simple bands usually had names, although names may have been informal and may have simply referred to some prominent geographical feature associated with the band's usual territory.

Resource availability influenced the formation of such small groups. Simple bands often were associated with the hunting of nonmigratory game animals, such as deer, guanaco, moose, or small mammals, which occupy a limited territory on a year-round basis and are found either singly or in small herds. The foraging activities of simple bands usually did not generate any significant surpluses of food, which necessitated the year-round hunting of game animals. Effective hunting required only a few male hunters who had intimate knowledge of the seasonal shifts in range of these animals within their territory. The game resources of such areas could be exploited most effectively by a small and highly mobile population. In addition, such bands depended on the seasonal collection of wild roots, berries, nuts, and other edible plants, as well as on limited fishing and shellfish collection.

Composite bands consisted of a larger aggregation of families, sometimes numbering in the hundreds. In contrast to simple bands, composite bands included unrelated extended families. Although leadership in composite bands was informal, it was more defined. Such leaders frequently have been called **big men.** Big men did not hold formal offices, and leadership was based on influence rather than authority over band members. **Influence** is merely the ability to convince people that they should act as you suggest. **Authority** is the recognized right of an individual

CONCEPT REVIEW Political Organization

FORM	CHARACTERISTICS	ASSOCIATED EQUALITIES AND INEQUALITIES
Bands (a) Simple	Local, economically self-sufficient, residence group. Single extended family, usually numbering 25 to 50 people. Family head with leadership based on influence.	Egalitarian
(b) Composite	Local economically self-sufficient residence group. Several extended families, usually numbering from 50 to several hundred individuals. Big man leadership based on influence.	Egalitarian
Tribes	Several economically self-sufficient residence groups. Usually numbering between 1,000 to 20,000 people. A few formal leadership positions with limited authority, with access based on inheritance and/or achievements. Group cohesion maintained by sodalities.	Primarily egalitarian with some societies showing the traits of ranking.
Chiefdoms	Several economically interdependent residence groups. Usually numbering from a few thousand up to about 30,000. Centralized leadership, with a hereditary chief, with full formal authority.	Ranked societies
States	Usually numbering from the tens of thousands up to several million. Centralized leadership, with formal full authority, supported by a bureaucracy.	Stratified societies

to command another person to act in a particular way. Thus, a big-man leader could not, by virtue of his position, make demands or impose rules on the members of the band, and his decisions were not binding on others. Because big-man status did not involve a formal office, no prescribed process for attaining leadership status existed. A man might emerge as the leader through a variety of personal accomplishments or qualities, such as his proven ability in hunting or warfare, the supernatural powers he possessed, or merely his charisma. There was no set tenure in the position, which was filled by a man until he was informally replaced by some other leader.

Like simple bands, many composite bands were nomadic and moved within a relatively well-defined range. Because of their greater size, composite bands were not as cohesive as simple bands and were politically more volatile. Disputes between families could result in some members joining another band or the band splitting into two or more bands.

The formation of composite bands resulted from economic pressures that facilitated or necessitated the cooperation of a larger number of individuals than found in a single extended family. As in the case of simple bands, the behavior of the principal game animals was an important influence. Composite bands were associated with the seasonal hunting of migratory animals that form large herds, such as bison and caribou. Migratory herd animals usually appeared only seasonally in the range of a particular composite band as the herd moved between its summer and winter ranges. Because bison and caribou migrated in herds that sometimes numbered in the tens of thousands, there was no difficulty in locating the herds on the open grasslands and tundra. Unlike the nonmigratory-animal hunters, who secured game steadily throughout the year, hunters of migratory animals took most of their game only twice a year, as the herds passed through their territories during migrations.

Successful hunting of large herds of animals requires maneuvering the herd into situations where they could be slaughtered. Herds might be run over a cliff, into a holding pen, or into a lake, where hunters in boats could kill them. Regardless of the method used, all these strategies required more hunters than were available in a simple band. Thus, composite bands were formed to provide enough hunters to control the movements of large herds of animals.

The Comanche of the Great Plains of the United States illustrate the nature of composite bands. These horse-raising, bison-hunting people were politically autonomous until the Red River War of 1875. During the early and middle years of the nineteenth century, the Comanche numbered about 6,000 to 7,000, divided between five and thirteen main bands. Comanche bands had only vaguely defined territories, and two or more bands frequently occupied the same general area or had overlapping ranges. Membership in Comanche bands was fluid: Individuals and families could shift from one band to another, or a number of families might join together to establish a new band. Some anthropologists have theorized that there were only five major bands, with a varying number of secondary bands appearing and disappearing from time to time.

A band consisted of a number of families, each headed by an older male who was "peace chief" or "headman." One family head also served as the peace chief for the entire band. There was no formalized method of selecting either the family heads or the head of the band. As the Comanche say, "No one made him such; he just got that way." A Comanche peace chief usually was a man known for his kindness, wisdom, and ability to lead by influencing other men. Although a war record was important, peace chiefs were not chosen from among the most aggressive or ambitious men. Such men usually remained war leaders—great warriors who periodically recruited men to raid neighbors—but frequently had little influence outside war and raiding.

A band peace chief was responsible for the well-being of the band. Through a consensus of the family heads, he directed the seasonal movement of the band and the bison hunts. He had voluntary assistants, and every morning he usually sent out two men to scout the area around the camp for enemy raiding parties. He also sent a crier through the camp periodically to announce plans for the movement of the camp, an upcoming hunt, or some other cooperative activities. During bison hunts, the peace chief called on a number of men from the camp to police the hunt and restrain overly eager hunters from scattering the herd and spoiling the hunt for others.

In an extraordinarily individualistic and egalitarian society, Comanche band leaders had to strive for and maintain consensus. If a dispute arose and a consensus could not be reached, individuals and families were free either to shift residence to another band or even to form a new band under another leader.

Comanche bands were economically and politically autonomous units. Rarely did two or more bands come together for any unified action, and never did leaders of the bands come together to discuss issues. At the same time, there was a strong consciousness of common identity, of being Comanche. Comanche freely traveled between bands to visit, marry, and even shift residence. There was an informally reached general consensus on whether relations with a particular neighboring group were friendly or hostile. Comanche bands usually refrained from attacking other Comanche bands, although on occasion some did ally themselves with non-Comanche groups.

Thus, on the band level of political organization, populations are fragmented into numerous independent political units that operate only at the local-group level. These various communities share a common cultural identity and usually attempt to maintain harmonious relations with one another, but they lack any political structure capable of organizing the various communities into a single unit for collective actions.

Tribes

Tribes, in contrast to bands, have formally organized institutions that unite the scattered residential communities, give the society greater cohesiveness, and make possible a more united response to external threats. These institutions are called **sodalities.** Sodalities may be based on (1) large kin groups, such as clans and lineages; (2) nonkinship units, such as age sets; or (3) voluntary associations, such as warrior societies. Sodalities unify geographically dispersed communities into political units.

Although tribal-level societies usually are egalitarian, with leadership dependent in part on the persuasive abilities of individuals, formalized political offices with institutionalized authority exist. Tribes vary greatly in structure, but here only one tribal-level society is examined.

In the eighteenth century, the Osage were a horticultural people, numbering between 10,000 and 12,000, in what is today the state of Missouri. They were divided into five permanent, named villages. Membership in the five villages was formal; an individual belonged to the village in which he or she was born. If a man married a woman from another village, he moved to her village (matrilocal), but he always remained identified with his home village. The Osage were also divided into twenty-four named patrilineal clans, which were grouped in Earth and Sky divisions.

Thus every Osage had two formal identities; village and clan. The villages were economically independent of one another. Each had its own fields tended by the women of the village. Twice a year, in the summer and fall, every village organized a bison hunt and moved onto the plains for a collective village hunt. Every village also had two *ka-hi-ga*, leaders, one representing the Sky clans and the other the Earth clans. These two positions were hereditary within specific clans and lineages. Usually, but not always, the eldest son was chosen to succeed his father as *ka-hi-ga*. The authority of the *ka-hi-ga* was limited. Their primary role was to keep peace and harmony among the families in the village, and thus they acted as mediators in disputes. Their other major role was to organize and lead the village on the bison hunts, alternating leadership on a daily basis.

All twenty-four clans were represented in each village. Clans were organized at the tribal level. The clan leaders were ritual leaders, or shaman, who were formally inducted into their positions through elaborate tribal initiation rites. These men had authority over the ritual knowledge of their particular clan. Collectively, the shaman of all twenty-four clans controlled all ceremonies, including those associated with warfare. The clan shaman, meeting in council, made all decisions concerning war and peace with neighboring groups.

Thus, although there were some formalized political and religious offices that bequeathed some limited authority and prerogatives, on the whole, tribal societies were basically egalitarian. Few positions were hereditary, and most leaders were selected on the basis of personal qualities and individual merit.

Second, there was little economic specialization, either individual or regional, among tribes. Except for cooperation in communal hunts, families produced their own food and manufactured their own clothes and other material goods. From an economic perspective, each band or village was virtually a self-contained unit, capable of sustaining itself without support from other communities; therefore, it was not economic necessity, convenience, or efficiency that led to the supra-community political organization of tribes. It is likely that external threats, either real or perceived, necessitated the cooperation in warfare of a large group of people and was the major factor that united geographically dispersed communities.

Thus, warfare—the existence and activities of hostile human neighbors—was an important force in creating the political integration of separate communities.

Chiefdoms

Like tribes, chiefdoms were multicommunity political units. Unlike tribes, chiefdoms had a formalized and centralized political system. A chiefdom was governed by a single chief, who usually served as both political and religious head of the polity. The chief had authority over members of the chiefdom, and the position often was hereditary within a single kin group, which based its rights primarily on supernatural powers. Thus, a chiefdom was a ranked or stratified society with access to resources based on inherited status. With authority and power conferred by supernatural beings, governing was not by consensus but by decree.

Most chiefdoms were associated with horticultural societies in which craft or regional specialization in production had emerged. There was a need for regularized exchanges of goods either between geographically dispersed communities or, at times, within a single community. This economic exchange was managed through redistribution, with the chief occupying the central position in the flow of goods (see Chapter 6).

In earlier periods, chiefdoms probably were found throughout much of the Old World. During more recent periods, such political systems were primarily concentrated in Oceania (Polynesia, Micronesia, and Melanesia) and in the Americas (the Caribbean and portions of South America and the northwestern coast of North America).

The Polynesian-speaking people of Tahiti, an island in the southeastern Pacific, have many characteristics typical of a chiefdom. This relatively large, mountainous, volcanic island had a population of about 100,000 at the time of European discovery. Tahiti was divided among about twenty rival chiefs.

The economy of Tahiti was based largely on farming. Taro, breadfruit, coconuts, and yams were the main crops; pigs and chickens were also raised, and fish and other seafood supplemented the food supply. Food production was sufficient not only to meet the needs of the population but also to produce surpluses for export to other islands. Although sufficient food was produced in all regions, there were significant regional differences in types of food produced because Tahiti varied ecologically.

Tahitian society had at least three, and possibly four, distinct classes, depending on how finely one wants to divide the units. *Arii,* or chiefs, and their close relatives formed the ruling elite. The *arii* were divided into two groups: the *arii rahi,* or sacred chiefs, and the *arii rii,* or small chiefs. Under these chiefs were the *raatira,* or subchiefs, and the *manahune,* or commoners. The sacred chiefs were viewed as descended from the gods, whereas the commoners were merely created by the gods for their use. The subchiefs were the offspring of intermarriage between the sacred chiefs and commoners, whereas the small chiefs were the products of still later intermarriages between sacred chiefs and subchiefs. Once these four classes were established, class endogamy became the rule.

The sacred chiefs, viewed as gods on earth, evoked both reverence and fear. Whatever the highest ranking sacred chiefs touched became *tabu,* or sacred, and could not be used for fear of supernatural punishment. Such a chief had to be carried on the back of a servant, lest the ground touched by his feet became *tabu.* He could not enter the house of another individual for the same reason. The lifestyle of the chief's family differed from that of other individuals: They had larger and more elaborate houses, the largest canoes, insignia of their rank, and particular clothing.

Unlike band- and tribal-level societies, resources in chiefdoms were individually owned. Land was owned mainly by the chiefs and subchiefs, but ultimate authority rested with the sacred chiefs within the polity. Although sacred chiefs could not withhold the title to lands from the families of subchiefs, they could banish an individual subchief. Crafts were specialized, and craftspeople were attached to particular sacred chiefs and produced goods for them. Communal fishing equipment was made by these craftspeople, and the chiefs regulated their use. Thus, the sacred chiefs directly controlled craft production and communal fishing. The chiefs could make unlimited demands on the property of the sub-chiefs and commoners. If someone refused, the chief could have the recalcitrant banished or make him or her a sacrificial victim. Theoretically, the sacred chief was the head judicial figure in the polity, but some believe that the chief seldom intervened in disputes between individuals; the chief usually used such powers only against people who challenged his authority.

The sacred chief in each polity was the focal point for redistributive exchanges. The chief periodically demanded surplus production from all his subjects for a public redistribution. Such events were associated with special occasions: a rite of passage for a member of the chief's family, the organizing of a military attack, religious ceremonies, or the start of the breadfruit harvest. During such ceremonies, the chief distributed the goods collected to all his subjects.

States

Although they had a centralized political system, chiefdoms were kinship-based structures. As a result, the number of people who could be effectively integrated into a chiefdom was limited. In Polynesia, most chiefdoms ranged from only a few thousand to 30,000 persons. Polities with larger populations require a political structure based on institutions other than kinship.

States, like chiefdoms, have a centralized political structure. But the presence of a bureaucracy distinguishes states. A chiefdom is basically a two-level system: (1) the chiefs, who have varying levels of authority and power, and (2) the commoners, or the great mass of the populace. A state has at least three levels: (1) the ruling elite, (2) a bureaucracy, and (3) the populace.

In states, as in chiefdoms, highest authority and power reside in the ruling elite, the formal political head or heads of the polity. States vary greatly in the types of political leaders and in the basis for the leaders' authority and power. Leaders in the earliest states frequently were consid-

Courtesy of Garrick Bailey

In state-level societies, authority is enforced by the military and/or police.

ered to be the descendants of gods, and thus themselves gods on earth. The Incas of Peru and the pharaohs of Egypt were leaders who ruled as gods. Other political leaders have legitimated their positions with claims of having been chosen by God. Early European kings legitimated their claims to leadership on such a basis; and as English coins still proclaim, the queen rules *Dei gratia*—by the "grace of God." Other states have evolved political leadership that uses strictly secular ideas to justify its power. In countries where leaders are elected by a vote of the populace, rule is legitimated by the internalized acceptance of such ascendance to office. Even strictly secular kingdoms, dictatorships, and oligarchies can, if in power for a sufficient time, have their rule accepted by the populace as "legitimate."

Although they differ greatly in political leadership, states all share one characteristic: the presence of a bureaucracy that carries out the day-to-day governing of the polity. In simple terms, a bureaucrat is a person to whom a political leader delegates certain authority and powers. The bureaucrat thus acts on behalf of the political leader. Lacking any inherent authority or powers personally, bureaucrats depend on the continued support of political leaders. The emergence of bureaucracies allowed for qualitative and quantitative changes in political systems. Using bureaucrats as intermediaries, political leaders could expand the size of their polities geographically and demographically, while strengthening their political control over the population. Bureaucrats could engineer such expansion without threat of revolution and political fragmentation because they lacked any personal claims to independent political legitimacy.

The emergence of states increased the complexity of political units. Bureaucracies allowed for specialization in governmental functions and made possible the effective integration of large land areas and populations into political units. Chiefdoms seldom exceeded 30,000 persons, whereas modern states such as China may have populations of one billion people.

SOCIAL CONTROL and LAW

All societies have clearly defined rules that govern the relationships between members, but not all individuals in any society will conform to these rules. Thus, among all peoples there exist formal and informal ways to correct the behavior of individuals. In general, we call these mechanisms social control. One form of social control is called law.

Social Control

Social control refers to the diverse ways in which the behaviors of the members of a society are constrained into socially approved channels. All cultures have certain behavioral norms that most people learn and begin to conform to during enculturation. But all societies have individuals who, to one degree or another, deviate from those norms. Violations of norms usually result in sanctions or punishments for the offender, which serve to correct the behavior of particular people and to show others the penalties for such deviance. The severity of sanctions and the process by which sanctions are imposed differ greatly, depending on the seriousness culturally attached to the violated norm, the perceived severity of the violation, and the overall political and legal system of the people.

Children who get into mischief usually are corrected by their parents. In our own society, parents may impose sanctions ranging from "time outs" to scolding to withdrawing privileges. The correcting of children trains individuals in proper behavior at an early age.

The community also applies informal sanctions against individuals—both children and adults—who are not behaving properly. Gossip, or fear of gossip, serves as an important method of social control in most societies. Most people fear the contempt or ridicule of their peers, so most individuals try to conform to behavioral norms. People attempt to hide behavior that would be the subject of gossip, scandal, and ridicule. Individuals whose known behavior consistently violates social norms may find themselves ostracized by friends and relatives (the severest of informal punishments). Informal economic penalties also may be imposed. A family may withdraw economic support in attempts to modify the errant behavior of a member.

A wide variety of supernatural sanctions may assist in controlling individual behavior, and in some cases these supernatural sanctions are automatically imposed on particular types of behavior. Supernatural sanctions can be specifically directed. In many societies, including some Christian ones, an individual may place a curse on another person by calling on a supernatural being. Fear of sorcery or witchcraft (see Chapter 11) frequently serves as another important form of social control. Most victims are people who offended a witch or sorcerer in some way, often through a breach of social norms.

Law

Law is the highest level of social control, and legal punishments usually are reserved for the most serious breaches of norms. The question of how law can be distinguished from other forms of social control is not easy to answer. In societies with court systems the distinction is formalized, but in societies without such formalized legal systems the division is not as clear.

E. Adamson Hoebel (1954, 28) defined law in the following way: "A social norm is legal if its neglect or infraction is regularly met, in threat or in fact, by the application of physical force by an individual or group possessing the socially recognized privilege of so acting." Law so defined was and is present in virtually every society. Leopold Pospisil, building in part on Hoebel's work, defined law as having four attributes: *authority, intention of universal application, obligatio,* and *sanction.*

In a legal action, some individual or group must have publicly recognized authority to settle a case or punish a violation. In societies with courts the authority is obvious, but in societies that lack courts the authority becomes less clear. What emerges frequently is an ad hoc authority; that is, because of the peculiarities of the case, a particular individual or group becomes recognized by the community as the authority responsible for its resolution. In some cases, the victim may be the recognized authority. In the victim's absence (as in the case of murder), the victim's family, clan, or kin group may be placed in the role of authority. Such ad hoc authority is discussed later in some of the examples.

Implicit in all legal actions is the intention of universal application, which means that in identical cases the sanction imposed is the same. Although one might argue that no two legal cases have been or will ever be identical, the notion of universal application requires that the law be consistent and thus predictable; the arbitrary imposition of sanctions is not law.

Obligatio refers to the legal relation between two or more living individuals. All individuals are immersed in a complex web of rights and duties, and every individual has both certain rights and certain duties to others. In some cases, an individual's rights and the correlative duties of others are well defined; in other cases, some ambiguity exists. Most civil legal cases and arguments in our own court system focus on questions about rights and duties. For example, when two drivers argue after a traffic accident, they argue about who was properly exercising rights and who was negligent regarding duties. An act breaches the law only if the abridgment of one's individual rights resulted from another person's failure to perform a legitimate duty.

Whereas Hoebel limited legal sanctions to physical sanctions, Pospisil argued that this definition is too narrow. A legal sanction does not have to be some form of corporal punishment, nor does it have to involve the loss of property. Based on his work with the Kapauku of New Guinea, Pospisil contended that the impact of psychological sanctions can be more severe than actual physical punishment. For this reason he stated, "We can define a legal sanction as either the negative behavior of withdrawing some rewards or favors that otherwise (if the law had not been violated) would have been granted, or the positive behavior of inflicting some painful experience, be it physical or psychological" (Pospisil 1958, 268).

LEGAL SYSTEMS

Two main levels of legal systems can be defined on the basis of complexity and formality: (1) **self-help systems** and (2) **court systems.**

Self-Help Systems

Self-help systems, also called *ad hoc systems,* are informal and exist in the absence of any centralized or formalized legal institutions capable of settling disputes. Such systems are associated with band-level societies and most tribal-level societies. All legal actions concern only the principal parties and/or their families.

Self-help legal systems take two main forms: (1) familial and (2) mediator. In familial systems, all actions and decisions are initiated and executed by the families or larger kin groups involved. Mediator systems add a neutral third party—the mediator—who attempts to negotiate and resolve the dispute peacefully.

In familial systems, legal actions are handled by the families involved. A legal offense only indirectly concerns the community as a whole. When an individual and/or family determines that its rights have been violated, the imposition of the proper sanction falls to the plaintiffs, who assume the role of authority. Such a system has some problems in implementation but not as many as one might anticipate. This is not a system of "might makes right." Cases arise in which the physically weak are victimized by the strong. However, in cases of legal redress there is a community consensus in support of the victim and usually a recognized means by which even the weakest members of the community can gather enough support to impose appropriate sanctions on the strongest.

The Comanche exemplify how a familial legal system operated and how victims weaker than their opponents could obtain redress. A frequent Comanche offense was "wife stealing." Most older Comanche men were polygynous, and some wives were much younger than their husbands. Among young Comanche men it was considered prestigious, although illegal, to steal the wife of another man. Under Comanche law the injured husband could demand either his wife back or some property, usually horses, in compensation. The husband had the responsibility of imposing these sanctions. The community played no direct role, but a husband could not ignore the loss of a wife; nonaction would result in ridicule by the community and a decline in prestige.

In imposing these sanctions the husband was allowed to use whatever physical force was needed, short of killing the individual. In cases in which the men involved were physical equals, they met to negotiate the husband's demands. Behind these negotiations was the potential threat that the husband might physically assault the defendant.

In cases where the husband presented no physical threat to the defendant, there were institutionalized means that enabled the husband to gain the physical backing he needed. Although lowering his prestige in the community, he could call on his relatives for support and with his kinsmen present, negotiate with the defendant. The defendant always had to stand alone. Even if the defendant asked his kinsmen for support, they would not have responded for fear of community ridicule.

If the husband was an orphan or lacked kinsmen to negotiate successfully, another cultural avenue was open. The aggrieved man could call on any man he wanted to prosecute his case. He usually sought the assistance of a powerful war leader, and such a request was so prestigious that a war leader could not refuse. But making such a request greatly lowered the husband's prestige, and usually it required extreme social pressure to cause a man to ask for assistance. Once the request was made, the issue was between the defendant and the war leader. On approaching the defendant the war leader would call out, "You have stolen my wife," and then proceed to exact whatever demands the husband had requested. For his action the war leader received nothing in payment other than the admiration of the community; the husband received the settlement. Although this process most commonly was used in wife-stealing cases, it could be used for other issues as well. Thus, Comanche legal institutions gave any individual the means to marshal overwhelming physical force in the protection of his rights.

The mediator system is more formalized. Under this system, disputes are still between individuals and families, and the offended party and/or his or her family fills the position of authority. However, a third party is called on, usually by the offending individual or his or her family, to attempt to negotiate a mutually agreeable solution. The mediator has no authority to impose a settlement. The aggrieved party and/or family must agree to accept the compensation negotiated.

The Nuer, a pastoral tribal society of the Sudan, provide an example of how mediator systems operate. The Nuer live in small villages of related families. Although villages are tied together through lineages and clans, there is no effective leadership above the village level. The only formalized leaders who transcend the local units are *leopard-skin chiefs,* whose position is indicated by the wearing of a leopard-skin cloak. These men have no secular authority to enforce their judgments, only limited ritual powers to bless and curse.

The most important function of leopard-skin chiefs is mediating feuds between local groups. The Nuer are an egalitarian, warrior-oriented people. Disputes between individuals frequently result in physical violence and sometimes death. The killing of a Nuer requires that his kinsmen exact retribution. Any close patrilineal kinsman of the murderer may be killed in retaliation, but initially the victim's kinsmen attempt to kill the murderer himself. Immediately after a murder the killer flees to the house of a leopard-skin chief. This dwelling is a sanctuary, and as long as the man stays in the chief's house he is safe. The victim's kinsmen usually keep the house under surveillance in order to kill the murderer if he ventures out.

The leopard-skin chief keeps the murderer in his house until a settlement is arranged. The chief will wait until tempers have cooled, which usually requires several weeks, before he begins to negotiate the case. He approaches the murderer's family about paying cattle to the victim's family in compensation. After the murderer's family has agreed to pay, the chief offers the victim's family cattle in compensation. Initially the victim's family invariably refuses, saying that they want blood, that cattle cannot compensate them for the death of their beloved kinsman. The leopard-skin chief persists, usually gaining the support of more distant relatives of the victim, who also pressure the family to settle. The leopard-skin chief may even threaten to place a curse on the family if they continue to refuse to settle for a payment rather than blood. The family eventually accepts cattle, usually about forty head, as compensation. Even though the matter is formally settled, the killer and his close patrilineal kinsmen will avoid the family of the victim for some years so as not to provoke spontaneous retaliation.

Court Systems

A number of factors distinguish a court system from a self-help system. First, legal authority resides not with the victim and/or his or her family but with a formalized institution, the court, which has the authority to hear disputes and to unilaterally decide cases and impose sanctions. Fully developed court systems exist only in societies that have centralized formal political leadership, that is, in chiefdoms or states. Second, most court systems operate with formal public hearings, presided over by a judge or judges, with formally defined defendants and plaintiffs. Grievances are stated, evidence is collected and analyzed, and, in cases of conflicting evidence, oaths or ordeals may be used to determine truthfulness.

Court systems may be divided into two categories: (1) **courts of mediation** and (2) **courts of regulation**. All court systems mediate disputes as well as regulate behavior; but, as societies become increasingly complex, the primary focus of the courts shifts from mediating disputes to regulating behavior. This shift results in a qualitative difference not only in the courts but in the nature of the law itself. Associated with this shift is an increasing codification of the laws. Laws and their associated sanctions become standardized and rigid, and civil laws are steadily transformed into criminal laws. Court systems begin to emerge with the concept of "crime against society"—the need to control individual acts that might endanger the society as a whole, as opposed to acts that threaten only individuals. Herein lies the distinction between criminal law and civil law.

Courts of Mediation In courts of mediation few laws are codified, and the judges follow few formalized guidelines as to what constitutes a legal violation or the sanction that should be imposed. Judges have tremendous latitude in their actions. What they apply is a reasonable-person model. Using prevalent norms and values, they ask the

CONCEPT REVIEW Legal Systems

FORM	CHARACTERISTICS	ASSOCIATED POLITICAL SYSTEM(S)
Self-Help		
(a) Familial	Legal concepts based on accepted social norms and behaviors of the society.	Band
	Ad hoc sanctioning authority limited to victim and/or victim's family, with implicit support of other community members.	
(b) Mediator	Legal concepts based on accepted social norms and behaviors of the society.	Found among composite bands and most tribal peoples.
	Ad hoc sanctioning authority limited to victim and/or victim's family, with implicit support of other community members.	
	Use of a third-party mediator, with limited if any authority, to negotiate a settlement.	
Courts		
(a) Mediation	Legal concepts based on the reasonable-person model.	Some tribal peoples have rudimentary court systems. However, true court systems appear with chiefdoms and smaller states.
	Formal judges who have the authority to hear cases and impose sanctions.	
(b) Regulation	Laws and sanctions are formally codified.	States
	Formal judges who have the authority to hear cases and impose sanctions.	

question, "How should a reasonable individual have acted under these circumstances?" To determine this, an individual's actions have to be examined within the social context in which the dispute occurred: What was the past and present relationship between the parties involved? What were the circumstances leading up to the event? Thus, judges attempt to examine each case as a unique occurrence. Although some sanctions are imposed as punishments, other sanctions are designed to restore as fully as possible a working, if not harmonious, relationship between the parties involved.

One difficulty in attempting to describe courts of mediation is our limited knowledge of such systems. Polities having courts of this nature were some time ago brought under European colonial rule. Their courts were soon modified by and subordinated to European colonial courts, which were more regulatory in nature. The example we use is that of the Barotse judicial system, as described by Max Gluckman. The Barotse made up a multiethnic state in southern Africa that at the time of Gluckman's study in the 1940s had been under British rule for forty years. More serious offenses had been removed by the British from the jurisdiction of this court. Despite these factors, the basic Barotse legal concepts aptly illustrate a mediation type of court system.

The Barotse state had two capitals—a northern capital, where the king resided, and a subordinate southern capital, ruled by a princess. All villages in the state were attached to one or the other of these capitals. The capitals were identical in structure; each had a palace and a council house. Courts of law were held in the council house.

The titular head of the court was the ruler; in practice, the ruler seldom was present at trials. In the center at the back of the house was the dais, or raised platform, where the ruler sat if present. There were three ranked groupings of judges. The highest ranking group of judges were the *indunas,* or "councilors," who sat to the right of the dais. The second-highest ranking group was the *likombwa,* or "stewards," who sat to the left. These two groups were divided into senior members, who sat in the front, and junior members, who sat behind. The third group consisted of princes and the husbands of the princesses, who represented their wives. This group sat at a right angle to the *likombwa.*

A case was introduced by a plaintiff, who was allowed to state his or her grievance at length with no interruption; the defendant was then allowed the same privilege. The statements of witnesses for both sides followed. There were no attorneys for either side; the judges questioned and cross-examined the witnesses. After all the testimony had been heard, the judges began to give their opinions, starting with the most junior *indunas,* followed by the others in order of increasing seniority. The last judge to speak was the senior *induna,* who passed judgment on the case, subject to the ruler's approval.

In judging a case, a reasonable-person model was used. With the Barotse, the reasonableness of behavior was related to the social and kinship relationships of the individuals involved. Also, a breach of the law usually did not happen in isolation, and many individuals were at fault; so one case frequently led to a number of related cases. In passing judgment and imposing sanctions, the judges considered numerous factors. One of the most important was the kinship relationship between parties. The judges attempted to restore the relationship and reconcile the parties—but not

without blaming those who had committed wrongs and not without imposing sanctions. The judges' opinions frequently took the form of sermons on proper behavior. As Gluckman (1973, 22) notes:

> Implicit in the reasonable man is the upright man, and moral issues in these relationships are barely differentiated from legal issues. This is so even though . . . [they] distinguish "legal" rules, which the . . . [court] has power to enforce or protect, from "moral" rules which it has no power to enforce or protect. But the judges are reluctant to support the person who is right in law, but wrong in justice, and may seek to achieve justice by indirect . . . action.

Courts of mediation have great potential for meeting the basic social purpose of the law, which is the maintenance of group cohesiveness. There is one serious drawback: Such a system is workable only in a culturally homogeneous political unit; that is, it works only if the judges and the parties involved share the same basic norms and values.

Courts of Regulation   In the second millennium B.C. the Code of Hammurabi, the earliest known set of written laws, was created in Babylon. The code covered a variety of laws. One section dealt with physicians. It set the prices to be charged for various types of operations, based on the ability of individuals to pay. It also decreed, among other things, that if a surgeon operated on an individual using a bronze knife and the patient died or lost his eyesight, the surgeon's hand was to be cut off. The laws defined in the Code of Hammurabi reflect the emergence of regulatory laws. The role of the court was no longer merely to arbitrate disputes and strive for reconciliation but to define the rights and duties of members of an increasingly heterogeneous community.

Courts of regulation were a natural outgrowth of state-level polities, which evolved socially and economically distinct classes and encompassed numerous culturally distinct peoples. As relationships between individuals in the population became depersonalized, the law, too, became increasingly depersonalized. This change in the nature of law was compounded by the political incorporation of diverse peoples who frequently had conflicting cultural norms and values. The use of a reasonable-person model is workable only as long as there is a general consensus on what is "reasonable." In increasingly stratified and multiethnic societies, the possibility of such consensus declined. Mediation of disputes works well in small, kinship-based societies, where all parties recognize the need for reconciliation through compromise. In sharply divided societies, however, the need for mediation is not as great because reconciliation in itself is not seen as a gain. Compromise is viewed only in terms of what is lost. Laws were thus created to bring order and stability to the interactions between individuals, particularly between individuals who were not social equals. With law divorced from social norms and values, justice was no longer simply a moral or ethical issue but came to be viewed in terms of consistency, or precedent.

The separation of law from social norms and values also allowed for the "politicization" of the laws. Laws were created to serve political ends, as various groups vied with one another for the creation of laws that would protect, express, or further their own goals, interests, and values. This situation is particularly evident in stratified societies. Given the cultural pluralism, religious diversity, regional differences, and economic inequality of the United States, it would be impossible to create a code of laws that could equally protect the interests of all classes and that would be consistent with the norms and values of all groups. As a result, many people find themselves subject to laws and sanctions, many of which they judge either immoral or unethical; at times, people find that laws violate their own cultural values (e.g., abortion, capital punishment, the draft). With the emergence of states and courts of regulation, law ceased to be an expression of social norms and values and became their molder.

Summary

1. Systems of equality and inequality, political organization, and social control are three distinct but overlapping aspects of culture.

2. Fried's typology of egalitarian, ranked, and stratified societies provides a useful description of the range of diversity in inequality.

3. In egalitarian societies all productive resources are open to use by all members of the society. Differences in material wealth, power, and prestige are minimal and based on the personal abilities and achievements of the individual. Most foragers and many horticultural peoples are egalitarian, with economic exchange within the group taking the form of reciprocity.

4. In ranked societies access to productive resources is limited by kin group membership.

There are a set number of honored positions (chiefs, titles, offices), which are primarily hereditary within particular lineages and/or kin groups. There are significant differences in rewards. Redistribution is characteristic of ranked societies.

5. Stratified societies are defined by three characteristics: (1) They have marked inequalities in access to all three kinds of rewards; (2) this inequality is based largely on unequal access to productive resources; and (3) the inequality is strongly heritable. Stratification takes two different forms: (1) caste systems and (2) class systems. The market economy is characteristic of stratified societies.

6. Four major categories of political organization are bands, tribes, chiefdoms, and states. Found among foraging societies, the band is the simplest and least formal level of political organization. Two forms of band organization exist: simple bands and composite bands. In simple bands, the highest level of political organization is the extended family, with the highest level of political leadership being the heads of the various families. These simple bands are economically self-sufficient and politically autonomous.

7. Composite bands are larger than simple bands and include a number of distinct families. Leadership in composite bands is vested in "big men," or informal leaders, who have influence but not authority.

8. At the tribal level formal institutions transcend local residence groups and bind the geographically scattered members of the society into a cohesive unit. The key element in tribal societies is sodalities, which may be either kinship-based, as in the case of clans, or nonkinship-based, as in the case of warrior societies or age grades. Leadership in such groups is more structured, with formal political offices.

9. Chiefdoms have formal, hereditary leadership, with centralized political control and authority. The associated redistributive economic exchange system focused on the chief serves to integrate economically the various communities within the political unit.

10. The state is the most complex level of political organization. States have centralized power and control, but the key characteristic of a state is the presence of a bureaucracy—individuals acting on behalf of the political elite, thus enabling the centralized power figures to maintain control of a greater number of individuals.

11. Social control consists of the various methods used to control and channel the behavior of individual members of a society into approved behavior. Law and legal systems are merely the highest level of social control. Law is defined as having four attributes: (1) authority, (2) obligatio, (3) intention of universal application, and (4) sanction. By this definition, all societies have law.

12. In societies without centralized political systems, legal systems are self-help. In self-help

systems, the responsibility and authority for determining a breach of the law and imposition of the proper sanction fall to the victim or his or her family (or both).

13. Law in societies with centralized political systems is handled by courts. Court systems in turn usually can be categorized as either courts of mediation or courts of regulation. In relatively homogeneous societies, most court systems take as their primary objective the mediation of disputes between individuals and the restoration of harmonious social relationships. In more heterogeneous groups, courts usually become more regulatory in nature, with formally defined laws and sanctions.

KEY TERMS

inequality	big men
egalitarian	influence
ranked	authority
stratified	sodalities
class	social control
caste	law
simple bands	self-help legal systems
composite bands	court legal systems
tribes	courts of mediation
chiefdoms	courts of regulation
states	

SUGGESTED READINGS

Berreman, Gerald D., and Kathleen M. Zaretsky. *Social Inequality: Comparative and Development Approaches.* New York: Academic Press, 1981.

A collection of papers discussing social inequality in a number of societies.

Cohen, R., and Elman Service, eds. *Origins of the State: The Anthropology of Political Evolution.* Philadelphia: Institute for the Study of Human Issues, 1978.

A collection of essays from various perspectives examining the development of state-level political systems.

Danziger, Sheldon, and Peter Gottschalk. *America Unequal*. New York: Russell Sage, 1995.

Two economists analyze the growing wealth differences in the United States and propose solutions using government policies.

Domhoff, G. William. *Who Rules America: Power and Politics in the Year 2000*. 3rd ed. Mountain View, CA: Mayfield, 1998.

An economist's analysis of the reasons for the increasing inequality in the United States and proposed solutions.

Fried, Morton. *The Evolution of Political Society*. New York: Random House, 1967.

A theoretical study that traces the development of political systems from egalitarian societies, through ranked, to stratified and state-level societies.

Gluckman, Max. *The Ideas in Barotse Jurisprudence*. Manchester: Manchester University Press, 1965.
———. *The Judicial Process Among the Barotse*. Manchester: Manchester University Press, 1973.

These two studies of the Barotse of Zambia not only describe a system in a non-Western state but also—and more important—illustrate the legal reasoning used in the Barotse court systems.

Hoebel, E. Adamson. *The Law of Primitive Man*. Cambridge, MA: Harvard University Press, 1964.

The first major comparative study of non-Western legal systems. Although somewhat dated, it remains a classic study.

———. *The Political Organization and Law-Ways of the Comanche Indians*. American Anthropological Association, Memoir 54, 1940.

Good description of the political structure and legal system of a band-level society.

Hurst, Charles E. *Social Inequality: Forms, Causes and Consequences*. Boston: Allyn and Bacon, 1992.

A textbook on inequality in the modern United States. Includes chapters on inequality based on race and gender as well as summaries of various explanations of inequality and stratification.

Mair, Lucy. *Primitive Government*. Baltimore: Penguin, 1966.

Concerned exclusively with African peoples, this is an excellent introduction to preindustrial political systems.

Newman, Katherine S. *Law and Economic Organization: A Comparative Study of Pre-Industrial Societies*. Cambridge: Cambridge University Press, 1983.

A cross-cultural analysis of sixty societies to show that legal institutions systematically vary with economic organization.

Service, Elman. *Primitive Social Organization: An Evolutionary Perspective*. New York: Random House, 1966.

Traces the evolution of political systems from bands to chiefdoms.

chapter 11

RELIGION *and* WORLD VIEW

Contents

All cultures have religions, by which we mean the belief in the existence of supernatural powers and the attempts to influence or control these supernatural powers by the performance of rituals.

Religious beliefs and rituals vary greatly among the world's peoples. In this chapter we are going to focus on the components of religion, the types of religious organizations, and theories concerning the kinds of individual or societal needs and wants met by religion. We will conclude with a discussion of witchcraft and sorcery.

Defining Religion

What is religion? How can we best define it so as to encompass all the diversity of religion found among humanity? Just as some societies have no formal government, so are there societies that lack a belief in any kind of all-powerful deity, comparable to the Judeo-Christian God. We need a definition that can be applied cross-culturally.

A nineteenth-century definition that many scholars still use is E. B. Tylor's **animism**, or "belief in spiritual beings." Most modern conceptions follow Tylor's lead: They specify that, at the least, all religions include beliefs that some kind of spiritual or supernatural powers exist. But Tylor's definition leaves out much about religion. By expanding on it we can present an overview of religion in cross-cultural perspective.

All religions consist of three major components: (1) beliefs about the nature and character of supernatural powers, (2) teachings or traditions, which tell of these supernatural powers, and (3) rituals intended to influence or direct these powers for the benefit of the group.

Supernatural Powers: Beings and Forces

"Beings" are not the only kind of spiritual powers that people believe in. Many religions posit the existence of other kinds of powers that are more like "forces" than "beings." For example, in aboriginal times the peoples of Polynesia believed in *mana*, a diffuse, impersonal, incorporeal power. *Mana* lent supernatural potency to things, which explained unusual qualities; or to people, which explained unusual success. People and objects could be infused with greater or lesser amounts of *mana*. Having a lot of *mana* explained why some chiefs always won battles, why some fishing equipment seemed to work so well, why certain gardens produced such fine crops, and so forth.

The widespread belief in powers such as *mana* make it useful to divide supernatural powers into beings and forces. Spiritual *beings* usually have qualities such as a bodily form, some way of appearing before people, a personality, and a fairly predictable way of responding to human actions. The characteristics people attribute to supernatural beings vary enormously: They can be capricious or consistent, stubborn or reasonable, vengeful or forgiving, amoral or just. Some beings have human origins, such as ghosts. Other kinds of beings have nonhuman origins, such as many gods or spirits.

Supernatural *forces* likewise have definite properties, which vary from people to people. Because forces usually have no will of their own—no power to refuse humans who know how to command or manipulate them in the proper manner—they often can be used for either good or evil purposes. In most cases, people believe that supernatural forces can be manipulated by humans who know the proper rituals.

Teachings

Belief in the existence of supernatural powers (beings and forces) is only part of religion. Religion also includes teachings—oral or written stories about the actions and deeds of supernatural powers. Teachings commonly tell of the actions of cultural heroes and supernatural powers of long ago. Sometimes they explain how the entire universe was created. They may recount how and why people, animals, plants, and natural features originated. Teachings explain how a

peopl
they
why
ways
who

N
tradi
chur
eties
as a
cour
ings
relig
whi
giou
cast
pco
wor
tea

Ch
to
use
gay
to
Ge
of
es
lu
wi
A
gi
in

ples culturally derived from Europe—Western
are more likely to believe that God gave the earth
to humans to conquer and exploit than to preserve and protect.

In contrast, Westerners might show more
respect for other living things if (as in some cultures) the sacred traditions of our religious heritage recounted how some of us came from bears,
some from coyotes, some from whales, and so
forth. We might hesitate to destroy a forest if the
scriptures told us explicitly that trees are just as
precious to God as are humans. In short, if Western sacred teachings emphasized the importance

harmony with nature rather than sub-
re, perhaps the modern "ecological
ld be less of a crisis.
er, Judeo-Christian scriptures can be
d in many ways and used for many
not all of which involve the uncon-
bloitation of resources for profit or ma-
gratification. The Amish communities
America, for example, are thoroughly
, but they reject much of the materialism
n society.

ple's sacred teachings—and this is the
point we are trying to make—are more
ies they recite on appropriate occasions.
more than satisfy idle curiosity and help
time. These sacred stories are part and
f a people's world view: their fundamen-
ptions of nature and society and how
ught to relate to the world and to one
. They therefore affect how people behave
everyday lives.

ls

ns include behaviors as well as beliefs and
. People everywhere believe that gods,
, demons, devils, and other supernatural
take an active interest in worldly affairs,
larly in the lives of human beings. Such
can be asked for blessings or aid, or some-
they can be commanded to do things for or
ple. Similarly, people can use supernatural
to cause helpful or harmful effects. Because
e believe that supernatural beings and
forces can make natural events occur and can
intervene in human affairs, all cultures prescribe
certain behaviors that are used to interact with
and influence various powers.

The organized performance of behaviors intended to influence supernatural powers is
known as **ritual**. Rituals are always stereotyped:
There are definite patterns of speech or movement, or definite sequences of events, that occur
in much the same way in performance after performance. In general, people performing rituals
want supernatural powers to do things on their

Hinduism regards certain substances and activities as spiritually defiling or polluting. Ritual bathing—here in the Ganges River—removes the pollution.

behalf: to make someone (or everyone) healthy or fertile, to bring rain, to make the crops grow, to save their souls, to bring back the game, to provide blessings, and so forth. People may pray, worship, make sacrifices, and follow ritual procedures scrupulously to ensure that their gods, their personal spirits, or the ghosts of their dead ancestors intervene favorably in their lives.

The performers of ritual often want supernatural powers to harm their enemies in some way: to make them sick or barren, to bring floods or pestilence to their land, to drive the animals out of their territory, to make their spears fly crooked in the upcoming battle, and so forth. If we can ask supernatural powers to harm our enemies, our enemies may have the same ability; they can cause supernatural harm to us, making us sick or prone to misfortune. So ethnographers commonly report that members of some societies believe that many or all illnesses, deaths, and accidents are caused by the supernatural powers of evil or enemy humans. And many kinds of rituals exist whose explicit purpose is to counteract the harm caused by other rituals performed by enemies.

Rituals the world over have symbolic aspects. They often occur in *places* that have symbolic significance to the performers. For example, they may be held where some mythological event occurred, or where the women who founded a matrilineage were born. Rituals often involve the display and manipulation of *objects* that symbolize an event (e.g., the cross), a holy person (statues of Jesus and Mary), a relationship (wedding rings, the symbol of holy matrimony), and a variety of other things. Symbolic significance usually is attached to the *language* and *behavior* of ritual, as in the Christian rituals of worship, hymn singing, prayer, baptism, communion, and confession.

Anthropologists classify rituals on two bases. The first basis is their conscious purposes—the reasons people themselves give for performing them. For example, there are divination rituals, which are performed to acquire information from a supernatural power about the future or about some past event. There are also curing, sorcery, sacrificial, and exorcism rituals. There are rituals to renew the world, to make a man out of a boy and a woman out of a girl, and to free the soul from a dead person's body. There are rituals held for single individuals, for kin groups, for people of similar age, for whole societies, and so forth.

The second basis of classification is when rituals occur, whether they are held on a regular schedule (like Sunday church services) or simply whenever some individual or group wants or needs them (like funerals or prayers for a sick person). If rituals are held regularly (seasonally, annually, daily, monthly, etc.) they are called *calendrical rituals*. *Crisis rituals* are organized and performed whenever some individual or group needs, wants, or asks for them for purposes of curing, ensuring good hunting or fishing, or other events that happen sporadically or unpredictably.

It is difficult to make meaningful generalizations about rituals since they vary so widely in form and significance. There is, however, one

Robert MacKinlay/Peter Arnold, Inc.

CONCEPT REVIEW Components of Religion

COMPONENT	CHARACTERISTICS
Supernatural Powers	
(1) Forces	Do not have any bodily or physical form; a diffuse, impersonal, incorporeal power.
(2) Beings	Have or can assume a bodily or physical form; they have a personality and a fairly predictable way of responding to human actions. (Ghosts, gods, spirits)
Teachings	The oral or written stories concerning the actions and deeds of supernatural powers.
Rituals	An organized performance of behaviors intended to influence supernatural powers.

general category of rituals that are commonly found among most peoples in the world: rites of passage.

Rites of Passage

Rites of passage are a specialized set of rituals associated with the **life cycle** of individuals; the culturally defined age categories through which a person passes between birth and death. An individual's life cycle usually includes stages such as birth, childhood, adolescence, adulthood, old age, and death. Each stage in the life cycle carries certain cultural expectations; as individuals move through these stages, their overall role in society changes. Sometimes these transitions between stages take place gradually and are not the subject of any particular notice, but more frequently they are sharply and formally defined by a rite of passage. A rite of passage is a public ceremony or ritual that marks a change in social status, usually brought about or related to increasing age. The most common of these rites are birth/naming rites, puberty rites, marriage rites, and burial/funeral rites. However, while most societies have such rituals they differ in relative importance from one group to the next and may or may not be religious in nature. In countries such as the United States and Canada such rites may be either religious or secular, and the religious forms of these rituals differ depending upon the individual's religious beliefs.

Birth/Naming Rites   When does an individual truly become a member of the society? In many cultures a baby's status is ambiguous until he or she is formally named. The formal naming of a child frequently is associated with the conferring of human status. For the Osage, a Native American people, the naming rite, bestowing human status, was the most important rite of passage. Osage parents often waited several months—in the case of a sickly child, possibly more than a year—before naming a child. If the child died before acquiring a name, he or she was quietly buried, and the family did not have to observe a year of mourning. After they were convinced the infant was going to survive, parents began to prepare for a naming ritual. A ritual specialist called a *non-hon-zhinga* (or "little-old-man") from the child's father's clan was chosen to organize and direct the ceremony. Little-old-men symbolically representing all the Osage clans gathered in the "lodge of mystery," a ritual structure in the village, to hold the ceremony. One at a time the leader gave a trade blanket to the little-old-men present, each of whom recited a long and complex ritual prayer asking Wa-kon-tah's (god's) blessing for the child and outlining the supernatural powers associated with his particular clan. After the clan prayers had been recited, the child was handed to each of the little-old-men, who in turn blessed the child. Some anointed the baby with water, others rubbed the child with cedar or touched the child with ground corn. Then the baby was seated on a specially prepared robe in the center of the lodge and given a name belonging to his or her clan by the leader. The giving of this name symbolized the acceptance of the child as a member of the particular clan. The ritual participation of members of the other clans indicated the acceptance of the child as an Osage. The ritual ended with the father of the child giving horses and blankets to the presiding little-old-man and lesser gifts to the other little-old-men. Only after the naming ritual might one say that Osage childhood truly began.

Puberty Rites   The transition from childhood to adolescence varies from society to society. In North American society there is no general public ritual or event that serves to mark this change in status; passage is informal and gradual. In many societies this transition is formal and abrupt. In Islamic societies children, unlike adults, do not fast during Ramadan, the major religious holiday. A person's first observance of Ramadan by fasting marks the beginning of adolescence, because it publicly indicates the individual's willingness to begin accepting adult duties and responsibilities.

In many preindustrial societies the onset of puberty is publicly announced by the performance of a rite of passage called a **puberty** (or **initiation**) **rite**. The significance and elaboration of such ceremonies vary cross-culturally and with the sex of the individual. Among some peoples puberty rites for males are the most elaborate and important, while many other societies emphasize rites for females. Another common difference is that a female puberty rite is usually for a particular girl soon after her menarche, while males are usually initiated in groups of boys of about the same age. During the ritual, the initiates are educated in the responsibilities of adulthood, being told of the changes that will be expected of them in their behavior, and often being told of ritual secrets as well. Physical trauma is a common part of puberty rites. Whipping, genital mutilation, tattooing, scarification, fasting, and similar acts indelibly mark this status transition in the mind if not on the bodies of the individuals.

About every four to five years, the BaMbuti, a foraging people of the Congo basin, together with neighboring village farmers, hold a male puberty rite. All boys between the ages of about eight and twelve are usually included. After the boys are assembled, they are taken to a special isolated initiation camp in the forest, where they live for about two weeks. Most of their time in camp is spent in learning songs and being instructed in their new roles as men. However, they are also subjected to ritual whippings, kept from sleeping, and forced to observe special food taboos. Finally the boys are circumcised (which they should endure without crying) and have their bodies painted with white clay, symbolizing their death as children and their rebirth as adults.

Initiation rites for females exhibit similar themes. Most often, they emphasize attainment of physical maturity, instruction in sexual matters and childbearing, and reminders of adult duties as wives and mothers.

Mescalero Apache are one people who have puberty ceremonies for girls. Each year, around the beginning of July, the people celebrate the attainment of womanhood in a ceremony that lasts four days and four nights. Apache girls in the region who have had their first menses in the last year go to a place where a large tipi is erected. During the ceremony, the girls are regarded as reincarnations of White Painted Woman, a spiritual being who gave many good things to the people. The girls are blessed by singers (specialists who have gone through lengthy training to learn the stories and chants) and by their relatives and friends. Those attending participate in traditional songs and dances dedicated to the four directions and to spirits associated with them. The Apache ceremony places a lot of emphasis on the girls becoming the "Mothers of the Tribe," perhaps because the Apache are a matrilineal people. On the fourth day, singers recount the history of the Apache and the girls are reminded of their ancestry and obligations. The ceremony honors the girls as individuals, reaffirms their commitment to the community and vice versa, urges them to act responsibly, and upholds and recreates Apache traditions annually. According to ethnographer Claire Farrer (1996, 89), "almost invariably, the girls report having been changed, not only into social women but also at a very basic level. They are ready to put aside their childhoods and become full members of their tribe and community." The ceremony thus helps the girls make the social transition to adulthood, with all its rights and responsibilities.

Among Apache, there are no painful ordeals. But ceremonies in some other cultures do involve pain. When a girl among the Tucuna Indians of the Amazon has her first menstruation, she is immediately placed in the loft of the large communal dwelling where she lives. She remains there until a special seclusion room next to the dwelling is constructed for her. She stays isolated in this room while preparations for her puberty rite are made. During this period the older women tell her about the danger from various spirits to which she as a woman is now subject, and they also inform her of what will be expected from her as a wife and mother. The ritual itself involves the presence of forty to fifty masked dancers who imitate spirits that both terrify and instruct her. Toward the end of the ceremony the girl is placed on a tapir hide in the middle of the house, and a group of elderly women slowly pull all the hair out of her head to the sound of a drum and rattle. The girl has to endure this pain without crying out. Although the Tucuna have an elaborate puberty rite for females, they have no such rite for males.

Marriage Rituals   Marriage denotes a major change in the social status of the two individuals involved, and in most societies it marks the beginning of true adulthood. As discussed in Chapter 7, marriages are governed by social, economic, and religious considerations. Clan or caste membership, which has religious significance, may affect whom you can or cannot marry (see also Chapters 8 and 10). However, social factors, such as family, as well as economic factors also affect choices. As a result marriage rituals usually show

considerable variability both between and within societies. Many marriage rituals focus on elaborate public exchanges of goods and valuables between the families of the bride and groom over a long period of time, the actual religious ritual portion of the wedding being limited. Certainly this is true of what might be termed the "ideal" wedding among Christian Americans. Prior to the ceremony itself, there are "showers" for the bride, given by her female friends and relatives. There are other parties for the groom, given by his male friends. Although the actual wedding ceremony and the exchanging of vows is the focal point of wedding activities, social activities such as eating, dancing, and displaying gifts usually occupy the better part of the day. The religious ritual part of a marriage is the critical or central part, but it is only a small part of what is primarily a social event. In this regard Christian American marriage rituals are similar to those of most peoples in the world. Marriages are usually social events with some religious elements.

Funerals   All peoples are faced with the problem of death and the disposal of the body of the deceased. All societies have beliefs about what happens to the soul or spirit of the individual after death. Some religions believe in reincarnation, others hold that the soul of the deceased travels to another world or even remains on earth. In some religions the ghost of the individual has to be ritually released from the body; in others, the ghost of the individual remains in the vicinity of the body for a period of time before leaving. Among some peoples it is thought that all ghosts are malevolent; others believe that ghosts of one's ancestors may act as supernatural helpers. The religious beliefs of a people strongly influence funeral rituals. Do you bury or cremate the body, and if so when, immediately or after a set number of days? How do you mourn the individual and for how long? Do you erect monuments to perpetuate the person's memory, or do you make the individual's name taboo and attempt to never think of him or her again? There are a wide range of different funeral practices.

Traditional Navajos believe that after death the ghost of the individual remains in the vicinity, and that all ghosts are malevolent. If possible, when a person is ill and expected to die, he or she is removed from the hogan (dwelling) and placed in a temporary open shelter. If the individual died in the hogan, a hole is made in the wall and the body is removed through the hole. One or two men of the family place the body on a horse, take it to a rock crevice or some other suitable area, and bury it under rocks and dirt. Jewelry and other prized possessions are also buried there, and the individual's horse would be shot at the gravesite. The burial party returns following the very same path that they had taken with the body. On the path they leave a black stone knife and a piece of sage. If the body was removed from the hogan through a hole in the wall, the hole is covered. The remaining personal property of the deceased person, saddles, blankets, clothes, and other items, is destroyed, the house where the individual died is abandoned, and his or her name is never spoken again. To the Navajos all ghosts, even those of loved relatives, are dangerous. All of these actions are meant to prevent the ghost from finding its way back to the family and doing harm to family members. Later in this chapter we will discuss the Lugbara, a people who have very different beliefs about ghosts.

TYPES of RELIGIOUS ORGANIZATIONS

There is no way to present an overview of the diversity of human religions without distortion. Nonetheless, a typology of religion is useful, because it gives a general picture of religious diversity among humanity.

Anthony Wallace has proposed a fourfold classification of religious organization. His typology is based on the concept of **cult.** A cult is an organized system of cultural beliefs and practices pertaining to control over specific supernatural powers. A cult is not the same as a religion. Rather, religion is a more inclusive concept:

A society's religion may include several cults, some of which are devoted to curing, some to controlling weather, some to praying to ancestors, some to foretelling the future, and so on.

Wallace distinguishes four kinds of cults: individualistic, shamanistic, communal, and ecclesiastical. Although any given culture usually has more than one of these kinds of cults, the cults are not randomly distributed among the peoples of the world. Rather, there is a rough evolutionary sequence to their occurrence. For example, many foraging bands and horticultural tribes, such as the Netsilik, !Kung, and Yanomamö, have only shamanistic cults, and ecclesiastical cults occur mainly in stratified chiefdoms and states. But the evolutionary matching of kinds of cults with kinds of economic and political organizations is very rough and general.

Further frustrating our desire to "pigeonhole" religions is the fact that in many societies there are several religions, sometimes at odds with one another. In the Caribbean nation of Haiti, voudon ("voodoo") persists even though the official hierarchy of the Catholic Church has tried to eliminate it for over a century.

But these complications should not obscure the general pattern. The religions of hunter-gatherer bands do differ generally and significantly from those of complex chiefdoms and states.

Individualistic Cults

The defining characteristic of **individualistic cults** is that individuals intentionally seek out particular spirits or other supernatural powers to protect and help them in their endeavors. Individualistic cults emphasize direct, personal interactions between people and the supernatural.

The most well-known example of individualistic cults is the **vision quest.** It is widespread among Native American peoples but is especially important for the Great Plains tribes. To the Plains Indians, the world is charged with spiritual energy and supernatural power. Power exists in inanimate objects such as rocks or mountains and in living animals and plants. Human beings require the aid of the supernatural in many activities—in hunting, warfare, and times of sickness or other troubles.

Spiritual power comes to individuals in visions. These visions play an important role in the religious life of the people because it is through them that people achieve the personal contact with the supernatural that is essential in various endeavors. Spiritual powers occasionally make contact with individuals for no apparent reason, coming to them as they sleep or even as they are walking or riding alone.

More often humans—especially young men—have to seek out these powers through an active search, or quest, whose purpose is to acquire a vision. There are places that supernatural powers are believed to frequent: certain hills, mountains, or bluffs. A young man goes to such a location alone. There he smokes and fasts, appealing to a power to take pity on him. Many young men fail at their quest, but others do achieve visions.

The supernatural power that contacts a man and the manner in which it manifests itself vary. Sometimes he only hears the spirit speak to him. Sometimes it comes in the form of a dreamlike story. In other instances it simply materializes before his eyes, taking the form of a bear, a bison, an eagle, or some other animal.

The power tells the man how it will help him. It might give him the ability to predict the future, locate enemies, find game, become a powerful warrior, or cure illness. It tells him the things he will have to do to keep his power—what songs to sing, how to paint his war shield, how to wear his hair, and so forth. It also tells the man some things he cannot do; for example, if the power comes from the bear, the man might be prohibited from killing "his brother," the bear. As long as he continues to behave in the prescribed manner, the power will be his supernatural protector, or guardian spirit. It aids him in his endeavors and gives him special powers other men do not have.

There is no known culture in which individualistic cults constitute the entire religion. Even among Plains Indians, in which this kind of cult

is unusually well developed, shamanistic and communal cults also exist.

Shamanistic Cults

A **shaman,** or **medicine man,** is a person with a culturally defined special relationship to supernatural powers, which he frequently uses to cure sickness. In many societies (especially among many foraging peoples), the shaman is the only kind of religious practitioner; that is, he practices the only kind of ritual and possesses the only kinds of abilities not available to ordinary people. Shamans seldom are specialized practitioners. They carry out their tasks whenever their services are needed, usually in return for a gift or fee; but otherwise they live much like everyone else.

Shamans are believed to possess several qualities. They have access to the power of spiritual beings, called *spirit helpers.* The effectiveness of a shaman in curing (or causing harm) is believed to derive from the potency of his spirit helpers and from his ability to contact them and get them to do his bidding. Contact with one's spirit helpers commonly is made by achieving an altered state of consciousness. This altered state (referred to as a *trance*) is reached in various ways: through intake of drugs, ritual chanting, or participation in rhythmic music. People quite often believe that one of a shaman's spirit helpers has physically entered (possessed) the shaman's body. The spirit takes over his body and speaks to the assembled audience through his mouth. When possessed, the shaman becomes a *medium,* or mouthpiece for the spirits—he may lose control over his actions, and his voice changes quality because a spirit is speaking through him.

The way in which a person becomes a shaman varies from people to people. Shamans usually are considered to have knowledge and powers lacking among ordinary folk. They acquire these in three major ways. In some societies they undergo a period of special training as an apprentice to a practicing shaman, who teaches the novice chants and songs and how to achieve the trance state. Many shamans must endure difficult deprivations, such as prolonged fasting, the consumption of foods culturally considered disgusting, or years of sexual abstinence. Finally, in many societies shamans are people who have experienced some unusual event. For example, they have miraculously recovered from a serious illness or injury, or they claim to have had an unusual dream or vision in which some spirit called them to be its mouthpiece.

In most cultures, the shaman's major role is curing. Again, how the shaman performs this role varies. By considering an ethnographic example of sickness and curing, we can see shamans in action. We also can use the case to suggest an answer to one of the questions frequently asked about shamanism: How does the belief that shamans have the power to make people well persist, even though many of their clients die?

The Jívaro are a rain forest people of Ecuador. Jívaro believe that most sickness is caused by the actions of their human enemies (rather than by natural causes). Jívaro shamans acquire their power from their control over their personal spirit helpers, which live in their bellies in the form of tiny magical darts. A man becomes a shaman by presenting a gift to an existing shaman, who regurgitates some of his spirit helpers, which the novice swallows. If the novice drinks a hallucinogenic drug nightly for ten days and abstains from sexual intercourse for at least three months—the longer the better—he will acquire the power to transform any small objects (insects, worms, plants, etc.) he ingests into magical darts.

The Jívaro recognize two kinds of shamans: bewitching shamans, who have the ability to make people sick, and curing shamans, who try to make people well by counteracting the evil deeds of bewitching shamans. By ingesting and storing many magical darts in his body, a bewitching shaman can later harm his enemies. He causes illness by propelling one or more magical darts into the body of his victim; unless the darts are removed by a curing shaman, the victim will die. To effect the cure, a curing shaman first drinks tobacco juice and other drugs, which give him the power to see into the body of the victim. The curer then "sucks" out and captures the magical darts with his mouth.

Many patients die, which means that curing shamans often are ineffective. How, then, does the belief in curing shamans persist? The answer is that the Jívaro believe that a kind of supernatural battle is waged between the bewitching and the curing shamans. Bewitching shamans have two special spirit helpers. One, called a *pasuk*, looks like an ordinary tarantula to people who are not shamans; the other takes the form of a bird. A bewitching shaman can order his *pasuk* or spirit bird to remain near the house of the victim, shooting additional magical darts into him as the curing shaman sucks them out. If the victim dies, it may be because the darts shot by the *pasuk* and spirit bird were too many for the curing shaman to remove. Or, because the supernatural power of shamans varies, it may be because the bewitching shaman has more power than the curing shaman.

Aside from serving as an example of shamanism, the Jívaro show how beliefs about supernatural causes and shamanistic cures for illness form a logically coherent system. If the patient recovers, as usually happens, the ability of the shaman to cure is confirmed. If the victim dies, this event, too, is explained in terms that are consistent with existing beliefs. Events in the real world—getting better or getting worse, living or dying—do not disprove the beliefs because the belief system itself covers such events and contingencies.

Communal Cults

Like shamanism, **communal cults** have no full-time religious specialists. Rituals organized communally frequently have leaders—often an elderly person or someone with a special interest in the outcome of some ritual—who manipulate the symbolic objects or who address the supernatural. But the cult leaders are unspecialized—they do not make their living as religious practitioners.

Communal rituals are held to intercede with the supernatural on behalf of some group of people, such as a descent group, an age group, a village, or a caste. To illustrate, we consider two widespread kinds of communal rituals organized by descent groups: **ancestral cults** and **totemism.**

Ancestral Cults Practically all religions hold that people have a spiritual dimension—what we call a *soul*—that lives on after the physical body has perished. Beliefs about the fate of the soul after death vary widely. Some religions, such as Hinduism, believe that it is reincarnated into another person or animal. Others hold that the soul passes into a spiritual plane, where it exists eternally with a community of other souls and has no further effects on the living. Still others believe that souls become malevolent after death, turning into ghosts that cause accidents or sickness or that terrify the living.

One of the most common beliefs about the fate of souls after death is that they interact with and affect their living descendants. A great many peoples hold such beliefs. They usually practice rituals to induce the spirits of their deceased ancestors to do favors for them or simply to leave them alone. Beliefs and rituals surrounding the interactions between the living and their departed relatives are called ancestral cults, or *ancestor worship.*

The Lugbara, a people of Uganda, illustrate ancestral cults. The patrilineage is an important social group to the Lugbara. Its members are subject to the authority of lineage elders. As the most important members of the lineage, elders are expected to oversee the interests and harmony of the entire group. They serve as the guardians of the lineage's morality, although they have no power to punish violations physically.

Lugbara believe that the spirit of a deceased person may become an ancestral ghost of her or his lineage. The ghost punishes living descendants who violate Lugbara ideals of behavior toward lineage mates. People who fight with their kinsmen (especially a relative older than oneself), who deceive or steal from their lineage mates, or who fail to carry out their duties toward others are liable to be punished by an ancestral ghost. Sometimes this happens because a ghost sees an offense committed and causes illness to the offender.

More commonly, the ghosts do not act on their own initiative to make someone sick. Rather, the ghosts act on the thoughts of an elder who is indignant because of the actions of some member of the lineage. John Middleton describes Lugbara beliefs about the power of lineage elders to cause illness by invoking ghosts.

> [The elder] sits near his shrines in his compound and thinks about the sinner's behavior. His thoughts are known by the ghosts and they then send sickness to the offender. He "thinks these words in his heart"; he does not threaten or curse the offender. For a senior man to do this is part of his expected role. It is part of his "work," to "cleanse the lineage home." Indeed, an elder who does not do so when justified would be lacking in sense of duty toward his lineage. (1965, 76)

In the Lugbara example we see how elders maintain harmony and cooperation in the lineage. This is a common feature of ancestral cults.

Totemism Totemism, another widespread form of communal cult, is the cultural belief that human groups have a special mystical relationship with natural objects such as animals, plants, and, sometimes, nonliving things. The object (or objects) with which a group is associated is known as its *totem.* The group most often is a unilineal kin group, such as a clan. The totem frequently serves as a name of the group, for example, the Bear clan, the Eagle clan.

The nature of the relationship between the members of the group and its totem varies widely. Sometimes the totem is used simply for identification of the group and its members, much like our surnames. Often there is a mystical association between the group and its totem object: People believe they are like their totem in some respects. Members of other groups also resemble their totems. In many populations—most notably among some of the aboriginal peoples of Australia—the members of a clan treat their totem like a clanmate, believing that the totem gave birth to their ancestors in a mythical period.

The welfare of the clan is mystically associated with the welfare of the totem, so periodically the clan gathers for rituals that ensure the reproduction of its totem.

Ecclesiastical Cults

In Chapter 5 we saw that a high degree of specialization accompanied the development of civilization. Among New World peoples such as the ancient Incas, Aztecs, Mayans, and Toltecs, and in the Old World cities of ancient Mesopotamia, Egypt, China, Japan, and India, this specialization extended into the religious dimension of cultural systems. Rather than organizing rituals on a communal basis—in which a wide range of people controlled and participated in the performance— a formal bureaucracy of religious specialists controlled most public rituals. The religious bureaucracy probably also had a large voice in formulation of the religious laws, which prescribed certain kinds of punishments for those who violated them.

These religious specialists are known as **priests.** It is instructive to compare priests with shamans. In addition to their more specialized status, priests differ from shamans in several respects. First, most shamans perform their ritual functions without aid from other shamans; indeed, as we have seen, many peoples believe that enemy shamans engage in supernatural battles with one another. In contrast, priests are organized into a hierarchical *priesthood* under the sponsorship of a formal government, the state. Second, priests undergo a lengthy period of special training because they must master the complex rituals needed to perform their role. Third, the priesthood was at or near the top of the social ladder in ancient civilizations, so individual priests lived much better than the population at large. Fourth, shamans typically perform mainly crisis rituals whenever some person requires their services. The rituals at which priests officiate tend to be calendrical—they occur at regular intervals because the gods that the rituals are intended to appease demand regular praise or sacrifice.

A final difference is especially revealing. With the development of a priesthood comes a strong distinction between priest and layperson. The layperson has little control over the timing and

CONCEPT REVIEW Religious Organization

FORM	CHARACTERISTICS
Individualistic Cults	Each individual has a personal relationship with one or more supernatural powers, who serve as his or her guardians and protectors. The aid of the powers is solicited when needed.
Shamanistic Cults	Some individuals—shamans—are believed to have contact with the supernatural that ordinary people lack. They use these powers primarily for socially valuable purposes to help (especially cure) others in need. They may also act on behalf of their band or village to cause supernatural harm to the group's enemies.
Communal Cults	The members of a particular group gather periodically for rituals that are believed to benefit the group as a whole or some individual member. There are no full-time religious specialists, as is also true of individualistic and shamanistic cults.
Ecclesiastical Cults	The hallmark of ecclesiastical cults is the presence of full-time religious practitioners who form a religious bureaucracy. The practice of religion is carried out by formal, specialized officials—priests—who perform rituals that benefit the society as a whole. The priesthood is usually supported by redistributive tribute.

content of religious performances or the content of teachings. The population at large relies on the priesthood to keep it in proper relation to supernatural powers. This creates a sense of spiritual dependence on the priesthood and on the state apparatus that sponsors it, a dependence that reinforces the high degree of stratification found in states.

These state-sponsored cults are called *ecclesiastical* (meaning "of or pertaining to the church") because their priesthood was highly organized and their rituals usually were held in grandiose buildings that served as temples. The entire ecclesiastical cult was under the control of the government. Officials exacted tribute or taxes to finance the construction of temples, the livelihood of the priesthood, the sacrifices that often accompanied state rituals, and other expenses needed to support and organize religious activities on a fantastically large scale.

There is little question that **ecclesiastical cults** provided a body of traditions and belief that supported the domination of the ruling dynasty. (This is not to say that this function totally explains these cults or that it constitutes their entire significance.) This is seen by the content of the cults' beliefs, traditions, and rituals, which almost invariably express the dependence of the entire population on the ruler's well-being and on the periodic performance of rituals. A common belief of official state religions is that the ruler is a god-king: He not only rules by divine mandate but is himself a god or somehow partakes of divine qualities. This was true of most of the ancient civilizations.

Many official rituals of ecclesiastical cults are held to keep the entire polity in beneficial relationship with supernatural beings. For example, the state religion of the ancient Aztecs taught that the gods had to be periodically appeased or they would cause the world to end in a cataclysm. To keep the gods' goodwill, the priesthood periodically performed human sacrifice at temples, offering the heart of the victim (usually a war captive) to the deities. The ancient Egyptians believed that their pharaoh would rule in the afterlife—just as

in the present world—so when he died, he took much of his wealth, his wives, and his servants into the next world with him.

Ecclesiastical cults everywhere consumed enormous resources, but they did not wipe out other kinds of cults. Common people usually continued to rely on local shamans for curing, to practice magic, to believe in witches and sorcerers, and to worship their ancestors. In China, for example, each household and lineage continued to revere its own ancestors.

Most Christian denominations—Catholic and the diverse Protestant sects—have an ecclesiastical character. In medieval Europe, the authority of the Catholic Church was tightly interwoven with the exercise of secular power, although there often was conflict between pope and king. Only in the past few centuries has the formal alliance between the power of government and the power of God been broken for any length of time. (Informally and unofficially, religion continues to prop up political systems—God seems always to be on "our side," according to many religious people in our own and other modern nations.) We should not assume that even this official separation between church and state will necessarily be permanent.

THEORIES of RELIGION

So far as we know, every culture has religion. The fact that religion is universal is a bit surprising, for two reasons. First—with regard to beliefs—it can never be proved that supernatural powers such as ghosts, gods, devils, demons, angels, souls, *mana*, and so forth exist, much less that myths about them are true. Indeed, from an outsider's ("nonbeliever's") perspective, other people's religious beliefs and myths often seem merely superstitious. Yet in every culture we know about, many, most, or all people believe in supernatural powers.

Second—with regard to rituals—religious behavior may not be effective at achieving the goals the performers have in mind. From an outsider's perspective, many rituals seem to be a huge waste of time and resources. For example, when a Trobriand Islander plans a yam garden, he does some things that "work" in the way he thinks they do: He clears the land, removes weeds, and so forth, just as anyone should for success. But a Trobriander believes that acts that many outsiders consider superfluous are also necessary for success in gardening. He hires a person who knows powerful magic to perform rites that will keep his yams from leaving his garden at night and roaming around, because he knows that other people are performing magic to steal his yams by luring them into their own gardens. We—meaning those outside the culture's belief system—easily understand what the Trobriand gardener gets out of the first kind of activity: a yam harvest, if nature cooperates. But what does he get from the magical rites and spells? How did Trobrianders come to believe that magic is needed?

We can state this second problem another way to see the major puzzling thing about rituals. When the Trobriander clears land, plants a crop, and weeds his garden, his actions are effective in attaining the goal he has in mind—they work in more or less the way he thinks that they do. But when the garden magician performs rites and spells to keep his client's yams from being stolen by a neighbor during their nightly wanderings, his actions do not achieve the result he has in mind. Yams do not "really" roam around; the magic does not "really" work. (Again, remember that these statements are made from an outsider's perspective.) How, then, did the Trobrianders get the idea that they do?

If rituals do not work the way the performers imagine they do, why do so many people believe in the power of ritual? Perhaps they work in some other way. They may have other effects that people find useful or satisfying. As for sacred traditions, if they are not accurate historical accounts, perhaps they are symbolic statements that help people make sense of reality and give meaning to real-world things and events.

We have all heard people who consider themselves sophisticated and educated say that reli-gious beliefs rest on simple ignorance and super-stition—"they believe because they don't know any better." The ethnocentrism of such remarks is apparent: Superstition is something that someone else believes in but you do not. Yet many of your own beliefs seem superstitious to others, and probably many of the accepted "scientific truths" of the year 2000 will be considered superstitious by people living in the next century. Besides, even if we think that such beliefs and practices are superstitious, we have not explained why they are universal.

Anthropologists have proposed three types of functions of religion: the **intellectual** (or **cognitive**), the **psychological,** and the **social.**

Intellectual/Cognitive

Scholars who focus on cognitive functions of religion begin with the assumption that humans demand explanations for the world around them. Religious beliefs help satisfy the uniquely human desire to understand and explain things and events. Without religion, much of the world would be incomprehensible and inexplicable, which (these scholars argue) would be intolerable to the mind of a conscious, reasoning, problem-solving species like *Homo sapiens.* For example, religion satisfies human curiosity by providing explanations for the movements of the sun, moon, and stars. *Origin myths* explain things like the creation of the sky, land, and water; where animals and plants come from; and where people got their language, tools, rituals, and other customs and beliefs. The essential purpose of religion, in the intellectual view, is to provide people with explanations.

A very influential scholar who followed the intellectual approach was Sir James Frazer. Frazer claimed that "savages"—as he called peoples whom he imagined were living representatives of the earliest cultures—usually believe in some kind of magical power that can be manipulated by people who perform the proper rites and spells. He saw this belief as a prescientific one: People wanted to influence natural

Psychological approaches hold that religion helps people cope with personal emotional traumas, such as the death of a loved one and fear of one's own death. These people from Surinam are hoisting a coffin at a funeral.

Martha Cooper/Peter Arnold, Inc.

occurrences and other people, but they did not understand true scientific cause-and-effect relations. Believers in magic thought, for example, that a magician could cause harm to people by performing rites and spells on things that were once in contact with their victims, such as hair, nails, feces, or even footprints. Such beliefs had a kind of logic —by doing something to things once in contact with a man, you can do something to him—but the logic was based on false premises. Frazer thought that people gradually realized their logical errors and eventually gained knowledge of true scientific cause and effect. Frazer thus believed that magic and science are alternative world views: Each provides people with an intellectual model of the way the world works and a means to manipulate events and people. But whereas magical beliefs are false, scientific theories are objectively correct, in Frazer's view. Because science is a superior system of knowledge, Frazer thought it is in the process of replacing magical and religious beliefs.

The idea that religious beliefs provide people with explanations for things and events is correct, as far as it goes, but it is an incomplete explanation for religion. Religion does satisfy curiosity about the world, but this is not its only function. "Savages" possess and use practical knowledge just as we do—a Trobriander knows that he must care for his yams as well as perform garden magic. Conversely, many "civilized" and "scientific" folk believe in and practice religion, even many of those who make their living as scientists! Religious beliefs do not take the place of practical or scientific knowledge; in some way that we do not fully understand, they supplement it.

Psychological

The notion that religion helps people cope psychologically with times of trouble, stress, and anxiety is a common one. Sicknesses, accidents, misfortunes, injustices, deaths, and other trials and tribulations of life can be handled emotionally if one believes that there is a reason and meaning to them or that one's troubles can be controlled or alleviated by means of ritual.

In anthropology a well-known psychological theory of religion is that of Bronislaw Malinowski, whom we introduced in Chapter 4. Malinowski thought that religion serves the valuable function of giving people confidence when they are likely to be unsuccessful despite their best efforts. There are always natural phenomena that people cannot control and that constantly threaten to ruin their plans and efforts. Belief in the power of ritual to control these (otherwise uncontrollable) elements instills confidence and removes some of the anxiety that results from the uncertainties of life.

Another specific psychological theory of religion holds that, as self-conscious beings, we humans are aware of our own mortality. Knowing that we will eventually die causes us great anxiety and leads us to worry about our own death. Experiencing the serious illness or death of one's parent or other relatives likewise produces grief and psychological stress for most people. We must have some way of coping emotionally with the grief over the death of our loved ones, and with the anxiety caused by the knowledge of our own mortality. Religion helps us cope by denying the finality of death, that is, by inculcating beliefs about the existence of a pleasant afterlife, in which our immortal souls live forever.

The notion that beliefs in life after death help to calm our fears and alleviate our anxieties seems reasonable. However, this theory is tainted by an ethnocentric assumption: Although most religions do include beliefs about some kind of afterlife, in a great many cultures the afterlife is far from pleasant. From a psychological perspective, religion has two "faces." On the one hand, it does—for some people, some of the time, in some respects—help us cope emotionally with times of trouble and hardships. On the other hand, beliefs about the supernatural often create fears and anxieties that would not otherwise exist. Pleasant afterlifes ("Heaven") offer us comfort and hope. But what psychological benefit does the threat of eternal damnation ("Hell") offer?

Social

"Societies need religion to keep people in line," you may have heard people say. The idea here is that religion instills and maintains common values, leads to increased conformity to cultural norms, promotes cohesion and cooperation, promises eternal reward for good deeds and eternal damnation for evil acts, and so forth. Those who champion the social function (also called the *sociological*) theory hold that religion exists because of the useful effects it has on human societies. Rather than helping individuals cope emotionally, religion helps societies maintain harmonious social relationships between individuals and groups. It encourages people to respect the rights of others and to perform their proper duties.

Consider the Ten Commandments, for example, which serve as a moral code for Christians and Jews. Two prescribe how people ought to feel and act toward God and other people, and eight

CONCEPT REVIEW Theories of Religion

FUNCTION	THEORY
Intellectual/Cognitive	Religious beliefs help satisfy the human desire to understand and explain things and events.
Psychological	Religion helps people psychologically cope with times of trouble, stress, and anxiety (sicknesses, accidents, misfortunes, injustices, deaths, etc.).
Social	Religion instills and maintains common values, conformity to cultural norms, promotes cohesion and cooperation, promises reward for good deeds and punishment for bad deeds.

proscribe actions, including the five "thou shalt nots" (see Exodus 20:3–17). Note that five of the divinely ordered prohibitions are against the commission of acts that could result in harm to others, such as killing and stealing. God gave us commandments that will, if obeyed, lead to good relations with others and therefore promote earthly social order. More general Judeo-Christian moral guidelines are the Golden Rule ("do unto others as you would have them do unto you") and love of one's neighbor (Matthew 19:19), both of which are useful prescriptions for harmonious social life.

Another social function of religion is to enhance the cohesion of society by making people feel their interdependence on one another and on their traditions. Emile Durkheim, a French sociologist of the early twentieth century, was influential in formulating this perspective. Durkheim's view was that the main function of religion in human society is to promote *social solidarity,* meaning that religion has the effect of bringing people together and enhancing their sense of unity, cohesion, and reliance on their society's customs. Groups of people who share the same beliefs and who gather periodically to perform common rituals experience a feeling of oneness and harmony. Religion exists, Durkheim believed, because it is socially useful or—stated differently—functional for society as a whole.

SORCERY and WITCHCRAFT

No anthropological discussion of religion is complete without some discussion of the misuse of supernatural power. In all societies there are individuals who out of jealousy, envy, or maliciousness use their knowledge of supernatural power to try to harm their relatives, neighbors, and other members of the community. The individuals involved in the illicit, or socially disapproved, use of knowledge fall into two broad and frequently overlapping categories called sorcerers and witches.

Sorcery

Sorcery is the performance of rites and spells intended to cause supernatural forces to harm others. In some cultures, sorcery may be carried out by almost anyone because everyone learns to harm their enemies by sorcery as an ordinary part of enculturation. Among other peoples, sorcery is a more specialized practice: Only certain people inherit or acquire the knowledge of how to recite the spells and perform the rites correctly.

In 1890, Sir James Frazer proposed that magic (including sorcery) is based on two kinds of logical principles or assumptions. Both involve a symbolic identification of something (e.g., an object or action) with something else (e.g., an event or a person).

One kind of logical principle on which magic is based is called the *imitative principle,* the premise that like produces like. That is, if an object resembles (is like) a person and the sorcerer mutilates the object, then the same effect will happen to the person. The so-called voodoo doll is a familiar example of the imitative principle. An image or effigy is made of the enemy; some act is performed on the effigy; and the enemy supposedly experiences the same fate. The effigy symbolically represents the person, so to mutilate the effigy is believed to harm the person. In another kind of imitative magic, the magician or sorcerer mimics the effects she or he wants to produce.

The second kind of logical premise underlying magic and sorcery is called the *contagious principle of magic,* the assumption that power comes from contact. That is, things that were once in contact with someone can be used in rites and spells to make things happen to that person. By performing the correct rites and spells on such objects as hair clippings, bodily excretions, nail parings, infant umbilical cords, or jewelry and clothing, harm can be done to one's enemies. In societies in which sorcery rests on the contagious principle, people must be careful to dispose of objects they have been in contact with, lest one of their enemies use them for sorcery. As with the imitative principle, a symbolic identification is made between the objects and the victim. But in the case of the contagious principle, the symbolic equation comes from previous contact rather than from resemblance: By acquiring possession of something once belonging to a person, supernatural power is acquired over that person.

Whether based on the imitative or contagious principle, beliefs about sorcery are affected by the *patterned* relationships between individuals and groups. In all societies, certain kinds of social relationships are especially likely to be fraught with built-in conflicts. Co-wives of a polygynous man may be jealous over their husband's favors or be in competition over an inheritance for their children. People who have married into a kin group or village may be viewed as outsiders who retain loyalty to their own natal families. Two men who want the same woman, or two women who want the same man, have reasons to hate one another. Men who are rivals for a political office have conflicts of interest.

These and other kinds of relationships are sources of strain and conflict. Which relationships are likely to cause strain and conflict vary with the way the society is organized: Brothers-in-law are allies in one society, but their interests regularly conflict in another society, for instance. In any case, the relationships most likely to be troublesome are patterned.

If you were brought up in a culture that explained illness or accident by sorcery, and if you or a relative became ill or suffered a misfortune, you would not suspect just anyone of harming you. You would ask, Who has a motive to perform evil magic against you? Who envies you? Who would profit from your sickness or death? Who harbors a grudge against you? With whom have you recently quarreled? These people are your prime suspects, and they are the ones you or your family are most likely to accuse.

Members of most cultures reason in much the same way. They believe that sorcerers do not strike randomly, but harm only their enemies or people toward whom they feel anger, envy, or ill will. But bad feelings are more likely to exist in certain kinds of relationships than in others,

within a single society. Accusations of sorcery, therefore, usually follow the prevalent lines of conflict: Because people who stand in the same kinds of relationships are likely to accuse one another again and again, sorcery accusations are patterned.

Witchcraft

Witchcraft is another explanation that people in many societies give for misfortune. There is no universally applicable distinction between sorcery and witchcraft. Whereas sorcery usually involves the use of rites and spells to commit a foul deed, here we define **witchcraft** as the use of psychic power alone to cause harm to others. Sorcerers manipulate objects; witches need only think malevolent thoughts to turn their anger, envy, or hatred into evil deeds. (Our own language's distinction between the two—witches are female, sorcerers usually male—is not useful cross-culturally.) Many cultures believe in the existence of both kinds of malevolent powers, so sorcery and witchcraft often are found among the same people. Like sorcery accusations, accusations of witchcraft are likely to be patterned, for people most often believe that both witches and sorcerers harm only people they dislike, hate, envy, or have a conflict with.

Cultures vary in the characteristics they attribute to witches and in how witches cause harm. A few examples illustrate some of the diversity.

- The Navajo associate witches with the worst imaginable sins—witches commit incest, bestiality (sex with animals), and necrophilia (sex with corpses); they change themselves into animals; they cannibalize infants; and so on.
- The Nyakyusa of Tanzania hold that witches are motivated mainly by their lust for food; accordingly, they suck dry the udders of people's cattle and devour the internal organs of their human neighbors while they sleep.
- The Azande of the southern Sudan believe that witches possess an inherited substance that

leaves their bodies at night and gradually eats away at the flesh and internal organs of their victims. Witches, as well as their victims, are considered to be unfortunate, because the Azande believe that a person can be a witch without even knowing it. Witches can do nothing to rid themselves permanently of their power, although they can be forced to stop bewitching some particular individual by ridding themselves of bad feelings against their victim.

- The Ibibio of Nigeria believe that witches operate by removing the spiritual essence (soul) of their enemies and placing it into an animal; this makes the victim sick, and he dies when the witches slaughter and consume the animal. Sometimes Ibibio witches decide to torture, rather than kill, a person. In that case they remove the victim's soul and put it in water or hang it over a fireplace or flog it in the evenings; the afflicted person will remain sick until the witches get what they want out of him or her.

Such beliefs, it might appear to someone who does not share them, are logically outrageous; no one's soul leaves his or her body at night to cavort with other witches, for example. It might seem that these beliefs are socially harmful as well; beliefs in witchcraft, fear of witchcraft, and accusations of witchcraft engender conflict and aggression among a people. Finally, the treatment many suspected and "proven" witches receive offends our notions of social justice. As we know from the witch hunts of European and American history, the truly innocent victims of witchcraft often are the accused witches, who sometimes are cruelly executed for crimes they could not have committed.

Interpretations of Sorcery and Witchcraft

Anthropologists wonder why beliefs in witches and sorcery are so widespread, given their seemingly harmful effects and the injustices that frequently result from them. What value or benefit could a human group possibly derive from accusations of sorcery and witchcraft?

In line with the overall theoretical approaches discussed earlier, the answers fall into two categories: cognitive and sociological. (In the following discussion, for simplicity, we use the term *witchcraft* to refer to both witchcraft and sorcery because the ideas presented have been applied to both kinds of beliefs.)

Cognitive Interpretations   The most influential of the various cognitive approaches is that witchcraft explains unfortunate events. The argument is that most people find the idea of coincidence or accident intellectually unsatisfying when some misfortune happens to them or their loved ones, so they search for other causes. Their logic is something like this: I have enemies who wish me harm, and harm just came to me, so my enemies are responsible.

The best example of how people account for misfortune by reference to the actions of witches comes from among the Azande. The Azande attribute prolonged serious illnesses and many other personal misfortunes to witchcraft. Ethnographer E. E. Evans-Pritchard describes their beliefs:

> Witchcraft is ubiquitous. . . . There is no niche or corner of Zande culture into which it does not twist itself. If blight seizes the groundnut crop it is witchcraft; if the bush is vainly scoured for game it is witchcraft; if women laboriously bail water out of a pool and are rewarded by but a few small fish it is witchcraft; . . . if a wife is sulky and unresponsive to her husband it is witchcraft; if a prince is cold and distant with his subject it is witchcraft; if a magical rite fails to achieve its purpose it is witchcraft; if, in fact, any failure or misfortune falls upon any one at any time and in relation to any of the manifold activities of his life it may be due to witchcraft. (1976, 18)

All this does not mean that the Azande are ignorant of cause and effect and therefore attribute every misfortune to some witch who is out to get them. When a Zande man seeks shelter in a granary and its roof falls and injures him, he blames witchcraft. But Zande know very well that granary roofs collapse because termites eat the wood that supports them. They do not attribute the collapse of granaries in general to witchcraft; it is the collapse of this particular granary at this particular time with this particular person inside that is caused by witchcraft. Do not granaries sometimes fall with no one sitting inside them? And do not people often relax in granaries without the roof falling? It is the coincidence between the collapse and the presence of a particular person— a coincidence that many other peoples consider bad luck—that witchcraft explains.

Another benefit people gain is that witches serve as scapegoats. When things are going poorly, people do not always know why. Witchcraft provides an explanation. It also provides people with a means to do something about the situation: identify, accuse, and punish the witch responsible. If, as often is the case, things still do not improve, there are always other yet-to-be-identified witches! People can blame many of their troubles on witches—evil enemies conspiring against them—rather than on their personal inadequacies or on bad luck.

Sociological Interpretations One sociological hypothesis is that witchcraft reinforces the cultural norms and values that help individuals live harmoniously with one another. Every culture has notions of how individuals ideally ought to act toward others (Chapter 2). Witches typically are the antithesis of these cultural ideals. They act like animals, or actually change themselves into animals. They mate with their relatives. They often put on a false front, pretending to be your friend by day while they eat your liver by night. They have no respect for age or authority. They are in league with the forces of evil. (In the Judeo-Christian tradition, witches made compacts with the Devil, agreeing to be his servant in return for worldly pleasures.) All the most despicable personal characteristics of people are wrapped up in the personality of witches, whom everyone is

supposed to hate. So witches symbolize all that is undesirable, wicked, and hateful. Just as one should despise witches, so should one hate all that they stand for. In short, by providing a hated symbol of the abnormal and the antisocial, the witch strengthens cultural conceptions of normatively approved social behavior.

Another argument is that witches provide an outlet for repressed aggression, and thus beliefs about witches lower the overall amount of conflict in a society. Writing about the Navajo in 1944, Clyde Kluckhohn argued that Navajo culture emphasizes cooperation and maintenance of good relationships between members of the same extended household. When bad feelings do develop within the household, Navajo culture requires people not to express them. But pent-up hostilities have an outlet in the form of witches, whom people are allowed to hate and gossip about. Because most people the Navajo believe to be witches are members of distant groups, usually little action is taken against them. Solidarity between relatives of the in-group is preserved by displacing hostility to people of the out-group.

Another sociological hypothesis is that witchcraft beliefs serve as a mechanism of social control. This might work in two ways. First, many people believe in the existence of witchcraft but do not know which specific members of their community are witches. This leads individuals to be careful not to make anyone angry, since the offended party may be a witch. Second, individuals who fail to conform to local cultural norms of behavior are most likely to be suspected and accused of being witches. People who are always mad at somebody; who carry grudges for prolonged periods; who are known to be envious and resentful of the success of others; who have achieved wealth but selfishly refuse to share it in the culturally accepted manner—such violators of these and other standards for behavior frequently are believed to be the likely perpetrators of witchcraft. Fear of being accused and punished presumably increases adherence to norms and ideals of behavior.

SUMMARY

1. There are three components that religions all share: (1) beliefs about the nature of supernatural powers (beings and forces), (2) teachings about the past deeds of these powers, and (3) rituals intended to influence them. All known human societies have such beliefs and teachings and practice such rituals, so all have religion.

2. One category of rituals that are widely distributed among the world's peoples are rites of passage. These are rituals that denote the changes in an individual's social status within the group. The four most common types of rites of passage are (1) birth/naming ceremonies; (2) puberty rites; (3) marriage rituals; and (4) funerals.

3. Religions may be classified according to the types of cults they include, although any such classification is inadequate to depict the diversity of the world's religions. Cults may be characterized as individualistic, shamanistic, communal, and ecclesiastical. In a generalized way, there is an evolutionary sequence to cults, in that they tend to be associated with different degrees of cultural complexity.

4. Religion is universal despite the facts that beliefs and teachings can never be proved true or false. One puzzling thing about religion is what it does for people as individuals or for society as a whole. Various social scientists have proposed that religion performs (1) intellectual/cognitive, (2) psychological, and (3) social functions. No consensus exists about which of these functions is most important. Religion probably fulfills all these "needs," but none seems able to explain religion itself or the great diversity of human religions.

5. Most religions include a belief that supernatural beings or forces cause or influence group or personal misfortune, such as deaths, illnesses, and "accidents." The malevolent powers of sorcerers and witches are blamed for misfortune in a great many societies. Accusations of sorcery and witchcraft tend to be patterned and to reflect prevalent conflicts and tensions in the organization of society. Many anthropologists argue that witchcraft and sorcery beliefs and accusations have positive cognitive and social benefits.

KEY TERMS

animism
ritual
rites of passage
life cycle
puberty rites
cult
individualistic cults
vision quest
shamanistic cults
shaman (medicine man)
communal cults
ancestral cults
totemism
priests
ecclesiastical cults
intellectual/cognitive functions of religion
psychological functions of religion
social functions of religion
sorcery
witchcraft

SUGGESTED READINGS

Numerous books provide basic introductions to the anthropological study of religion, including the following.

Guthrie, Stewart. *Faces in the Clouds: A New Theory of Religion.* Oxford: Oxford University Press, 1993.

Theoretical treatment of religion and other topics. Argues that humans everywhere tend to attribute human-like qualities to natural phenomena (to "anthropomorphize" nature and other things), and that this tendency helps to explain religion. Also applies the idea of anthropomorphism to topics such as art, science, and advertising. Readable and thoughtful.

Howells, William. *The Heathens: Primitive Man and His Religions.* Salem, WI: Sheffield, 1986.

This book was originally written in 1948. Interpreted with the date of its first publication in mind, it is a good place to start for an overview of human religious diversity.

Klass, Morton. *Ordered Universes: Approaches to the Anthropology of Religion.* Boulder, CO: Westview, 1995.

An introductory textbook in the anthropological study of religion and religious diversity. Although some definitions and concepts are nonstandard, this book is generally quite user-friendly.

Lehman, Arthur C., and James E. Myers, eds. *Magic, Witchcraft, and Religion.* 5th ed. Palo Alto, CA: Mayfield, 2001.

An excellent reader prepared mainly for undergraduates.

Levack, Brian P., ed. *Anthropological Studies of Witchcraft, Magic and Religion.* New York: Garland, 1992.

Reprints of twenty-one influential articles published at various times in the twentieth century. Especially good on witchcraft and religion.

The following ethnographies examine religion and religious movements.

Boyer, Dave, and Stephen Nissenbaum. *Salem Possessed.* Cambridge, MA: Harvard University Press, 1974.

Historical study of the witchcraft outbreak in 1692 in Salem, Massachusetts. Shows that the accusations closely reflected long-standing lines of conflict in the community.

Evans-Pritchard, E. E. *Witchcraft, Oracles, and Magic Among the Azande.* Abridged ed. Oxford: Clarendon, 1976.

An abridgement of the 1937 edition that loses little of the information found in the original. One of the best descriptions of witchcraft among an African people ever written.

Geertz, Clifford. *The Religion of Java.* Glencoe, IL: The Free Press, 1960.

One of the great case studies of non-Western religions.

Grim, John A. *The Shaman: Patterns of Religious Healing Among the Ojibway Indians.* Norman: University of Oklahoma, 1983.

Empirical study of Ojibway shamans that also compares Ojibway with shamanism in other parts of the world.

Keesing, Roger. *Kwaio Religion.* New York: Columbia University Press, 1982.

Study of the religion of a Solomon Island society.

Kluckhohn, Clyde. *Navaho Witchcraft.* Boston: Beacon, 1967.

Well-written study of witchcraft among the Navajo of the Southwest, originally published in 1944.

Luhrman, T. M. *Persuasions of the Witch's Craft: Ritual Magic in Contemporary England.* Cambridge, MA: Harvard University Press, 1989.

Detailed and lengthy ethnographic study of witchcraft and the use of magic in England. One focus is how people maintain beliefs in the powers of magical rituals.

Malinowski, Bronislaw. *Coral Gardens and Their Magic.* New York: American Book Company, 1935.

A detailed description of garden magic and horticultural practices in the Trobriand Islands.

Neihardt, John G. *Black Elk Speaks.* 2d ed. Lincoln: University of Nebraska Press, 1961.

A very popular and readable account of an Ogalala Sioux holy man and an excellent introduction to the religious beliefs and practices of this American Indian people.

chapter 12

ART *and the* AESTHETIC

Contents

There is much more to human life than the acquisition of food and other necessities. In all societies there is both a sense of and a desire for the aesthetic: those things that appeal to the eye, the ear, the taste, the touch, the emotions, and the imagination. Such sensory experiences are important for their functional value, but also because their color, form, design, sound, taste, or feel are pleasurable in their own right. These experiences are sought after to stimulate our imaginations and emotions through the creation of feelings of happiness, fear, and even anger. These expressions of the aesthetic are what we call art—the subject of this chapter.

According to Richard Anderson, it is the artistic component, the designs, that transforms an object from the realm of the utilitarian to the realm of art. Thus, it is ornamentation placed on the object—not the functional design of the object—that defines it as art.

The Shakers (a religious communal group that reached its height in the early nineteenth century in the United States) were "plain folk" who emphasized the utilitarian. The qualities of simplicity and function were incorporated into everything they made and used in their communities. Their wooden furniture was simple, delicate, and superbly crafted, with stark straight lines or gentle curves. Veneering of wood was considered "deception," and paint was not used. There were no carvings, extravagant turning, or inlays. In keeping with their idea of natural purity, only light stains and varnishes were used. Some Shakers said that their designs came from heaven, communicated to them by angels. The beauty of Shaker furniture is in its masterful simplicity of form. Form and superb craftsmanship, not ornamentation, make Shaker furniture art.

So at what point is a piece of wood, stone, or ivory transformed into a work of art? When does noise become music, body movements become dance, and words become poetry, literature, or song lyrics? Are there any limitations on what can be considered art? Can the preparation and serving of food be considered art? Is the painting or alteration of the human body art?

In this chapter we use a broad definition of art. Something becomes **art** when its purely utilitarian or functional nature is modified for the purpose of enhancing its aesthetic qualities and thus making it more pleasurable for our senses. Most of the time art is displayed publicly or used in social events such as gatherings or ceremonies. In such contexts, art objects sometimes take on an additional function: They become a means of communication. Thus, Western artists often claim that they are trying to "make a statement" through their artwork, although we all recognize that the artistic message is in the eye of the beholder. In other cultures, artistic creations communicate messages, which have both religious and secular meanings.

Obviously, art is inseparable from the **aesthetic,** and the aesthetic is an elusive quality since it is subjective. Anthropologists since Franz Boas have argued that there are no universal standards as to what is considered beautiful or pleasurable. Something that members of one society might find beautiful or pleasing, others might consider ugly, disgusting, or even repulsive.

Each culture, as well as every individual, has its own ideas as to what is aesthetically pleasing, and aesthetics change within a culture over time. For example, if one examines European or Chinese art over the past 2,000 years, one finds dramatic changes in both the nature and the complexity of designs. Thus, not only is the idea of what is beautiful subjective, but it is also ever changing.

THE PERVASIVENESS of ART

In the urban, industrial world, we usually think of artistic creation as a separate and distinct kind of activity. We often think of art only in terms of "fine art": painting, sculpture, music, and dance. If pressed further, we might add great architecture, literature, drama, and even poetry. We tend to categorize as art only those things whose sole or basic value is aesthetic.

The notion that art is a conceptually separate realm of social and cultural existence is not found among all peoples. American Indian peoples had

Rafel Salvatore/Documentary Educational Resources

All known peoples appreciate the aesthetic value of certain objects, actions, images, and sounds. This Latin American man makes fine musical instruments.

no word for art in their languages. Similarly other traditional peoples also frequently lack words for art. The basic reason is that art is integrated into virtually every aspect of their lives and is so pervasive that they do not think of it as something separate and distinct. The idea of "art for art's sake" is a recent Western cultural phenomenon that in some ways both distracts and diminishes the reality of human creative expressions. If we define art broadly, then it permeates virtually every aspect of our lives. All of us search for and attempt to create that which is aesthetically pleasing and, thus, we are all "artists." Creative artistic expressions are found in even the most mundane and commonplace daily acts. Consider, for example, three behaviors that most of us think of as "mundane" rather than "artistic": dressing for the day, residing in a particular place, and eating.

The search for the aesthetic is reflected in the appearance of our persons, our homes, and our meals, as well as in our places of worship, recreation, and work. Much of our day is filled with music, song, dance, drama, comedy, literature, and sports, which we listen to, participate in, and

sometimes create. Art, anthropologists recognize, is a cultural universal. But beyond this the artistic impulse is seen in the everyday lives of individual human beings, for we are all both producers and consumers of art.

Forms of Artistic Expression

Art permeates most aspects of human activity, from clothing and furniture to music and theater, but space constraints limit our discussion to certain categories: body arts, visual arts, and performance arts.

Body Arts

People around the world are highly creative in altering their physical appearance. Almost anything that can be done to the body is probably being done or has been done in the past. This section focuses on physical alterations, body painting, and tattooing and scarification.

Physical Alterations   In most societies people attempt to physically alter their bodies. Head and body hair is treated in many different ways. In Western societies hair is styled and often artificially colored. Some people shave their heads, their beards, and even their legs and armpits. Others let their beards and/or mustaches grow and style them in various ways. In most Western societies these actions are mainly a matter of fashion or personal taste; in other societies such actions may have cultural meaning.

In parts of Africa the status of a woman—e.g., whether she is unmarried or married, or is a mother or a widow—is indicated by hairstyle. Among the Hopis, adolescent girls of marriageable age wear their hair in a large whorl on each side of their head, creating the so-called "butterfly" hairstyle. After marriage they wear their hair long and parted in the middle. Children among the Omahas had their hair cut in patterns indicative of their clan membership.

The wearing of beards is not always a matter of personal taste and fashion. In many societies, for example, Hasidic Jews, Mennonites, Amish, some Muslim sects, and Sikhs, wearing a beard is an act of religious belief. In the ancient world social status was frequently associated with beards. In Egypt only the nobility could have beards. Not only were noblemen bearded, but women of the nobility frequently wore artificial beards to indicate their social rank. In contrast, in ancient Greece only the nobility were allowed to be clean-shaven; men of commoner status had to let their beards grow.

Hair alterations usually are reversible, for hair will grow back. Other parts of the body are altered on a permanent basis. Cranial deformation or head shaping has been widely practiced among the peoples of the world. By binding a baby's soft skull, the shape of the skull can be permanently changed, flattening the back and the forehead or lengthening the head. In parts of France cranial deformation was virtually universal until the eighteenth century. A baby's face was tightly wrapped in linen, resulting in a flattened skull and ears. In the Netherlands, babies wore tight-fitting caps that depressed the frontal portion of the skull. The elite classes of the ancient Andean civilizations elongated the skull, as did the ancient Egyptians. Some peoples of central Africa bound the heads of female babies to create elongated skulls that came to a point on the back.

Some peoples permanently altered other parts of the body as well. In China the feet of female children of high-status families were bound at the age of five or six to deform them and keep them small. This deformation also served as a visible indication of the fact that the family was wealthy and its women did not have to do physical labor. In parts of Africa and among some Native American peoples holes were cut in earlobes or the lower and upper lips were expanded so that ear plugs and large lip plugs could be inserted. Some of these plugs were up to three inches in diameter. Some central African pygmy peoples file their front teeth into points, which in their culture enhances their attractiveness. In parts of Africa, a series of rings were placed around a girl's neck over a period of time, so that when womanhood was achieved the shoulders were pressed down, making the neck appear longer.

Such alterations continue in modern nations. Much of the lucrative work of plastic surgeons in contemporary Western nations is concerned with altering physical appearance by changing the shapes of the eyes, nose, mouth, and jowls, or increasing or decreasing the size of breasts, lips, thighs, hips, or waistlines.

Body Painting   Painting is a temporary manner of changing an individual's appearance. Some peoples paint only their faces, while others paint almost their entire bodies. Face painting is more common than body painting. When face painting is mentioned, most people think first of American Indians and "war paint." American Indian peoples did paint their faces for war. The Osages, before attacking their enemy, would blacken their faces with charcoal, symbolic of the merciless fire and their ferocity. In other Native American groups the designs and meaning varied. Among some, face painting was individualized, each man

These Australian aborigine boys have their bodies painted for a dance. Body painting is commonly used in many cultures for ceremonial and ritual occasions.

John Cancalosi/Peter Arnold, Inc.

using different colors and designs to create a ferocious appearance. Among others, the manner in which a man might paint his face depended upon a vision and his spiritual helpers (see Chapter 11). However, not all face painting was associated with war. Faces were often painted for religious rituals. In ritual face painting the painted symbols usually had some form of religious significance. In addition, many Native American peoples painted their faces to enhance their social appearance. Thus, Native Americans painted their faces for a variety of reasons—warfare, religious rituals, and appearance.

Like face painting, body painting is widely distributed among the world's peoples. In some cases, body painting has religious significance

and meaning; in other cases, it is purely secular, designed to enhance the physical appearance of the person. Many peoples in Papua New Guinea cover their faces and limbs with white clay when a relative or important person dies, as a sign of mourning and respect for the deceased. Among the aboriginal peoples of Australia, bodies were painted with red and yellow ocher, white clay, charcoal, and other pigments. During rituals individuals were painted, at times with elaborate designs covering most of the body. The colors and designs were standardized and had symbolic meaning. Ritual specialists who knew these designs were charged with the actual painting. Among many Australian peoples, body painting was also a secular and daily activity, performed by family members on one another. Individuals could use whatever colors and designs pleased them, so long as they were not ritual designs.

Tattooing and Scarification Tattooing and the related practice of scarification are widespread. Tattoo designs, achieved by etching and placing a colored pigment under the skin, have been practiced by diverse peoples. When the skin is too dark for tattoo designs to be seen, people may use scarification, the deliberate scarring of the skin to produce designs on the body.

Tattooing has a long history as an art form. Tattooing was practiced in ancient Egypt, as well as by the ancient Scythians, Thracians, and Romans in Europe. The ancient Bretons, at the time of the Roman conquest, were reported to have had their bodies elaborately tattooed with the images of animals. In the fourth century A.D., when Christianity became the official religion of the Roman Empire, tattooing was forbidden on religious grounds. Tattooing virtually disappeared among European peoples until the eighteenth century when it was discovered in the Pacific and Asia by sailors and reintroduced to European peoples as purely secular art.

Robert Brain noted an important difference between body painting and tattooing and scarification: Paint is removable; tattooing and scarification are indelible and permanent. As a result, tattooing and scarification are usually associated with societies in which there are permanent differences in social status. Among some people, tattooing was limited to a few lines on the face, chest, or arms. Among others, complex designs covered most of the body from the face to the legs. In some cases, every adult had some tattoos. Although the significance and meaning of tattoos varied, most had socioreligious significance and the more fully tattooed an individual was, the greater the social status.

Among the Osages of North America, only men who had earned thirteen war honors in battle were entitled to be tattooed. These tattoos, consisting of thirteen elongated triangles, were placed on the chest, radiating out from the neck like a necklace. These men were also entitled to have their wives and daughters tattooed on the chest, back, arms, and hands. For the women these tattoos were considered prayers for long life, children, and good health.

The adornment of the body by tattoos is most highly elaborated in the islands of Polynesia. In fact, the word *tattoo* itself is Polynesian. The word, like the practice of tattooing sailors, came into use as a result of the voyages of Western explorers and whalers in the seventeenth and later centuries. Tongans, Samoans, Marquesans, Tahitians, Maoris, and most other Polynesian peoples practiced tattooing, which everywhere was connected to social distinctions such as class or rank, sex, religious roles, and specialization.

Many Maoris had large parts of their bodies covered with tattoos: the torso, thighs, buttocks, calves, and, most notably, the face. Several instruments were used by skilled tattoo artists to incise the curvilinear patterns characteristic of most Maori tattoos. Apparently, no anesthetic was used to relieve the pain and, in fact, tolerating the pain of the procedure may have been part of its cultural significance. The most skilled tattoo artists were rewarded with high prestige and chiefly patronage, and their craft was in such high demand that they traveled widely over New Zealand's two major islands.

Maori men and women were tattooed, although men's bodies were more thoroughly covered. For both sexes, tattoos were seen not merely as body ornamentation or expression of one's personal identity. Having tattoos brought certain privileges. Men who did not undergo tattooing could not build canoe houses, carve wood, make weapons, or weave nets. Untattooed women could not help in the gardens with sweet potatoes, the Maori staple vegetable crop.

Maori facial tattoos, called *moko,* have special importance. Women were tattooed on the lips and chin, often near the time of their marriage. In many cases, virtually the whole male face was tattooed. Not just any *moko* design could be worn by just any male, for designs were related to factors such as hereditary status, locale of birth, and achievement in battle. Social restrictions thus were placed on the wearing of facial tattoos, suggesting that they were important symbols of group identity and personal achievement.

In all of Polynesia, it was the people of the Marquesas whose bodies were most covered by tattoos. The highest ranking chiefs even had tattoos on the soles of their feet. Alfred Gell argues that this relatively thorough covering of the body in the Marquesas was necessary to wrap the body in images in order to protect it from spiritual dangers.

Decorating the body by cutting and creating scars, or scarification, is done for numerous reasons. Depending on the culture, both men and women may be scarred. Sometimes the scarred design is on the face; in other cases, the chest, breast, back, and even the legs and arms may be elaborately covered with such designs. Sometimes scarification is part of the puberty rite or some other initiation rite. Among the Nuer of the southern Sudan, a series of horizontal cuts is made on the foreheads of men who have completed male initiation rituals. On young men, these cuts symbolically mark and communicate their maturity and courage. After they scarify, these cuts become permanent symbols of Nuer manhood.

Visual Arts

Visual arts are produced out of material, tangible objects, so they are part of the material culture of a people. They may be religious or secular in meaning and use. Usually they are permanent in that they are meant for long-term use, but sometimes they are created for a one-time use only and then destroyed. Visual arts encompass a wide range of objects, such as basketry, ceramics, textiles, clothing, jewelry, tools, paintings, masks, and sculpture. Metal, wood, stone, leather, feathers, shells, paper made of fibers, pigments, and other materials are used in their creation. The main factors that transform a material item into a visual art are form and ornamentation.

Form   The physical form or shape of an object is a reflection of its utilitarian function, the materials available, the technical knowledge and skill of the person producing it, and the general lifestyle of the society. Nomadic or seminomadic foraging and pastoral people often produce items that are light in weight and easily transportable. The Inuit precisely carved small art objects out of soft soapstone and ivory and decorated many of their portable tools with figures of animals. Shields and hides were elaborately painted among many nomadic peoples of the American plains, who also heavily decorated their clothing and moccasins with shells and beadwork. On the other hand, Native Americans of the western United States, especially the southwest, used pigment to paint or hard stones to etch images of animals, celestial objects, people, mythological beings, and other things on rocks. The prehistoric people who created these images might have moved on the landscape according to season, but their art was stationary and long lasting. Today we know these images as pictographs and petroglyphs, also called rock art.

The availability of wood, stone, clay, hides, and other natural materials does influence what people can create and how. The kinds of tools the artist uses to paint, etch, or sculpt also are important influences on the final artwork. Metal tools have advantages over stone tools in giving artistic form to a raw material. Peoples also differ in their technical knowledge of how to work stone or wood, and how to model clay or metals.

Within these natural and technical limitations, the form of an object is the result of the interplay of utilitarian function and aesthetic style. If one examines prehistoric stone tools, one finds a bewildering variety of forms. In North American archaeology, extensive typologies have been created to classify projectile point types, which differ in size, relative length and width, and shape (straight, concave, convex, or even serrated). Some are unnotched; others are notched on the bases or sides. Great variability is also present in the vessel shapes and decoration of pottery from one group to another, as well as within the same group of people over time.

Ornamentation   Ornamentation is design added to the physical form of an object. Humans are highly creative in developing ways of adding ornamentation to material items. Ornamental designs may be woven or carved into an object. They may be painted, incised, or sewn onto an object, or a combination of these techniques may be used.

In basketry and textiles, designs are commonly woven onto the item during its construction. Different colors of plant fibers, either natural or artificially dyed, are used for the designs of baskets. Different colored yarns are used in weaving textiles. However, not all textile designs are created using fibers of contrastive colors. By using different types of weaving techniques, designs may be created in single-color baskets and textiles.

Carving creates a design by removing parts of the original material. Wood, stone, clay, ivory, shell, and bone may have carved designs. An object may be carved in three dimensions so that the form itself becomes the design, as in a piece of sculpture. Or the form of the object may remain the same, with only shallow relief carving of a design on the surface.

Painting is possibly the oldest method of ornamentation. European cave paintings date back at least 20,000 years. To make colored pigments, various materials may be mixed with water, oil, or fat, such as charcoal, plant materials, and natural mineral pigments. Paintings can be applied to wood, stone, clay, textiles, paper, or leather. Paintings can be applied to flat surfaces, such as cave walls, exposed rocks or cliff walls, wooden furniture, or canvas. They may be made on round or irregular surfaces, such as pottery, masks, and sculpture.

Incising is done by scratching lines into the surface. Like painting, incising appears to be one of the earliest ways of adding designs to an item. Incising is most commonly used on ivory, bone, and shell. In these cases, the scratched lines are frequently accentuated by adding some type of colored pigment, usually black or dark in color, so one can more readily see the design itself. Incised designs are also occasionally used for decorating clay pots and leather.

Sewing is often used to ornament cloth or leather. Glass, bone, or shell beads may be sewn on to form designs, as on moccasins or clothing. Designs may be created with various colored threads of hair, plant fiber, quills, or metal, or by sewing different colors of fabrics together, as in a patchwork quilt.

This discussion has only touched upon some of the ways in which people add ornamentation to and create design on objects. When it comes to ornamenting objects, humans are highly creative.

Although meaningful cross-cultural studies of visual arts are difficult, comparative studies have been made of stylistic elements found in ornamental designs. Working with the idea that art reflects the creator's idea of society, John Fischer studied the use of stylistic elements in twenty-eight different societies around the world. He divided the societies on the basis of their degrees of social equality and inequality (see Chapter 10), feeling that the artistic expressions of egalitarian (primarily foraging) societies would differ from those of socially stratified (primarily intensive agricultural) societies. Stylistic elements were examined in terms of relative complexity, use of space, symmetry, and boundedness. Fischer found that in egalitarian societies designs tended toward repetition of similar, symmetrical design elements, with large areas of empty space without enclosures. In more stratified societies, ornamentation was characterized by asymmetrical designs that integrated unlike elements and more fully filled enclosed areas. Fischer interpreted these differences as symbolically reflecting the differing social realities of egalitarian and stratified people. Egalitarian peoples tend to live in small, scattered isolated groups, while in stratified societies people live in crowded communities.

Performance Arts

Performance arts encompass music, song, and dance, which use voice, instruments, and/or movement to delight the senses and communicate. (Theater/drama also is a performance art, but we do not cover it here.) Music, song, and dance are closely interrelated. Dancing is usually to the accompaniment of music, especially of rhythms created partly by drumming, clapping, or other kinds of percussion. Singing often is accompanied by instrumental music. Traditional religious ceremonies and pageants commonly integrate music, song, and dance.

Music and song often are part of religious rituals. For example, Osage rituals integrated music, song, physical movements (including dance), and theatrical performances in such a manner as to communicate ideas that could not be expressed by words alone. In his studies of Osage religious rituals, Francis LaFlesche argued that these rituals were not merely prayers for supernatural assistance, but were educational as well. They were a manner of recording and transmitting the collective knowledge of the society, communicating social messages to the assembled participants. Thus, even within a society the purposes of performance arts may differ significantly, depending upon whether they are religious or secular in nature.

People raised in the Judeo-Christian religious tradition are quite familiar with the many functions of music in religious services. The lyrics of familiar hymns sung to praise God are an integral part of worship rituals. Music also helps to create the mood and sense of reverence for the service and is capable of altering the emotional state of the participants. The shared experience of singing in unison may help draw the congregation together, enhancing what many Christian denominations call their fellowship. In these and other ways, music is important in making the congregation receptive to the messages delivered in the sermon and prayers.

Music and other forms of performance arts are essential to the religious experience for diverse peoples. The voudon ("voodoo") religion of the Caribbean incorporates performance arts into religious ceremonies. Followers of voudon consider themselves to be people who "serve the spirits" (*loa*). Many *loa* originated and now live in West Africa, the area where the ancestors of modern Afro-Caribbean people were enslaved beginning about 1500. Voudon temples are elabo-

This photo of a Northwest Coast house and family crest ("totem") pole was taken in the late nineteenth century. The painting on the house is identified as a bear by the prominent teeth, large central nostrils, paws, and ears protruding from the house top.

rately decorated with sacred objects, paintings, and symbolic representations of various *loa,* which show the devotion of the worshippers and make the temple attractive to the spirits. Through drumming, music, and energetic dancing, voodoo worshippers induce the *loa* to leave their spiritual homes and take over the bodies of those who worship them. When the *loa* possess their human servants, the latter speak with the voices of the *loa,* wear the *loa's* favorite clothing, eat their foods, drink their beverages, and generally assume their identity. Visiting petitioners with problems can ask questions of the worshipper/*loa,* who may answer with directions about what course of action to take. Voudon drumming, music, and dancing are so integrated into temple rituals that the religion is unimaginable without it.

Among many peoples, music, dance, and other forms of performance arts are essential elements of curing ceremonies. !Kung shamans use percussion, song, and dance to induce the trance state they believe is necessary for curing sick people. The power to heal, !Kung believe, comes from a substance called *n!um,* which when heated up by dancing and trance allows shamans to draw sickness out of people. While women produce a definite rhythm by clapping and singing, the curers circle the fire in short, synchronous dance steps. The combination of music and dance causes the *n!um* inside their bodies to boil up into their heads, inducing trance. In this spiritually powerful state, shamans then heal by placing hands on the sick and shrieking to drive out the affliction.

Music is essential to the healing process among other African peoples. The Tumbuka-speaking peoples of northern Malawi combine singing, drumming, and dancing in all-night curing sessions. Some kinds of illnesses are caused by a category of spirits called *vimbuza,* which are the powerful spiritual energy of foreign peoples and wild animals (especially lions). *Vimbuza* cause various kinds of illnesses and even death when they possess someone. Tumbuka believe that health requires a balance between cold and hot forces (similar to the bodily "hu-

mours" of old Europe). When *vimbuza* enter the bodies of people, they create an imbalance between hot and cold forces, causing the buildup of heat that is culturally interpreted as sickness.

Tumbuka diviner-healers diagnose illnesses and direct elaborate healing ceremonies that include drumming, music, and dance. The most essential part of the curing ritual is a group gathering in which every individual present is expected to contribute to the music making. Even patients participate. As the sick person dances to the drums and music, the heat inside her or his body increases, which causes the possessing spirit to expend excess energy and cool off. As the balance between hot and cold is restored, the individual is cured, at least temporarily.

In the early 1980s, the authors of this book first heard about a medical field that uses music in the treatment of biomedical and psychological disorders. At the time, we thought the field now called music therapy was a new mode of treatment and a new occupation. As the previous examples illustrate, other cultures have long recognized the connection between music and healing and have integrated the performance arts into their treatments.

Few comparative studies of performance arts have been made. Alan Lomax's comparative studies of dance and song rank with the most ambitious. Lomax and his collaborators analyzed film footage of peoples from around the world, comparing body movements in everyday activities with their movements. They found that dance movements were formalized repetitions of the movements in daily life. Lomax further argued that the form of dance was correlated with the relative complexity of the society.

In his comparative study of songs, Lomax found that differences in song styles were also correlated with societal complexity. The songs of less complex peoples, such as egalitarian foragers, included more vocables (sounds instead of words). Words were not enunciated as clearly in their songs, and there was greater repetition of vocables and words. The songs of most complex peoples included fewer vocables, less repetition, and more words, which were clearly enunciated. Although Lomax's conclusions concerning the correlation between dance and song and relative cultural complexity have been challenged, there are some interesting parallels between his findings and those of Fischer on stylistic elements in ornamental designs.

ART and CULTURE

Art is embedded in a cultural context. Three of many features of this context are religion, gender, and identity.

Secular and Religious Art

Certain artistic products are sacred and others are not. There are sacred and secular designs, dances, songs, music, and literature. This division between secular and sacred cuts across many forms of art and across most cultures.

In contemporary urban society, the greatest artistic energies are expended in the creation of secular art, although such art may at times include religious themes. This was not always true. The great art of earlier periods was largely concerned with religion, partly because religious and political authorities often sponsored artists and their creations. The pyramids and great temples of ancient Egypt were related to conceptions of the afterlife and other dimensions of the supernatural world; the pharaohs were gods on earth.

In classical Greece, religion was the central focus for many of their highest artistic accomplishments. The Parthenon in Athens was the temple of Athena, while most of their public statuary depicted gods such as Poseidon, Zeus, Apollo, and Venus. Much Greek drama had strong religious overtones and was associated with the god Dionysus. In Rome, secular art became more prominent. The great buildings were usually palaces and theatres, and public monuments honoring the triumphs of living heroes filled Roman cities. With the advent of the Middle Ages religion regained preeminence. The great buildings

of the Medieval and the Renaissance periods were cathedrals, while the greatest artists of the time labored to fill these buildings with frescos, mosaics, paintings, statuary, and other artistic works, as well as music, song, and pageantry dedicated to the worship of God.

The 1700s began the emphasis on reason and science, the industrial revolution, the rise of capitalism, and the beginnings of modern political democracy. Ever since, Western art has become increasingly secular. The largest buildings in our cities are no longer dedicated to religion, but to government, commerce, or athletics. Contemporary painters choose secular subjects, from realistic landscapes and buildings to abstract designs and cans of Campbell's soup. The most illustrious composers and performers today seldom produce or perform religious music, but focus on secular and, at times, even irreligious themes. For those of us who learned our culture in a society dominated by secular art, it is important to remember that for most peoples and for most of human history, religion and religious art have been preeminent. The most elaborate artistic achievements of a great many peoples are associated with religious ceremonies: visual arts, music, dances, ornamentations, architecture, and their associated mythologies.

For example, much of the art of the Navajo is bound to their religion. In curing ceremonies the singer (a shaman) addresses and calls on the Holy People, who are spiritual beings believed by Navajo to have the power to restore sick people to harmony and beauty.

For the ceremony, the singer creates images of the Holy People out of sand, called sandpaintings. Navajo sandpaintings are visual and sacred representations that are created, used in a single ceremony, and then destroyed. Most sandpaintings are stylized scenes of events involving various Holy People that occurred in the mythological past. Each sandpainting is part of a ceremony that also includes other sacred objects (such as rattles and prayer sticks) and lengthy songs or chants recited by the singer. The songs/chants that are recited over the sandpainting and the patient may last for hours. Most songs/chants tell of the myths depicted in the specific sandpainting.

In their years of learning to become singers, Navajo singers must memorize the lengthy songs and chants that they recite over sick people to restore their harmony with the world. Singers also learn to make precise sandpaintings that represent specific mythical scenes and events.

There are hundreds of sandpaintings. Most ceremonies involve a combination of many sand-paintings used in association with particular chants. Because some are quite large and ex-tremely detailed, they often take hours to create. But all must be exact representations of the ideal model of the mythical scene or event depicted. Most scenes represented in the sandpaintings are from particular myths familiar to the patient and audience.

Sandpaintings are made for the express pur-pose of inducing the Holy People to come to the hogan where the ceremony is held. The Holy People are attracted by the beauty of the sand-painting, the compelling chants recited by the singer, and the manipulation of powerful ritual objects. During the ceremony, the patient usually sits on the sandpainting, which contains draw-ings of the Holy People whose presence in the hogan imbues the images of the Holy People. After each phase of the ceremony is finished, the sandpainting is destroyed.

Navajo sandpaintings and the singing of curers clearly have strong religious overtones, but the division between secular and religious purposes is not always clear. The kachina dolls of the Hopis are small figurines carved out of cottonwood root and painted to look like one of the kachina or supernatural beings which are a central focus of their religious life. Traditionally, these dolls were given to girls at ceremonial dances by people wearing kachina costumes and masks. The dolls themselves are not ritual items, but rather a way to help the children learn about and recognize the 500 or so different kachina spirits.

Similarly, the Hispanic peoples of New Mexico have a tradition of producing *bultos,* which are carved wooden crucifixes and figures of saints, and *retablos,* which are flat wooden boards painted with images of Christ or saints. Today in New Mexico dozens of artists produce and sell *bultos* and *retablos.* Some of these paintings and figures of saints find their way into churches or family chapels and altars, but the majority are used in a more secular context as decorative art for the home. Religious symbolism is often used to deco-rate clothing and other items of everyday use, blurring the distinction between secular and sacred art.

Religious considerations have other effects on secular art. The use of certain types of motifs or themes may be forbidden. The Koran prohibits the use of human images, which are viewed as idolatry. Thus, many Islamic peoples extended this ban to include any pictorial representation of humans or animals. As a result, much of the art of Islamic peoples is devoid of naturalistic represen-tations, focusing instead on elaborate geometric or curvilinear designs. The Shakers emphasized singing and dancing as important parts of their religious services, but prohibited the use of musi-cal instruments. Religious beliefs frequently place limits on secular artistic expressions.

Art and Gender

Gender differences often are reflected in body, visual, performance, and other forms of art. Colors and designs in clothing and body decora-tion sometimes are considered male or female. Gender also influences who creates and/or per-forms certain types of visual, performance, or verbal arts. The BaMbuti pygmies of the African rain forest have a ritual performance involving dance and music they call *molimo.* At night after the women and children retire to their huts, the men make *molimo* music. Women are not sup-posed to know that the *molimo* is just a long, flutelike instrument, but to believe it to be some kind of forest animal. In fact, women seem to know all about the *molimo.*

Among the Plains Indians, beadwork and quillwork were produced by women. The only men who produced beadwork and quillwork were *berdaches,* men who dressed and acted as women. Although both women and men painted hides, there were distinct differences in subject matter. Women painted only geometric designs. The hide containers, called *parafleches,* used for the storage of food and clothing were made by women and were only painted in geometric designs. Representational designs of people, horses, and other animals and supernatural beings were only painted by men. Tepees and buffalo robes were painted by either men or women depending upon whether the design was to be geometric (by women) or representational (by men).

Some visual art objects are made for specific rituals or ceremonies. Initiation rites are usually held for only one sex. The art produced for them, therefore, is sometimes "sex-specific." In the highlands of New Guinea, long bamboo flutes are played at male initiation ceremonies. Women are not supposed to know about the existence of flutes. Many initiation ceremonies also include carved and painted masks, supposedly kept secret from women and uninitiated boys.

Performance arts often are carried out during religious ceremonies. Men have historically played the dominant role in most religions. Not surprisingly, in most societies men dominate the performance arts associated with religion. For example, even though many of the Hopi kachinas are female, in traditional kachina dances all dancers, even those impersonating female spirits, are men. In ancient Greek drama, the roles of women were played by men. In the West, women were not allowed to participate in certain performance arts long after they had become secularized. The role of Juliet, in the original production of Shakespeare's play, was performed by a young boy, for women could not be actors in Shakespeare's time. It was not until the late seventeenth century that women could perform in the English theater.

Social Functions of Art

Does art exist solely to satisfy the human desire for the aesthetic? Perhaps, but if so why have humans expended such energy in its creation? Perhaps art also has a critical role in human social life and cultural existence. Through the use of art people can simultaneously express their identities as members of particular groups, while at the same time demonstrating their unique individuality. Through the production, consumption, and use of art, we can express our personal individuality, our group identities (including ethnic affiliation), and even our social status.

Individuality   Many of us attempt to express our individuality by creating art or displaying art, as shown by the widespread appeal of handmade goods produced by skilled craftspeople. The attraction of handmade over machine-made goods has been, since the advent of the industrial revolution in the nineteenth century, their individuality. This individuality is not solely the result the differing technical skill of the makers, but rather that the makers have consciously tried to make every item unique by varying colors and designs. Thus, if one looks at Oriental rugs, American Indian jewelry, pottery and baskets, Maya textiles from Guatemala, or wood carvings from New Guinea, rarely are two items identical. If they are, it is probably because they were produced for the commercial market.

Similarly, our clothing and houses express our individuality. Even though we usually conform to the norms of our society in clothing styles, most of us abhor uniforms, and thus we enhance our clothes in some manner so as to make them uniquely ours. Similarly in dwellings or buildings people attempt to express individuality. All Maori dwellings were carved and painted, but different designs and images were used. Today in suburban North America builders of subdivisions usually vary the houses by using a range of floor plans, building materials, and colors. Many residents of older neighborhoods, though, still consider the new subdivisions to be lacking in character, style, and individuality.

Social Identity   Art is also a means of expressing social identity, publicly displaying what kind of person you are or which group of people you identify with. In the 1960s and early 1970s, long hair, beads, and baggy clothes decorated with peace signs and upside-down flags denoted "hippies." Some traveled the country in old Volkswagen minibuses or school buses that were hand painted in strange colors and designs. Clothing styles, hairstyles, and other art forms are commonly used to indicate social group identity, from the black leather jackets painted with club emblems of motorcycle gangs to the shepherd crook spears and red sashes of the Cheyenne Dog Soldier society.

A widespread use of art to express social membership has to do with ethnic affiliation. Clothing styles and decoration are important visual markers of ethnic identity. Plaid kilts are markers of Scots, as much as beaded clothing and feather headdresses are of American Indians. A woman in Guatemala wearing a *huipuli* is a Maya. If you see a man wearing a cowboy hat and boots in Europe, you can guess that he has probably never ridden a horse or seen many cows.

Ethnicity is expressed in more than clothing. The full range of artistic forms—body, visual, performance, and verbal arts—is employed to display one's ethnic identity. Thus, we speak of ethnic literature, and ethnic foods. Despite our use of the word *ethnic* in such contexts, ultimately, of course, all art is ethnic art, since it is associated with a specific ethnic group and everyone is a part of some ethnic group.

Social Status Finally, relative social status within societies is reflected in the use of art. As discussed earlier, body arts are frequently an indicator of social status. Other art forms also indicate status. In many ranked and stratified societies the rights to make use of certain art forms may be the property of families or status groups. Only certain individuals will have the right to wear or use particular colors or designs, sing particular songs, dance particular dances, and even tell particular stories. This control over the use or performance of particular artistic expression is a symbolic indicator of individual social status.

Similarly in contemporary society we use art to demonstrate our relative status. We display our status in our homes, automobiles, furnishings, and clothing, communicating to the world our affluence. We also demonstrate our status in what we hang on our walls, read, listen to, and watch. In our consumption of visual, performance, and verbal arts the evaluation, of course, is more subjective and difficult to measure. But for many people opera, ballet, and classical music have higher status than comedy, square dancing, and country-western or rap music. Classical literature has higher status than romance novels, science fiction, and comic books. Personal taste obviously still plays a significant role in our artistic choices, but relative social rankings of art forms also plays a role.

SUMMARY

1. All cultures have artistic objects, designs, songs, dances, and other ways of expressing their appreciation of the aesthetic.

2. People around the world change their bodily appearance by such means as physical alterations, application of body paints, tattoos, and scarification. These changes in the appearance of the body are termed *body arts*.

3. Visual arts are those material artistic expressions that appeal to the eye. These arts include clothing, pottery, textiles, houses, basketry, and practically all other material objects.

4. Performance arts refer to those arts that use sound and movement for aesthetic purposes. These arts include music, song, dance, and theater.

5. Some arts are secular and others sacred. At times the differences between the two are difficult to determine.

6. Art serves a range of social purposes. Art can define and reinforce gender differences in a society. Differences in the use of art can define the boundaries of ethnic groups, serving as ethnic boundary markers. Art also serves to define the relative status differences in a society.

KEY TERMS

art   visual arts
aesthetic   performance arts
body arts

SUGGESTED READINGS

Boas, Franz. *Primitive Art.* New York: Dover Publications, Inc., 1955 (original 1927).

The first systematic treatment of the subject by an anthropologist. Despite its original publication date nearly 75 years ago, this book remains insightful today.

Brain, Robert. *The Decorated Body.* New York: Harper & Row, 1979.

Faris, James C. *Nuba Personal Art.* London: 1972.

The Garland Encyclopedia of World Music. 10 volumes (editors Bruno Nettl, Ruth Stone, James Porter, and Timothy Rice). New York: Garland Publishing, 1997.

This very useful reference includes large volumes dedicated to the music of particular world regions, such as Australia and the Pacific, Africa, and North America. Not all volumes are yet available. Each volume has dozens of articles written by experts on various specific cultures of the region, or on various topics about the region's music.

Mead, Sidney Moko. *Te Maori: Maori Art from New Zealand Collections.* New York: Harry N. Abrams, 1984.

chapter 13

GLOBALIZATION *and* ETHNICITY

Contents

According to the nightly news commentaries we are living in a time of unprecedented economic growth. Almost daily we hear of new millionaires and billionaires being made as a result of the rising stock market. The greatest economic problem seems to be the difficulty of finding enough skilled workers to fill the new jobs being created. We are told that the new technology has revolutionized the global economy and that, as we enter the new millennium, we stand at the threshold of a new era of unparalleled prosperity for the world's peoples. Is this true? Can this new information and communication technology solve the problems confronting humanity? Are we at the threshold of a new, utopian era in human history? Then why do these same newscasts report an ever-increasing number of small-scale wars? Why are people killing each other in places such as the Congo, Sudan, Kosovo, the Middle East, Spain, Northern Ireland, Kashmir, Afghanistan, Timor, Irian Jaya, and the Philippines? The list of conflicts grows longer, and few seem to be resolved. On one hand the world appears to be coming together in a new global economy, while on the other it appears to be coming apart politically. In this chapter, as anthropologists, we are going to examine the modern world by looking at three interrelated issues: the global economy, demographic changes, and ethnic conflicts.

THE MODERN WORLD

The world today is a far different place from what it was when your grandparents were young. The Second World War was a major watershed in world history. In 1940 the United States, together with the major countries of Europe, dominated world affairs politically and economically. Japan was the only non-Western country in the world that was truly autonomous. The native peoples of the Americas had been conquered, and most countries of Africa, Asia, and the Pacific were colonial possessions of or under the indirect domination of one or another Western power.

The British, French, and Soviet empires were the largest, but Belgium, the Netherlands, Spain, Portugal, Italy, and even the United States had overseas possessions. There was global trade, but no integrated global economy. Overseas possessions were the economic monopolies of the "home country" or colonial power. Thus India, South Africa, Nigeria, and the other British colonies served as monopolized sources of raw materials for English factories, as well as protected markets for English manufactured goods. Trade both among and within these empires was highly controlled and regulated. Although conflicts existed in many parts of the world, they were usually between rival Western powers. Western leaders in Washington, London, Paris, Berlin, Moscow, and other European capitals made the important political and economic decisions concerning all of the world's peoples.

With most of the world divided into colonial empires, there could be no integrated global economy. Even if there had not been political trade barriers, the highly integrated multinational corporations of today could not have existed. Global communications, travel, and shipping were slow, inadequate, and expensive. Thus markets were protected not only by trade barriers, but frequently by geography as well.

Three major changes have occurred since the end of World War II that have profoundly changed the course of world history by making the global economy possible. The first of these changes was the collapse of the European colonial empires, which eliminated many of the political barriers to global trade. This change started in 1945 and ended in the late 1980s with the collapse of the Soviet Union. Non-Western peoples throughout the world were given the freedom to manage their own affairs. For the first time, these peoples were allowed to sell their own raw materials and products on a global market. For the first time, the peoples of India, Pakistan, Kenya, Indonesia, and elsewhere were able to purchase goods from any country they wished. For the first time, these former colonies could establish local industries to compete directly with those of Europe and North America.

The second change was the development of new technologies that not only increased the production of manufactured goods and food, but allowed for the development of transportation systems that could move goods, raw materials, food, and people at greatly reduced cost. Today we can extract more raw materials and produce more manufactured goods and food with only a fraction of the physical labor required prior to World War II. The costs of shipping goods and materials as well as the time in transit have been dramatically reduced. Air freight now carries lighter, higher-cost goods, while faster and larger oceangoing ships carry heavier products and raw materials at a much lower cost. Ships and trains have been replaced by airplanes for international business travel. Trips that in 1940 required days, weeks, or even months have been reduced to hours or at most little more than a day.

The third and latest change has been the development of information and communications technology. Telephone communication has been supplemented by the Internet. Today letters, messages, photos, music, videos, and even whole databases can be sent or accessed, while products can be bought or sold and money transferred twenty-four hours a day, instantaneously, via the Internet. The information and communications technology has not merely made the world "smaller"; for many purposes, it has made geography irrelevant.

The Global Economy

For better or worse, the market principle (discussed in Chapter 6) increasingly integrates the local economies of the world into a **global economy** in which manufactured goods, foodstuffs, raw materials, labor, and even technical services are marketed worldwide (see Figure 13.1). The prices that farmers in the United States, Australia, Argentina, and elsewhere receive for their wheat, corn, and other crops are not determined by local or national markets, but ultimately by global supply and demand. Similarly, the price that an oil company receives for a barrel of oil is set by the international market. No one is totally immune to global market pressures. Manufacturers of goods, whether automobiles, machine tools, home appliances, clothes, shoes, or toys, have to compete in the global market. Even workers have also come into direct global wage competition: Increasingly, companies are willing to move their production facilities to countries with lower labor costs to remain competitive.

Until the 1950s, the industrialized regions of the world were concentrated in Europe and North America, with Japan being the only non-Western country that had industrialized to any significant degree. The rest of the world served basically as a source of raw materials and a market for the manufactured goods of these regions. Starting in the 1960s, other countries in Asia, such as Hong Kong, Taiwan, South Korea, and Singapore, began emulating Japan's success. At first they used their low labor costs to produce textiles, clothing, footwear, and other labor-intensive products that undercut the prices and invaded the markets of the established "first-wave" industrial countries. At the same time, Japan was expanding its heavy industry (steelmaking, shipbuilding, and automobiles), as well as its electronic industries. In recent years, industrialization has spread to Thailand, Malaysia, Korea, Indonesia, and China. These countries are now competing with Western Europe and North America not only in heavy industry, but in high-tech industries as well. The countries of Asia have the fastest growing economies in the world.

The changing economic relations between the United States and the rest of the world over the past fifty years illustrates the increasing degree of global interdependence. Just before World War II, more than 50 percent of U.S. exports consisted of foodstuffs and raw materials such as oil, raw cotton, wheat and other grains, and tobacco. Imports were dominated by products that did not occur naturally or grow well domestically, notably tropical foodstuffs and raw materials such as rubber, sugar, coffee, and silk. The United States was self-sufficient in most minerals critical

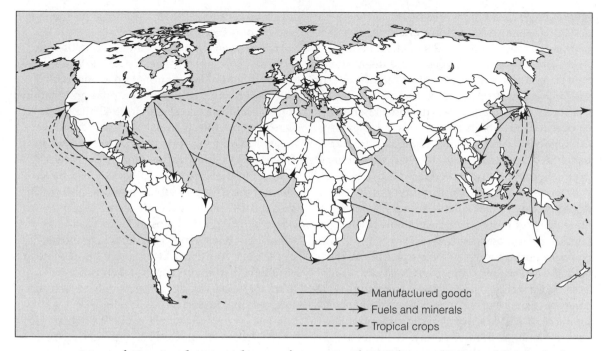

Figure 13.1 Map of Commodities and Manufacturing Flow The modern world is linked together by the flow of materials and manufactured goods, creating a global economy.

for industry, including iron, copper, coal, and petroleum. Indeed, the United States was an exporter of these items. In turn, American industrial output was more than sufficient to meet domestic needs for most categories of manufactured goods.

The postwar era has seen major shifts in both the kinds and the quantities of goods that the United States imports and exports. As the volume of trade has increased, the nature of American imports and exports has changed. The United States now has to rely on other countries for many of the critical raw materials for industries and fuels that it once produced. The increasing dependence of Americans on the importation of metals, petroleum, and other raw materials is the result of several factors. The expanding economy of the United States has resulted in an increased consumption of energy fuels and raw materials. At the same time, either domestic energy and raw-material reserves have declined in production or production cannot be increased to meet demands.

While the United States has become increasingly dependent on foreign sources for basic energy needs and raw materials, the nature of American industry itself has been changing. The American shoe industry is almost gone, replaced by factories in Brazil, Italy, Taiwan, and South Korea. Segments of the American electronics industry have lost out to foreign competition; most television sets, radios, and videocassette recorders are now produced in Japan, Hong Kong, Singapore, or Southeast Asia. The American garment industry is rapidly losing its domestic market to clothing imported from South Korea, Hong Kong, Cambodia, and Taiwan. The American automobile industry, traditionally the bulwark of the manufacturing economy, has lost a significant portion of both its domestic and its world markets to Europe, Japan, and South Korea. In 1950, American factories produced 75 percent of all motor vehicles manufactured in the world, dominating not just their own domestic market but most of the world market as well. Today, American production has dropped to less than 20 percent of the world's total, and almost 25 percent of the automobiles sold in the United States are imported. A similar loss of the domestic market has occurred for the American steel industry. Today the United States depends on foreign sources for much of its basic needs in manufactured goods. To pay for these increased imports, the United States has shifted from being primarily an exporter of raw materials to being an exporter of specialized manufactured goods. Today, in terms of overseas dollars earned, America's largest export industry is entertainment: movies, television programs, and music.

An important consequence of globalization has been the loss or weakening of the national identities of corporations. In the past a company and its products were clearly American, or German, or Japanese. In today's world of global trade and multinational corporations such identities are becoming increasingly ambiguous or irrelevant. Firestone is a century-old American tire company. Its tires are made in plants in the United States and its headquarters is in Nashville. However, today it is a wholly owned subsidiary of Bridgestone/Firestone, a Japanese corporation. Similarly, Chrysler is now a subsidiary of Daimler-Chrysler, a German corporation. Jaguar, the great English car company, although still making its cars in England for export to the United States, is today part of Ford. Regardless of where their corporate headquarters are located, companies are increasingly acting as global, not national entities. It is not unheard of for an American company to borrow money from banks in Europe, or an American branch of a European bank, to finance the building of new plants in Asia, to manufacture goods to be marketed in Latin America or the United States. Corporations are collectively owned by and are accountable to their stockholders, an anonymous multinational group of investors. Corporations think in terms of profits for their investors, not national interest. As a result, corporations can and do move their facilities from country to country in search of cheaper labor,

lower taxes, and less demanding governmental regulations. (See Figure 13.2.)

These recent changes in the world economic system would not have been possible without the development of international financing, which has made money available to capital-poor nations for economic development. In 1945, the World Bank and the International Monetary Fund were created to help war-ravaged Europe and Japan reestablish their industrial plants. These two institutions have played a pivotal role in the creation of the existing global economic system. The World Bank has been a major conduit for economic development loans to Third World nations. The World Bank's role in making loan money available to Third World countries has now been supplemented by numerous European, American, and Japanese banking houses that have become international financiers.

Loans provided to these capital-poor countries have allowed them to adopt high-cost technology more quickly and increase their economic productivity. With these funds, Third World countries have constructed irrigation projects, expanded their transportation systems, developed or expanded port facilities, and, in some cases, developed their own manufacturing industries. In the past decade alone, these loans have

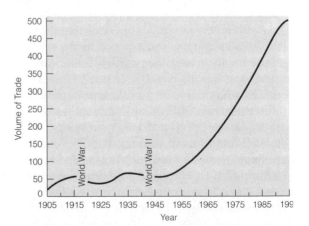

Figure 13.2 Growth of World Trade: 1905–1990

amounted to hundreds of billions of dollars. An unappreciated consequence of these loans is a stimulation of the exports of industrialized nations, because most of these funds are used to purchase needed technology and equipment from Japan, Europe, and the United States. At the same time, most of the economic development projects funded by these loans have focused on increased production of raw materials needed by these same industrialized countries.

International financing adds still another dimension to the increasing interdependence of nations. In a capitalist world, money flows both ways across international boundaries in search of greater profits. United States banks, companies, and individuals have more than $4 trillion invested in other countries. Conversely, foreign companies, banks, and individuals have a similar amount invested in the United States. Of the $3.5 trillion in U.S. government debt, 38 percent is owed to foreign individuals or banks, with the Japanese owning the largest share. The Japanese banks in turn also have made more than $290 billion in loans to other Asian countries. The citizens of these countries have a direct, vested interest in the continued economic prosperity of the others. The loans the U.S. government made to Mexico a few years ago, and the recent international loans to South Korea, were not made out of friendship or humanitarian concern, but out of economic self-interest.

Today neither the United States nor any other country in the world even approaches economic self-sufficiency. Virtually all peoples are integrated into the global economy. We depend on one another for critical energy fuels, raw materials, and particular categories of foodstuffs and manufactured goods. Without these imports we could not sustain our economy or even adequately provide food, clothing, and shelter for our population. In turn, other countries depend on us, both as a source for particular manufactured goods and foodstuffs and as a market for their products. Although some countries and regions may be more critical than others because they provide some particular essential goods or resources, all are important in maintaining the current global economic system.

Demographic Changes and the Global Economy

The postwar period has also been a time of rapid population growth. Advances in medical science have lowered infant mortality rates, eradicated many deadly diseases, and lengthened life expectancies. As a result, in the last fifty years, the world population has jumped from only slightly more than 2.5 billion to 6 billion (see Figure 13.3). This population growth has not been equally as pronounced among all the world's peoples. The population growth rate during this period in

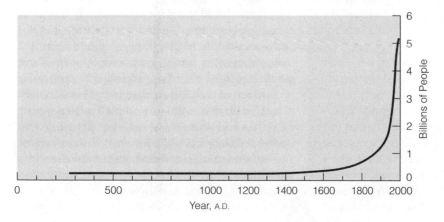

Figure 13.3 Growth of World's Population

Europe, North America, and the former Soviet Union has fallen well below the world rate. In some European countries the birth rate of the native ethnic group has fallen so low that their populations will actually start to decline within the next generation. The highest rates of population growth—those of Latin America, Asia, and Africa—are in the least economically developed regions of the world.

Although the world as a whole has profited from globalization, not everyone has equally benefited. The global economy has resulted in a dramatic skewing in the distribution of wealth, not just between individuals, but between countries and regions of the world as well. In 1960 it was estimated that the richest 20 percent of the world's peoples had 30 times more income than the poorest 20 percent. By 1999 this ratio had risen to 74 to 1 and growing. The problem is not just that the rich are getting richer; the standard of living of the poor is actually declining. Since 1980 the average per capita income in more than a third of the countries of the world has declined. Today 1.2 billion people are surviving on incomes of less than $1 a day, and 800 million people are suffering from malnutrition. In contrast, the total assets of the three richest billionaires in the world exceed those of the poorest 600 million people, while the richest 200 individuals in the world have a combined wealth that exceeds the annual income of the poorest 2.4 billion people.

The difficulty is not just that a wealth gap exists, but that the differences are rapidly increasing, and there appears to be no way to reverse the trend. To fully participate in the global economy, people have to be connected to the Internet. A so-called "digital divide" has emerged among the world countries. In the United Kingdom there are 30 personal computers for every 100 people; by contrast, in Malawi there is only one computer for every 10,000 people. It is not merely that most of the individuals in the world do not have access to computers, nor the educational skills to use them; their countries lack the necessary telecommunications infrastructures as well. To develop the infrastructure alone would be extraordinarily expensive. It has been estimated that these underdeveloped countries would have to spend up to 1.5 percent of their gross domestic product annually to develop the needed technological infrastructure. The underdeveloped countries not only lack the needed capital for technological development, but most are deeply in debt. In 1980 the forty most heavily indebted poor countries of the world had a total debt of $55 billion. By 1999 the debts of these countries had grown to $260 billion. Unable to even meet the annual interest payments on their debts, these countries lack the money to maintain their existing inadequate infrastructures, let alone expand them.

The population explosion has created extreme economic and population pressures in many of the less-developed rural regions of the world, contributing to outmigrations of peoples. Mass movements of people are not new. Migrations of populations came in the wake of European expansion. However, both the nature and the geographical direction of population movements since World War II differ from those of earlier periods. Earlier migrations were primarily movements of European and African peoples. Since 1945, there have been two main patterns of human migration: (1) rural-to-urban migration, and (2) migration of peoples from poorer countries to richer countries.

During the nineteenth and early twentieth centuries, the development of major urban centers was associated with industrial economies. Increasing demand for industrial workers was the primary factor in the growth of cities. In industrialized societies this trend toward urbanization has continued. In addition, major urban centers have emerged in nonindustrialized countries. Just before World War II, about 50 percent of the total population of the United States and Europe was urban, compared with only about 8 to 10 percent for Africa and Asia and 25 percent for Latin America. Today, about 75 percent of Americans and 70 percent of Europeans are city dwellers. However, the urban populations of Asia and Africa have jumped to between 25 and 30 percent, and in Latin America the urban population

Population growth contributes to social problems in the Third World, including unemployment and overcrowding in urban areas. This is a shantytown in Rio de Janeiro, Brazil.

has increased to more than 60 percent. The growth rate of urbanization has thus been highest outside Europe and North America. In fact, the world's five most rapidly growing cities are located in nonindustrialized nations: Bandung (Indonesia), Lagos (Nigeria), Karachi (Pakistan), Bogotá (Colombia), and Baghdad (Iraq). Most Third World cities lack the large industrial complexes capable of employing the great masses of people migrating into them, but their small-scale industries, transportation services, and government jobs, although limited, offer greater economic opportunities than do the overcrowded rural regions of the adjacent countryside.

Most migration has been within countries, but a growing trend has been toward international migration. It has been estimated that 125 million people presently live in countries in which they were not born, and this is probably a conservative estimate. Most evident has been the migration from the nations of Latin America, Asia, and Africa to the highly industrialized countries of North America and Europe. As their industrial economies expanded during the 1950s and 1960s, many Western European countries began experiencing labor shortages. West Germany initiated a "guest worker" program to recruit foreign laborers, first in southern Europe, Italy, and Spain, and later in Yugoslavia and Turkey. Concurrently, French factories began recruiting Arab workers from what were France's North African colonies, particularly Algeria. In the 1950s, England began experiencing an influx of West Indians from its possessions in the Caribbean. In the 1960s, a wave of Pakistani and Indian immigrants also settled in England.

By the early 1970s, when the economic growth of Western Europe began to slow, large non-European communities were well established in most of the major cities. When West Germany ended its guest worker program in 1974, it had 2.5 million foreign workers, more than 10 percent of its total labor force. Through various means the West German government tried to repatriate these guest workers and their families, but failed. France, England, and other Western European countries have considered stricter immigration laws to stop the continuing influx of African and Asian workers, but the number of new immigrants is increasing despite tighter controls. Today almost 10 percent of the population of Western Europe are recent immigrants, most from Asia and Africa. As a result, Western European countries, which once had relatively homogeneous populations, are now home to a number of culturally and ethnically diverse peoples.

This change in patterns of human migration is equally evident in the United States. Since World War II, about 25 percent of American population growth has been the result of immigration, and migration patterns to the United States have changed dramatically. In the 1960s, the flood of immigrants began to increase. From only about 300,000 persons per year in the 1960s, the number of immigrants jumped to more than 700,000 per year by the 1980s. Today, more than a million legal and illegal immigrants enter the United States every year. As the number of immigrants increased, their origin shifted markedly. Proportionally, the number of Latin American immigrants remained about the same (one-third), while European immigration declined. The major change was in the number of Asian arrivals, from less than 10 percent of all immigrants in 1950 to more than 40 percent by the 1980s. As a result, between 1980 and 1990 the number of Asian Americans more than doubled, from 3.5 million (1.5 percent) to almost 7.3 million (2.9 percent), whereas the number of Latin Americans increased almost 50 percent, from 14.5 million (6.4 percent) to more than 22 million (9 percent). These figures are only for legal immigrants; if the number of illegal immigrants could be added, the shift would have been much greater, since most of these immigrants are Asians or Latin Americans. The ethnic diversity of the U.S. population is increasing.

This massive migration of peoples has alleviated some of the economic and population pressures in many underdeveloped countries. At the same time, it is bringing peoples from extremely diverse cultural backgrounds into direct daily contact with one another.

Ethnicity and Conflict

The news media today present us with a seemingly unending stream of stories of massacres, bombings, and fighting from virtually all corners of the globe. The Irish Republican Army bombs a building in London, a group of Tutsis are killed by Hutus, Sikhs assassinate the prime minister of India, the bodies of Muslims murdered by Serbs are uncovered in Bosnia, a group of Maya Indians in Mexico are massacred, the Basques attack a police post in Spain, and the list goes on. These and the vast majority of the 150 or so ongoing armed conflicts in the world are ethnic conflicts. However, not all ethnic movements are violent. In

Canada, citizens of the province of Quebec prepare for still another vote on whether to remain part of Canada or secede. American Indian tribes throughout the United States push in federal courts for greater tribal sovereignty and power. In Great Britain, Scotland and Wales have now established their own separate parliaments. Throughout the world ethnic groups are increasingly asserting their rights within the political system in many countries, and by armed violence in others. Why, in this time of globalism, is the world fragmenting along ethnic lines?

Ethnicity   It is difficult for most Americans to understand the causes and bitterness of ethnic conflicts in other parts of the world. The United States is home to more ethnic groups than any other single country in the world. While there are ethnic conflicts and rivalries, they are not a major problem. There are no serious secessionist movements. We are, as we commonly hear, "all Americans."

To understand ethnic conflict in other parts of the world, and the common American misunderstanding of its nature and magnitude, we need first to see what is meant by **ethnic group**. An ethnic group is a formal, named grouping of people who see themselves as sharing a common cultural-historical tradition that distinguishes them from other groups. Membership is determined by ancestry. There is in ethnic identity a strong psychological and/or emotional component that divides the world into categories of "us" and "them." The two main attributes that help to define and identify an ethnic group and its members are (1) an origin myth or history and (2) ethnic boundary markers. The **origin myths** of the group are those commonly known (at least to the members) cultural-historical events that define the group's uniqueness as a people. **Ethnic boundary markers** are those overt characteristics of the population that serve to publicly identify members of the group, both to each other and to "others." Such markers may include differences in language, religion, physical characteristics, clothing, house styles, food, and so forth.

Thus defined, there are a vast number of ethnic identities in the world, many of which appear to be subgroups of larger groupings. For example, there is an "American" ethnic identity, which encompasses a large number of smaller or subgroups: German American, Italian American, African American, and so on. There is an origin myth and ethnic boundary marker that defines and distinguishes Americans. Embedded in the American identity are the more particularistic origin myths and boundary markers that distinguish some Americans as German Americans and others as Italian Americans or African Americans.

How many such subgroups are found in the American population is difficult to determine. What we see is that there are differing levels of ethnic identity. Although the boundary is frequently unclear, some ethnic identities are purely social identities, while other ethnic identities are both social and political. A **nationality** is an ethnic group with a separate political identity, while a **subnationality** has only a social identity. German American, Italian American, and African American are primarily social (subnational) identities embedded in the larger social and political (national) identity as American. The trait that distinguishes a subnationality from a nationality is the concept of a discrete and separate **homeland**. A homeland is the geographical area, defined by history, that in their beliefs collectively and exclusively belongs to the members of that nationality. Implicit in the idea of homeland is that the members of the group have the right to political autonomy within and sovereignty over their homeland. It is nationalities and nationalism, not subnational groups, that are the primary and most dangerous source of ethnic conflict.

To see how powerful and resilient ethnic nationalities are and the potential danger posed by the rise of nationalism, let's examine two cases that we often hear about in the news: Northern Ireland and Israel/Palestine, places where the ethnic conflicts have proved particularly bitter.

In 1922, after several centuries of British colonial domination and periodic rebellions by the native Irish, the Irish Free State (now the Republic of Ireland) was established. However, not all of Ireland was given independence. In the seventeenth century, to control the Irish, the British evicted Irish farmers from the northernmost portion of the island and colonized the region with Scottish Presbyterians, who became known as the Scotch-Irish. The Scotch-Irish did not identify themselves as Irish and had no desire to become part of an independent Ireland. Recognizing the wishes of the Scotch-Irish, at independence the British partitioned the island. The northern six counties became Northern Ireland and remained part of the United Kingdom. Many Irish did not and do not accept the legality of this partitioning of Ireland. To them, Northern Ireland is part of the Irish homeland and thus should be part of the Republic of Ireland.

Beginning in 1968, the Irish Republican Army, a secretive guerrilla army that is illegal in the Republic of Ireland, waged a war with the object of reuniting Northern Ireland with the Republic of Ireland. Bombings, ambushes, and assassinations claimed the lives of more than 2,200 persons. In May, 1998, voters in Northern Ireland overwhelmingly approved an accord that would end the bloodshed and provide for a political solution to the conflict. Unfortunately, all of the provisions of the accord have yet to be met.

The news media frequently report the problems in Northern Ireland as conflict between the British and the Irish or between Catholics and Protestants; in reality, it is neither. The root of the problem is the conflicting claims of two rival nationalities: the Irish and the Scotch-Irish. The Scotch-Irish have emerged over the past four hundred years as a distinct nationality that claims the northern part of Ireland as its homeland. In contrast, the Irish see the area as an integral and inalienable part of the Irish homeland. Only time will reveal whether the 1998 accord will counterbalance the parties' claims.

Jews began returning to their historic homeland in Palestine in 1882. During the early twentieth century, Jewish settlements in Palestine grew, and in 1948 the state of Israel was proclaimed by the Jewish settlers. For the past fifty years,

Members of the Irish Freedom Movement demonstrate in London against the continued British presence in Northern Ireland.

Reuters/Bettmann

conflict between Israelis and Palestinians has been constant, varying only in the intensity and form of violence. The problem is similar to that in Northern Ireland, in that two nationalities—Israelis and Palestinians—claim the same geographical region as their legitimate homeland. Although some progress has been made toward peaceful settlements of the conflicts between Israelis and Palestinians, the agreements are tenuous. The situation remains extremely volatile, and it seems impossible to resolve these conflicts to the satisfaction of both nationalities.

These two conflicts vividly illustrate the strength of nationalist sentiments. In both cases we see groups of educated, rational human beings who are willing to sacrifice their lives and economic well-being in unending conflicts for what they consider to be their nationality's legitimate rights to their homeland.

With the end of the colonial empires in Africa, Asia, and Oceania, many people naively believed that the issue of nationalism had been resolved. After all, "they" all had independence. What many did not realize was that the new national boundaries were the same as the old colonial boundaries. These were (as some termed them) "artificial countries," consisting of numerous distinct nationalities, many of whom harbored old hatreds for one another. Boundaries and political structures had been created and held together only by Western military force. Internal ethnic conflicts within these new countries were inevitable, as secessionist movements quickly emerged in country after country following independence. The collapse of the colonial world also served to encourage minority nationalities in Europe and North America in their quest for increased local autonomy, if not total independence.

To understand the magnitude or potential magnitude of this problem, one need only realize that the world is divided into less than two hundred countries, which are home to between 3,000 and 5,000 distinct ethnic nationalities. As a result, the populations of most countries encompass a number of distinct nationalities. China officially recognizes fifty-six distinct nationalities. Some estimates are as high as three hundred ethnic nationalities in Indonesia. Ethiopia has at least seventy nationalities. Only a handful of countries are peopled by members of a single nationality and are thus ethnically homogeneous.

The Nature of Ethnic Conflict   To understand ethnic conflict it is important to first distinguish between ethnic conflicts and wars. Wars are fought between countries using formally organized armies. The primary objective of a war is to attack and destroy the other army for the purpose of changing or maintaining the political status quo. In contrast, ethnic conflicts are between peoples for the purpose of changing or maintaining the social status quo. In ethnic conflicts the people themselves, men, women, children, old and young, not the opposing army, are the primary target of aggression. As a result ethnic conflicts are fought with much greater emotional intensity and savagery. Even if, as frequently happens, an ethnic conflict takes the form of a standard war, pitting countries and armies against one another, there are still no noncombatants. Every member of the opposing ethnic population is a potential target. The wars between the U.S. government and Native Americans are an ideal example of this form of conflict. There were formal battles between organized groups of Indians and the U.S. army. However, most fighting took the form of attacks by Indian groups on white settlements and travelers, and attacks on Indian villages by the U.S. army. The majority of the casualties on both sides were women, children, and the elderly. In reply to the accusation of the killing of Indian children, General Phil Sheridan once remarked, "Nits make lice."

Not all wars are ethnic conflicts, and not all ethnic conflicts take the form of war. The nature of ethnic conflict varies depending upon the set of cultural historical events that have brought the groups into conflict, the relative size and power of the groups, and their objectives. Recognizing that ethnic conflicts take many forms, here we are just going to examine one form of conflict: ethnic cleansing. By **ethnic cleansing** we mean the deliberate and systematic attempt by the dominant ethnic group to eliminate a rival ethnic group or groups within a geographical region. Ethnic cleansing takes three main forms: sociocide, genocide, and relocation.

Sociocide consists of destroying the ethnic identity of a people for the purpose of assimilating the group into the dominant society. It is im-

portant to note the difference between assimilation and sociocide. The assimilation of small ethnic groups by larger, more dominant ones occurs with some regularity. Much of American social history is the history of the assimilation of immigrant European peoples. Germans, Poles, Italians, Hungarians, and others came to the United States in great numbers during the late nineteenth and early twentieth centuries. Within a generation or two most of these people had abandoned their language, discarded most of their traditional customs, begun intermarrying with earlier immigrant families, and become "Americanized." These people wanted to become "American" and they did so voluntarily. In contrast, sociocide is the forced destruction of a group's ethnic identity. This is accomplished by the elimination of their communities and their ethnic boundary markers: language, dress, and other distinguishing customs. During the late nineteenth and early twentieth centuries the U.S. government deliberately attempted to destroy Native American tribal identity. Indian children were placed in boarding schools, where, physically separated from their parents and home communities, they were taught to speak only English, dressed in European-style clothes, instructed in Christianity, and in general taught contempt for their traditional beliefs and cultural practices. Even until the middle part of the twentieth century, in Australia, the children of Australian aborigine families were commonly taken from their parents and given to white parents to adopt. In most cases they were not told who their birth parents were or anything about their ethnic group. In both the United States and Australia the idea was to separate the children from their communities so that they could become part of the "white" world. This was for their "own good." As Captain Pratt, who established the first American Indian boarding school, said, "One has to destroy the Indian to save the man."

In human history many smaller peoples have fallen victim to sociocide. Joseph Stalin attempted it with the tribes of Siberian Russia. Within the last decade, the Bulgarian government attempted to force the minority Turkish population to adopt Christian Slavic names, stop speaking Turkish in public, and close the mosques. Today in India, Hindu nationalist groups are calling for the "Indianizing" of resident Christian and Muslim communities.

Genocide is the deliberate and systematic attempt to physically destroy the unwanted ethnic population. The objective may be the total destruction of the group, the reduction of their numbers, or a stimulus for the surviving members of the group to migrate. Regardless of the actual objective, the process is the same: the indiscriminate slaughter of men, women, and children of the targeted ethnic group.

Today, when we think of genocide, we think of recent events in Bosnia or Rwanda, or of the killing of millions of Jews and Gypsies by the Nazis during World War II. However, genocide has been a recurrent event in human history. During the colonial period the English, Dutch, French, Spanish, Portuguese, and Belgians were periodically guilty of genocide. In American history there are numerous incidents of massacres of Native American peoples. Genocide is and has been a far too common response to ethnic conflict and rivalry.

Relocation is the forced resettlement of an unwanted ethnic group in a new geographical location. The forced relocation of the population may be in conjunction with genocide, as in Bosnia and Kosovo, or separate from it. Sometimes the unwanted group is forced outside the boundaries of the country, becoming what today we term *refugees*. In other cases the targeted group is forcibly moved to a new area within the boundaries of the state, where it is assumed that they will pose less of a problem or threat.

Relocation has been an aspect of ethnic conflict throughout human existence. The Jews were expelled from ancient Israel by the Romans. The English cleared Northern Ireland of the Irish. The Five Civilized Tribes were removed, over the Trail of Tears, from their homes in the southeastern states by the U.S. government and resettled in Indian Territory. During World War II Stalin had

the Chechen, ethnic Germans, and several other ethnic groups whose loyalties were questionable removed to Kazakhstan, Siberia, and other remote areas of the Soviet Union. Following World War II millions of Germans were expelled from Poland, Czechoslovakia, and other eastern European countries. Few groups of peoples have not, at one time or another, been expelled from all or parts of their original homelands. Many of the ethnic problems in the world today originate in these historic expulsions. The problems of Northern Ireland and Israel/Palestine are far from uncommon.

There is no simple or easy solution to ethnic conflict. Attempts by governments of multiethnic states to accommodate cultural differences and nationalistic aspirations also have a high failure rate. We need only look at the disintegration of the Soviet Union, Yugoslavia, and Czechoslovakia and the continuing ethnic problems of countries such as Indonesia and India. Ethnic conflict is and will be the major destabilizing factor in world politics for the foreseeable future.

THE CONSEQUENCES of an INTERDEPENDENT WORLD

The world has changed greatly over the past fifty years. This is true both for us as individuals as well as citizens of different countries.

For us as individuals, the consequences of these changes are both direct and indirect. Whether in Los Angeles, London, Kuala Lumpur, or Lagos, urbanization is resulting in increased daily contact between individuals from diverse ethnic and cultural backgrounds. In cities throughout the world, people are finding that employers and employees, customers and vendors, landlords and tenants, doctors and patients—in other words, individuals whose actions affect the quality of their everyday lives—are increasingly individuals with whom they do not share a common cultural heritage and who have different social norms and values. In the United States and Canada, when our grandparents spoke of ethnic diversity, they spoke primarily about the differences between Irish, Italians, Ukrainians, French, Germans, Poles, and so forth. Although there were some cultural differences among these groups, they all basically shared a common cultural tradition. Today immigrants to the cities of the United States and Canada are from all parts of the world—Ethiopia, Nigeria, India, Pakistan, Iran, Iraq, Mexico, Colombia, China, Vietnam, and Afghanistan, to name only some countries of origin. These new immigrant populations often represent cultural traditions and have norms and values very different from those of earlier European immigrant peoples.

It is at the international level where the problems and consequences become greatest and most dangerous. The global economy and the resultant economic interdependence of the world's peoples requires a steady flow of communications, manufactured goods, foodstuffs, and raw materials among countries and regions of the world. No region or country today is economically self-sufficient. Any major disruption in the flow of this exchange could conceivably have catastrophic economic repercussions. The vulnerability of even a country such as the United States was made clear in 1973 when the Arab oil-producing countries embargoed shipments of oil to the United States in retaliation for American support of Israel. The result was a major shortage of petroleum products that created lines at gasoline stations throughout the country.

Wars are a major threat to the global economy, and increasingly wars take the form of ethnic conflicts. For the most part ethnic conflicts have been confined to regions of the world of little if any direct significance to the global economy. As long as an ethnic conflict does not threaten the strategic interest of one or more of the major countries of the world, it is either ignored or contained. Thus we see ethnic conflict and political anarchy spreading throughout central Africa.

However, as we enter the new millennium, wars, particularly ethnic wars, have added a new and far more threatening dimension. Wars have traditionally been fought with guns and bombs with the intent of killing people and destroying property. In these traditional wars small, militarily impotent, ethnic groups have had only limited abilities to inflict damage on their enemies, let alone the global economy. This situation is now changing. In the fall of 2000, Israeli teenage computer hackers, acting on their own, attacked and destroyed anti-Israeli Web sites in Iraq and Lebanon. Arab hackers quickly retaliated by attacking and closing a wide range of Israeli government Web sites. With these attacks, the first known cyber war started. It is only a matter of time before these hackers, motivated by nationalist sentiments, begin attacking financial institutions, corporations, and other venerable facilities identified as supportive of enemy groups. Cyber warfare is a natural arena for ethnic conflict in that it requires little in the way of equipment and logistical support. All a cyber attack requires is a single dedicated skilled individual and a computer. Such an individual can act with anonymity from almost any place on earth, almost immune from detection and elimination. In such wars more technologically sophisticated and powerful countries and ethnic groups are at a disadvantage, since their economic infrastructure is far more vulnerable to cyber attacks than those of smaller, less technologically sophisticated countries and groups. Cyber warfare may well prove the great equalizer in ethnic conflicts. Cyber warfare also has the potential for being far more expensive and damaging to the global economy than traditional warfare.

Recognizing that war, particular ethnic conflicts, poses a threat to the global economy and thus to all of us, we have to work toward minimizing the potential for conflicts. Population pressures and related economic problems and inequities increase the possibilities for such conflicts. Whether we want to view the existing and potential problems of the world in a purely humanistic way or in terms of pragmatic self-interest, the answers are the same. Conflict among the oil-producing countries of the Persian Gulf is an issue that directly affects the world's peoples.

Starvation in Africa is not simply an African problem. Economic development projects in Latin America, Africa, or Asia serve the needs not only of the local peoples, hopefully lessening the possibility of conflict, but also benefit the global economy and thus, at least indirectly, all of the world's peoples.

Why should you study the cultural systems of people from some other region of the world? The reason is simple. These "strange and exotic" people no longer live half a world away; they live in your city, your neighborhood, and maybe next door. They may soon be your schoolmates, your colleagues, your customers, or your employer—if they are not already. You depend on these people, directly or indirectly, for much of the food you eat, the clothes you wear, the tools you use, the gasoline that powers your car, and possibly the car itself. You in turn have to sell, either directly or indirectly, goods or services so that you can afford to buy what they produce. In the modern world there is no escape from cultural differences. Like it or not, we are living and will continue to live in a multicultural world. In this interdependent world we are all going to have to accommodate the beliefs, cultural practices, and ethnic aspirations of all of us as equals. In this new world there can be no place for ethnocentrism and ethnic extremism.

SUMMARY

1. The global economy emerged after World War II. The collapse of colonial empires and the rise of technology have allowed for a truly integrated world economic system. The market principle now works globally. The prices we can charge and the prices we pay for labor, services, and products are determined by a global marketplace.

2. Over the past fifty years the world population has grown from 2.5 billion to 6 billion people. Most of this growth has been and is in the economically underdeveloped Third World countries. In search of jobs and economic opportunity, a massive migration of peoples is occurring from rural areas to urban centers and from Third World countries to the more industrialized countries.

3. Nationalism is increasing in the world. Ethnic conflicts are becoming more common and destructive. There are between 3,000 and 5,000 ethnic nationalities in the world, but only 200 separate countries. Most countries are multinational, and most of the conflict is the result of minority nationalities wanting to establish their own independent nations.

4. Ethnic cleansing, the elimination of an ethnic group in a particular region, takes three main forms: sociocide, genocide, and relocation.

5. The growing integration of the global economy and population migrations have far-reaching consequences. Today, all of the peoples of the world are dependent on others for their economic well-being. Vast cultural differences still separate the world's peoples. The domination of Western peoples in the world is waning, and a time of economic and political power-sharing among all of the different peoples of the world is emerging.

KEY TERMS

global economy
demographic changes
origin myth
ethnic group
ethnic boundary
   markers
nationality

subnationality
homeland
ethnic cleansing
sociocide
genocide
relocation

SUGGESTED READINGS

Black, Jan Knippers. *Inequity in the Global Village.* Bloomfield, CT: Kumarian Press, 1999.

Addresses the wealth differences that are developing with globalization and some of the consequences of these growing differences.

Bodley, John H. *Anthropology and Contemporary Human Problems,* 3rd ed. Mountain View, CA: Mayfield, 1996.

A good place to start in glimpsing the relevance of anthropology to modern problems. Provides insights on war, poverty and hunger, population, and environmental destruction.

Burger, Julian. *Report from the Frontier: The State of the World's Indigenous Peoples.* Cambridge, MA: Cultural Survival, 1987.

A general survey of the plight of indigenous peoples of the world.

Gupte, Pranay. *The Crowded Earth: People and the Politics of Population.* New York: Norton, 1984.

Overview of the social, economic, and political dimensions of population growth and control.

Moynihan, Daniel Patrick. *Pandemonium: Ethnicity in International Politics.* New York: Oxford University Press, 1993.

A good general introduction to the problem of increasing nationalism and conflict.

United Nations. *On the Threshold: The United Nations and Global Governance in the New Millennium,* 19–21 January 2000. Available on the United Nations Web site (http://www.unu.edu).

Provides a good summary discussion of many of the economic and social problems brought about by globalization.

chapter 14

THE FUTURE *of* INDIGENOUS PEOPLES

Contents

I n this book we have emphasized the cultural diversity of humanity. How much of this diversity will persist into the future? In recent centuries, technologies, adaptations, political organizations, religious traditions, and other aspects of culture have changed drastically for most of the world's peoples. As a result, there is far less cultural diversity at the start of the twenty-first century than there was at the end of the nineteenth.

A discussion of some reasons for the disappearance of preindustrial ways of life is followed by advocacy for the rights of indigenous peoples to preserve their cultural systems, if that is their choice.

INDIGENOUS PEOPLES TODAY

Since Columbus' voyage to the New World in 1492, there have been numerous technological changes and massive migrations of human populations. The migrations of European (and African) peoples to the Americas, Australia, and New Zealand are well known, but North Americans are less aware that similar migrations also occurred throughout the Old World. The Norwegians, Swedes, and Finns have expanded northward, displacing the native Sami (or Lapp) herders. Russians settled portions of Siberia, displacing the native "tribal" herding and foraging peoples. In southeast Asia, the Chinese expanded at the expense of neighboring "tribal" peoples. Malay, Chinese, and Javanese settlers now occupy portions of Borneo. In southern Africa, the San foragers have lost most of their land to immigrant European (Boer) and Bantu-speaking peoples. In every region of the world, and in almost every country, the same pattern is being repeated: Stronger, usually numerically larger and more technologically advanced peoples are displacing or conquering and absorbing their smaller, less technologically advanced, indigenous neighbors.

By **indigenous peoples,** we are referring specifically to the smaller, culturally distinct, foraging, farming, and herding peoples of the world. Sometimes these groups are termed "tribal" peoples. Others have called them "Fourth World" peoples. Representing no physical (military) threat to the governments of the countries that unilaterally claim sovereignty over them, they are politically powerless. Occupying the most isolated and least accessible regions of the world, they are the last surviving preindustrial peoples, living on or in some cases beyond the frontiers of the modern world and the global economy. Subject to the whims and needs of their politically dominant neighbors, they have managed to survive mainly because they have nothing that their neighbors yet want.

The global economy and the associated population explosion are creating an ever-growing demand for food, raw materials, and energy (Chapter 13). As a result, the remaining strongholds of these indigenous peoples are now being invaded. The last great forested regions of the world are being cut for timber or cleared for farmland and pasture. Dams for hydroelectric power are being constructed in formerly isolated areas, flooding vast valley and canyon systems. Oil and gas fields and mining operations are being developed and expanded, destroying land areas and polluting rivers and lakes. We commonly speak of the destruction of habitats and are concerned about rare and endangered plants and animals. Indigenous peoples are the endangered peoples of world. Should we not show at least as much concern about their survival and future? What are their rights? Do they possess any cultural knowledge of value in the modern world?

The legal rights of indigenous peoples first became an issue when Columbus landed in the Americas. Debates took place in Spain about whether the native peoples of the Americas—or for that matter any indigenous people—had any inherent rights to their land, resources, or political autonomy. Although legal particulars differed from one colonial power to another as well as over time, a basic consensus was reached early in the colonial period. An indigenous people had some rights based on prior occupancy. However, more "civilized" peoples could unilaterally claim jurisdiction over them and make use of any land and resources that were either unutilized or underutilized. Civilized peoples had both a right and an obligation to uplift indigenous peoples and act in their "best interest." This responsibility was the so-called "white man's burden." Civilized peoples also had the right to travel and trade wherever they wanted without interference from indigenous peoples. Finally, if an indigenous people resisted, the civilized people had the right to use military force against them. Racism, ethnocentrism, and social Darwinist ideas about the inevitability and desirability of progress provided the moral justification for the treatment of indigenous peoples.

Such attitudes and policies influenced the governing of most indigenous peoples in the colonial possessions of European nations. When Asian and African countries gained independence in the twentieth century, the leaders and the dominant ethnic groups of many of the new nations adopted similar attitudes and policies. The modern boundaries of most existing countries are legacies of European colonialism. In most cases, the political and legal systems of these countries are also Western-derived or heavily Western-influenced. Such attitudes, governmental policies, and legal concepts often form the basis for the treatment of indigenous peoples and other ethnic groups within a Third World nation. The present-day policies toward indigenous and small ethnic groups in Africa, Asia, and Latin America parallel nineteenth- and early twentieth-century U.S. Indian policy.

Governments in Latin America, Africa, and parts of Asia face serious economic, political, and social problems. Many of these governments—including those democratically elected—are under pressure from their dominant ethnic group to pursue policies that lead to the displacement or assimilation of the smaller indigenous peoples whose territories lie within their national boundaries. Indigenous people living in remote, "undeveloped" regions are forced to move aside in the nterest of what the dominant ethnic group defines as the "greater good" for their nation.

Sometimes this greater good consists of opening undeveloped areas to settlers. Indonesia has long had a plan to resettle peasants from over-populated Java onto its outer islands, which are said to be "underpopulated." Although often considered a modernized nation, Brazil has some of the poorest people in the world living in its northeastern area. It is also one of the few countries with a frontier—the vast tropical rain forest of Amazonia. In the 1970s, Brazil constructed highways intended to open Amazonia to resettlement and to mineral, timber, grazing, and agricultural exploitation.

One people who are threatened by the opening up of Brazil's Amazonian frontier are the Yanomamö, mentioned earlier. Until the early 1970s, most of the approximately 9,000 Yanomamö were relatively isolated from outside influences. In 1974, the Brazilian government constructed a road through the southern part of Yanomamö territory, and workers involved in forest clearing and road building exposed them to new diseases such as influenza and measles. In some regions the resulting epidemics killed as many as one-half of the Yanomamö. Dirt airstrips constructed during the 1980s also made Indian territory accessible to Brazilian gold prospectors. In the late 1980s thousands of gold seekers—most of them impoverished—poured into the area in search of wealth. By early 1990, as many as 45,000 prospectors had invaded traditional Yanomamö lands and extracted gold worth an estimated one billion dollars.

Brazil's National Indian Foundation is charged with protecting native peoples and territories from invasion and plunder, but it has been unable to control violence against the Yanomamö and other indigenous groups. In 1990, Brazil's former president ordered the landing strips destroyed to reduce future access, but by 1996 miners had returned to Yanomamö lands. The Yanomamö have already lost rights to two-thirds of their Brazilian territory, and deaths caused by violence and disease are likely to continue.

Another common justification for the neglect of the territorial rights of indigenous peoples is the desire to improve a country's balance of trade. The Philippines, Indonesia, Congo, and other countries earn foreign exchange by leasing rights to harvest timber from their tropical hardwood forests to multinational companies, although much of the "unexploited" forest is needed as fallow by indigenous shifting cultivators. Debts owed to foreign banks and international lending agencies encourage some nations to open up their hinterlands to resource development, pushing their indigenous inhabitants aside. In countries such as Brazil and Mexico, minerals, cattle, timber, vegetables, coffee, and other exports are sold to Europe and North America to earn foreign exchange to help pay off international debts. The new rationalizations for the forced removal and exploitation of the territories of indigenous peoples include "developing" the whole country; solving "national problems" by providing land to peasants; making payments on debts owed to foreign banks and international lending institutions; and making the country's products "competitive" in international markets.

The indigenous peoples who remain in cultural communities are learning to protect themselves through international political action. In increasing numbers, indigenous peoples around the world are fighting attempts to dispossess them of their traditional territories and resources. Many are resisting efforts to assimilate them into the cultural mainstream of their nations. They are publicly objecting to racist and ethnocentric attitudes about their beliefs and customs.

The Kayapó of Brazil provide an example. In the 1980s, the government of Brazil sought World Bank funding for the construction of two enormous hydroelectric dams on Amazon River tributaries. Eighty-five percent of the land that would have been flooded belongs to one or another indigenous Indian population. Organized by leaders of the Kayapó tribe, members of twenty-nine Brazilian Indian groups protested the dams. In early 1988, two Kayapó leaders traveled to Washington with anthropologist Darrell Posey to speak against the project to officials of the World Bank and to members of Congress. When the

Victor Englebert/Photo Researchers, Inc.

The physical and cultural survival of Amazonian Indians, and millions of other indigenous peoples, is threatened by the encroachments of more powerful peoples.

World Bank deferred action on the loans, Brazil brought charges against the three protestors under a law that forbids "foreigners" from engaging in political activity harmful to the nation.

The Kayapó and Yąnomamö cases well illustrate the problem facing indigenous peoples. During this century many Brazilian politicians have championed the rights of indigenous peoples and succeeded in passing protective legislation. However, the ever growing economic needs and demands of the majority population seem in the end always to overwhelm humanitarian desires. Since 1900, more than one-third of the indigenous Brazilian "tribes" have disappeared, while the surviving two-thirds have lost most of their populations and lands.

Only political intervention by the international community holds the possibility of protecting the rights of indigenous peoples. Chapter 1, Article 1 of the Charter of the United Nations recognizes the right of a people to self-determination. However, the United Nations also recognizes the sovereignty and territorial integrity of existing states. Thus indigenous peoples are in effect "nonpeople" as far as the United Nations is concerned. Since most countries in the world have their own internal problems with indigenous peoples, it is doubtful that the international political community will ever take action to protect the rights of indigenous peoples.

VANISHING KNOWLEDGE

Despite the increased political sophistication of indigenous peoples around the world and the protests of concerned citizens in many countries, there is no doubt that many preindustrial cultures are in danger of extinction. Even if the people themselves survive the onslaughts of lumbering, mining, damming, grazing, farming, and building, their way of life is liable to disappear. Most people would agree that genocide is a crime of the highest degree. But destruction or alteration of a culture is another matter—is it not possible that indigenous peoples themselves would be better off if they joined the cultural mainstream of their nations?

Yes, many peoples do want to acquire formal education, get jobs, improve their living standards, and generally "modernize" their societies. For many peoples and for many individuals within an indigenous culture, contact with the wider world offers new opportunities and new choices. Young people especially are attracted by the material goods, entertainments, new experiences, and sheer variety of activities found in towns and cities. They should have these opportunities and these choices. But indigenous peoples and their ways of life often are overwhelmed by forces over which they have no control. It is not that most indigenous peoples are given the opportunity to carefully weigh the options available to them, so that they can make informed choices about whether it is best for them to preserve or modernize their ways of life. Today, as in the past, their traditions are disappearing more often because powerful national governments want to open up their territory or because private entrepreneurs or corporations want to exploit their resources.

Anthropologists are especially concerned with the rights of indigenous peoples for several reasons. First, because of our interest in cultural diversity, we are more aware of what has happened to non-Western cultures in the past several centuries. Second, we identify with indigenous peoples partly because so many of us have worked among them. Third, our professional training gives us a relativistic outlook on the many ways of being human, so we can appreciate other peoples' customs and beliefs as viable alternatives to our own. Finally, the fieldwork experience often affects our attitudes about our own societies—deep immersion in other cultural traditions leaves some of us not so sure about our commitment to our own.

Whether one is an anthropologist or not, one can appreciate the rights of any group of people to have their lives, property, and resources secure from domination by powerful outsiders. The most important factors in considering the rights of indigenous peoples to be left alone are ethical ones. Do not people everywhere have the right to live their lives free from the unwanted interference of those more powerful and wealthier than themselves? Does any government, regardless of its "problems," have the right to dispossess people from land they have lived on and used for centuries? Is the demand of citizens in Japan, Europe, North America, or anywhere else for wood, minerals, meat, electricity, or other products a sufficient justification for relocating a people or taking land away from them? (Our American readers who follow politicians' statements about human rights violations in Iran, Iraq, China, Bosnia, and other countries might wonder why they have so little to say about the rights of indigenous peoples.)

Surely, most of us agree on the answers to such questions. Ethical concerns for the human rights of indigenous peoples, combined with a respect for their cultural traditions, are the primary reasons for granting their rights to survive as living communities.

But if the ethical arguments alone (based on shared values about human rights) are not compelling, there are other arguments (based on practical concerns, and even on the self-interest of the dominant majority). The long-term welfare of all humanity may be jeopardized by the loss of cultural diversity on our planet.

Think about the cultural heritage of humanity as a whole. Consider *all* the knowledge accumulated by *all* humanity over hundreds of generations. Imagine, in other words, Human Culture—here defined as the sum total of all knowledge stored in the cultural traditions of all humans alive today.

Some of the knowledge existing in present-day Human Culture has been widely disseminated in the past few centuries by means of written language. We may call it *global knowledge* (not meaning to imply that it is "true" or "universally known"). Although some global knowledge will be lost or replaced, much of the knowledge stored in writing (or, more recently, on computer disks) will be preserved and added to over the coming decades and centuries.

Other knowledge comprising Human Culture is *local knowledge*—it is stored only in the heads of members of particular cultures, many of which are endangered. Most local knowledge will disappear if those cultural traditions disappear—even if the people themselves survive.

How much of this local knowledge is knowledge that may (today, tomorrow, someday) prove useful to all humanity? Of course, no one knows. But no one can doubt that the rest of the world has much to learn from indigenous cultures. In fact, much of what was in the past only the local knowledge of some indigenous culture has been incorporated into global knowledge, as a consequence of contact with the West and other colonizing people. We conclude this book with a small sample of some of the medical and adaptive wisdom of indigenous peoples, whose local knowledge has already contributed so much to the world.

Medicines We Have Learned

"The Medicine Man Will See You Now," proclaimed a headline in a 1993 edition of *Business Week*. The accompanying article described a California pharmaceutical company that sends ethnobotanists and other scientists into rain forests to learn from indigenous shamans. Companies as well as scholars are beginning to understand that the traditional remedies long used by preindustrial peoples often have genuine medical value. In fact, many of the important drugs in use today were derived from indigenous knowledge. Here we can only provide a few examples of the medicines originally discovered by indigenous peoples that now have worldwide significance.

Malaria remains a debilitating, although usually not fatal, sickness in tropical and subtropical regions. Its main treatment is quinine, a component of the bark of the cinchona tree. Europeans in the seventeenth century learned of the value of quinine from Peruvian Indians.

The Madagascar periwinkle has long been used in folk medicine to treat diabetes. Researchers first became interested in the plant as a substitute for oral insulin, but it seems to have little value for this purpose. However, during the course of their investigation, scientists discovered that extracts from periwinkle yielded dramatic successes in treating childhood leukemia, Hodgkin's disease, and some other cancers. Drugs based on the plant—notably vincristine and vinblastine—remain the major treatments for these otherwise fatal diseases.

Muscle relaxants are important drugs to surgeons. A popular one is curare, made from the chondodendron tree. Taken in large amounts, curare can paralyze the respiratory organs and lead to death. This property was recognized by South American Indians, who used it as arrow poison for hunting birds, monkeys, and other game, and from whom medical science learned of the drug's value.

The ancient Greeks and several North American Indian tribes used the bark of willows for relief from pain and fever. In the nineteenth

century, scientists succeeded in artificially synthe-
sizing this compound that today we call *aspirin*.

There is no way of knowing how many plants
used by surviving indigenous peoples could
prove to be medically effective. The potential is
great. According to pharmacologist Norman
Farnsworth, about one-fourth of all prescribed
drugs in the United States contain active ingre-
dients extracted from higher plants. The world
contains more than 250,000 species of higher
plants. Although as many as 40,000 of these
plants may have medical or nutritional values
that are undiscovered by science, only about
1,100 of these have been well studied. Botanists
and medical researchers are coming to realize
that indigenous peoples already have discovered, through centuries of trial and error, that
certain plants are effective remedies for local
diseases. The future value of their medical wisdom to all of humanity is largely unknown, but
probably great.

Adaptive Wisdom

Many preindustrial peoples have lived in and
exploited their natural environments for centuries. Over their history, they have selected those
crops and varieties that grow and yield well in
the conditions of their local habitat. They have
learned to control insect pests and diseases that
attack the plants on which they depend, and to
do so without the need for expensive and often
polluting artificial chemicals. They often have
learned how to make nature work for them with
minimum deterioration of their environments.
They have, in short, incorporated much adaptive
wisdom into their cultural traditions.

Following are a few possible benefits that all
humanity might gain by preserving the ecological
knowledge of indigenous peoples.

Preservation of Crop Varieties In all cultivation
systems, natural selection operates in the fields.
Like wild plants, crops are subject to drought,
disease, insects, and other natural elements,
which select for the survival of individual plants

best adapted to withstand these hazards. In addition, crops are subject to human selection. For
example, crop varieties most susceptible to
drought or local diseases are harvested in smaller
quantities than drought- and disease-resistant
varieties. Perhaps without knowing it, the culti-
vator replants mainly those varieties best adapted
to survive the onslaughts of drought and local
diseases. This "tuning" of plant varieties to the
local environment, with all its hazards and fluctuations, goes on automatically so long as the crops
harvested from the fields are replanted in the
same area. Thanks to the unintentional and intentional selection by hundreds of generations of
indigenous cultivators around the world, each
species of crop (e.g., beans, potatoes, wheat)
evolved a large number of land races, or distinct
varieties adapted to local conditions.

Over the course of human history, several
thousand species of plants have been used for
food but less than a hundred of these were ever
domesticated. Of all the plants that have been
domesticated, today only a handful provide significant amounts of food for the world's people.
In fact, a mere four crops—wheat, rice, maize,
and potato—provide almost one-half the world's
total consumption of food.

Since around 1950, plant geneticists and agricultural scientists have developed new varieties
of wheat, corn, rice, and potatoes that are capable
of giving higher yields if they receive proper
amounts of water and fertilizers. These new
strains were developed by crossing and recross-
ing native land races collected from all over the
world. The aim was to achieve a "green revolution" that would end world hunger by increasing
production. Many new varieties are hybrids,
which means that farmers must receive a new
supply of seeds yearly from government or private sources.

Ironically, having been bred from the genetic
material present in their diverse ancestors, the
new strains now threaten to drive their ancestors
to extinction. As the seeds of artificially bred
varieties are planted by farmers in Asia, Africa,
and the Americas, the traditional varieties—the

land races that are the product of generations of natural and human selection—fall into disuse and many have disappeared.

Why should we care? Increasingly, agricultural experts are realizing the dangers of dependence on a few varieties. If crops that are nearly identical genetically are planted in the same area year after year, a new variety of pest or disease eventually will evolve to attack them. The famous Irish potato famine of the 1840s was directly related to the genetic uniformity of the potato because all the potatoes in Ireland were apparently descended from only a few plants. More than a million people died as a result of the potato blight, and a million more immigrated to North America. The United States has also suffered serious economic losses: The corn blight of 1970 destroyed about 15 percent of the American crop. Losses would have been less severe had most American farmers not planted a single variety of corn.

Many plant breeders are alarmed at the prospect of losing much of the genetic diversity of domesticated plants. Today they are searching remote regions for surviving land races that contain genes that one day might prove valuable.

(The seeds are stored in seed banks for future study.) They have been well rewarded—although no one knows how much of the genetic diversity of crops such as wheat and corn has already disappeared.

The knowledge of indigenous peoples is an important resource in the effort to preserve land races. In many parts of the world—the Andes, Central America, Amazonia, the Middle East, and elsewhere—cultivators still grow ancient varieties of crops. They know where these varieties yield best, how to plant and care for them, how to prepare them for eating, and so on. In the Andes, for instance, hundreds of potato varieties survive among the Quechua Indians as a legacy of the Inca civilization. Many have specific ecological requirements, and some are even unique to a single valley. Research is now under way to determine how well specific land races will grow in other areas, to help solve food supply problems elsewhere. It is important to preserve the genetic information encoded in these varieties for future generations. Indigenous peoples who still retain the hard-won knowledge of their ancestors and who still use the often-maligned

Lumber mills such as this one near San Jeromino, Guatemala, are contributing to the destruction of the world's forests.

N. Kemp/PhotoResearchers, Inc.

"traditional crop varieties" are important informational resources in the effort to save the genetic diversity of crops on which humanity depends.

"Undiscovered" Useful Species   In addition to their familiarity with local crop varieties with potential worldwide significance, many indigenous peoples cultivate or use crop species that currently are unimportant to the rest of the world. One example is amaranth, a grain native to the Americas that was of great importance to the Indians in prehistoric times. The great Mesoamerican civilizations made extensive use of the plant in their religious rituals. This led the Spanish conquerors, in their anxiety to root out heathenism, to burn fields of amaranth and prohibit its consumption. Otherwise, it—like maize, potatoes, beans, squash, and other American crops—might have diffused to other continents. Amaranth remains an important food to some indigenous peoples of highland Latin America, who retain knowledge of its properties and requirements. Its unusually high protein content might someday make it valuable to the rest of the world.

Other plants used by native peoples have the potential to become important elsewhere. Quinoa, now grown mainly in Peruvian valleys, has twice the protein content of corn and has long been recognized as a domesticate with great potential. The tepary bean, now grown mainly by the Tohono O'odham (Papago) of the American Southwest, can survive and yield well under conditions of extreme drought, which might make it cultivable in other arid regions of the world. Another legume, the winged bean, has long been cultivated by the native peoples of Papua New Guinea, and it has helped nourish people in fifty other tropical countries.

Humans use plants for more than food. Indigenous peoples have discovered many other uses for the plants found in their habitats. Scientific researchers today are attesting to the validity of much native knowledge about the use of plants as sources of fuel, oils, medicines, and other bene-ficial substances, including poisons. Forest peoples of Southeast Asia use the toxic roots of a local woody climbing plant as a fish poison. The root is so powerful that a mixture of 1 part root to 300,000 parts water will kill fish. From the indigenous tribes, scientists learned of the toxicity of these roots, which allowed them to isolate the rotenoid that now is used as an insecticide spray for plants and as dips and dusting powders for livestock.

Scientists no doubt will rediscover many other useful plants that today they know nothing about—if the tropical forests in which most endangered plant species are found last long enough. Their task will be easier if the original discoverers—indigenous peoples—are around to teach them what their ancestors learned.

Cultural Alternatives

There is another kind of practical lesson we might yet learn from surviving indigenous peoples. Industrialized humans have developed technologies that discover, extract, and transform natural resources on a scale undreamed of a century ago. To North Americans and to many other citizens of the developed world, *progress* is almost synonymous with "having more things." Yet whether our economies can continue to produce ever-increasing supplies of goods is questionable. Many of us are frightened by the thought that economic growth might not continue. The widespread foreboding that we will be forced to accept a stagnation or even a decline in our levels of material consumption no doubt contributes to the interest today's undergraduates have in careers most likely to yield high incomes.

But humanity survived for many thousands of years without TVs, VCRs, BMWs, CDs, and PCs. Billions of people throughout history lived under conditions many modern people consider backward, with consumption levels we consider minimal. As we have seen in previous chapters, there is little evidence to suggest that their lives typically were as nasty, brutish, and short as often portrayed. Indeed, native peoples around the world more often were the victims rather than the beneficiaries of what we call progress.

In a sense, we all are victims of the mentality of progress—of that restless desire to earn more and to have more. If the industrial bubble does not burst in our lifetime, most of us who live in the developed world will spend our lives in continuous effort to maintain or increase our consumption of goods. We will do so despite the fact that we can never catch up with the Joneses because there will always be other Joneses whom we have not yet caught. We will do so despite the fact that our efforts will never be sufficient to get us all we want because no one can consume goods as fast as companies can turn them out and advertisers can create new desires for them. We will do so despite the fact that many of our marriages and families will be torn apart by the effort, and many of us will suffer psychologically and physically from stress-related disorders. Sadly, most of us pursue our dollars and goods unthinkingly because we remain ignorant of any alternative way of living.

The world's remaining indigenous peoples provide us with such alternatives. They do not and did not live in a primitive paradise. Subjugation of neighboring peoples, exploitation by the wealthy and powerful, subordination of women,

warfare, and other ideas and practices many of us find abhorrent exist among some preindustrial peoples, just as among modern industrial nations. Yet we also find other cultural conditions that some of us long to recover: closer family ties, greater self-sufficiency, smaller communities, more personal and enduring social relations, and "more humane," "more moral" values. No anthropologist can tell you whether life is better or worse in preindustrial communities; indeed, we cannot agree on the meaning of *better*. We do know that humanity is diverse. We know that this diversity means that human beings—ourselves included—have many alternative ways of living meaningful and satisfying lives. In the end, it is these cultural alternatives provided by indigenous peoples that might have the greatest value to humankind.

Perhaps a people themselves are the only ones qualified to judge the quality of their lives, to decide what it will take to lend meaning and dignity to their existence. We hope to have convinced you that there are many ways of being human. We hope you have learned to appreciate some of the alternative ways of living experienced by various human populations. We hope you will agree that some of these alternatives are worth preserving, both in their own right and for the long-term well-being of all humanity.

SUMMARY

1. As European influences and industrial economies swept the world during the past few centuries, the lives of indigenous peoples were dramatically altered. Many groups have disappeared altogether. Many others are threatened with relocation, reduction of their traditional lands and resources, and loss of their cultural autonomy through assimilation.

2. Rationalizations for policies harmful to the interests of indigenous peoples have changed since the colonial era, but modern governments continue to violate their rights. Common official

justifications for such violations include resettling people from overpopulated to "underpopulated" areas; lumbering and mining operations; developing energy resources; producing crops and livestock for internal and external markets; improving trade balances; and paying off debts owed to international lending agencies and multinational banks.

3. The cultures of surviving preindustrial peoples are in danger of destruction. Ethical considerations alone are a sufficient reason these peoples should be allowed to remain in their communities, on their traditional lands, living in the ways of their ancestors, if that is their choice.

Pragmatic considerations also are important because these people still retain a vast body of knowledge—knowledge that is of great potential value to all humanity.

4. Science already has adapted several important medicines and treatments from indigenous peoples. Many other plants with medical value probably will be discovered, if the tropical forests and the cultural knowledge of their indigenous inhabitants last long enough.

5. Adaptive wisdom is also to be found in the traditions of indigenous peoples. Land races of important crops still survive and might contain genetic materials from which useful foods might someday be bred. Crops that today are used primarily by indigenous peoples—such as amaranth, quinoa, tepary bean, and the winged bean—might eventually have worldwide significance. Nonfood plants used by indigenes are also important as insecticides, oils, fibers, and other products.

6. Finally, indigenous people provide us with alternative cultural models that should reduce our anxieties about the likelihood of eventual decline in our material living standards. The diversity of the human species shows that we can live meaningful and wholly satisfying lives in the future without the technologies and huge quantities of consumer goods we now consider necessary to our economic welfare. The remaining preindustrial cultures allow us to see that there is more than one narrow road to personal fulfillment, cultural health, and national dignity and prestige.

KEY TERM

indigenous peoples

SUGGESTED READINGS

Bodley, John. *Victims of Progress*, 4th ed. Palo Alto, CA: Mayfield, 1999.

A good overview of tribal peoples in the modern world and how they are being destroyed by industrial civilization.

Cultural Survival. *State of the Peoples: A Global Human Rights Report on Societies in Danger.* Boston: Beacon Press, 1993.

Together with other publications of the Cultural Survival organization, an excellent source on the threats to indigenous peoples around the world.

Davis, Shelton H. *Victims of the Miracle: Development and the Indians of Brazil.* Cambridge: Cambridge University Press, 1977.

A study discussing economic development in Brazil and the resulting destruction of Indian communities.

Denslow, Julie Sloan, and Christine Padoch, eds. *People of the Tropical Rain Forest.* Berkeley: University of California Press, 1988.

Written for the general public, this edited work is a broad introduction to both indigenous and recent peoples living in the tropical forests of Latin America, Asia, and Africa. Some articles discuss what can be learned from indigenous peoples about developing the forest in a sustainable manner.

Harrison, Paul. *The Greening of Africa.* London: International Institute for Environment and Development, 1986.

Shows how indigenous cultivation systems and scientific ecological principles can be integrated to alleviate Africa's food shortages.

Paine, Robert. *Dam a River, Damn a People?* Copenhagen: International Work Group for Indigenous Affairs, 1982.

A study discussing the effects of a hydroelectric project in Norway on the indigenous Lapp, or Sami, population.

Plotkin, Mark J. *Tales of a Shaman's Apprentice.* New York: Penguin, 1993.

In part an adventure story of an ethnobotanist, this book describes the author's experiences in the Amazon forest while searching for useful medicines. An interesting place to start for an overview of the medical knowledge of indigenous peoples.

Sponsel, Leslie E., ed. *Indigenous Peoples and the Future of Amazonia.* Tucson: University of Arizona Press, 1995.

Articles discussing Amazonian cultures and their prospects for survival.

Suzuki, David, and Peter Knudtson. *Wisdom of the Elders.* New York: Bantam Books, 1992.

Lucid (although often romanticized) overview of how preindustrial cultures view nature and their relation to it. Sees many parallels between "scientific" and "native" knowledge of nature.

Weyler, Rex. *Blood of the Land: The Government and Corporate War Against the American Indian Movement.* New York: Vintage, 1982.

A polemical attack on the U.S. and Canadian governments and corporate development of Indian resources.

appendix

ANTHROPOLOGY
and the INTERNET

The use of the Internet for educational purposes has exploded since the 1990s. As modern college-age students know, you can use the Internet to access an enormous amount of information about every imaginable subject. Unfortunately, the sheer number of Web sites (numbering in the hundreds of millions) means that somehow you have to find the ones that house the Web pages that contain the information you want. You also must have some way of evaluating the accuracy and completeness of a site once you've located it.

The one crucial point to make about the information you obtain from the Internet is: *Don't believe everything that appears on your computer monitor.* Internet sources are incredibly variable in quality and accuracy, because no one has the authority to remove "bad" Web pages from the Internet. Anyone who knows how to do so can publish a Web page full of factual errors, irrelevancies, personal opinions disguised as fact, and other forms of "garbage." Therefore, anything you see or read on the Internet should be checked with other sources, like your library! It is a really bad idea to conduct a research project or write a paper using only materials you've acquired from the Internet. Use it as a starting point only.

There is no fail-safe way to evaluate the quality and accuracy of Internet materials, but here is a good rule of thumb: In general, sites posted and maintained by academic departments in universities, professional organizations, libraries, museums, and government institutions are the most reliable. Sites posted and maintained by "unaffiliated individuals" should be evaluated critically for the reliability of their content.

A good print resource for you in beginning to use the Internet for anthropology is David L. Carson's *Researching Anthropology on the Internet* (Wadsworth, 2001). This booklet may be bundled with copies of the text. Wadsworth also provides two dedicated Web sites, which should be your first stop when exploring the Internet.

Accompanying Web site to *Essentials of Cultural Anthropology*:

http://anthropology.wadsworth.com/

The Wadsworth Anthropology Resource Center contains a wealth of information and useful tools for both instructors and students. After logging on, click the button on the left half of the screen called Course Material. Find the link to Bailey and Peoples, *Essentials of Cultural Anthropology,* click on it, and proceed to the book page. At the book page you have several options. You can take a book tour to get an overview of the text and the course. Instructors will be interested in accessing the Instructor's Resources (password protected). Students should proceed to the section of the site called Student Resources. There you will find study aids such as flashcards that can be used to help you master the vocabulary and terminology of anthropology. The online practice quizzes for each chapter are useful study tools.

A special section of the Anthropology Resource Center can be found by clicking on the button called Applying Anthropology. This section of the Web site serves as an online resource center for anthropology students, with an emphasis on how anthropology is applied to real world problems. There is an essay on careers in anthropology. Short video clips from the film *Anthropologist at Work* accompany this essay, distributed by the American Anthropological Association. The Applying Anthropology site has information on careers in anthropology outside the academic setting, including advice on organizations, student internships, and hot links to graduate programs in applied anthropology.

Another valuable Internet tool is InfoTrac College Edition:

http://www.infotrac-college.com/wadsworth

If your instructor has ordered the text with the optional InfoTrac College Edition, you should receive a free four-month password with the purchase of each new copy of the text. InfoTrac College Edition is an active online library of more than 800,000 published articles in the sciences, social sciences, and humanities. Once you have accessed the address listed above, click on "Enter InfoTrac College—Thomson Learning Edition." You will be taken to a page that asks for a password. Enter the password you were given and provide the information requested. After you have done this, you can perform searches by either subject or key words. Your instructor may use InfoTrac College Edition to create a customized reader to accompany selected chapters or the entire text. Or you may be assigned to access a special section of the Wadsworth Anthropology Resource Center.

The Student Guide to InfoTrac College Edition, prepared by Kathryn Coe of the University of Missouri, Columbia, consists of exercises based on 16 core subjects vital to the study of anthropology. These exercises utilize InfoTrac College Edition's huge database of articles. The exercises help you to narrow down the search of articles related to each subject and ask questions that enable you to see the ideas more clearly and pique your interest. The study guide is interactive, and your instructor may ask you to e-mail your responses to the online questions in the guide.

After your first visit to both the Wadsworth Anthropology Web site and the InfoTrac College Edition site you should bookmark both sites. They are both invaluable resources for your study of cultural anthropology and starting points to anthropology and the Internet.

Notes

Chapter 1

Snow (1995) is a brief source on forensic anthropology.

Chapter 2

A Definition of Culture

The distinction between trial and error and social learning is from Boyd and Richerson (1985) and Pulliam and Dunford (1980), who also discusses the advantages of social learning. The material on the Yąnomamö and Semai is drawn from Chagnon (1983) and Dentan (1968), respectively.

Cultural Knowledge

The Hanunóo plant classification example is described in Conklin (1957). Information on Navajo witchcraft is from Kluckhohn (1967). Reichel-Dolmatoff (1971) describes shamanism among the Tukano. Aveni (1995) describes how some cultures experience and measure the passage of time.

Chapter 3

The Power of Language

Some of the discussion about the important properties of language is from Hockett (1960).

How Language Works

The examples on Thai aspiration and Nupe tones are taken from Fromkin and Rodman's (1988) text. Examples of Kosraen phonemes are from the author's (J. P.) own knowledge.

Language and Culture

The American farmers' classification of livestock is described by Tyler (1969). We thank University of Minnesota undergraduate Toni K. Olesiak for correcting a factual error in an earlier edition. A concise discussion of the Whorf-Sapir hypothesis is in D. Brown (1991).

Social Uses of Speech

Farb (1974) and Trudgill (1983) discuss male and female speech and Javanese "levels" of speech. Chagnon (1983) describes the Yąnomamö name taboo. Thanks to Kathryn Meyer and Gary DeCoker for help with the example of Japanese honorifics.

Chapter 4

Nineteenth Century: Origins

Unilineal evolutionary theory is best known from the works of Tylor (1865, 1871) and Morgan (1877). The times and places of the founding of the first anthropology programs in the United States are from Black (1991).

Early Twentieth Century: Development

The best single source of writings on Boas is a collection of his articles (1966). The critique of historical particularist assumptions is drawn from Harris (1968). Malinowski's ideas about the functions of institutions, behaviors, and beliefs are presented in his 1944 book, reprinted in Malinowski (1960). Good sources on structural-functionalism are Radcliffe-Brown (1922, 1965) and Nadel (1951).

Mid-Century Evolutionary Approaches

See L. White (1949, 1959). Steward's most influential articles are in two volumes (1955, 1977).

Anthropology Today: Divisions

Marvin Harris (1977, 1979, 1985) was instrumental in the development of modern materialistic thought. More recent and more technical sources on cultural evolution and adaptation are Johnson and Earle (1987) and Smith and Winterhalder (1992).

Methods of Studying a Culture: Ethnographic Fieldwork

The discussion of Trobriand suicide is from Malinowski (1926). The problems of collecting genealogical information from the Yąnomamö are recounted in Chagnon (1983).

Chapter 5

Hunting and Gathering

Dobyns (1983) provided most of the information on the distribution of foragers in North America used in Figure 5.1. Denevan (1992) discusses the use of fire to provide habitat for game animals among prehistoric Native Americans. Information on specific foragers is taken from the following sources: BaMbuti (Turnbull 1962), Hadza (Woodburn 1968), Western Shoshone (Steward 1938, 1955), !Kung (Lee 1979, 1993), Northwest Coast (Ferguson 1984; Piddocke 1965; Suttles 1960, 1962, 1968). Kelly (1995) is an excellent overview of foragers.

Agriculture

On the benefits and costs of agriculture, see M. Cohen (1977). Readable books on the origins of farming in various world regions are B. Smith (1995) and Diamond (1997). Comparative information on foraging working hours are from Sahlines (1972) and M. Cohen (1977). M. Cohen (1989) overviews evidence about the health of prehistoric foragers. Sources used to draw the North American portion of the map on the distribution of horticulture are Dobyns (1983) and Doolittle (1992). See Bradfield (1971) on dry land gardening among the Western Pueblo. Material on shifting cultivation is from Conklin (1957), Freeman (1970), and Ruddle (1974). Differences between extensive and intensive agriculture are set forth in Boserup (1965) and Griff (1974). Material on intensive agriculture in the New World is drawn from our general knowledge and from Donkin (1979). E. Wolf (1966, 1969) remains valuable on peasants.

Pastoralism

Porter (1965) discusses the subsistence risk reduction benefit of pastoralism. Schneider (1981) shows the negative relation between the distribution of the tsetse fly and cattle pastoralism in Africa. A short source on the Karimojong is Dyson-Hudson and Dyson-Hudson (1969).

Chapter 6

Sahlins (1965) first distinguished the three forms of exchange.

Reciprocity

Malinowski (1922) describes Trobriand *wasi*. The Maring discussion is from Rappaport (1968) and Peoples (1982).

Redistribution

Alkire (1977) and Sahlins (1958) describe tribute in Micronesia and Polynesia.

Market Exchange

See Neale (1976) on money. Schneider (1981) describes some African monies. Pospisil (1978) discusses the multiple uses of money among Kapauku. Bohannon (1955) describes Tiv exchange spheres. On Philippine *suki*, see W. Davis (1973). On Haitian *pratik*, see Mintz (1961).

Chapter 7

Marriage: Definitions and Functions

The material on Nayar marriage is from Gough (1959).

Marriage: A Cross-Cultural Perspective

Goldstein (1987) describes Tibetan polyandry and its advantages to husbands and the wife. Chagnon (1983) discusses the importance of marriage alliances among the Yąnomamö. Kuper (1963) describes Swazi bridewealth. See Lee (1979) on !Kung brideservice. See Goody and Tambiah (1973) and Harrell Dickey (1985) on dowry.

Postmarital Residence Patterns

The frequencies of different residence patterns are as reported in Pasternak (1976, 44). Among those who have discussed the influences on residence patterns are Ember and Ember (1971, 1972), Goody (1976), and Pasternak (1976), but none of them should be held responsible for the ideas presented in this section.

Family and Household Forms

Murdock (1949) showed how forms of postmarital residence produce various forms of the family and household. Pasternak, Ember, and Ember (1976) suggest an economic hypothesis for why extended families exist.

Chapter 8

Unilineal Descent

Data on the frequencies of patrilineal and matrilineal descent are from Divale and Harris (1976). Firth (1936, 1965) describes the function of Tikopian lineages and clans. See Eggan (1950) on Hopi matrilineal descent.

Cognatic Descent

Cognatic descent in Polynesia is discussed in Firth (1968), Howard and Kirkpatrick (1989), and Douglas Oliver (1989). Material on the Maori *hapu* is from Firth (1959). The Samoan *'aiga* is described in M. Ember (1959), Holmes and Holmes (1992), and Douglas Oliver (1989).

Bilateral Kinship

Material on Iban kindred is from Freeman (1968, 1970).

Influences on Kinship Systems

Sources for this discussion are Aberle (1961), Divale (1974), Divale and Harris (1976), C. Ember (1974), Ember and Ember (1971), and Ember, Ember, and Pasternak (1974).

Classifying Relatives: Kinship Terminologies

Aberle (1961) and Pasternak (1976) provide statistical data on the correlation between forms of kinship and terminological systems.

Chapter 9

Cultural Construction of Gender

The Hua material is from Meigs (1988, 1990).

Gender Crossing and Multiple Gender Identities

The main source of information on particular Native American peoples is Roscoe (1998). Nanda (2000) is a source for much of the conceptual discussion. Particular information on the Zuni is from Roscoe (1991). Hoebel (1978) discusses Cheyenne *berdache*.

The Sexual Division of Labor

Table 9.1 was put together from data in Murdock and Provost (1973). On female hunting among BaMbuti pygmies and Agta, see Turnbull (1962) and Estioko-Griffin (1986), respectively. On the possibility that strenuous exercise inhibits ovulation, see Graham (1985). The childcare compatibility idea is from Brown (1970b). The discussion of why female contributions to subsistence tend to decline with intensification uses information in Martin and Voorhies (1975), Boserup (1970), Burton and White (1984), and White, Burton, and Dow (1981). The Kofyar material is from Stone, Stone, and McC. Netting (1995).

Gender Stratification

The general discussion in this section relies on material in di Leonardo (1991), Leacock (1978), Morgen (1989), Rosaldo and Lamphere (1974), Quinn (1977), and Sacks (1982). The information about Andalusia is from Gilmore (1980, 1990). The suggestion that women's status improves with age in many cultures is from J. Brown (1988). Information on the Iroquois is from Albers (1989) and J. Brown (1970a). On BaMbuti and Aka sexual egalitarianism, see Turnbull (1962) and Hewlett (1992). The idea that women's control over key resources frequently leads to high overall status is discussed in Sanday (1973, 1981). Yoruba material is from Barnes (1990). Schlegel (1972) and Whyte (1978) discuss why matrilineality and matrilocality tend to give women high status, all else equal. Information on Chinese wives is from M. Wolf (1972) and our general knowledge.

Chapter 10

Systems of Equality and Inequality

The classification of societies into egalitarian, ranked, and stratified was proposed by Fried (1967). Woodburn (1982) discusses the reasons for the egalitarianism among foragers. The material on Tikopia is from Firth. (1936).

Castes in Traditional India

The Indian caste system and its relationship to Hinduism are discussed in Dumont (1980), Hiebert (1971), Mandelbaum (1971), and Tyler (1973).

Classes in Industrial Societies: The United States

Material on the distribution of income and assets is from U.S. Bureau of the Census (1997).

Forms of Political Organization

The definitions and ideas concerning political structure were influenced by Steward (1955), Service(1962), Cohen and Service (1978), Krader (1968), and Fried (1967). Ethnographic examples were taken from the following sources: Comanche from Hoebel (1940) and Wallace and Hoebel (1952).

Social Control and Law

For the basic definition of law as well as many of the concepts about legal systems, we relied upon Hoebel (1954), Pospisil (1958), Fallers (1969), Bohannan (1968), Newman (1983), and Gluckman (1972, 1973). Ethnographic examples were taken from the following sources: Comanche from Hoebel (1940), Osage from Bailey (1995), Nuer from Evans-Pritchard (1940, 1973a), and Barotse from Gluckman (1972, 1973).

Chapter 11

Defining Religion

An excellent recent summary of *mana* is Shore (1989). The idea that Judeo-Christian myths provide a world view conducive to environmental destruction is taken from L. White (1967).

Rites of Passage

The basic concepts are taken from Van Gennep (1960). The description of Osage child-naming is based on LaFlesche (1928). The information on male initiation of the BaMbuti is from Turnbull (1962). The female puberty rite of the Apache is taken from Farrer (1996) and that of the Tucuna from Ninuendju (1948). The other data are from conversations with students and colleagues.

Varieties of Religious Organization

Wallace (1966) formulated and named the kinds of cults. The vision quest material is from Lowie (1956). Harner (1973b) describes Jivaro shamanism. Middleton (1965) describes the Lugbara ancestral cult. The idealist interpretation of totemism is from Levi-Strauss (1963).

Theories of Religion

The Trobriand magic example is from Malinowski (1954). Frazer's intellectual theory is from Frazer (1963). Geertz (1965) argues that religion provides meaning. Malinowski (1954) argued that magic and religion serve to alleviate anxieties during times of stress or uncertainty. The theory that ritual behavior creates social solidarity goes back to Durkheim (1915). The cross-cultural study indicating the association between supernatural punishment and inequality is from Swanson (1960, 166).

Witchcraft and Sorcery

The distinction between imitative and contagious magic is taken from Frazer (1963). Fortune (1932) describes Dobu sorcery. The witchcraft examples are from Kluckhohn (1967, Navajo), Wilson (1951, Nyakyusa), Evans-Pritchard (1976, Zande), Offiong (1983, Ibibio), and Middleton (1965, Lugbara). Kluckhohn (1967) hypothesizes that Navajo witchcraft beliefs reduce overt, socially disruptive hostilities.

Chapter 12

Art and the Aesthetic

Many of the ideas for this chapter came from Hunter and Whitten (1976) and Anderson (1989). On Shaker art, we consulted the classic study by Andrews and Andrews (1937). For changes in Chinese art, we consulted the Nelson Gallery (1975). Other sources of general information used in this chapter include Lipman and Winchester (1974) and Hobson (1987). Specific information on art in particular cultures is drawn from Colton (1959; Hopi) and Connelly (1979; Hopi), Hoebel (1978; Cheyenne), Kalb (1994; New Mexico), and Hail (1983; Plains Indians).

Forms of Artistic Expression

The general discussion of body arts is based primarily on Brain (1979). Information on Polynesian tattooing is from Gell (1993), Hage et al. (1995), and Simmons (1983). Close (1989) provides a good summary of the archaeological debate over style versus function. The comparative information on style in visual arts is from Fischer (1961). For performance arts we drew from the studies of Kaeppler (1978) and Lomax (1962, 1968). Good sources on voudon are Metraux (1972) and Wade Davis' (1985) controversial book. We drew information on !Kung healing from Lee (1993) and Shostak (1983) and on Tumbuka healing from Friedson (1998). A recent source of case studies on various performances and healing is Laderman and Roseman, eds. (1996). An informative and heavily illustrated source for students on Native American dance is Heth (1992). For a discussion of the individual in art see Warner (1986).

Art and Culture

Information on the use of sandpaintings and song/chants in Navajo curing ceremonials is taken from Sandner (1991) and Reichard (1950, 1977). BaMbuti *molimo* is described in Turnbull (1962).

Chapter 13

The Modern World

The global economy, demographic changes, and ethnic conflicts are developing at such a rate that most academic articles and books are outdated before they are published.

As a result we have used Internet Web sites for most of the current data used in this chapter. The most important of these sources are the Web sites of BBC World News, the United Nations, Migration News, and the Center for Comparative Genocide Studies.

For background studies we drew on a variety of traditional sources. General economic and population data were drawn from Hepner and McKee (1992), Jackson and Hudman (1990), Stamp (1973), World Bank (1982, 1992), and the CIA (1993). Data on the changing magnitude of world trade were obtained from Rostow (1978). There is a vast body of literature in anthropology and sociology on ethnicity and related issues. Our ideas on the nature and significance of ethnicity have been most strongly influenced by the studies of Frederick Barth (1958 and 1969), Joan Vincent (1974), Bud B. Khlief (1979), Nathan Glazer and Daniel Moynihan (1963 and 1975), John Bennett (1975), Robert E. Norris (1990), Joseph Himes (1974), DeVos and Romanucci-Ross (1975), Ronald Cohen (1978), Sol Tax (1967), Bernard Nietschmann (1989), Donald Horowitz (1985), and Richard Jackson and Lloyd Hudman (1990). For discussions of international legal and political issues, see Gudmundur Alfredsson (1989) and Lee Swepton (1989). For additional data concerning particular ethnic groups and historical events, we have drawn on a number of sources: Gerner (1994), Hajda and Beissinger (1990), Charles Foster (1980), John Bodley (1982), Robert Carmack (1988), Alice B. Kehoe (1992), John T. McAlister (1973), Dale Eickelmen (1989), Richard Handler (1988), and Richard Price (1979), as well as basic reference sources.

Chapter 14

Indigenous Peoples Today

For the best general discussion of the evolution of European attitudes to indigenous peoples, see Berkhofer (1978). Germany's policies toward the Herero are discussed in Bodley (1982). S. Davis (1977) discusses the impact on indigenous tribes of Brazil's efforts to develop the Amazon Basin. Specific material on the plight of the Yanomamö is from *Newsweek* (April 9, 1990:34) and from the Commission for the Creation of the Yanomamö Park (1989a, b), published in *Cultural Survival Quarterly*. The experiences of the Kayapó are recounted by T. Turner (1989).

Vanishing Knowledge

The *Business Week* issue referred to is from March 1, 1993. The examples of medicines we have learned about from indigenous peoples are taken from Lewis and Elvin-Lewis (1977). Farnsworth (1984) argues that many more plants will be discovered to have medical uses. A good discussion of the insights of "traditional medicine" is in Fabrega (1975). The discussion of the erosion of the genetic diversity of major food crops is from our general knowledge and Harlan (1975). The material on amaranth is from Sokolov (1986).

Glossary

adaptation Process by which organisms develop physical and behavioral characteristics allowing them to survive and reproduce in their habitats.

aesthetic Qualities that make objects, actions, or language more beautiful or pleasurable, according to culturally relative and variable standards.

affines In-laws, or people related by marriage.

agriculture Adaptation based primarily on the planting, tending, and harvesting of domesticated plants (crops).

ancestral cults A type of communal cult centered around rituals performed to worship or please a kin group's ancestors.

animism Belief in spiritual beings.

anthropological linguistics Subfield that focuses on the interrelationships between language and other aspects of a people's culture.

anthropology The study of humankind (*Homo sapiens*) from a broad perspective, especially focusing on the biological and cultural differences and similarities between populations and societies, of both the past and the present.

applied anthropology Subfield whose practitioners use anthropological methods, theories, and concepts to solve practical real-world problems; practitioners often are employed by a government agency or private organization.

archaeology The investigation of past cultures through excavation of material remains.

art Any human action that modifies the utilitarian nature of something for the primary purpose of enhancing its aesthetic pleasure or symbolic communication.

authority The recognized right of an individual to command another to act in a particular way; legitimate power.

balanced reciprocity The exchange of goods considered to have roughly equal value; social purposes usually motivate the exchange.

band A small foraging group with flexible composition that migrates seasonally.

big men Political leaders who do not occupy formal offices and whose leadership is based on influence, not authority.

bilateral kinship Kinship system in which individuals trace their kinship relations equally through both parents.

bilocal residence Postmarital residence is with either the wife's or the husband's parents, according to choice.

body arts Artificial artistic enhancement or beautification of the human body by painting, tattooing, scarification, or other means.

bound morpheme A morpheme attached to a free morpheme to alter its meaning.

brideservice Custom in which a man spends a period of time working for the family of his wife.

bridewealth Custom in which a prospective groom and his relatives are required to transfer goods to the relatives of the bride to validate the marriage.

caste Stratification system in which membership in a stratum is in theory hereditary, strata are endogamous, and contact or relations between members of different strata are governed by explicit laws, norms, or prohibitions.

chiefdoms Centralized political systems with authority vested in formal, usually hereditary, offices or titles; exchange in such systems is often organized by redistribution.

civilization A form of complex society in which many people live in cities.

clan A named unilineal descent group, some of whose members are unable to trace how they are related, but who still believe themselves to be kinfolk.

class System of stratification in which membership in a stratum can theoretically be altered and intermarriage between strata is allowed.

classification of reality Ways in which the members of a culture divide up the natural and social world into named categories.

cognatic descent Form of descent in which relationships may be traced through both females and males.

cognatic descent group A group of relatives created by the tracing of relationships through both females and males.

communal cults Cults in which the members of a group cooperate in the performance of rituals intended to benefit all.

comparative perspective The insistence by anthropologists that valid hypotheses and theories about humanity be tested with data from a wide range of cultures.

composite bands Autonomous (independent) political units consisting of several extended families that live together for most or all of the year.

consanguines "Blood" relatives, or people related by birth.

consultant (informant) A member of a society who provides information to a fieldworker, often through formal interviews or surveys.

court legal systems Systems in which authority for settling disputes and punishing crimes is formally vested in a single individual or group.

courts of mediation Court systems in which sanctions imposed are designed more to restore harmonious relations between parties than to punish.

courts of regulation Court systems that use codified laws, with formally prescribed rights, duties, and sanctions.

Crow kinship terms Associated with matrilineal descent; in this system paternal cross cousins are called father or father's sister, while maternal cross cousins are called son or daughter if ego is a male, and niece or nephew if ego is a female.

cult Organized practices and beliefs pertaining to interactions with and control over specific supernatural powers.

cultivation See agriculture.

cultural anthropology (ethnology) The subfield that studied the way of life of contemporary and historically recent human populations.

cultural construction of gender The idea that the characteristics a people attribute to males and females is culturally, not biologically, determined.

cultural identity The cultural tradition a group of people recognize as their own; the shared customs and beliefs that define how a group sees itself as distinctive.

cultural knowledge Information, skills, attitudes, conceptions, beliefs, values, and other mental components of culture that people socially learn during enculturation.

cultural relativism The notion that one should not judge the behavior of other peoples using the standards of one's own culture.

culture (as used in this text) Shared, socially transmitted knowledge and behavior.

culture shock The feeling of uncertainty and anxiety an individual experiences when placed in a strange cultural setting.

demographic change Any change in population, increases and decreases in numbers, as well as shifts in the relative gender, age, and settlement patterns.

descent The tracing of kinship relationships back to previous generations.

descent group A group whose members believe themselves to be descended from a common ancestor.

dialect A regional or subcultural variant of languages.

domestication The process by which people control the distribution, abundance, and biological features of certain plants and animals, in order to increase their usefulness to humans.

domestic group Individuals, usually relatives, who reside together in a single household.

dowry Custom in which the family of a woman transfers property or wealth to her upon her marriage.

ecclesiastical cults Highly organized cults in which a full-time priesthood performs rituals believed to benefit believers or the whole society; occur in complex societies.

egalitarian society Form of society in which there is little inequality in access to culturally valued rewards.

enculturation/socialization The transmission of culture to succeeding generations by means of social learning.

endogamous rules Marriage rules requiring individuals to marry some member of their own social group or category.

Eskimo kinship terms In this system mother's and father's siblings are called aunt and uncle, while their children are called cousins. English kinship terminology is of the Eskimo type.

ethnic boundary markers Any overt characteristics that can be used to indicate ethnic group membership.

ethnic cleansing The deliberate and systematic attempt by the dominant ethnic group to eliminate or remove a rival ethnic group or groups from a geographical region.

ethnic group A named social group based on perceptions of shared ancestry, cultural traditions, and common history that culturally distinguish that group from other groups.

ethnocentrism The attitude or opinion that the morals, values, and customs of one's own culture are superior to those of other peoples.

ethnography A written description of the way of life of some human population.

ethnology The study of human cultures from a comparative perspective; often used as a synonym for cultural anthropology.

exchange Transfer of goods (or rights to goods) between individuals or groups.

exogamous rules Marriage rules prohibiting individuals to marry a member of their own social group or category.

entended family A group of related nuclear families.

extended household A group of related nuclear families that live together in a single household.

fieldwork Ethnographic research that involves observing and interviewing the members of a culture to describe their contemporary way of life.

foraging See hunting and gathering.

forensic anthropologists Physical anthropologists who identify and analyze human skeletal remains.

form of descent How a people trace their descent from previous generations.

free morpheme A morpheme that can be used alone.

functionalism Theoretical orientation that analyzes cultural elements in terms of their useful effects to individuals or to the persistence of the whole society.

gender crossing The adoption of social roles and behaviors normatively appropriate for the opposite biological sex from one's own.

gender stratification The degree of inequality between males and females based on culturally defined differences between the sexes. May be based on social status (rank, prestige) and/or on access to resources, wealth, power, or influence.

generalized reciprocity The giving of goods without expectation of a return of equal value at any definite future time.

genocide The deliberate and systematic attempt to physically destroy an unwanted ethnic population.

global economy A worldwide integrated system of buying and selling of goods, materials, labor, and services in the global market.

grammar Total system of linguistic knowledge that allows the speakers of a language to send meaningful messages and hearers to understand them.

group marriage Several women and several men are married to one another simultaneously.

Hawaiian kinship terms In this system mother's and father's siblings are called mother and father, while their children are called brother and sister.

herding Adaptation based on control and breeding of domesticated livestock, which are taken to naturally occurring pasturelands.

historical particularism The theoretical orientation emphasizing that each culture is the unique product of all the influences to which it was subjected in its past, making cross-cultural generalizations questionable.

historic archaeology Field that investigates the past of literate peoples through excavation of sites and analysis of artifacts and other material remains.

holistic perspective The assumption that any aspect of a culture is integrated with other aspects, so that no dimension of culture can be understood in isolation.

homeland A geographical region over which a particular ethnic group feels it has exclusive rights.

horticulture A method of cultivation in which hand tools powered by human muscles are used.

human variation Refers to physical differences between human populations; an interest of physical anthropologists.

hunting and gathering Adaptation based on harvest of only wild (undomesticated) plants and animals.

idealism A contemporary theoretical orientation holding that cultural knowledge and behavior patterns are largely independent of the material conditions of life; claims that each culture must be analyzed separately, on its own terms, and mistrusts cross-cultural comparisons.

incest taboo Prohibition against sexual intercourse between certain kinds of relatives.

indigenous peoples Culturally distinct peoples who have occupied a region longer than peoples who have colonized or immigrated to the region.

individualistic cults Cults based on personal relations between specific individuals and specific supernatural powers.

inequality Degree to which individuals, groups, and categories differ in their access to rewards.

influence The ability to convince people they should act as you suggest.

initiation rite A rite held to mark the sexual maturity of an individual or a group of individuals of the same sex.

intellectual/cognitive functions of religion The notion that religious beliefs provide explanations for puzzling things and events.

intensive agriculture A system of cultivation in which plots are planted annually or semiannually; usually uses irrigation, natural fertilizers, and (in the Old World) plows powered by animals.

interviews Collection of cultural data by systematic questioning; may be structured (using questionnaires) or unstructured (open-ended).

Iroquois kinship terms In this system father's brother is called father, and mother's sister is called mother, while their children are called brother and sister. Father's sister is called aunt and mother's brother is called uncle, while their children are called cousins.

key consultant (informal) A member of a society who is especially knowledgeable about some subject, and who supplies information to a fieldworker.

kindred All the bilateral relatives of an individual.

kin group A group of people who culturally conceive themselves to be relatives, cooperate in certain activities, and share a sense of identity as kinfolk.

kinship terminology The way a people classify their relatives into labeled categories, or into "kinds of relatives."

kin terms The words (labels) that an individual uses to refer to his or her relatives of various kinds.

law A kind of social control characterized by the presence of authority, intention of universal application, obligation, and sanction.

levirate Custom whereby a widow marries a male relative (usually a brother) of her deceased husband.

lexicon All the words that exist in a single language.

limited-purpose money Money that may be used to purchase only a few kinds of goods.

lineage A unilineal descent group larger than an extended family whose members can actually trace how they are related.

market Exchange by means of buying and selling, using money.

marketplace Location where buyers and sellers meet for the purpose of acquiring goods and making money.

marriage alliances The relationships created between families or kin groups by intermarriage.

materialism The theoretical orientation holding that the main influence on human ways of life is how people produce and distribute resources from their environment.

matrilineal descent Form of descent in which individuals trace their primary kinship relationships through their mothers.

matrilocal residence Couple live with or near the wife's parents.

mechanized agriculture Cultivation system in which machinery powered by oil, gasoline, electricity, and other inanimate energy sources provides the major energy inputs to farms.

monogamy Each individual is allowed to have only one spouse at a time.

morpheme A combination of phonemes that conveys a standardized meaning.

morphology The study of the units of meaning in language.

multiple gender identities The recognition, present in some cultures, of more than two sexes, with the third and fourth identities often called by terms such as *man-woman* and *woman-man*.

multipurpose money A money that can be used to purchase a very broad range of goods and services.

nationality An ethnic group that claims a right to a discrete homeland and to political autonomy and self-determination.

negative reciprocity Exchange motivated by the desire to obtain goods, in which the parties try to gain all the material goods they can.

neolocal residence Couples establish a separate household apart from both the husband's and wife's parents.

nomadism Seasonal mobility, often involving migration to high-altitude areas during the hottest and driest parts of the year.

norm Shared ideas and/or expectations about how certain people ought to act in given situations.

nuclear family A family unit consisting of only parents and children.

Omaha kinship terms Associated with patrilineal descent; in this system matrilineal cross cousins are called mother and mother's brother, while patrilineal cross cousins are called son and daughter if ego is a female and niece and nephew if ego is a male.

origin myth The collective history of an ethnic group that defines which subgroups are part of it and its relationship to other ethnic groups.

paleoanthropologists Physical anthropologists who specialize in the investigation of the biological evolution of the human species.

participant observation The main technique used in conducting ethnographic fieldwork, involving living among a people and participating in their daily activities.

pastoralism See herding.

patrilineal descent Form of descent in which individuals trace their most important kinship relationships through their fathers.

patrilocal residence Couples live with or near the husband's parents.

patterns of behavior The behavior that most people perform when they are in certain culturally defined situations.

peasants Rural people who are integrated into a larger society politically and economically.

performance arts Forms of art such as music, percussion, song, dance, and theater/drama that involve sound and/or stylized body movements.

phoneme The smallest unit of sound that speakers unconsciously recognize as distinctive from other sounds; when one phoneme is substituted for another in a morpheme, the meaning of the morpheme alters.

phonology The study of the sound system of language.

physical (biological) anthropology The subfield that studies the biological aspects of humankind.

polyandry One woman is allowed to have multiple husbands.

polygamy Multiple spouses.

polygyny One man is allowed to have multiple wives.

postmarital residence pattern Where a newly married couple go to live after their marriage.

prehistoric archaeology Field that uses excavation of sites and analysis of material remains to investigate cultures that existed before the development of writing.

priest A kind of religious specialist, often full-time, who officiates at rituals.

primatologists Those who study primates, including monkeys and apes.

prophet A person who claims to have dreams or visions in which he or she received a message from a supernatural power.

psychological functions of religion The emotional satisfaction people derive from religion.

puberty (initiation) A religious ceremony that symbolically transforms the individual from a child to an adult.

ranked society Society in which there are a fixed number of statuses (e.g., titles, offices) that carry prestige, and only certain individuals are eligible to attain these statuses.

reciprocity The transfer of goods for goods between two or more individuals or groups.

redistribution The collection of goods or money from a group, followed by a reallocation to the group by a central authority.

relocation The forced resettlement of an unwanted ethnic group to a new geographical location.

rite of passage A public ceremony or ritual recognizing and marking a transition from one group or status to another.

ritual Organized and stereotyped symbolic behaviors intended to influence supernatural powers.

role A social position in a group, with its associated and reciprocal rights (privileges) and duties (obligations).

self-help legal systems Informal legal systems in societies without centralized political systems, in which authorities who settle disputes are defined by circumstances of the case.

semantic domain A class of things or properties that are perceived as alike in some fundamental respect; hierarchically organized.

sexual division of labor The kinds of productive activities (tasks) that are assigned to women versus men in a culture.

shaman (medicine man) Part-time religious specialist who uses his special relation to supernatural powers for curing members of his group and harming members of other groups.

shamanistic cults Cults in which special individuals (shamans) have relationships with supernatural powers that ordinary people lack.

simple bands Autonomous or independent political units, often consisting of little more than an extended family, with informal leadership vested in one of the older family members.

social control Mechanisms by which behavior is constrained and directed into acceptable channels, thus maintaining conformity.

social distance The degree to which cultural norms specify that two individuals or groups should be helpful to, intimate with, or emotionally attached to one another.

social functions of religion The effects of religion on maintaining the institutions of society as a whole.

social learning The process of learning by means of imitating or communicating with others.

society A territorially distinct and largely self-perpetuating group whose members have a sense of collective identity and who share a common language and culture.

sociocide The deliberate and systematic attempt to destroy the ethnic identity of a people for the purpose of assimilating them into the dominant society.

sociolinguistics Specialty within cultural anthropology that studies how language is related to culture and the social uses of speech.

sodalities Formal institutions that cross-cut communities and serve to unite geographically scattered groups; may be based on kin groups (clans or lineages) or on non-kin-based groups (age grades or warrior societies).

sorcery The performance of rites and spells for the purpose of causing harm to others by supernatural means.

sororate Custom whereby a widower marries a female relative of his deceased wife.

state A centralized, multilevel political unit characterized by the presence of a bureaucracy that acts on behalf of the ruling elite.

stereotypes Preconceived mental images of a group that biases the way they are perceived and how their behavior is interpreted.

stratified society Society with marked and usually heritable differences in access to wealth, power, and prestige; inequality is based mainly on unequal access to productive and valued resources.

subnationalities A subgroup within a larger nationality, which lacks the concept of a separate homeland and makes no claim to any inherent right to political autonomy and self-determination.

surplus The amount of food (or other goods) a worker produces in excess of the consumption of herself or himself and his or her dependents.

surveys Methods used by fieldworkers to gather information from a lot of individuals or families very quickly. Common survey instruments include censuses and formal questionnaires.

symbols Objects, behaviors, and so forth whose culturally defined meanings have no necessary relation to their inherent physical qualities.

tone languages Languages in which changing voice pitch within a word alters the entire meaning of the word.

totemism A form of communal cult in which all members of a kin group have mystical relations with one or more natural objects from which they believe they are descended.

tribe Autonomous political unit encompassing a number of distinct, geographically dispersed communities that are held together by sodalities.

tribute The rendering of goods (typically including food) to an authority such as a chief.

unilineal descent Descent through "one line," including patrilineal and matrilineal descent.

unilineal descent group A group of relatives all of whom are related through only one sex.

unilineal evolution The nineteenth-century theoretical orientation that held that all human ways of life pass through a similar sequence of stages in their development.

values Shared ideas or standards about the worthwhileness of goals and lifestyles.

vision quest The attempt to enlist the aid of supernatural powers by intentionally seeking a dream or vision.

visual arts Arts that are produced in a material or tangible form, including basketry, pottery, textiles, paintings, drawings, sculptures, masks, carvings, and the like.

Whorf-Sapir hypothesis The idea that language profoundly shapes the perceptions and world view of its speakers.

witchcraft The use of psychic powers to harm others by supernatural means.

world view The way a people interrupt reality and events, including how they see themselves as relating to the world around them.

Bibliography

Aberle, David F.
1961 "Marilineal Descent in Cross-Cultural Perspective." In *Matrilineal Kinship*, edited by David M. Schneider and Kathleen Gough, pp. 655–727. Berkeley: University of California Press.

Adams, Richard N.
1982 *Paradoxical Harvest.* Cambridge: Cambridge University Press.
1988 "Energy and the Regulation of Nation States." *Cultural Dynamics* 1:46–61.

Albers, Patricia C.
1989 "From Illusion to Illumination: Anthropological Studies of American Indian Women." In Sandra Morgen, ed., 1989, pp. 132–170.

Alfredsson, Gudmundur
1989 "The United Nations and the Rights of Indigenous Peoples." *Current Anthropology* 30:255–259.

Alkire, William H.
1977 *An Introduction to the Peoples and Cultures of Micronesia.* 2nd ed. Menlo Park, CA: Cummings.

Allen, James P., and Eugene J. Turner
1988 *We the People: An Atlas of America's Ethnic Diversity.* New York: Macmillan.

Anderson, Richard L.
1989 *Art in Small-Scale Societies.* 2nd ed. Englewood Cliffs, NJ: Prentice Hall.

Andrews, Edward Deming, and Faith Andrews
1937 *Shaker Furniture: The Craftsmanship of an American Communal Sect.* New Haven: Yale University Press.

Aveni, Anthony
1995 *Empires of Time.* New York: Kodansha America.

Avery, Robert B., Gregory E. Elliehausen, and Arthur B. Kennickell
1987 "Measuring Wealth with Survey Data: An Evaluation of the 1983 Survey of Consumer Finances." Paper presented at the 20th Congress of the International Association for Research on Income and Wealth, Rocca di Papa, Italy.

Bailey, Garrick
1995 *The Osage and the Invisible World: From the Works of Francis La Flesche.* Norman: University of Oklahoma Press.

Barnes, Sandra T.
1990 "Women, Property, and Power." In Peggy Reeves Sanday and Ruth Gallagher Goodenough, eds., *Beyond the Second Sex.* 1990, pp. 253–280.

Barth, Fredrik
1969 *Ethnic Groups and Boundaries.* Boston: Little, Brown and Company.

Bennett, John, ed.
1975 "The New Ethnicity: Perspectives from Ethnology." 1973 Proceedings of the American Ethnological Society. St Paul, MN: West Publishing Co.

Berkhofer, Robert F., Jr.
1978 *The White Man's Indian: Images of the American Indian from Columbus to Present.* New York: Knopf.

Berlin, Brent, and Paul Kay
1969 *Basic Color Terms—Their Universality and Evolution.* Berkeley: University of California Press.

Bertelsen, Judy S., ed.
1977 *Nonstate Nations in International Politics: Comparative System Analyses.* New York: Praeger.

Black, Nancy Johnson
1991 "What Is Anthropology?" In *Introduction to Library Research in Anthropology*, edited by John Weeks, pp. 1–5. Boulder, CO: Westview Press.

Boas, Franz
1966 *Race, Language and Culture.* New York: Free Press (original 1940).

Bodley, John H.
1982 *Victims of Progress.* 2nd ed. Palo Alto, CA: Mayfield Publishing Company.

Bohannan, Paul
1955 "Some Principles of Exchange and Investment Among the Tiv." *American Anthropologist* 57:60–70.
1968 *Justice and Judgement Among the Tiv.* London: Oxford University Press.

Boserup, Ester
1965 *The Conditions of Agricultural Growth.* Chicago: Aldine.
1970 *Woman's Role in Economic Development.* New York: St. Martin's.

Boyd, Robert and Peter J. Richerson
1985 *Culture and the Evolutionary Process.* Chicago: University of Chicago Press.

Bradfield, Maitland
1971 "The Changing Pattern of Hopi Agriculture." Royal Anthropological Institute of Great Britain and Ireland Occasional Paper, no. 30. London: Royal Anthropological Institute.

Brain, Robert
1979 *The Decorated Body.* New York: Harper & Row.

Brown, Donald E.
1991 *Human Universals.* New York: McGraw-Hill.

Brown, Judith K.
1970a "Economic Organization and the Position of Women Among the Iroquois." *Ethnohistory* 17:131–167.
1970b "A Note on the Division of Labor by Sex." *American Anthropologist* 72:1073–1078.
1988 "Cross-Cultural Perspectives on Middle-Aged Women." In *Cultural Constructions of 'Woman,'* edited by Pauline Kolenda, pp. 73–100. Salem, WI: Sheffield.

Burger, Julian
1987 *Report from the Frontier: The State of the World's Indigenous Peoples.* Cambridge, MA: Cultural Survival, Inc.
1990 *The GAIA Atlas of First Peoples.* New York: Anchor Books.

Burton, Michael L., and Douglas R. White
1984 "Sexual Division of Labor in Agriculture." *American Anthropologist* 86:568–583.

Carmack, Robert, ed.
1988 *Harvest of Violence.* Norman: University of Oklahoma Press.

Central Intelligence Agency
1993 *The World Factbook 1992.* Washington, DC: Government Printing Office.

Chagnon, Napoleon A.
1983 *Yanomamö: The Fierce People.* 3rd ed. New York: Holt, Rinehart and Winston.

Close, Angela E.
1989 "Identifying Style in Stone Artifacts: A Case Study from the Nile Valley." In Donald Henry and George Odell, eds. "Alternative Approaches to Lithic Analysis." *Archaeological Papers of the American Anthropological Association,* no. 1, pp. 3–26.

Cohen, Mark Nathan
1977 *The Food Crisis in Prehistory.* New Haven and London: Yale University Press.
1989 *Health and the Rise of Civilization.* New Haven, CT: Yale University Press.

Cohen, Ronald
1978 "Ethnicity: Problem and Focus in Anthropology." In *Annual Review of Anthropology,* vol. 7, 1978, edited by Bernard Siegal. Palo Alto, CA: Annual Reviews Inc.

Cohen, Ronald, and John Middleton, eds.
1970 *From Tribe to Nation in Africa.* Scranton, PA: Chandler Publishing Company.

Cohen, Ronald, and Elman Service
1978 *Origins of the State: The Anthropology of Political Evolution.* Philadelphia: Institute for the Study of Human Issues.

Cohen, Theodore F.
1987 "Remaking Men." *Journal of Family Issues* 8:57–77.

Colton, Harold S.
1959 *Hopi Kachina Dolls.* Albuquerque: University of New Mexico Press.

Commission for the Creation of Yanomami Park (CCPY)
1989a "Brazilian Government Reduces Yanomami Territory by 70 Percent." *Cultural Survival Quarterly* 13:47.
1989b "The Threatened Yanomami." *Cultural Survival Quarterly* 13:45–46.

Conklin, Harold C.
1957 "Hanunóo Agriculture." FAO Forestry Development Paper, no. 12. Rome: Food and Agriculture Organization of the United Nations.

Connelly, John C.
1979 "Hopi Social Organization." In William Sturtevant, ed. *Handbook of North American Indians* 9:539–553.

Coombes, Annie E.
1994 *Reinventing Africa: Museum, Material Culture, and Popular Imagination in Late Victorian and Edwardian England.* New Haven, CT: Yale University Press.

Davis, Shelton H.
1977 *Victims of the Miracle.* Cambridge: Cambridge University Press.

Davis, Wade
1985 *The Serpent and the Rainbow.* New York: Warner Books.

Davis, William G.
1973 *Social Relations in a Philippine Market.* Berkeley: University of California Press.

Denevan, William M.
1992 "The Pristine Myth: The Landscape of the Americas in 1492." *Annals of the Association of American Geographers* 82:369–385.

Dentan, Robert Knox
1968 *The Semai: A Nonviolent People of Malaya.* New York: Holt, Rinehart and Winston.

DeVos, George, and Lola Romanusci-Ross, eds.
1975 *Ethnic Identity: Cultural Continuities and Change.* Palo Alto, CA: Mayfield Publishing Co.

Diamond, Jared
1991 *Gender at the Crossroads of Knowledge.* Berkeley: University of California Press.

di Leonardo, Micaela, ed.
1997 *Guns, Germs, and Steel.* New York: Norton.

Divale, William T.
1974 "Migration, External Warfare, and Matrilocal Residence." *Behavior Science Research* 9:75–133.

Divale, William T., and Marvin Harris
1976 "Population, Warfare, and the Male Supremacist Complex." *American Anthropologist* 78:521–538.

Dobyns, Henry
1983 *Their Number Became Thinned.* Knoxville: University of Tennessee Press.

Donkin, Robin
1979 *Agricultural Terracing in the Aboriginal New World.* Tucson: University of Arizona Press.

Doolittle, William E.
1992 "Agriculture in North America on the Eve of Contact: A Reassessment." *Annals of the Association of American Geographers* 82:386–401.

Dumont, Louis
1980 *Homo Hierarchicus: The Caste System and Its Implications.* Chicago and London: University of Chicago Press.

Durkheim, Emile
1915 *The Elementary Forms of the Religious Life.* London: George Allen and Unwin Ltd.

Dyson-Hudson, Rada, and Neville Dyson-Hudson
1969 "Subsistence Herding in Uganda." *Scientific American* 220:76–89.

Eggan, Fred
1950 *Social Organization of the Western Pueblos.* Chicago: University of Chicago Press.

Ember, Carol
1974 "An Evaluation of Alternative Theories of Matrilocal versus Patrilocal Residence." *Behavior Science Research* 9:135–149.

Ember, Melvin
1959 "The Nonunilinear Descent Groups of Samoa."*American Anthropologist* 61:573–577.

Ember, Melvin and Carol R. Ember
1971 "The Conditions Favoring Matrilocal versus Patrilocal Residence." *American Anthropologist* 73:571–594.

1972 "The Conditions Favoring Multilocal Residence." *Southwestern Journal of Anthropology* 28:382-400.

Ember, Melvin, Carol R. Ember, and Burton Pasternak
1974 "On the Development of Unilineal Descent." *Journal of Anthropological Research* 30:69–94.

Estioko-Griffin, Agnes
1986 "Daughters of the Forest." *Natural History* 95:36–43.

Evans-Pritchard, E. E.
1940 *The Nuer.* Oxford: Clarendon.
1976 *Witchcraft, Oracles, and Magic among the Azande.* Abridged edition. Oxford: Clarendon Press.

Fabrega, H., Jr.
1975 "The Need for an Ethnomedical Science." *Science* 189:969–975.

Fagan, Brian M.
1986 *People of the Earth.* Boston: Little, Brown and Company.

Fallers, Lloyd A.
1969 *Law Without Precedent.* Chicago: University of Chicago Press.

Farb, Peter
1974 *Word Play.* New York: Alfred A. Knopf.

Farnsworth, Norman R.
1984 "How Can the Well Be Dry When It Is Filled with Water?" *Economic Botany* 38:4–13.

Farrer, Claire F.
1996 *Thunder Rides a Black Horse.* 2nd ed. Prospect Heights, IL: Waveland Press.

Ferguson, R. Brian
1984 "A Reexamination of the Causes of Northwest Coast Warfare." In *Warfare, Culture, and Environment,* edited by R. Brian Ferguson, pp. 267–328. Orlando, FL: Academic Press.

Figler, Stephen K.
1981 *Sport and Play in American Life.* Philadelphia: Saunders College Publishing.

Firth, Raymond
1936 *We, the Tikopia.* Boston: Beacon Press.
1959 *Economics of the New Zealand Maori.* 2nd ed. Wellington: Government Printer.
1965 *Primitive Polynesian Economy.* New York: Norton.
1968 "A Note on Decent Groups in Polynesia." In *Kinship and Social Organization,* edited by Paul Bohannan and John Middleton, pp. 213–223. Garden City, NY: The Natural History Press.

Fischer, John
1961 "Art Styles as Cultural Cognitive Maps." *American Anthropologist* 63:80–84.

Fogelson, Raymond D.
1989 "The Ethnohistory of Events and Nonevents." *Ethnohistory* 36:133–147.

Fortune, Reo
1932 *Sorcerers of Dobu.* New York: E.P. Dutton.

Foster, Charles, R., ed.
1980 *Nations Without a State: Ethnic Minorities of Western Europe.* New York: Praeger.

Frazer, Sir James George
1963 *The Golden Bough.* Abridged ed. Toronto: The Macmillan Company (original 1911–1915).

Fried, Morton
1967 *The Evolution of Political Society.* New York: Random House.

Friedson, Steven
1998 "Tumbuka Healing." In *The Garland Encyclopedia of World Music*, vol. 1, edited by Ruth M. Stone, pp. 271–284. New York: Garland Publishing, Inc.

Frigout, Arlette
1979 "Hopi Ceremonial Organization." In *Southwest*, edited by Alfonso Ortiz, pp. 564–576. *Handbook of North American Indians*, vol. 9. Washington, DC: Smithsonian Institution.

Fronkin, Victoria, and Robert Rodman
1988 *An Introduction to Language*. 4th ed. New York: Holt, Rinehart and Winston.

Geertz, Clifford
1965 "Religion as a Cultural System." In *Anthropological Approaches to the Study of Religion*, edited by Michael Banton. Association of Social Anthropologists Monographs, no. 3. London: Tavistock Publications.

Gell, Alfred
1993 *Wrapping in Images*. Oxford: Clarendon Press.

Gerner, Deborah J.
1994 *One Land, Two Peoples: The Conflict over Palestine*. Boulder, CO: Westview Press.

Gilmore, David D.
1980 *The People of the Plain*. New York: Columbia University Press.
1990 *Manhood in the Making*. New Haven, CT: Yale University Press.

Glazer, Nathan, and Daniel P. Moynihan
1963 *Beyond the Melting Pot*. Cambridge: Harvard University Press.

Glazer, Nathan, and Daniel P. Moynihan, eds.
1975 *Ethnicity: Theory and Experience*. Cambridge: Harvard University Press.

Gluckman, Max
1972 *The Ideas in Barotse Jurisprudence*. Manchester: Manchester University Press.
1973 *The Judicial Process Among the Barotse*. Manchester: Manchester University Press.

Goldstein, Melvyn C.
1987 "When Brothers Share a Wife." *Natural History* 96(3):38–49.

Goody, Jack
1976 *Production and Reproduction*. Cambridge: Cambridge University Press.

Goody, Jack, and S. J. Tambiah
1973 *Bridewealth and Dowry*. Cambridge: Cambridge University Press.

Gough, E. Kathleen
1959 "The Nayars and the Definition of Marriage." *Journal of the Royal Anthropological Institute* 89:23–34.

Graham, Susan Brandt
1985 "Running and Menstrual Dysfunction: Recent Medical Discoveries Provide New Insights into the Human Division of Labor by Sex." *American Anthropologist* 87:878–882.

Griffen, Joyce
1980 *Navajo Funerals, Anglo-Style*. Museum of Northern Arizona Research Paper 18.

Grigg, David
1974 *The Agricultural Systems of the World*. Cambridge: Cambridge University Press.

Hage, Per, Frank Harary, and Bojka Milicic
1995 "Tattooing, Gender and Social Stratification in Micro-Polynesia." *Journal of the Royal Anthropological Institute*. (N.S.) 2:335–350.

Hail, Barbara A.
1983 *Hau, Kola!: The Plains Indian Collection of the Haffenreffer Museum*. Bristol, RI: Haffenreffer Museum of Anthropology, Brown University.

Handler, Richard
1988 *Nationalism and the Politics of Culture in Quebec*. Madison: University of Wisconsin Press.

Harlan, Jack R.
1975 "Our Vanishing Genetic Resources." *Science* 188:618–621.

Harner, Michael J.
1973a *The Jivaro*. Garden City, NY: Doubleday-Anchor.
1973b "The Sound of Rushing Water." In *Hallucinogens and Shamanism*, edited by Michael J. Harner, pp. 15–27. London: Oxford University Press.

Harrell, Stevan, and Sara A. Dickey
1985 "Dowry Systems in Complex Societies." *Ethnology* 24:105–120.

Harris, Marvin
1968 *The Rise of Anthropological Theory*. New York: Thomas Y. Crowell.
1977 *Cannibals and Kings*. New York: Random House.
1979 *Cultural Materialism*. New York: Vintage Books.
1985 *Good to Eat*. New York: Simon and Schuster.

Hepner, George F., and Jesse O. McKee
1992 *World Regional Geography: A Global Approach*. St. Paul, MN: West Publishing Company.

Herdt, Gilbert H.
1997 *Same Sex, Different Cultures: Gays and Lesbians Across Cultures*. Boulder, CO: Westview Press.

Hewlett, Barry S.
1992 *Intimate Fathers*. Ann Arbor: University of Michigan Press.

Hickerson, Harold
1970 *The Chippewa and Their Neighbors: A Study in Ethnohistory*. New York: Holt, Rinehart and Winston.

Hiebert, P. G.
1971 *Konduru: Structure and Integration in a Hindu Village.* Minneapolis: University of Minnesota Press.

Himes, Joseph S.
1974 *Racial and Ethnic Relations.* Dubuque, IA: Wm. C. Brown Company.

Hockett, Charles F.
1960 "The Origin of Speech." *Scientific American* 203:88–96.

Hoebel, E. Adamson
1940 *The Political Organization and Law-ways of the Comanche Indians.* American Anthropological Association, Memoir 54.
1954 *The Law of Primitive Man.* Cambridge: Harvard University Press.
1978 *The Cheyennes.* 2nd ed. New York: Holt, Rinehart and Winston.

Holmes, Lowell D., and Ellen Rhoads Holmes
1992 *Samoan Village Then and Now.* 2nd ed. Fort Worth, TX: Harcourt Brace Jovanovich.

Horowitz, Donald L.
1985 *Ethnic Groups in Conflict.* Berkeley: University of California Press.

Howard, Alan, ed.
1971 *Polynesia: Readings on a Culture Area.* Scranton, PA: Chandler Publishing.

Howard, Alan, and John Kirkpatrick
1989 "Social Organization." In *Developments in Polynesian Ethnology,* edited by Alan Howard and Robert Borofsky, pp. 47–94. Honolulu: University of Hawaii Press.

Hunter, David E., and Phillip Whitten, eds.
1976 *Encyclopedia of Anthropology.* New York: Harper & Row.

Johnson, Allen W., and Timothy Earle
1987 *The Evolution of Human Societies.* Stanford, CT: Stanford University Press.

Kaeppler, Adrienne L.
1978 "Dance in Anthropological Perspective." In Bernard Siegel, ed. *Annual Review of Anthropology,* 7:31–49. Palo Alto, CA: Annual Reviews, Inc.

Kahn, J., et al., eds.
1979 *World Economic Development.* Boulder, CO: Westview Press.

Kalb, Laurie Beth
1994 *Crafting Devotions: Tradition in Contemporary New Mexico Santos.* Albuquerque: University of New Mexico Press.

Kammer, Jerry
1980 *The Second Long Walk: The Navajo-Hopi Land Dispute.* Albuquerque: University of New Mexico.

Keesing, Roger M.
1982 *Kwaio Religion.* New York: Columbia University Press.

Kelly, Robert L.
1995 *The Foraging Spectrum.* Washington, DC: Smithsonian.

Khlief, Bud B.
1979 "Language as Identity: Toward an Ethnography of Welsh Nationalism." *Ethnicity* 6 (4):346–357.

Kluckhohn, Clyde
1967 *Navajo Witchcraft.* Boston: Beacon Press.

Kolb, Albert
1971 *East Asia.* London: Methuen and Co. Ltd.

Krader, Lawrence
1968 *Formation of the State.* Englewood Cliffs, NJ: Prentice-Hall.

Kroeber, Alfred
1963 *Cultural and Natural Areas of Native North America.* Berkeley and Los Angeles: University of California Press (original 1939).

Laderman, Carol, and Marina Roseman, eds.
1996 *The Performance of Healing.* New York: Routledge.

LaFlesche, Francis
1928 "The Osage Tribe: Two Versions of the Child-Naming Rite." *43rd Annual Report of the Bureau of American Ethnology, 1925–1926,* pp. 23–164. Washington, DC: Government Printing Office.

Langness, L. L., and John C. Weschler, eds.
1971 *Melanesia: Readings on a Culture Area.* Scranton, PA: Chandler Publishing.

Lappé, Frances Moore, and Joseph Collins
1977 *Food First.* New York: Ballantine Books.
1986 *World Hunger: Twelve Myths.* New York: Grove Press.

Lawrence, Peter
1964 *Road Belong Cargo.* Manchester: Manchester University Press.

Leacock, Eleanor
1978 "Women's Status in Egalitarian Society: Implications for Social Evolution" *Current Anthropology* 19:247–75.

Lee, Richard B.
1968 "What Hunters Do for a Living, or, How to Make Out on Scarce Resources." In *Man the Hunter,* edited by Richard B. Lee and Irven DeVore, pp. 30–48. Chicago: Aldine.
1969 "!Kung Bushman Subsistence: An Input-Output Analysis." In *Environment and Cultural Behavior,* edited by Andrew P. Vayda, pp. 47–79. Garden City, NY: Natural History Press.

1979 *The !Kung San.* Cambridge: Cambridge University Press.
1993 *The Dobe Ju/'hoansi.* 2nd ed. Fort Worth, TX: Harcourt Brace Jovanovich.

Lefkowitz, Mary
1995 *Not Out of Africa: How Afrocentrism Became an Excuse to Teach Myths as History.* New York: Basic Books.

Lenski, Gerhard E.
1966 *Power and Privilege.* New York: McGraw-Hill.

Levenson, Jay A., ed.
1992 *Circa 1492: Art in the Age of Exploration.* New Haven and Washington, DC: Yale University Press and The National Gallery of Art.

Lévi-Strauss, Claude
1963 *Totemism.* Boston: Beacon.

Lewis, Walter H., and Memory P. F. Elvin-Lewis
1977 *Medical Botany.* New York: John Wiley and Sons.

Lipman, Jean, and Alice Winchester
1974 *The Flowering of American Folk Art.* New York: The Viking Press.

Lipsky, George
1962 *Ethiopia: Its People, Its Society, Its Culture.* New Haven, CT: Human Relations Area Files Press.

Lomax, Alan
1962 "Song Structure and Social Structure." *Ethnology* 1:425–51.
1968 "Folk Song Style and Culture." *American Association for the Advancement of Science Publication,* no. 88. Washington, DC.

Lowie, Robert H.
1956 *The Crow Indians.* New York: Holt, Rinehart and Winston (original 1935).

Malinowski, Bronislaw
1922 *Argonauts of the Western Pacific.* New York: E. P. Dutton and Company.
1926 *Crime and Custom in Savage Society.* London: Routledge and Kegan Paul.
1954 *Magic, Science and Religion.* Garden City, NY: Doubleday and Company, Inc.
1960 *A Scientific Theory of Culture and Other Essays.* New York: Oxford University Press (original 1944).

Maloney, Clarence
1974 *Peoples of South Asia.* New York: Holt, Rinehart and Winston.

Mandelbaum, David G.
1970 *Society in India.* 2 vols. Berkeley: University of California Press.

Martin, Phyllis, and Patrick O'Meara
1977 *Africa.* Bloomington: Indiana University Press.

Martin, M. Kay, and Barbara Voorhies
1975 *Female of the Species.* New York: Columbia University Press.

McAlister, John T., ed.
1973 *Southeast Asia: The Politics of National Integration.* New York: Random House.

McDonald, Kim
1995 "Unearthing Sins of the Past." *The Chronicle of Higher Education,* October 6, A12,20.

McVey, Ruth T., ed.
1962 *Indonesia.* New Haven, CT: Human Relations Area Files Press.

Meigs, Anna S.
1988 *Food, Sex, and Pollution: A New Guinea Religion.* New Brunswick, NJ: Rutgers University Press.
1990 "Multiple Gender Ideologies and Statuses." In Peggy Reeves Sanday and Ruth Gallagher Goodenough, eds., 1990, pp. 99–112.

Metraux, Alfred
1972 *Voodoo in Haiti.* New York: Schocken Books.

Middleton, John
1965 *The Lugbara of Uganda.* New York: Holt, Rinehart and Winston.
1970 *Black Africa: Its People and Their Cultures Today.* New York: Macmillan.

Mintz, Sidney W.
1961 "*Pratik*: Haitian Personalistic Economic Relationships." *Proceedings of the American Ethnological Society,* 54–63. Seattle: University of Washington Press.

Moore, Omar Khayyam
1957 "Divination—A New Perspective." *American Anthropologist* 59:69–74.

Morgan, Lewis Henry
1877 *Ancient Society.* New York: World Publishing.

Morgen, Sandra, ed.
1989 *Gender and Anthropology: Critical Reviews for Research and Teaching.* Washington, DC: American Anthropological Association.

Murdock, George Peter
1949 *Social Structure.* New York: The Free Press.
1959 *Africa: Its People and Their Culture History.* New York: McGraw-Hill.

Murdock, George P., and Caterina Provost
1973 "Factors in the Division of Labor by Sex: A Cross-Cultural Analysis." *Ethnology* 12:203–225.

Nadel, S. F.
1951 *The Foundations of Social Anthropology.* London: Cohen & West.

Nanda, Serena
2000 *Gender Diversity: Crosscultural Variations*. Prospect Heights, IL: Waveland Press.

Naroll, Raoul
1962 *Data Quality Control—A New Research Technique*. New York: The Free Press.

Neale, Walter C.
1976 *Monies in Societies*. San Francisco: Chandler and Sharp.

Newman, Katherine S.
1983 *Law and Economic Organization: A Comparative Study of Pre-Industrial Societies*. Cambridge: Cambridge University Press.

Nietschmann, Bernard
1988 "Third World War: The Global Conflict over the Rights of Indigenous Nations." *Utne Reader* (Nov./Dec.):84–91.

Ninuendju, Curt
1948 "The Tucuna." In *Handbook of South American Indians*, vol. 3, edited by Julian Steward, 713–725. *Handbook of South American Indians: The Tropical Forest Tribes*. Bureau of American Ethnology Bulletin 143. Washington, DC: U.S. Government Printing Office.

Offiong, Daniel
1983 "Witchcraft Among the Ibibio of Nigeria." *African Studies Review* 26:107–124.

O'Leary, Timothy, and David Levinson, eds.
1991 *Encyclopedia of World Cultures*. 10 vols. Boston: G. K. Hall.

Oliver, Douglas L.
1989 *Oceania: The Native Cultures of Australia and the Pacific Islands*. Honolulu: University of Hawaii Press.

Pasternak, Burton
1976 *Introduction to Kinship and Social Organization*. Englewood Cliffs, NJ: Prentice Hall.

Pasternak, Burton, Carol R. Ember, and Melvin Ember
1976 "On the Conditions Favoring Extended Family Households." *Journal of Anthropological Research* 32:109–123.

Peoples, James G.
1982 "Individual or Group Advantage? A Reinterpretation of the Maring Ritual Cycle." *Current Anthropology* 23:291–309.
1985 *Island in Trust*. Boulder, CO: Westview Press.

Piddocke, Stuart
1965 "The Potlatch System of the Southern Kwakiutl: A New Perspective." *Southwestern Journal of Anthropology* 21:244–264.

Pieterse, Jan Nederveen
1992 *White on Black: Images of Africa and Blacks in Western Popular Culture*. New Haven, CT: Yale University Press.

Porter, Philip W.
1965 "Environmental Potentials and Economic Opportunities—A Background for Cultural Adaption." *American Anthropologist* 67:409–420.

Pospisil, Leopold
1958 *Kapauku Papuans and Their Law*. Yale University Publications in Anthropology, no. 54.
1978 *The Kapauku Papuans of West New Guinea*. 2d ed. New York: Holt, Rinehart and Winston.

Price, Richard, ed.
1979 *Maroon Societies: Rebel Slave Communities in the Americas*. Baltimore: Johns Hopkins University.

Pulliam, H. Ronald, and Christopher Dunford
1980 *Programmed to Learn*. New York: Columbia University Press.

Quinn, Naomi
1977 "Anthropological Studies on Women's Status." *Annual Review of Anthropology* 6:181–225.

Radcliffe-Brown, A. R.
1922 *The Andaman Islanders*. Cambridge: Cambridge University Press.
1965 *Structure and Function in Primitive Society*. New Haven: Yale University Press.

Rappaport, Roy
1968 *Pigs for the Ancestors*. New Haven: pp. 308–311. Yale University Press.

Rasmussen, Knud
1979 "A Shaman's Journey to the Sea Spirit." In *Reader in Comparative Religion*, edited by William A. Lessa and Evon Z. Vogt, pp. 308–311. New York: Harper & Row.

Reichard, Gladys A.
1950 *Navaho Religion*. NJ: Princeton University Press.
1977 *Navajo Medicine Man Sandpaintings* New York: Dover Publications.

Reichel-Dolmatoff, Gerardo
1971 *Amazonian Cosmos*. Chicago: University of Chicago Press.

Robinson, Harvey
1967 *Monsoon Asia: A Geographical Survey*. New York: Praeger.

Rohner, Ronald P.
1975 *They Love Me, They Love Me Not: A Worldwide Study of the Effects of Parental Acceptance and Rejection*. New Haven, CT: HRAF Press.

Rosaldo, Michelle Z., and Louise Lamphere, eds.
1974 *Women, Culture, and Society*. Stanford, CT: Stanford University Press.

Roscoe, Will
1991 *The Zuni Man-Woman*. Albuquerque: University of New Mexico Press.
1998 *Changing Ones: Third and Fourth Genders in Native North America*. New York: St. Martin's Press.

Rostow, W. W.
1978 *The World Economy: History and Prospect.* Austin: University of Texas.

Ruddle, Kenneth
1974 *The Yukpa Autosubsistence System: A Study of Shifting Cultivation and Ancillary Activities in Colombia and Venezuela.* Berkeley: University of California Press.

Sacks, Karen
1982 *Sisters and Wives.* Urbana: University of Illinois Press.

Sahlins, Marshall
1958 *Social Stratification in Polynesia.* Seattle: University of Washington Press.
1965 "On the Sociology of Primitive Exchange." In *The Relevance of Models for Social Anthropology,* edited by Michael Banton, pp. 139–236. London: Tavistock.
1972 *Stone Age Economics.* New York: Aldine Publishing Company.
1995 *How "Natives" Think: About Captain Cook, for Example.* Chicago: University of Chicago Press.

Sanday, Peggy R.
1973 "Toward a Theory of the Status of Women." *American Anthropologist* 75:1682–1700.
1981 *Female Power and Male Dominance.* Cambridge: Cambridge University Press.

Sanday, Peggy Reeves, and Ruth Gallagher Goodenough, eds.
1990 *Beyond the Second Sex.* Philadelphia: University of Pennsylvania Press.

Sandner, Donald
1991 *Navajo Symbols of Healing.* Rochester, VT: Healing Arts Press.

Sapir, Edward
1964 "The Status of Linguistics as a Science." In *Edward Sapir,* edited by David G. Mandelbaum, pp. 65–77. Berkeley: University of California Press (original 1929).

Schlegel, Alice
1972 *Male Dominance and Female Autonomy.* New Haven, CT: HRAF Press.

Schneider, Harold K.
1981 *The Africans.* Englewood Cliffs, NJ: Prentice-Hall.

Scudder, Thayer
1982 *No Place to Go: Effects of Compulsory Relocation on Navajos.* Philadelphia: ISHI.

Shore, Bradd
1989 "*Mana* and *Tapu*." In *Developments in Polynesian Ethnology,* Alan Howard and Robert Borofsky, editors, pp. 137–173. Honolulu: University of Hawaii Press.

Shostak, Marjorie
1983 *Nisa: The Life and Words of a !Kung Woman.* New York: Vintage.

Simmons, Dave
1983 "Moko." In *Art and Artists of Oceania,* pp. 226–243. [Palmerston North:] Dunmore Press.

Smith, Bruce
1995 *The Emergence of Agriculture.* New York: Scientific American Library.

Smith, Eric Alden, and Bruce Winterhalder, eds.
1992 *Evolutionary Ecology and Human Behavior.* New York: Aldine de Gruyter.

Snow, Clyde
1995 "Murder Most Foul." *The Sciences* (May/June):16–20.

Sokolov, Raymond
1986 "The Good Seed." *Natural History* 95:102–105.

Stamp, L. Dudley
1973 *A Commercial Geography.* 9th ed. London: Longman.

Steward, Julian H.
1938 *Basin-Plateau Sociopolitical Groups.* Bureau of American Ethnology Bulletin 120.
1955 *Theory of Culture Change.* Urbana: University of Illinois Press.
1977 *Evolution and Ecology: Essays on Social Transformation,* edited by Jane C. Steward and Robert F. Murphy. Urbana: University of Illinois Press.

Steward, Julian, and Louis Faron
1959 *Native Peoples of South America.* New York: McGraw-Hill.

Stone, M. Priscilla, Glenn Davis Stone, and Robert McC. Netting
1995 "The Sexual Division of Labor in Kofyar Agriculture." *American Ethnologist* 22:165–186.

Suttles, Wayne
1960 "Affinal Ties, Subsistence, and Prestige Among the Coast Salish." *American Anthropologist* 62:296–305.
1962 "Variations in Habitat and Culture on the Northwest Coast." In *Man in Adaptation: The Cultural Present,* edited by Yehudi A. Cohen, pp. 128–141. Chicago: Aldine.
1968 "Coping with Abundance: Subsistence on the Northwest Coast." In *Man the Hunter,* edited by Richard B. Lee and Irven DeVore, pp. 56–68. Chicago: Aldine.

Swanson, Guy
1960 *The Birth of the Gods.* Ann Arbor: University of Michigan Press.

Swepton, Lee
1989 "Indigenous and Tribal Peoples and International Law: Recent Developments." *Current Anthropology* 30:259–264.

Szwed, John F., ed.
1970 *Black America.* New York: Basic Books.

Tax, Sol, ed.
1967 *Acculturation in the Americas.* New York: Copper Square Publishers.

Thernstrom, Stephen, ed.
1980 *Harvard Encyclopedia of American Ethnic Groups.* Cambridge, MA: Harvard University Press.

Trudgill, Peter
1983 *Sociolinguistics.* Middlesex, England: Penguin.

Turnbull, Colin M.
1962 *The Forest People.* New York: Simon and Schuster.

Turner, Terence
1989 "Kayapo Plan Meeting to Discuss Dams." *Cultural Survival Quarterly* 13:20–22.

Turner, Victor
1967 *The Forest of Symbols.* Ithaca, NY: Cornell University Press.

Tyler, Stephen A., ed.
1969 *Cognitive Anthropology.* New York: Holt, Rinehart and Winston.

Tyler, Stephen A.
1973 *India: An Anthropological Perspective.* Pacific Palisades, CA: Goodyear Publishing Company.

Tylor, Edward B.
1865 *Researches into the Early History of Mankind and the Development of Civilization.* London: J. Murray.
1871 *Primitive Culture.* London: J. Murray.

United Nations Development Programme
1995 *Human Development Report 1995.* New York: Oxford University Press.

United States Bureau of the Census
1997 *Statistical Abstract of the United States 1997.* Washington, DC.

Urban, Greg, and Joel Sherzer, eds.
1992 *Nation-States and Indians in Latin America.* Austin: University of Texas.

Van Gennep, Arnold
1960 *The Rites of Passage.* Chicago: University of Chicago Press.

Vayda, Andrew P., ed.
1968 *Peoples and Cultures of the Pacific.* Garden City, NY: The Natural History Press.

Vincent, Joan
1974 "The Structuring of Ethnicity." *Human Organization* 33:375–379.

Wagley, Charles
1968 *The Latin American Tradition: Essays on the Unity and the Diversity of Latin American Culture.* New York: Columbia University Press.

Wallace, Anthony F. C.
1966 *Religion: An Anthropological View.* New York: Random House.
1969 *The Death and Rebirth of the Seneca.* New York: Vintage Books.

Wallace, Ernest, and E. Adamson Hoebel
1952 *The Comanches: Lords of the South Plains.* Norman: University of Oklahoma.

Weyler, Rey
1982 *Blood of the Land.* New York: Vintage Books.

White, Douglas R., Michael L. Burton, and Malcolm M. Dow.
1981 "Sexual Division of Labor in African Agriculture: A Network Autocorrelation Analysis." *American Anthropologist* 83:824–849.

White, Leslie
1949 *The Science of Culture.* New York: Grove Press.
1959 *The Evolution of Culture.* New York: McGraw-Hill.

White, Lynn
1967 "The Historical Roots of Our Ecologic Crisis." *Science* 155:1203–1207.

Whyte, Martin King
1978 *The Status of Women in Preindustrial Societies.* Princeton, NJ: Princeton University Press.

Wilson, Monica
1951 *Good Company.* Oxford: Oxford University Press.

Winthrop, Robert H.
1991 *Dictionary of Concepts in Cultural Anthropology.* New York: Greenwood Press.

Wolf, Eric
1966 *Peasants.* Englewood Cliffs, N.J: Prentice-Hall.
1969 *Peasant Wars of the Twentieth Century.* New York: Harper and Row.

Wolf, Eric R., and Edward C. Hansen
1972 *The Human Condition in Latin America.* New York: Oxford University Press.

Wolf, Margery
1972 *Women and the Family in Rural Taiwan.* Stanford, CA: Stanford University Press.

Woodburn, James
1968 "An Introduction to Hadza Ecology." In *Man the Hunter,* edited by Richard B. Lee and Irven DeVore, 49–55. Chicago: Aldine.
1982 "Egalitarian Societies." *Man* 17:431–451.

World Bank
1992 *World Development Report 1992.* New York: Oxford.

Worsley, Peter
1968 *The Trumpet Shall Sound.* New York: Schocken Books.

Photo Credits

Index